CW01091261

Leaders and Leadership in Japan

Leaders and Leadership in Japan

edited by
IAN NEARY
University of Essex

JAPAN
LIBRARY

LEADERS & LEADERSHIP IN JAPAN

First published 1996 by
JAPAN LIBRARY

Japan Library is an imprint of Curzon Press Ltd
St. John's Studios, Church Road, Richmond, Surrey TW9 2QA

British Library Cataloguing in Publication Data
A CIP catalogue entry for this book is available
from the British Library

ISBN 1–873410–41–7

Typeset by LaserScript, Mitcham, Surrey, in Bembo 12 on 12pt.
Printed and bound in England by Bookcraft, Midsomer Norton, Avon

Contents

Preface

The European Association for Japanese Studies has organized a conference once every three years since 1976. Indeed its conferences are now recognized as the most important international Japanese Studies conferences. The Seventh Triennial meeting, held in Copenhagen in August 1994 was attended by over 400 participants from 34 countries and in the course of four days a total of 169 papers were presented at eight sections.

Each of the sections adopted a theme or themes to provide coherence to its sessions. The difficulties of writing about leadership in contemporary Japan suggested that it might be a fertile theme for the History, Politics and International History section. Thirty papers were read in this section in the course of the conference, nearly all related in some way to the theme of leadership. Watanabe Osamu of Hitotsubashi University was to have provided the keynote paper for our session but illness shortly before the conference prevented him attending.

One set of papers interpreted the theme in terms of Japan's leadership in the international community; in South-East Asia, Eastern Europe or the international system in general. Faced with the problem of selecting papers for publication, since not all could fit into one volume, it was decided not to use those which looked at Japan as leader, as opposed to leaders in Japan.

The task of editing these papers has been a rather drawn out process which must have been frustrating for those who provided a final version of their paper within weeks of the conference. To them I must apologize. Collecting and then imposing some kind of uniformity on the twenty papers from fifteen countries took much longer than expected. Thanks are due to the publisher, Paul Norbury, for his patience and to Lynn Baird, secretary at the Contemporary Japan Centre, for her efficiency. Finally, I would like to reiterate the thanks of all those who took part in the Copenhagen conference to the organizers of the event at which all these papers were presented.

IAN NEARY
Fukuoka, October 1995

About the Contributors

Ian Neary is a professor in the Department of Government, University of Essex. He has published books and articles on Burakumin, the pharmaceutical industry and is currently engaged on a research project on human rights in Japan, Taiwan and South Korea.

Shigekazu Kondō is an Associate Professor at the Historiographical Institute University of Tokyo. He was a visiting scholar at the University of Bonn 1991–2. His specialization is the role of documentation in the political structure of medieval Japan.

Detlev Taranczewski studied Japanese history and philology, political sciences and sociology at the University of Frankfurt am Main (Germany); mediaeval Japanese history at Tokyo Metropolitan University and Japanese language at Waseda University. Since 1984 he has been at the University of Bonn where his special field of research is the social, economic and constitutional history of mediaeval Japan.

Willy Vande Walle is Professor and Director of the Department of Oriental Studies at the University of Leuven. He is currently working on a book-length study on Count de Montblanc and his relationship with Japan.

Seija Jalagin teaches in the Department of History at the University of Oulu.

Herman J. Moeshart is an Assistant Curator of the Collection of Photography at the University of Leiden. He has published the *Diary of Dirk de Graeff van Polsbroek, Dutch Minister Resident* *in Japan (1859–1870)* (in Dutch, Van Gorcum, Assen, 1987 and in Japanese translation by Yushodo, 1995). He is currently working on a thesis on the Dutch in Japan, 1850–1900.

Alistair Swale is a lecturer in politics at the University of Waikato.

Annette Skovsted Hansen has degrees in Japanese Studies from the Universities of Copenhagen and Columbia, New York. She is currently a PhD candidate at the University of Copenhagen working on a thesis entitled 'The creation of tool and myth in nation building: perceptions of language change and usage in universal education and mass communication, 1860–1910'.

Selçuk Esenbel is an Associate Professor of History at the Department of History, Bosphorus University (Bogizi), Istanbul, Turkey. She is the author of *Even the Gods Rebel: Peasants of Takaino and the 1871 Nakano Uprising in Japan* (1995 AAS Monographs).

Ewa Palasz-Rutkowska is an Assistant Professor in the Japanese and Korean Department, Warsaw University, where she specializes in the history of modern Japan. Her work on the Japanese army in the 1930s and Japanese-Polish cooperation has been published in Japanese, Polish and English.

Ernst Lokowandt is a Professor at Tōyō University, Tokyo. He has studied at the Universities of Bonn and Kokugakuin and has published extensively in German and Japanese on aspects of state formation and the Shintō religion in Meiji Japan.

Ian Nish presently Emeritus Professor of International History, University of London has taught at University of Sydney and London School of Economics. He is author of *The Anglo-Japanese Alliance, Alliance in Decline, Japanese Foreign Policy*, and most recently *Japan's Struggle with Internationalism, 1931–3*.

John Crump is a Senior Lecture in Politics at the University of York. He is the author of *Hatta Shuzo and Pure Anarchism in Interwar Japan* (Macmillan, 1993), a Japanese version of which is to be published by Aoki Shoten.

Christoph Brumann is instructor for social and cultural anthropology at the University of Cologne, Germany. He has published articles on utopian communities, alternative culture, and money gift-giving in Japan. He is currently working on a comparative study about the survival conditions of utopian communities world-wide.

Gerhard Krebs has studied in universities in Germany and Japan and taught in the universities of Waseda and Freiburg. From 1990 to 1995 he was a member of the research staff of the 'German Institute for Japanese Studies' (Siebold Foundation).

Henry Oinas-Kukkonen is a Lecturer in the Department of History at the University of Oulu. He has written on the relationship between the United States and the Japanese Communist movement during the Occupation.

Peter Lowe is a fellow of the Royal Historical Society and Reader in History at University of Manchester. His principal research interest concerns British and American foreign policies in East Asia during the twentieth century. His latest publication is: (edited with T.G. Fraser), *Conflict and Amity in East Asia: Essays in Honour of Ian Nish* (Macmillan, 1992).

Olavi K. Fält is a professor of history at the University of Oulu, Finland. He is author of several books in Finnish on Japan and *The interpretation of the crisis years of 1930–1941 in the Japanese English-language press* (1985) and *The Clash of Interests: the transformation of Japan in 1861–1881 in the eyes of the local Anglo-Saxon press* (1990) both published in English by Jyvaskyla.

Bert Edström is Senior Research Fellow at the Center for Pacific Asia Studies, University of Stockholm, Sweden. He is the author of *Japan's Quest for a Role in the World* (Stockholm, 1988) and the editor of *Current Developments in Asia Pacific* (Stockholm, 1993) and *Japan's Global Role: Implications for Sweden* (Stockholm, 1994).

J.A.A. Stockwin is Nissan Professor of Modern Japanese Studies and Director of the Nissan Institute of Japanese Studies at the University of Oxford. He is author of various books on Japanese politics and is engaged on a long-term study of political change in Japan.

David Williams is a Senior Research Fellow in Japanese Politics at the University of Sheffield. He is the author of *Japan: Beyond the End of History* (1994) and *Enemies of Open Political Science* (1996).

Leaders and Leadership in Japan

IAN NEARY

'The most general characteristic of leadership is its ubiquity' begins one well-used American textbook on political leadership. (Mughan and Patterson 1992: 1) But, as the editors of the same textbook point out, although the study of leadership has a venerable tradition, from Plato through Machiavelli, most of the early writings on the subject were concerned with the normative issues of who should become leaders and how they should conduct themselves, rather than considering the nature of leaders or the structures in which they act. It is only fairly recently that there has been sustained attention to leadership as an object of study.

Power, its pursuit and exercise, has long been accepted as a legitimate object of study by historians and political scientists but since the early 1980s there has been an attempt to distinguish between power and leadership. Burns, for example, argued that, 'Leadership is an aspect of power but it is also a separate and vital process in itself'. (Burns 1978: 21). This stress on process emphasises the relationship between the leaders and followers enabling the analyst to consider leadership on a continuum at one end of which are wielders of absolute power and at the other are those leaders who are so sensitive to the needs of the followers that the leadership element almost entirely dissolves. This notion of leadership as process also underlines its dynamic and multi-layered character, a leader may at one stage of his or her career closely identify with and be sensitive to the feelings of the followers and at another time be distant and insensitive or may at one moment in time be receptive to one sector of the supporting groups and not others. The attempt to separate power from leadership is rarely entirely successful, even Burns who set himself the task of 'disenthralling ourselves from our over-emphasis on power' (Burns 1978: 11) still considers that both 'power and leadership are measured by the degree of production of intended effect'. (Burns 1978: 28) In this, his approach is very close to that of Lukes who suggests that, as a minimum, discussions of leadership and power look at 'two questions: in the difference that is made and the making of that difference . . . the first an interest in the outcomes and second an interest in the focus of power.' (Lukes 1986: 5) And, we will usually find a leader positioned at the focus of power.

One nineteenth-century trend, as exemplified by Thomas Carlyle, was to write history as the product of the actions of great men. However, an alternative nineteenth-century tradition, that of the socialist and Marxist approaches to history, which flows into the twentieth century through Plekanov, via Gramsci and into the writings of post-Marxists (?) such as Foucault, has tended to concentrate on structure and argue that direct attribution of responsibility to individual power holders for any particular sets of outcomes will rarely make sense. Foucault, for example, argues that,

> . . . we know perfectly well that even if we reach the point of designating all [the] people, all those 'decision makers', we will still not really know why and how the decision was made, how it came to be accepted by everybody, and how it is that it hurts a particular category of person, . . (Kritzman 1988: 103)

On the other hand, C. Wright Mills, among others, has argued that it

> . . . . is now sociologically realistic, morally fair and politically imperative to make demands upon men of power and to hold them responsible for specific courses of events. (Wright Mills 1959: 100)

Studies of leaders and leadership are almost inevitably subscribing to this latter approach asking such questions as: Did the intervention of an individual or collective agency make a difference? Or, did it do so in the way intended? Leaders and leadership will be judged strong or weak to the extent that they can product intended effects. Judgements about the possession or location of power and ability of leaders depend on assessing what Goldman calls 'the truth of certain subjunctive conditionals

– most of them counterfactuals. (Goldman 1974: 789) At which 'branching' or 'turning' points could or did the exercise of power (leadership) make a difference?

Studies of leadership have usually concentrated on the 'great men' of history, the Napoleons, Churchills and Reagans and it may well be that the actions of such individuals 'made a difference' to the lives of thousands or millions of others. But leaders also operate at less exalted levels and indeed it may be that the way they emerge and the way they interact with their followers may tell us a great deal about a particular society. Our interest is, of course, Japan. Is there anything distinctive about the structures within which Japanese leaders work either at the high or low levels? Are there any characteristic features of Japanese leadership or the way it is studied?.

* * *

There is plenty of evidence of leaders and leadership in Japan's history. The earliest histories, the *Kojiki* and *Nihongi*, describe men and, more rarely, women making decisions which were crucial in taking Japan in certain directions. The family feuds of the Gempei wars, the creation of the Kamakura shogunate and the battles of the period of 'Warring States' are replete with tales about the actions of leaders.

The two papers on pre-modern history which appear in this collection look not so much at the highest level of society but rather at aspects of leadership at the local level. Kondō Shigekazu considers the nature of the leadership system in the medieval family based on documents of the thirteenth and fourteenth centuries. He shows how the system of inheritance changed during the Kamakura period eliminating the previously existing equality of siblings so that only one son, usually the eldest, would inherit the family estate. This new system stimulated rivalry between brothers in powerful families leading directly or indirectly to the Onin wars. Contrary to the conventional wisdom that society was changed by the Onin wars, he argues that 'the changes in society caused the civil war'. Moreover, contrary to Murakami Yasusuke and others who argue that the '*ie*' society has existed continuously since the twelfth century, Kondō argues that it is of much more recent origin and was not the only pattern of family organization.

Detlev Taranczewski's study of leadership in villages of late medieval Japan shows the importance of contracts, the role played by locally-appointed leaders and traces the emergence of a 'proto-parliamentary institution' where 'the representatives and leaders of the villages . . . [deliberated on] . . . their common political, economic and agricultural problems'. Given the discussion about whether democratic practice can take root in Japan, this is an important example.

The activities of the three 'great unifiers', Oda Nobunaga, Toyotomi Hideyoshi and Tokugawa Ieyasu created the conditions that made 250 years of Tokugawa peace possible. At the local level the daimyo had considerable discretion in the way they chose to govern local affairs and they, in turn, gave village communities significant amounts of local autonomy. We had expected offers of papers on some aspects of leadership in this period but none were forthcoming.

Leaders of the heroic mould were familiar faces in Japanese history before the Meiji restoration. In the mid-nineteenth century there are the actions of local leaders who precipitate and lead the movement which overthrew the Tokugawa shogunate. Unfortunately, there were no offers of papers about this group either, but there was a contribution about one of the Europeans who sought to introduce Japan and the Japanese to the wider world. Willy Vande Walle introduces us to Charles de Montblanc who was agent for the Satsuma clan in the 1860s, then in 1870 he briefly served the new Meiji government acting as its *chargé d'affaires* in Paris. How important he was is open to some doubt. He was variously called a 'charlatan', 'dabbler in exoticism' and a 'fortune-hunter eager to establish . . . . a reputation as an expert on Japan'. Nevertheless, he was one of a group of foreigners who were cleverly used by the leaders of Japan in this transitional period to make an impact on and find out more about the rather threatening outside world.

Western perceptions of what was happening in Japan just before and just after the Restoration are Seija Jalagin's main theme. Focusing on the leadership, she demonstrates how the Western image of the Emperor changed over a period of fifteen years from being that of a divine but politically weak figure to a modern constitutional monarch capable of leading, at least by example. This, she argues, reflects less what was actually happening in Japan and more the hopes and aims of the Westerners living there.

It is often asserted that Japan had never been invaded or occupied by a foreign power during recorded history until the arrival of the Allied forces in August 1945. Yet, as Herman

Moeshart shows, strictly speaking, this is not true. In March 1861 a Russian ship dropped anchor off Tsushima and the Russians began to build a settlement that would have been the base for its control of the island which has a strategically important location between Kyushu and Korea. International pressure, mainly from the British, forced the Russians to evacuate the following September. The Russian threat receded and the influence of the British in Edo increased. This attempt by the Russians to seize control of Japanese territory was further proof of the real dangers posed by the Western powers.

There was a clearly identifiable group which, individually and collectively, provided the leadership for a Japan which was under political, economic and cultural threat from the Western powers in the mid-nineteenth century. As expected, the conference attracted several papers in this group. If Montblanc's influence on the course of Japan's history was marginal despite several visits, Herbert Spencer's contribution was much more important although he never actually visited the country. As Alistair Swale demonstrates Mori Arinori's 'progressive conservatism' was rooted in Spencer's thought and thus the ideas of Spencer had a strong influence on the development of the Meiji educational system.

One might have expected that education reform and language reform would have taken place hand in hand, with central government taking a leading role in both. However, despite the fact that there were many people in and around government, including Mori Arinori, who were acutely aware of the need to standardize the written language, in Annette Skovsted Hansen's words, 'official language reforms appear to have been few, largely limited to script reform, and only launched after they had more or less taken effect in reality'. Government did not lead, it followed. But who? She demonstrates that there was no individual or single group which played a critical role in this process. Intellectuals provided a definition of the problem of language reform, writers experimented with possible solutions and the residents of Tokyo, many of them recent immigrants from rural Japan, generated practical solutions to the problem of the creation of a standard dialect. Only after this process was complete, or at least well underway, did government venture to suggest standard reforms in 1900.

Not only language had to change. Almost every aspect of everyday life was affected by the Meiji restoration. Selçuk Esenbel shows how 'attire, household environment, and manners and ethics' were affected by the Westernisation process. Here government did take a lead with its decision in 1872 that the bureaucratic élite should adopt Western dress and hair-styles, but this did not resolve the problem. At least among the élite groups there were no simple solutions, certainly not the often quoted 'Western at work, Japanese at home' and she presents ample evidence that the private inner rooms of Japanese life, both literally and figuratively, had become hybrid mixtures by the late nineteenth century. The self perception of the modern in-dividual required a Western cultural identity as well as a 'Japanese' one – a bi-cultural context to the 'civilizing process'.

Consideration of leadership in the Meiji period would not be complete without mention of the role of the Emperor. Here we have two papers. Ewa Palasz-Rutkowska considers the role of the Emperor within the structures created by the Meiji constitution in comparison with the role of the monarch within the frameworks of the Polish constitution of 1791 and the Prussian constitution of 1850. Ernst Lokowandt essays a similar comparative exercise but concentrates on the provisions of the Imperial House Law comparing it, on the one hand, to con-temporary equivalents in Prussian, Bavaria and Hanover and on the other with Japanese tradition. Whereas Palasz-Rutkowska concludes there was nothing unique in the role assigned to the Emperor, Lokowandt argues that the Meiji state was founded on the Imperial Family since the Imperial House Law was the basis of the constitution. This placed primary emphasis on the Tennō right to rule deriving from his divine ancestors alone.

To be sure, the Meiji constitution blurred, perhaps deli-berately, the locus of political responsibility. The framers of the constitution wanted a political structure that resembled the parliamentary systems of European monarchies while retaining real power in the hands of an oligarchy that had formed around and identified with the Emperor. Moreover, the imperial institution and its mystique were prompted from the late nineteenth century to disable criticism of its activities. The result was, in Maruyama's well known paragraph.

> An uncertain sharing of responsibility was preferred so that no person could be pointed out as bearing the ultimate responsibility for decisions. It is obvious that the mechanism of the Emperor-system state had within it the danger of developing into a colossal system of irresponsibility. (Maruyama 1964: 44)

The military occupied a privileged position within the Meiji government structure which interfered with the ability of the civilian government to control events at times of crisis. However, it would be wrong, therefore, to depict the government as dominated at all times by the military and military ambition. Katō Tomosaburō (1861–1923) was an admiral of the Imperial Navy 1913–23, Prime Minister 1922–3 but, perhaps most importantly, leader of the Japanese delegation at the Washington Naval Conference in 1921. Despite having been a strong supporter of the 'Big Navy' option following the Great War in Europe, he was quickly persuaded of the need to limit the size of Japan's fleet in the course of the negotiations in Washington where he even won the reputation of being pacifist. While Prime Minister, he oversaw the withdrawal of troops from Siberia and Tsingtao and the reduction in the size of both the army and navy. He realized that any future war could only be fought on the basis of the total mobilization of the states resources and that finance for such a war effort could not be found domestically. Only the US could supply the necessary financial resources, 'we can therefore only conclude', he wrote, 'that a war with America is to be avoided'. Ian Nish's view is that he was a good leader, flexible and able to face unpopularity when he realized that military capability was not the only criterion for policy-making. His Prime Ministership shows that it was possible for military officers to oversee military contraction, at least in the 1920s.

Leaders do not only make a difference at the international and national levels of politics. Iwasa Sakutarō (1879–1967) was an anarchist-communist who was active in Japan from the 1920s when the anarchist movement was at its peak until the mid-sixties when support and interest had dwindled so far as to be almost non-existent. John Crump's brief biography demonstrates that Iwasa conspicuously refused to lead in any sense in which the word is usually understood and yet he did make a difference being an inspiration to all in the movement until his death. However, ironically perhaps, there was a notion of leadership in Iwasa's revolutionary theory which ascribed to the anarchist communist revolutionaries the leading role in the process (revolution?) that would bring about anarchist-communism. Crump argues that requiring the masses to trust the good intentions of revolutionary leaders is fraught with peril and contradicts the aim of creating the leaderless condition of anarchist communism.

Iwasa's leadership by example was very similar to the role played by a number of his contemporaries who were instrumental in establishing communes which aimed to demonstrate that people could live together sharing property. Several such communities were set up in Japan before the war and a number still exist. Christoph Bruman considers the role of the founders of four such communes; three men, Nishida Tenko, Ozaki Masutarō, Yaoi Nisshō, and one woman, Fukuzato Niwa. Bruman shows that contrary to what Nakane might lead us to expect, these were not 'weak leaders'. They were powerful and colourful personalities who were able to attract followers by their practical examples and sincerity.

Fifty years after the end of the Pacific war it is tempting to speculate about what would have happened if Japan had won, or at least had not been as so convincingly defeated. If the Japanese had been able to claim some kind of victory, would this have been ascribed to the brilliant leadership of the Emperor ably assisted by Prince Konoe, on the one hand, and such military expertise as provided by Tōjō Hideki, on the other? Would Western observers of Japan be writing commentaries on the importance of the individual leader within Japanese society and history from Shōtoku Taishi through Tokugawa Ieyasu to Nakasone Yasuhiro? Or is there a central truth in Nakane Chie's observations about the 'inability of Japanese soil to grow a charismatic leader'. (Nakane 1970: 70–1)

No-one attempted the perilous task of assessing the locus of leadership during the war years but Gerhard Krebs uses recently released US government documents to re-evaluate the career of a diplomat who played a key role in US-Japan relations both immediately before and after the Pacific War. Terasaki Hidenari was a diplomat posted to Washington less than a year before the outbreak of war. His main activity at that time was to set up an intelligence network to provide Japan with political, economic and military information about the USA. Immediately after the war, Terasaki and his American wife, Gwen, became the embodiment of good US Japanese relations. Despite the aversion of Japanese historians to dealing with the spy network period, Krebs argues there was no necessary incompatibility between involvement in intelligence gathering and post-war peace promotion. Terasaki provided the appropriate leadership for his country both in wartime and in peace.

Preparing for the occupation, US forces looked for potential leaders who would be able to provide an alternative leadership for the defeated nation and who would ensure that Japan would abandon its militarist ambitions. As the communists had provided the most uncompromising resistance to the war effort it was perhaps natural that the Americans should have investigated the possibility of giving assistance to the leaders of the Japanese communist movement whether in prison or in exile. Henry Oinas-Kukkonen describes this process. US officials first contacted Nosaka Sanzō while he was in Yanan with the Chinese communists and concluded he was a moderate, sensible and talented man whose programme, 'sounded like a paraphrase of the American Bill of Rights'. In autumn 1945 when Tokuda Kyuichi and Shiga Yoshio were released from prisons in Japan, they, too, were, evaluated by American officials. These three became the leading personalities in the reformed Japan Communist Party (JCP). Perhaps it was inevitable that the early plans for American cooperation with the JCP would be abandoned given the right wing bent of many of the commanders of the US occupying forces and the nature of the post-war international situation, but there was still room for co-existence in the first part of the occupation and it is interesting to conjecture about what more positive cooperation might have led to, both for the conduct of the occupation and the development of the Communist Party.

More than anyone else, with the possible exception of Yoshida Shigeru, Douglas MacArthur provided leadership for post-war Japan and a considerable amount has been published about him and the policies implemented by his administration. Peter Lowe provides a new perspective on MacArthur by summarizing British perceptions and reactions to his leadership based on Foreign Office documents. Overall, contemporary British impressions were that although a good deal had been achieved, 'extravagant claims were forthcoming on the extent of the achievement'. Free from the occupation Japan would, British observers thought, settle down within a political system which would be if not democratic, then at least liberal.

One topic on which MacArthur held strong views, often contrary to orders from Washington, was the retention of the Emperor. He held that the Emperor should be retained to give credence and support to the occupation's reform policies. Gerhart Krebs demonstrates that, ordered to collect evidence to demonstrate Hirohito's guilt for Japan's breaches of international law, GHQ under MacArthur's leadership struggled to produce evidence to show his innocence. Many senior Japanese officials, including Terasaki Hidenari, willingly cooperated in this enterprise. Olavi Fält's paper examines the changing image of the Emperor from the time of the Occupation until the end of the 1950s. At first, despite the profound constitutional changes, the emphasis was on the deep bond between the ruler and his people with only marginal changes being made to popularize his image. Following independence, the Emperor was projected as taking part, along with his people in the task of reconstructing Japan. The application of science was one part of this national project and many articles about him stressed his scientific achievements. His role as a family man, his love of gardening and his interest in sumo and baseball were also mentioned in the reports about him in the 1950s to create the image of an emperor in harmony with the new constitution.

Bert Edström brings our attention forcefully back to the issue of leadership and the question, Do leaders matter? More specifically, do Japanese Prime Ministers make a difference in the process of foreign policy-making. The constitution provides for the Prime Minister to act as decision-maker and a national spokesman. However, following a review of the record of post-war Prime Ministers, Edström concludes that there is little evidence of them providing positive leadership. This is mainly because the kind of people favoured by the Liberal Democratic Party (LDP) have been men of caution and experience rather than men with innovative ideas. Moreover, the task of the LDP leader has largely been to maintain the factional coalition which was the LDP, and thus the post has been filled by consensus builders rather than forceful leaders. Finally, he points out, Japan has not been well placed within the international system to play a more positive role even if the leaders had been there. Things are changing though. Japan is emerging as a hesitant but stronger actor in international affairs, at least regionally, and the LDP will inevitably change in response to reforms in the electoral system. As this takes place the factors which have constrained the leadership ability of the Prime Minister hitherto may become less significant.

The LDP could justifiably claim to have led Japan through the period of post-war recovery and its reward was virtually unchallenged control of the political structure. It was only the defections of such reformers as Osawa Ichirō which forced the general election in 1993 where it lost its majority in the lower house and, apparently, its mandate to rule. A grand coalition led by Hosokawa Morihiro oversaw the passage of legislation reforming the electoral system, but once he was forced to resign, it proved impossible to keep the coalition together. With the

LDP back in power in the summer of 1994, admittedly with the support of the Socialist Party and the Sakigake, some argued that the process of reform was over. Arthur Stockwin disagrees. The old '1955 system' cannot be put back together even if the LDP wins a clear majority in the next general election, the first under the new system.

Osawa Ichirō has been the most important single actor in Japanese politics since the late 1980s even though he has only rarely occupied senior government posts, yet little has been written about him in English. David William's paper on him, the final essay in this collection, is a first step towards filling this gap. First elected in 1969, Osawa was close to Tanaka Kakuei and a member of his faction. Osawa is ambitious and has a vision of politics in Japan where power would alternate between two conservative parties as in the USA. His actions in early summer 1993 broke the LDP's hold on power, his activities since then have been directed at creating a viable alternative to it. The success of the Shinshintō in the 1995 House of Councillors election suggest that he is more than half-way to realizing his vision. In terms of Burns definition of measurement of leadership – the 'degree of production of intended effect' – surely Osawa would score very highly.

★ ★ ★

Our rather serendipitous survey of Japanese history reveals no shortage of leaders or difficulty in discussing leadership in a more abstract sense. It has also identified gaps in the English-language literature about leaders in Japan. It is not only in this survey that there is little or nothing on the position of leaders in the Heian period and before, in the early years of the Tokugawa period and during the Fifteen Years War (1931–1945). Before ending this brief introduction, two comments on leadership in Japan – both being ideas that came up in informal discussion at the conference.

Firstly, there is the often-cited tendency of Japanese leaders to avoid taking on an up-front role preferring to exercise power by manipulating events from behind the scenes. Certainly there are examples in the Heian period of retired emperors exercising power at second and even third hand in very complex arrangements. In the Meiji period authority was wielded in the name of the emperor but, as our two papers on the emperor demonstrate, there was not much difference between this arrangement and counterparts in Europe. Tanaka Kakuei continued to exert political power after he resigned but he did not resign through choice and never lost the ambition to become Prime Minister once more. Osawa, his protégé, has exercised power as king-maker without ever actually being king, but no one would be so rash as to argue he has no personal ambition to become Prime Minister. There must be some doubt about whether this pattern of indirect rule has any salience for contemporary Japan.

Secondly, as a general rule and social scientists aside, it is usually those of a conservative persuasion who favour explan-ations of history and politics which emphasize the importance of human agency. Individuals are depicted as playing a crucial role in the course of events which lead to peace or war, success or failure. In contrast, those influenced by the socialist tradition are more apt to stress the role of impersonal forces, be they the nature of the class struggle within a country or the role of imperialism in the international arena. In Japan, however, we have the curious situation where it is the politicians of the right who place greatest stress on impersonal forces, particularly when it comes to a discussion of the war which began with fighting in Manchria in 1931 and culminated in defeat at the hands of the Allies in 1945. Throughout the first half of 1995 in discussions about the Japan's war responsibility, right-wing poli-ticians repeatedly argued that Japan was merely responding to a hostile international environment and therefore was not ultimately responsible for the war the resulting suffering, nor was it sensible to ascribe blame for the war to any individual or set of individuals.

This not only prevented any further discussion of the problem of the responsibility of the Emperor for the series of events that led to Pearl Harbor and beyond, it also blocked discussion of the role played by other leaders in the civil and military services in the decisions which led to war. As we have seen there were those like Katō Tomosaburō who in the early 1920s were convinced of the need to avoid war with the USA. We also know that even in the late 1930s this opinion was not uncommon among both military and civilian leaders. So what happened? Were the dynamics of the situation such that there really was nothing that any person or group of people could do to prevent the gradual broadening of the conflict? If there were people who could have 'made a difference', why did they hold back? These are not just questions of historic significance. Writers such as Karel Van Wolferen argue that there is very little difference between the system of irresponsibility that Maruyama identifies in pre-war Japan and the structure of power today. (Wolferen 1989) The study of leadership in both twentieth-century Japan and before needs to continue to expose the pattern of decision-making in the past so we can better understand the trends of the present.

BIBLIOGRAPHY

Burns, J.M., (1978) *Leadership*, New York: Harper and Row.
Goldman, A., (1974) 'On the Measurement of Power' *Journal of Philosophy*, 71, 231–252.
Kritzman, L.D. (Ed.), *Foucault: Politics, Philosophy, Culture: interviews and other writings of Michel Foucault, 1977–1984* London: Routledge, Chapman and Hall.
Lukes, S., (1986) *Power*, Oxford: Blackwell.
Maruyama, M., (1964) 'Japanese Thought', *Journal of Social and Political Ideas in Japan* April.
Mughan, A., and Patterson, S.C., (1992) *Political Leadership in Democratic Societies* Chicago: Nelson-Hall.
Nakane, C., (1970) *Japanese Society*, London: Pelican.
van Wolferen, Karel (1989) *The Enigma of Japanese Power* London: Macmillan.
Wright, Mills C., (1959) *The Causes of World War Three* London: Secker and Warburg.

2

Leadership in the Medieval Japanese Warrior Family

KONDŌ SHIGEKAZU

INTRODUCTION

The purpose of this paper is to consider leadership in the medieval Japanese warrior family between the twelfth and fourteenth centuries. That is, the *sōryō* system. '*Sōryō*' originally referred to controlling wholly divided fiefs, but later was used to refer to a person. The term is usually used in the latter sense, and primarily in the case where a fief is divided among siblings. Thus, a brother controls his brothers and sisters fiefs which they inherit from their mother or father. However, scholars are divided on the mechanics of the system.

There are two views concerning the relationship among brothers and sisters: some hold that the eldest brother dominated his brothers and sisters as their master, while the others hold that the eldest brother only represented his brothers and sisters who were independent of their eldest brother. There are also two views concerning the change of the *sōryō* system in the fourteenth century: first, that brothers and sisters became independent of their eldest brother, and second, that the eldest brother came to dominate his brothers and sisters more strongly. As a result, four theories about the *sōryō* system have been advanced:

1. Before the fourteenth century the eldest brother dominated his brothers and sisters, a system which broke down after the fourteenth century.
2. Before the fourteenth century the eldest brother dominated his brothers and sisters. This became stronger after the fourteenth century.

3. Before the fourteenth century the eldest brother represented his brothers and sisters. After the fourteenth century brothers and sisters became more independent of their eldest brother.

4. Before the fourteenth century the eldest brother represented his brothers and sisters. After the fourteenth century brothers and sisters became subject to their eldest brother.

The *sōryō* system was a subject of controversy in the 1950s and 60s. In a debate begun by Matsumoto Shinpachiro, he explained the *sōryō* system on the basis of the first of the above-mentioned theories and described the change in the fourteenth century as a 'feudal revolution.' But in the subsequent controversy it became clear that the domination of the eldest brother was not very strong. If the brothers and the sisters had their own fiefs, they were independent of their eldest brother. The *sōryō* system was built on the basis that the brothers and the sisters had their own fiefs, and the eldest brother could not strongly dominate his brothers and sisters who were independent of him.

In order to shed light on the overall debate I shall take up the case of the 'family council' that operated in the Shibuya family in Iriki Estate, Satsuma Province (west Japan).

MATERIAL

The Shibuya family and Iriki Estate are well known in European and American Japanese history research circles, for the documents of the Shibuya family and Iriki Estate were translated into English by Asakawa Kan'ichi and published by Yale University Press and Oxford University Press in 1929: *The Documents of Iriki*. (Asakawa was assistant professor of history and curator of the Japanese and Chinese collections in Yale University at the time). These documents were the ones held by the main line and by the Terao and Okamoto branch lines. However, Asakawa, and the editors of the second edition published in 1955, were unaware of other Iriki documents, those held by another branch family, the Yamaguchi. The documents of the Yamaguchi family were introduced to the scholarly world in 1963 by Gomi Yoshio, then associate professor of Kagoshima University.

I shall focus on two of these documents, both of which are included in *Kamakura Ibun*, volume 29, numbers 22292 and

22516 (*Kamakura Ibun* – edited by Takeuchi Rizō in 42 volumes contains 32866 documents of the Kamakura period (1185–1334) in chronological order).

THE SHIBUYA FAMILY AND IRIKI ESTATE

The Shibuya family was named after their original homeland the Shibuya Estate in Sagami Province (east Japan). Iriki Estate lay south in Kyūshū over 1000 km west of the Shibuya Estate. The Kamakura shogunate granted the Iriki Estate as a fief to the Shibuya family in 1247, as a result of a political upheaval that year. The then holder of Iriki Estate (a branch of the powerful Chiba family) had had its lands confiscated. In recognition of his loyal service the Iriki Estate was granted to Shibuya Jōshin and four other nearby estates to his four brothers. Iriki estate covers an area of about 200 square kilometres and includes nine villages. Jōshin transferred the Iriki estate in lots to his several sons. Jōshin's eldest son, Akishige, inherited the largest portion, made up of the three villages of Ichibino, Kiyoshiki and Kami-soeda. Akishige transferred Kami-soeda Village to his son Atsushige, who in turn transferred it in lots to his son Masashige and to his grandson Koreshige. Masashige was the *sōryō* of Kami-soeda Village. Koreshige named his holding in Kami-soeda Yamaguchi Village. Masashige did not recognize Yamaguchi Village, but Koreshige's successors came to be called the Yamaguchi family.

There was a boundary dispute between Masashige and Koreshige at the beginning of the fourteenth century. They took the dispute to the court of shogunate. Koreshige was the plaintiff and Masashige the defendant. There are two letters of refutation by Masashige in the document collection of the Yamaguchi family. According to the legal procedure of the shogunate, a letter of accusation was sent to the defendant and a letter of refutation to the plaintiff. After three rounds of exchange of accusation and refutation, the court subpoenaed the plaintiff and defendant and delivered its judgement. In the present case only two letters of refutation – by Mashige, and sent to Koreshige – remain, and we do not know the eventual judgement. However, the documents provide great insight into the Shibuya family council.

THE FAMILY COUNCIL OF THE SHIBUYA IN IRIKI

According to the first letter of refutation by Masashige dated the seventh month of the third year of Kagen (1305). Masashige's grandfather Akishige left it in his will that the inheritors of his holdings should resolve their disputes between themselves within the family council. Masashige obeyed his grandfather and waited for the family council to be held. But Koreshige did not obey his great-grandfather and brought the accusation to the court of the shogunate, since he was afraid that the illegality of his actions would come to light in the family council.

While Koreshige's original letter of accusation is not extant, his claims are known to us through Masashige's second letter of refutation (the first month of the next year, 1306), in which they are quoted. According to Koreshige, a family council was held. It investigated the boundary and advised the parties concerned to come to a compromise. Koreshige was disposed to obey the family council, though he was not satisfied with its decision but Masashige did not obey the family council, and Koreshige brought the accusation to the court of the shogunate.

Countering Koreshige's second accusation, Masashige stated his case in great detail in his second refutation. Masashige said: the family council was planned to be held on the thirteenth day of the fifth month of the second year of Kagen (1304) at the temple in Yamazaki. On the appointed day Masashige presented himself, but Koreshige did not appear. It was Koreshige who did not obey the family council. It is natural that cases of both parties contradicted each other, but it is noteworthy that both parties recognized the family council.

THE FAMILY COUNCIL AND THE *SŌRYŌ* SYSTEM

The family council that was held was based on what Akishige laid down in his testament, or '*okibumi*'. '*Okibumi*' or 'left letter' means the letter which should be left for future generations. *Okibumi* was written for a house or a village. *Okibumi* may be divided into two types: those which tell the history of a house or a village and those which provide the rules which the members of a house or a village should observe. When an *okibumi* was written on the occasion of an inheritance, it usually provided rules which inheritors should observe following the requirement of inheritorship.

The Shibuya family in Iriki made *okibumi* for generations. Akishige's *okibumi* is not extant, but we know from Masashiges second refutation that Akishige wrote his *okibumi* on the twenty–seventh day of the second month of the third year of Bun'ei (1266). It provided that the inheritors should solve their problems among themselves based on the family council, and that an offender who went against the family council should lose his suit. In addition, it makes clear that disputes should not be solved by unilateral action of the *sōryō*.

According to Masashige's first refutation, Akishige's *okibumi* was held by Akishige's eldest son Kimishige. Masashige referred to Kimishige as *sōryō*. As mentioned above, Akishige held Ichihino, Kiyoshiki and Kami-soeda villages in Iriki. He trans-ferred Ichihino to his eldest son Kimishige, Kiyoshiki in lots to his sons Arishige and Muneshige and Kami-soeda to his son Atsushige. Kimishige was the *sōryō* among the inheritors of Akishige's holdings. Mashashige was the *sōryō* between the inheritors of Atsushige's holdings, but Atsushige's holdings themselves were part of Akishige's holdings. Masashige should refer to Kimishige as *sōryō* to the extent that he obeyed Akishige.

The family council was held by the *sōryō* system of the inheritors of Akishige's holdings. It was not dictatorship but leadership in the family council which the *sōry ō* needed. The *sōryō* system did not mean the despotism of the *sōryō* but the unity of the family which the *sōryō* led.

GENERALITY OF THE FAMILY COUNCIL

Several studies have been made on the family council of the Shibuya, since the documents of the Yamaguchi were introduced by Gomi Yoshio. Kobayashi Kazutake showed some cases of the family council of several families besides the Shibuya: the case of the Takanashi family in Shinano Province (east Japan) and the case of the Kikuchi family in Higo Province (west Japan). In the Takanashi family, a dispute among the family was judged by the family council in 1338. The Kikuchi made two *okibumi* in 1338 and 1342. These *okibumi* provided that the domestic admini-stration should not be made by the *sōryō* but by the family council. It has been made clear by Kobayashi's study that the family council was not a special case of the Shibuya but a general case of the medieval warrior family.

One of Kobayashi's central and important points is that the family council had the same structure as the family union or '*ichizoku-ikki*' in the fourteenth to fifteenth century. '*Ikki*' means originally unifying people who have a common interest, but it also means the union which is formed through the act of unifying itself.

When the debate on the *sōryō* system first began, it was

commonly accepted that the *sōryō* system and the *ikki* stood opposite to each other. According to Matsumoto's theory, the *sōryō* system in which the eldest brother dominated his brothers and sisters broke down after the fourteenth century. The lords who became independent of their eldest brothers respectively formed the *ikki* not by blood but by a shared territorial bond. The change from the *sōryō* system to the *ikki* in the fourteenth century is thus regarded as a change from the society based on blood relationships to a society of shared territorial bond or a change from slave society to feudal society. The *ichizoku-ikki*, which was formed from the members of a family, is not referred to as a typical *ikki* but a transitional relationship, from the *sōryō* system to the *ikki*.

On the other hand, according to Kobayashi's study, the *sōryō* system and *ikki* are compatible. The structure of the *ikki* was already realized as the family council in the *sōryō* system. Kobayashi did not specifically point out the relation between the family council or the *ikki* and *sōryō* system, but it follows from his research that the *sōryō* system itself was formed through the principle of the *ikki*.

THE PRINCIPLES OF THE SŌRYŌ SYSTEM

The *sōryō* system unifies primarily brothers and sisters, though it could be enlarged from generation to generation. There were two principles which unified brothers and sisters: the first was that father or mother dominated sons or daughters absolutely, the second was that brothers and sisters were independent of each other.

The transfer of property from father or mother to son or daughter was distinguished from that between parties who did not have a blood relationship. A son or a daughter who got property from his or her father or mother had the duty to provide a comfortable life in old age and consolation after death to his or her father or mother. If a son or a daughter was undutiful, his or her father or mother could take back the property and transfer it to another son or daughter.

After a father's or a mother's death the eldest son as *sōryō* supervised the other sons and daughters performance of their filial duty as noted above. If a brother or sister was undutiful to his or her father or mother, the eldest brother as *sōryō* could take away the property, but could take the property from his brother or sister not under his own right but in his father's or mother's place. In the debate over the *sōryō* system several cases were offered to show the *sōryō* dominance. But almost all these cases can be explained by representation of the father's or mother's dominance. The father's or mother's dominance was strong, but the *sōryō* could not dominate his brothers or sisters independently of the father's or mother's dominance.

Another element to be considered is the difference between brothers and sisters. It was the general case that the eldest brother became the *sōryō*, but the father or mother could designate another son as the *sōryō*. Daughters could not be designated as *sōryō*. The *sōryō* inherited twice as much as his brother or sister. Even if the eldest son was not designated as *sōryō*, he could inherit at least one-fifth as much as the *sōryō*. Otherwise, brothers and sisters were on an equal footing.

A father or a mother could transfer holdings only to the eldest son. This was based on the absolute dominance of a father or a mother and not on the eldest brother's dominance. The eldest brother could not deny his brothers or sisters inheritance rights. If a father or a mother died before transferring the holdings, the eldest son could not monopolize the holdings, but the holdings would have to be divided among all sons and daughters.

The fact that brothers and sisters were on an equal footing and that each had holdings was divisive, and in fact disputes among them about inheritance of the holdings or the boundary of the territory were endemic in the thirteenth century. On the other hand, the absolute dominance of a father or a mother served to unify siblings; in order to do their duty to their father or mother, brothers and sisters had to be unified. These two factors formed the *sōryō* system.

THE SŌRYŌ SYSTEM AND HIGHER AUTHORITY

The *sōryō* system was a kind of self-governing system. This leads to the question of the relation between the *sōryō* system and higher authority. Let us now return to the boundary dispute in Kami-soeda Village, Iriki estate. Koreshige claimed that he brought the accusation to the court of the shogunate because Masashige did not obey the family council. With respect to Masashige's refutation that it was Koreshige who encroached the boundary, Koreshige held that if he had encroached the boundary, then Masashige should have requested a family council, and if Koreshige did not obey the family council, Masashige should have brought the accusation to the shogunate. These remarks came from his intention to present the fact that Masashige requested neither the family council nor the judge of the shogunate as proof that the Masashige's refutation was groundless. From these remarks we infer the following: while the family council was respected as a way to resolve troubles among the family, an appeal to higher authority was regarded as reasonable when the other party did not obey the family council.

In fact, there is an interesting example of an appeal to higher authority several decades later. Regarding a dispute over the right of possession involving an inheritance from Akishige's brother, in 1334 a letter of reconciliation, bearing the signatures of several members of the family as guarantor, was drawn up. Shigemoto, Akishige's grandson, Jōshin's great-grandson, also signed as the *sōryō* among all of Jōshin's inheritors. This letter contained the following provision: in accordance with the consensus of the family, an accusation should be brought to the higher authority against anyone who broke the provisions of the letter of reconciliation.

This was the principle that troubles within a family should be solved through the family's autonomy. Higher authority might receive an accusation if it were brought in accordance with the consensus of the family. In other words higher authority was expected to complement the family's autonomy.

DISSOLUTION OF THE *SŌRYŌ* SYSTEM

The *sōryō* system, as mentioned above, was formed on the grounds that brothers and sisters were on a equal footing and each possessed holdings, and it demanded division of holdings. The division from generation to generation made holdings smaller and smaller. But the lordship needed holdings kept at a certain size.

Division of holdings and keeping holdings at a certain size were appropriate in the twelfth century while land was being rapidly developed. Family heads enlarged their holdings and could divide them while maintaining them at a certain size. Moreover, the Kamakura shogunate was established at the end of this century, and since there were many lords who were against the shogunate, lords supporting the shogunate could enlarge their holdings through taking their opponent's holdings.

But the development of land and the reorganization of holdings passed their peak by about the middle of the thirteenth century. As lords could not enlarge their holdings any more, they had to transfer their holdings only to their eldest sons. A father could deny his son's or daughter's inheritance rights, but if a father died before transferring his holdings, nobody could deny the inheritance rights of the father's son and daughter. Families tried to change the inheritance system: some of them succeeded, but others failed. For example, with the Shibuya family in Iriki, the largest branch family, the Terao, failed to change the inheritance system, collapsed and in consequence entered the head family's service. On the other hand, the head family succeeded in changing the inheritance system, unified the holdings of the branch families through intermarriage and adoption and realized their lordship over the whole of Iriki at the end of the fifteenth century.

The establishment of the system that only the eldest son inherited his father's holdings conclusively changed the relationship among siblings. The absolute dominance of the eldest brother was built up and a new family structure appeared in which the eldest brother took his brothers as retainers. The relationship between siblings became similar to that between master and vassal, and the relationship between master and vassal became regarded as the enlarged relationship of the family. This point I would like to regard as the establishment of the so-called Japanese family or '*ie*'.

The change of the inheritance system also changed the character of disputes among brothers. While each brother had his own inheritance right on an equal footing, the brothers who were not the *sōryō* could inherit the holdings and could establish new branch families. They might have a dispute about, for example, the boundary, but they did not contest the post of the *sōryō*. But when the inheritance right was limited to only one brother, the brothers who were not the inheritor could no longer live as lords. They had to contest the post of the inheritor. The post of the only inheritor was also called *sōryō*. That is, the meaning of the word '*sōryō*' changed.

The significance of this change should be understood, for it bears on our view of the medieval period. For example, the so-called 'Onin Civil War' (1467–1477) was brought about by several internal troubles of the powerful warrior families. It is said that the Japanese society changed entirely after the Onin Civil War, but strictly speaking, the changes in society caused the civil war.

CONCLUSION

Fifteen years ago the most logical, systematic and influential theory about '*ie*' was presented by three professors, Murakami Yasusuke, Kumon Shunpei and Sato Seizaburo in their *Bunmei toshite no Ie Shakai* (*Ie* Society as a Pattern of Civilisation). The authors regarded the *sōryō* system as the original form of '*ie*' and tried to find the fundamental character of '*ie*' in the *sōryō* system. Then, they assert that the '*ie*' society has existed continuously from the twelfth century, and that it was as rational a system as the *sōryō* system. According to their theory, it is difficult for Japanese people to change the '*ie*' society, and it is not necessary, either.

But I cannot bring myself to accept this theory. In my opinion, the '*ie*' was not entirely different from the family which had developed within the *sōryō* system. The so-called '*ie* society is not guaranteed a long life. On the other hand, the *sōryō* system and the *ikki* show traditions other than '*ie* society. Japanese people have, like other peoples, various sorts of traditions, and Japanese society has, like other societies, the possibility of change.

BIBLIOGRAPHY

Asakawa, Kan'ichi, (1929) *The Documents of Iriki*. New Haven and London. 2d edit.Tokyo (1963): 1955

Gomi, Yoshio, 'Irikiin Yamaguchishi ni tsuite – Yamaguchi Monjo no Shōkai.' *Kadai Shigaku* 11: 1–14.

Kobayashi, Kazutake, (1987) 'Ikki no hō no Keisei – Ichizoku Ketsugō no Hōteki Seikaku.' *Shien* 46: 1–2: 29–50.

Kondō, Shigekazu, (1985) 'Ie Shakai wo Koete – Bunmei toshite no Ie Shakai Hihan' *Rekishi Hyōron* 418: 49–63.

Kondō Shigekazu, (1989) 'Chūsei Zaisan Sōzokuho no Seiritsu – Bunkatsu Sō zoku ni tsuite.' In Zenkindai Joseishi Kenkyūkai, ed., *Kazoku to Josei no Rekishi – Kodai Chūsei*. (1989) Tokyo: 320–343.

Mass, Jeffrey P. *Lordship and Inheritance in Early Medieval Japan: A Study of the Kamakura Sōryō System*. Calif., Stanford University Press.

Matsumoto, Shinpachiro, (1956) *Chūsei Shakai no Kenkyū*. Tokyo.

Murakami, Yasusuke, Kumon, Shunpei, Sato, Seizaburō, (1979) *Bunmei toshite no Ie Shakai*, Tokyo.

Oka, Kuninobu, 'Okibumi to Ichizokukan Sōron – Shibuya-Irikiinshi no Jirei o Sozai toshite.' In Kawazoe Shōji, ed., *Kyūshū Chūseishi Kenkyū*, Tokyo: 49–94.

Map 1

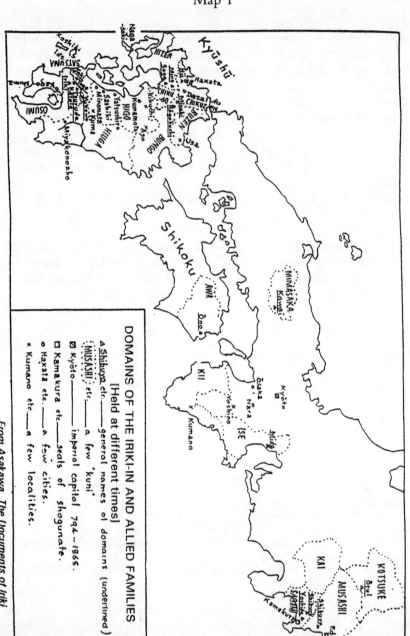

DOMAINS OF THE IRIKI-IN AND ALLIED FAMILIES
[Held at different times]

△ Shibuya etc.——general names of domains (underlined)
(MUSASHI)
☑ MUSASHI etc.——a few "kuni"
☑ Kyōto——imperial capital 794~1866.
☐ Kamakura etc.——seats of shogunate.
○ Hakata etc.——a few cities.
✕ Kumano etc.——a few localities.

From Asakawa, The Documents of Iriki

Map 2

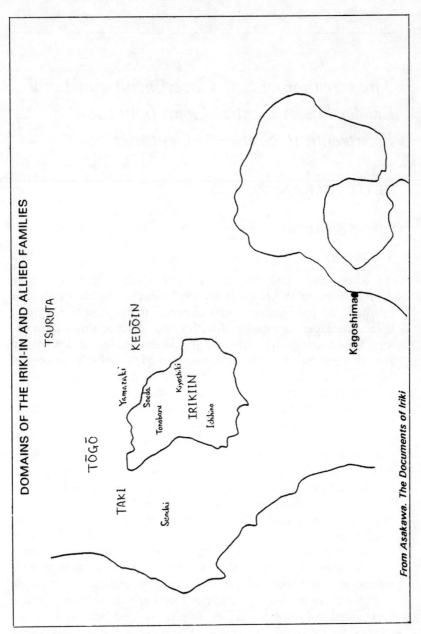

DOMAINS OF THE IRIKI-IN AND ALLIED FAMILIES

TSURUTA

TŌGŌ

TAKI

Sendai

Yamazaki

Soeda

Tonoharu

Kyoshiki

IRIKIIN

Ichihino

KEDŌIN

Kagoshima

From Asakawa, The Documents of Iriki

3

The Creation of Self-Government and Local Leadership in Central Japan from the Fourteenth to Sixteenth Centuries

DETLEV TARANCZEWSKI

INTRODUCTION

Terminology

It is an interesting phenomenon that many languages give preference to the English words 'leader' or 'leadership' – for example in publications on industrial management although these languages are equipped with words of an analogous meaning. Scrutinizing the contexts in which leader or leadership appear we can find many similarities to Max Weber's concept of 'charismatic rule'. But obviously there exist sufficient reasons to avoid the term 'rule' in certain contexts.

Characteristically, leadership seems to be the not-yet-institutionalized power of a person, leaders appear in new situations, acting between or against the existing institutions, in a constructive or destructive way. As an ideal type, the leader is a person who shows the way out of a deadlock situation, when the established institutions no longer function sufficiently. Leader or leadership stands for something new and individual. Certain very personal, individual traits seem to be the decisive qualification for a leader. Accordingly, it is no wonder leaders are the favourite subject of story-tellers as well as of historiographers.

The problem of leadership appears when new groups with common targets and tasks are being organized, leadership is one important element of explicitly or implicitly innovative political and social movements. (Here might be one reason why we cannot find a word equivalent to 'leader' in the contemporary sources except pejoratives like 'ringleader' (chōhonnin). A general problem seems to be that the conceptualization of social phenomena is an historical process with its own rules, and conceptualizations which satisfy the critical eye of scholars are necessarily posthumous ones.) Leadership appears as an aspect of peoples movements and peoples history, in that sense it owns a fundamentally 'democratic' aspect. (Weber 1985: 156)

PRECONDITIONS, THEORETICAL BACKGROUND AND SUBJECT

In my paper I am going to sketch some lines in the formative process of what seemed to me a new type of 'political culture' in the period from the fourteenth to sixteenth centuries – an era called High and Late Medieval in Japanese historiography. This new political culture is characterized by strengthening local self-government and by increasing local autonomy. During that process the ancient hierarchies which had determined everyday business in the various fields of central bureaucracy, *shōen*-estates, vassalty, and village administration, were being challenged by newly-emerging military, political, and economic tasks. The society of this period is characterized by increasing heterogeneity and complexity in all its spheres. Under the conditions of an unprecedented mobility of society, new leaders in the above sense appeared on the stage of local societies. I want to examine from what social layers and from what milieus they were re-cruited and what their main fields of activity had been.

Of the various useful theoretical approaches to my subject I found the theory of social conflict especially fruitful. By means of this theory we can discuss leadership as one aspect or element in the formation of the conflicting parties, in the articulation of the interests of the parties and in the manifestation of the conflict. This theory and its methods have been developed by social and political scientists, but the theory is flexible enough to create a 'historical study of social conflict'. Such research would complement the history of class conflicts which has a considerable tradition within the framework of socio-economic history and peoples history in Japanese historiography. Its weak point was that it fixed too much attention on vertical social conflicts neglecting the various historically extremely import-ant, horizontal forms.

I want to focus my discussion on the oscillation between conflict and cooperation in the irrigation of paddy fields. Of course, at first glance more stirring and colourful struggles may have happened in pre-modern Japanese history, but there has

hardly existed any form with the sustained intensity of irrigation conflicts, because they concerned the very basis of agriculture. The forms of regulations in this field can be expected to
have had an eminent influence on the constitution of local
society.

Under the conditions of the ancient state, irrigation of paddy
fields was controlled by the centralized bureaucracy. In the
medieval period beginning in the late eleventh century the
disintegration of the ancient state made room for new forms of
regulation. Inter-village relations which always had played a
crucial practical rôle for water control and which had been
buried under centre-oriented territorial institutions and juri-
dical framework for a long time now became a vacuum of
power to be filled by a new type of local leaders. Other historical
frame conditions to be mentioned here are the successive disintegration of the autonomy of the house and the replacement
of the function of social organization based on blood relations
(with status and career chances gained primarily by birth) by
more public forms which are based on contract between formally equal parties – be it between individuals or between
groups, in vertical (e.g. Vassalty) or in horizontal (e.g. *Ikki* –
associations) direction. Private elements in the rights on water
and on landed property increased, and generally speaking,
norms and institutions formerly guaranteed by the central state
were now more and more supplanted by norms created through
a process of negotiation of the (in many cases conflicting) parties
involved.

SETTLEMENTS, ESTATES AND THE STRUCTURE OF THE
VILLAGE COMMUNITY

Topography

As an example I chose a region near Kyoto. This region, which
came to be called 'Nishinooka' (Western Hills) in the sources
since the fourteenth century, is formed by a plain to the south-
west of Kyoto. It is about 4 km in extent in a west–east direction
and about 15 km in the north–south direction. Towards the
capital Nishinooka borders the Katsura, a river, wild in some
places, but usually easily meandering through a rubble bed
which is between 100 and 200m wide. In several places it is
shallow enough to wade through the river. In the west Nishinooka
rims the Arashiyama and the hill chains in the south. To the

north the Togetsu-Kyō bridge crosses Katsura river, already a tourist attraction in medieval times. In the utmost south, opposite Iwashimizu Hachimangū shrine, lies Yamazaki, since ancient times the most important port of the Yodo river.

TERRITORY, ESTATES, SETTLEMENTS

Since ancient time the Nishinooka region belonged to two different territorial units: the north was part of Kadono district, the south was included in Otokuni district. That meant in ancient times the region was not perceived as a unit by the central state.

At the beginning of the modern era about 50 settlements had developed in this region; at the end of the Middle Ages, in the sixteenth century, it might have been somewhat less. During medieval times the region was subdivided into a great number of estates, in most cases called *shōen*. Most of these estates were neither in territory nor institutionally congruent with settlements even if *shōen* and settlements were using identical names – a situation we often find in Central Japan. In some *shōen*-estates more than 30 lords held rights; in other cases, persons or institutions were lords over several *shōen* at once; some *shōen* were scattered in small plots over many settlements, in some settlements several different *shōen* were concentrated together.

The *shōen*-estates consisted of heterogeneous rights which were stratified hierarchically. The top positions were held by metropolitan circles like members of the imperial house, court nobles, high ranking temples and shrines. The next stratum in the hierarchy was held by direct delegates of the top authorities. Of special importance for our discussion is a 'middle class' of local holders of estate offices and income rights, like *geshi, kumon, daikan,* and *satanin.*

The *shōen*-hierarchy was only one of several competing forms of social, economic and political order in the region. Since the foundation of the Muromachi shogunate in 1336, the Ashikaga shoguns endeavoured to win especially these local *shōen* officials of *geshi* and *kumon* ranks as their vassals *(gohikannin)* by providing them with additional income from the estates they were administering. (Uejima 1973: 147–152)

THE STRUCTURE OF THE VILLAGE COMMUNITY

In medieval sources the word '*go*' often appeared as a special term for settlements as functional, political local units, as village communities. It is a term opposite to *shōen*, which has a strong connotation as a unit of metropolitan rule. The sources show that also in the village communities the middle-class *shōen* officials played key rôles. Some information on the constitution of village communities is scattered in the extant sources. For example, we know the names of all the fully qualified inhabitants of two *shōen* in 1459, which seem to have been identical with two villages of the same names. In one village /*shōen* called Kami-Kuze are listed 104 male inhabitants: 84 of them have 'peasant status' (*jige-bun*), 20 of them have 'warrior status' (*samurai-bun*), which belong to five different 'families'. The figures for the other village are 56 to 11 persons, the latter ones being divided into two 'families'. (DNK 10:6: 363–371)

Probably all persons listed here are heads of their households. As nuclear family households can be supposed to be prevailing already at this time, we can add four supposed household members to any peasant name, and one or two serfs. A peasant household would thus consist of six or seven members, and a warrior household might have contained a few more souls. In total we can roughly estimate between 700 – 800 inhabitants in Kami-Kuze and 450 – 500 inhabitants in Shimo-Kuze.

As other sources show, middle class *shōen* officials were recruited from members of the local warrior status. The sources also show, that these officials never held absolutely predominant and undisputed positions within the village. Their position could better be described as *primus inter pares*. In this point we can find a fundamental difference with the situation in the Eastern provinces. *Shōen* offices and vassalage of course give us a rough understanding of local hierarchies, but it is much more difficult to get a notion of the internal local self- government. The inner order of the village community is not congruous with the surrounding institutional milieu, each belongs to a different, relatively autonomous sphere.

Some hints in the sources suggest that age groups existed, which show a type of village communities often to be found in medieval Central and Western Japan (Fujiki 1987: 10–37). The basic institution seems to have been the assembly of all fully qualified members of the community, (*gōchū-dangō* – DNK 10:7: 98 sqq.), which perhaps took place in the tutelary shrine of the village (*gō–chinju*). A peasant council of elders (*jige-toshiyorishū* – DNK 10:7: 232) acted as a deliberative and decision-making body – probably in form of a *miyaza*. The young men's associations (*wakashu*) now and then caused a stir in the region as an executive body, mostly acting as military and police power.

It is not quite clear in what way the members of the local warrior status (*samurai-bun*) participated in the community organization. In fifteenth century western Japan, status discrimination was less rigorous than in the eastern parts of the country, and we can also suppose that the economic position of upper-class peasants and average-class warriors did not differ so much. Probably, the warriors had an exclusive organization like a *miyaza* or all *samurai-shū* of one village. In most cases the representatives of a village community in contact with estate and state authorities were members of the warrior status. On average, they were richer than the peasants, they were better educated, and they had more various connections to different circles in the outside world. But, on the other hand, there is no clear and fundamental difference between warriors and peasants except their status ascription. Perhaps village administration had a dual structure, where members of warrior status acted in certain cases as external representatives of the village community in agreement with the council of elders and the other bodies of village self-government.

The main economic basis of all villages was paddy-field rice agriculture. One of the most important tasks of the village community was to supply the – chiefly small-sized – farms belonging to the village with water, for no single farm was able to manage paddy-field irrigation alone. Probably more than 90% of the water came from the river Katsura. This implied that single villages also were not able to manage the irrigation of their fields on their own. Water was only available in cooperation – and conflict – with other villages.

CASE STUDIES ON CONFLICT AND COOPERATION FOR WATER

Cooperation on irrigation

Even more than struggles with the shogunate or with the *shōen* lordship for the reduction of taxes and corvées, the common task which had the strongest influence on the structure of the village community was the management of cooperation and conflict about the irrigation of paddy-fields. This problem was constantly urging farms and villages to cooperate and to join alliances surpassing the borders of a single village community.

We do not know much detail of how the irrigation of the

paddy-rice fields was organized under the ancient centralized bureaucratic state with the superior property rights it held over all the land. Generally, the regulations of the state in this field were strict, and as a rule the bureaucracy was restrictive against free local initiatives. Under the heterogeneous conditions of medieval society it demanded great political and technical flexibility, and its study promises us a viable approach to understanding the character of leadership in the Nishinooka region.

The earliest source I found on the subject of cooperation on irrigation between different villages in the Middle Ages dates from 1340 (KKM 1: 152). In a written contract the representatives of the three villages Kami-Kuze, Kawashima, and Terado promised each other a fair distribution of the water from an arterial irrigation canal they were using in common. The parties agreed in this document, that any offence of a village against this contract and the spirit of concord should be sanctioned by cutting off the water supply and by the punishment by all gods and buddhas, especially the tutelary deities of the villages.

In the text of the contract not the word *shōen* – estate –, but only the word *gō* – village, village community – is used. The village communities are appearing here, with their representatives on the top, as self-governing corporations with a legal status of their own. The villages present themselves as self-contained units, but of course this is only one aspect of their nature. Their relations to the state and to the metropolitan *shōen*–lordship reveal more complicated aspects: Two *shōen* were situated in the settlement known as 'Kawashima no gō'. One *shōen*, Minami no shō, was an estate of a high court noble family, the house Konoe, the other *shōen*, Kita no shō, had several metropolitan lords on its top, the houses Yamashina, Sanjō, and Saionji. Both *shōen* were parcelled out into several plots, and plots of both *shōen* lay intermingled with each other. The local administrators of both *shōen* were members of different families, each using the name of their residential village Kawashima as their surnames. The house of the Kawashima of Minamoto origin held sway over the southern estate, the north was under the rule of the Kawashima who had Taira as their *nomen gentile*. Both lineages were of different origin, but they were improving their relationship throughout the centuries by marriage. The representative of the whole village Kawashima who had signed the contract probably was a member of the northern Taira-Kawashima; from this time on members of this line appear as representatives of whole of Kawashima. They act as represent-atives and leaders of the entire village community, although the Minamoto-Kawashima in the South at first glance look much more powerful, as their connexions to the shogunate and as their landed property strewn over the whole Nishinooka region show. (On the other hand, local leadership perhaps was not their favourite career.)

In Terado, the conditions seem to have been even more complex than in Kawashima. Here, two important estates existed: the so-called Terado no shō, a *shōen* under the rule of Ninnaji temple – that meant nearly equivalence with rule of the Imperial house, because the superior abbot of Ninnaji used to be an Imperial prince. The other important estate in Terado belonged to the Sangoji temple. Besides these two large estates a number of smaller possessions of members of the court nobility were scattered over the territory of the village. Local rulers were, besides the chief of the Terado family who had signed the contract, the members of the families Takeda and Ōbatake. Each was bestowed with a *jitō–shiki* by Ashikaga Takauji, at least for a couple of years (MSS: 206 sq.). All these families had their possessions not only in Terado, but they also held plots of land scattered over the surrounding villages.

Only Kami-Kuze is structured quite simply. The only domin-ant lord of the Kami-Kuze no shō estate was Tōji temple (more precisely speaking: the tutelary shrine of Tōji temple, Chinju Hachimangū). The local administrator (*kumon*) at the time of the making of the contract was a member of Maita family, who used the name of the village he was residing in as his surname, as his colleagues from Kawashima and Terado had also done. Besides his rôle as owner of a local *shōen* administrator post he was a vassal of the Ashikaga shogun. However, also in this village the local administrator of the *shōen* was not without local rivals, as we have seen before: in the middle of the fifteenth century five different families of *samurai* status were residing in Kami-Kuze.

In short, all three representatives underwriting the contract were acting within a heterogeneous network of various social, economic, and political relations. They belonged to the local upper class of 'gentry', but they were not unrivalled. They did not act as rulers of their residential villages without local control – an ideal type of local rulership which is said to be char-acteristic of the Eastern provinces of medieval Japan. They were vassals of the *shogun* and *shōen* officers responsible to metropolitan lords, but in this contract they do not act as their agents. Here they are obviously acting merely as leaders and representatives of their own village communities. This is symbolized by the fact that the contracting parties use the term '*gō*' – village community. Nowhere in the document does the word *shōen* appear. At this *gō* – level of local society the sphere of metropolitan lordship, of central state and of *shōgun* vassalage is not dominant. The various offices and the connections the three underwriting village representatives were holding with other spheres of society may have been necessary attributes for their leadership, but they were not sufficient. An important component of their qualification as leading representatives must be looked for in their personalities.

Represented by their leaders, the three village communities entered an alliance on their own initiative, without regard to the boundaries and interests of lordship and state, and in a relationship of latent conflict with these authorities. In some sense this contract is an *ikki keijō*, an alliance contract, which is based on the spirit of equality of the contracting parties, and of freedom from the ties which determine their different social and political relationships. (Katsumata 1979: 240) This contract shows that in the middle of the fourteenth century the political and legal basis had been prepared for the increasingly autonomous local society of Nishinooka.

CONFLICT FOR IRRIGATION

The reverse side of cooperation for irrigation is conflict, and the historical sources of Nishinooka show us a veritable continuum of both phenomena. In fact, the associating power of social conflict sometimes seems even stronger than that of cooperation. The struggle for water in particular gives us a vivid impression of the nerves of the local society and of their dynamic forces. The historian Hōgetsu Keigo analysed the various intermingled irrigation conflicts of the middle ages in this region, and according to his research they begin to appear in the sources in the early fifteenth century and do not disappear throughout the medieval times (Hōgetsu, 1943: 272–316). Irrigation conflicts in fact last until modern times (the last major clash for which I was able to obtain information about took place in 1933).

Horizontal conflicts predominated – between farms, villages and alliances of villages. In most cases they were provoked by drought or by irrigation arrangements damaged by floods and the problems arising from the redistribution of water rights following these catastrophes. Typically the upstream villages enjoyed privileged access to the water for irrigation, and from time to time their privilege was disputed by four or five downstream villages.

The composition of the conflicting parties changed more or less from case to case, no alliance seems to have been absolutely stable. A net of alterable, fluctuating alliances and conflicts was woven which determined the political behaviour of individuals and of groups. On the other hand, certain constellations turned out to be relatively stable after some decades. The most famous alliance was formed by the so-called 'Eleven Village Communities of Nishinooka', which appeared in the early fifteenth century. The villages of Kami-Kuze, Terado, and Kawashima we have introduced above were members of this alliance, too. All these villages were using one arterial irrigation canal in common. Their opponent in many cases was the Matsunoo (alternative reading: Matsuo) shrine, which ruled over the territory in the northern part of Nishinooka where for long periods the water intake from Katsura river had been installed. But also this alliance of the eleven villages did not remain stable all the time. The village communities belonging to it changed parties sometimes, depending on their interests. Alliances were unstable as rivalry was keen. In this way in the region of Nishinooka was created from a network of alliances which always seemed to have implied possible shifts and future conflicts in the spirit of contract.

The village communities used to form their alliances (and conflicts as well) with little regard to the lords of the *shōen* estates. Their influence along with the increasing number of villages joining the alliances and the number of *shōen* getting involved. The solidarity of the ruled was stronger than the solidarity of the political rulers. Sometimes a *shōen* lord tried to get his plan carried out, but I could not find one single case when a *shōen* lord succeeded, except where the local powers were convinced that his aims would conform with their own interest. The reverse case of village communities roping in metropolitan lords to help them reach their aim occurred more often. Usually they had more staying power. It is really a fascinating spectacle to see the toughness and phantasy, the flexibility and impertinence of the village communities and their alliances in pursuing their plans.

In most conflicts 'peasants' (in the sense of inhabitants of a

village who enjoyed the full right of a member of village
community called by various names like *hyakushō, jigenin, domin*)
appear as the driving force, and often they show a considerable
militancy in their actions, but on the other hand, I did not find
any evidence of persons killed in militant actions. The process of
civilisation seemed to have advanced a little in the local society
of the fifteenth century, if we compare it with the extremely
violent irrigation conflicts in southern Yamashiro province about
200 years before (Hōgetsu 1943: 263–265).

CONCLUSION

The extant sources show only a few cases of peasants appearing
as leaders in Nishinooka. In this point Nishinooka differs from
the great alliance Yamashiro no kuni-ikki in 1485 where peasants in the above sense were also included in the leading groups.
As soon as various forces from outside the local society became
involved in a conflict, the leadership of the conflicting parties
shifted into the hands of members of the *samurai-shō*, a kind of
'middle class', which was characterized by a high degree of
social, political, and economic versatility. As we have seen above
they act as apparently autonomous authors of contracts between
several villages for the distribution of irrigation water, thus
creating new political rules and a local society based on contract
to a very great extent. In their most prominent rôle these local
leaders appear in the sources as conflict managers at the 'horizontal' inter-village level as well as on a 'vertical' level between
metropolitan lords and the villages.

During a long-lasting water conflict between the so-called
'Five Village-Communities' – a sub-group of the above-
mentioned 'Eleven Village Communities' – and the estate Nishi
no shō which lay on the opposite side of river Katsura, in 1496
an oral hearing (*taiketsu*) was held at the shogunates lawcourt.
Kuze Hironari, who was a local administrator (*kumon*) in the
Shimo-Kuze no shō in Shimo-Kuze village, one of the 'Five
Villages, was elected to be the speaker of all representatives of
the 'Five Villages'. They elected him, as is stressed in the source,
because he was distinguished by his versatility and eloquence.
They had made a good choice, and Hironari was highly praised
by the representatives of the other village and by the delegate of
temple Tōji, which was involved as a *shōen* lord in Kami– and in
Shimo-Kuze, that he had led the alliance to victory. This
example shows, that a decisive qualification of a leader was a

very individual one: the ability to lead a rational dispute.

As a matter of course, lawcourts were not the only and not the most important public forum. The village communities of Nishinooka created a relatively autonomous public space of their own. Nishinooka became the name of a new medieval local society which comprised many more village communities than the above-mentioned 'Eleven Villages'. The changing alliances for cooperation and conflict for irrigation with their rationalizing and civilizing effect on the local society worked as a constituent element in its formation. A similar political and symbolic rôle the tutelary shrines (*gō-chinju*) had played within the individual village communities, was more and more achieved during the fifteenth century by the 'Nishinooka Mukō-daimyōjin' shrine for the whole local society of Nishinooka. This shrine, which itself possessed a very old history, had been rebuilt by the surrounding villages in the beginning of the fifteenth century, and it was functioning now as a public space, as a forum where the representatives and leaders of the village communities were deliberating and passing resolutions about their common political, economic and agricultural problems. This shrine had been turned into a kind of proto-parliamentary institution by the local society itself. Thus the Mukō shrine of Nishinooka symbolizes and forms a fascinating medieval, as Malinowski called it, 'proto-democratic', culture. This culture shows a deep contrast to the society represented by the antique state and court-oriented Matsunoo shrine, the priests of which, the Hata, had opened up this region about one millenium before.

BIBLIOGRAPHY

Abbreviations:
DNK – *Dai-Nihon Komonjo, Iewake*
MSS – *Mukō-shi Shi, Shiryōhen*
KMM 1, 11 – 'Kawashima-ke Monjo 1, 11'
SKR 13 – *Shiryō Kyōto no Rekishi, Vol 13, Minami-ku*

Dai-Nihon Komonjo, (1925–1991), Iewake 10 (*Tōji Monjo*), vols. 1–9, ed. By Tōkyō Daigaku Shiryō Hensanjo, Tokyo, Tōkyō Daigaku Shuppankai.
Hōgetsu, Keigo, (1943) *Chūsei Kangai-shi no Kenkyū* Tokyo, Yoshikawa Kōbunkan. (Reprint 1983).
Fujiki, Hisashi, (1987) *Sengoku no sahō: Mura no funsō kaiketsu*, Tokyo, Heibonsha.
Katsumata, Shizuo, (1979) *Sengoku-hō Seiritsu-shi ron*, Tokyo, Tōkyō Daigaku Shuppankai.

'Kawashima-ke Monjo 1,' (1977) ed. By Kyōto Furitsu Sōgō Shiryōkan [Takeda Osamu], pp. 131–205 in *Shiryōkan Kiyō*, No. 5.
'Kawashima-ke Monjo 11,' (1978) Kyoto Furitsu Sōgō Shiryōkan [Takeda Osamu] 97–214, in Shiryōkan Kiyō, No. 6.
Mukōshi Shi, Shiryōhen, (1988) ed. By Mukō-shi Shi Hensan Iinkai, Kyōto-fu Mukō-shi; Mukō.
Shiryō Kyōto no Rekishi, (1992) Vol. 13, *Minami-ku*, ed. By Kyōto-shi, Heibonsha, Kyoto.
Tamaki, Reiko, (1986) '15 seiki kōhan no Otokuni ni okeru sōkoku ni tsuite, pp. 755–764, in *Nagaoka-kyō Kobunka Ronsō*, ed. By Nakayama Shūichi, Sensei Koki Kinen Jigyōkai, Kyoto, Dōhōsha Shuppan.
Uejima, Tamotsu, (1973) 'Kyōkō-shōen no nōmin to shōke no ikki: Yamashiro no kuni Kami-Kuze no shō', pp. 137–168, in *Shōen no sekai*, ed. By Inagaki Yasuhiko, Tokyo, Tokyo Daigaku Shuppankai.
Weber, Max, (1985) *Wirtschaft und Gesellschaft [Economy and Society]*, *Tübingen*: J.C.B. Mohr.

4

Le Comte des Cantons Charles de Montblanc (1833–1894),[1] Agent for the Lord of Satsuma

WILLY VANDE WALLE

The least one can say about Count de Montblanc is that he was a controversial figure. Some have considered him a far-sighted man, others have branded him a charlatan. On the credit side, one can point to his rôle as an intermediary at the negotiations in Paris of the Bakufu embassy headed by Ikeda Nagaoki (Bunkyū 01/12/29 – Genji 01/07/18, 1864), the second mission the Bakufu sent to Europe. He stayed in Japan twice, styled himself Shiroyama-haku and, according to popular tradition, had a concubine named Furansu Omasa. He was one of a few European Japan buffs and maintained close contacts with the centre of power, the Bakufu. (Monburan 1987) He is best remembered for his role at the Paris World Exhibition of 1867, when he forcefully and according to some, deviously, promoted the interests of the *daimyō* of Satsuma, trying to pass him off to the European public as the king of an independent kingdom of the Ryūkyūs. Such is more or less the image of the Count in Japan. Outside Japan he is hardly known at all, except among students of Japanese modern history.

Charles de Montblanc was descended from French nobility based in the south of France, who at the time of the French revolution sought refuge in Belgium. His father had inherited the château and barony of Ingelmunster (present day province of West Flanders), but the family made its actual home in Brussels. Even after the restoration of the French monarchy, they did not return to France. (Isomi 1989:63–4) Charles was born in Paris on 12 May 1833. In contrast with his younger brothers Albéric and Ernest, who exerted their so-called right of option and adopted Belgian nationality, he never abandoned his French citizenship.

Charles de Montblanc first came to Japan in 1858 aboard the warship that brought Baron Gros, Minister Plenipotentiary of France, to Japan. (Bassompierre 1953: 231) After the successful conclusion of the Tientsin Treaty (1858), Gros sailed from Shanghai to Yokohama with the purpose of concluding a commercial treaty, which was duly signed on 9 October 1858. It is not clear why the Count came to Japan, what itinerary he followed and how long he stayed, but he seems to have been entrusted with some scientific mission by the French Ministry of Foreign Affairs. (Bassompierre 1953: 232) After his visit to Japan, he is seen doing some research in the Philippines, which was supposedly part of his official assignment. (Isomi 1989: 64) At any rate he is back in France in 1861, the year when his father died. In 1867 he would visit Japan for the second time. In between, during the period from 1861 to 1867, he supposedly studied Japanese and the Japanese political system.

One may ask how he studied Japanese. Apart from the Japanese that he possibly may have picked up from Omasa, his most likely source of information was a young Japanese student by the name of Saitō Kenjirō. In his memoirs Tanabe Taichi mentions that Montblanc had hired the lad during his first stay in Japan and taken him back home. From the same passage in Tanabe's memoirs, we catch a glimpse of the kind of exoticism Montblanc liked to dabble in. Tanabe relates:

> When on a previous occasion, I accompanied Lord Ikeda of Chikugo to Paris, I was invited by Montblanc. I received permission from the mission to attend the supper. The Kenjirō lad had already cut his hair, but for the occasion he had put on a makeshift topknot, and wore a *haori* and *hakama*. Besides, there was a barbarian of the South Seas, who wore a patterned waistcloth on his tawny skin. These two waited upon us. Of course, there were no other western guests, except for the interpreter Blackman. But even so, one can imagine the kind of daily life he was leading. Montblanc was indeed a queer fellow, who liked to depart from convention and make a show of his eccentricity. (Tanabe 1966: 254, Takahashi 1967: 223)

After his first visit to Japan, the count apparently tried to establish his reputation as a Japan expert, and a splash of exoticism could do wonders. In particular, he tried to impose himself as a go-between for the Ikeda mission during its stay in Paris. Later, he played the Satsuma card and pursued a career as sole agent for the powerful southern fief. Mostly, his was a one man enterprise, and often he was pitted against a whole bureaucracy, sometimes that of the Bakufu or the French government, at other times it was a British company, such as Glover & Co, which was his opponent.

THE SHOGUNAL MISSION OF 1864

In 1864 a second shogunal mission (the first had visited Europe in 1862) led by Ikeda Nagaoki (1837–1879), was sent to Europe. Its ostensible purpose was to apologize for the assassination of Lieutenant Camus, commander of the French Legation guard in Yokohama, on 13 October 1863 (Medzini 1971: 58), but its real aim was to negotiate with the French government about the closure of the port of Yokohama. When it was reported that the envoys had reached Paris and had been received in audience by the Emperor on 3 May, the Japan buffs hurried to offer them their services. Von Siebold came all the way from his home-town of Würzburg, offering his advice both to the Ikeda mission and the French Foreign Ministry. (Medzini 1971: 61–2) During the month of May the mission had a meeting with Montblanc as well. The latter expressed the idea 'that the Bakufu should crush the feudal lords and create a central government. Montblanc compared Japan to the France of four centuries earlier, and he stressed the need for forceful action. (Jansen 1961: 214, Medzini 1971: 65, Osatake 1944: 108–9) From this it would appear that Montblanc was rather well disposed towards the Bakufu. In order to construct the kind of unified state he was advocating, he urged the Japanese to call on France to help in building up a navy and an army. In the meantime, he suggested Japan call on French troops stationed in Japan to weaken the military strength of the *daimyo*. Ikeda was much impressed by Montblanc and adopted his advice as the way to strengthen the position of the Bakufu. (Osatake 1944: 109) The purchase of arms was not within the purview of its powers, but the mission nevertheless looked into the matter and sounded out the possibilities, (Medzini 1971: 64) for the Bakufu had made the strengthening of its military power one of its top priorities. (Medzini 1971: 38) The result was that Japan buffs often found themselves brokering arms sales. A case in point was Von Siebold. At one point he was granted an interview with the French Emperor, who asked the scholar if Japan had a navy. This not being the case, the Emperor suggested ceding a few warships, no longer used by the French navy, but still in good condition. Von Siebold was authorized by the Emperor to broach the idea to the Japanese envoys. All this was going on against the backdrop of the negotiations between Ikeda and the French Foreign Ministry. It is probably no mere coincidence that during the meetings between the envoys and the Ministry following the consultation of Montblanc and Von Siebold, the purchase of arms was unreservedly discussed, whereas at the beginning of the negotiations the Japanese had been most reluctant to bring up the matter, for fear of arousing suspicion that Japan intended to challenge the foreign ships that came to her coastal waters. (Medzini 1971: 64)

From the preceding it would appear fair to assert that Montblanc exerted a considerable amount of influence on the Ikeda mission. In his report to the Bakufu, Ikeda expressly mentions the goodwill of the French Emperor, who had himself made the offer to cede some warships. (Osatake 1944: 111)

THE SATSUMA MISSION OF 1865

Though initially Montblanc was rather well disposed towards the Bakufu, he seems to have had a change of heart in October 1865. In that year Satsuma sent a mission to England to buy arms.[17] The mission consisted of nineteen members, and included observers and students. It was headed by Niiro Keibu (1832– 1889), *ōmetsuke*. Other important members were Godai Saisuke (Tomoatsu, 1835–1885), Matsuki Kōan (Terashima Munenori, 1832–1893), and Hori Sōichirō (Takayuki), a Nagasaki inter- preter. Since the Anglo-Satsuma war of 1863, Satsuma had been trying to establish a closer relationship with England. The ban on travel abroad for the purpose of study and trade was only lifted in May 1866. For that reason, the mission feigned *dappan* (drop out from the *han*), and all its members used pseudonyms. Niiro went under the name of Ishigaki Einosuke, Godai under that of Seki Kenzō, Matsuki under that of Idemizu Senzō. (Isomi 1989: 71)

After a voyage of more than two months the party arrived in London. They at once went to the Foreign Office to negotiate about the possibility of breaking the Bakufu monopoly on trade, and the free opening of ports within each fief. (Isomi 1989:71) They also travelled through England to visit the advanced industrial areas. Some day during the seventh month (moon calendar), a Japanese by the name of Shirakawa (Saitō) Kenjirō, who had left Japan clandestinely to accompany Montblanc to

France, appeared before the mission, saying he wanted to introduce them to Count de Montblanc. Niiro and Godai received the visitor. On this occasion Godai and de Montblanc became friends.

On 13 September, (Keiō 01/07/24) Niiro, Godai, Hori et al. left for the continent. (Isomi 1989: 71ff) They arrived in Ostend, where they spent one night. They described it as a place where 'tourists from all western countries flocked to, during the summer, and enjoyed themselves on the beach'. They were the first Japanese to set foot on Belgian soil. The next morning, they were met by de Montblanc, who invited them to his estate house in Ingelmunster and entertained them there. They stayed two nights in Ingelmunster then they left for Brussels, described by contemporaries as 'little Paris'. For two days they watched theatre, visited a company that manufactured steam engines and museums. In the afternoon of the thirtieth day (Keiō 01/07/30), i.e. 19 September, they 'met the minister in charge of foreign affairs, and talked about visiting manufacturers throughout the country. The talks lasted for several hours'.

THE BAKUFU MISSION LED BY TOKUGAWA AKITAKE

At the beginning of 1867, on the occasion of a private audience accorded to Léon Roches in Osaka, the new shogun Keiki imparted to Léon Roches his intention of sending his younger brother, Prince Akitake, to Paris, in the capacity of official representative to the Paris World Exhibition, as a gesture of goodwill to Napoleon III. (Medzini 1971: 136) The decision to participate in the Exhibition had been taken by the Bakufu a year earlier (Keiō 01/04, 1866). The prince, accompanied by the *gaikoju bugyō* Mukōyama Hayato no shō, left Yokohama on 15 February 1867 (Keiō 03/01/11) and arrived in Marseilles in the beginning of April. (Medzini 1971: 143, Isomi 1989: 79) After inspecting military installations in Marseilles and Toulon, they continued their journey to Paris, where they arrived on 11 April (Keiō 03/03/07) and would be staying until September in order to attend the World Exhibition.

When the party arrived in Marseilles, they were greeted by Shibata Takenaka, consul-general Fleury-Hérard, and a few officials of the *Gaikokukyoku* who had been sent ahead. They had some bad news. An embassy from Satsuma, posing as the representatives of the Kingdom of the Ryūkyūs, had arrived in Paris. They had rented an independent section at the exhibition to show the products of the Ryūkyūs, they had posted the name of the Kingdom of the Ryūkyūs above their section and were flying a flag of their own, featuring a cross in a circle. Thus the Bakufu mission found itself faced with a *fait accompli*.

On the 21 April (Keiō 03/03/17), the Japanese represent-atives were invited to the residence of de Lesseps, a commissioner-general for the Japanese exhibits, for a consultation. (Isomi 1989: 65, Montblanc 1865: 60) The reason why they were being bothered on this day, although a Sunday, was that the following day, Napoleon III would visit the premises of the Exhibition and inspect the progress of the preparations. (Isomi 1989:65) Repre-senting the Bakufu at this meeting were Tanabe Taichi, secretary to the Japanese Legation in Paris (Mukōyama was chargé d'affaires) and Yamanouchi Bunjirō. Besides a few French officials of the exhibition secretariat, the meeting was also being attended by Iwashita Sajiemaon, Satsumas 'special envoy to the exhibition', and Montblanc, representative in Europe for the said fief.

De Lesseps was at a loss as how to handle the feud between the two competing missions and asked that they find a solution among themselves. Tanabe protested against the independent position Satsuma had taken at the exhibition and demanded an explanation. Iwashita dodged the attack by saying that every-thing had been arranged by Montblanc. Being asked whence he had the right of presenting the Ryūkyūs as an independent kingdom, Montblanc replied that the previous year (Keiō 2), he had received wide powers of proxy from the Lord of Satsuma and he had simply done what he thought needed be done. (Takahashi 1967: 66) However, this was a rather free interpret-ation of the power of proxy granted to him, for he had actually been appointed 'advisor to Iwashita, as well as director and secretary, in order to take in hand the negotiating, concluding the signing of peace and friendship treaties the envoy might enter into in Europe'. Besides, Montblanc had not been officially certified by the secretariat as representative of Satsuma. (Takahashi 1967: 66–7) Montblanc, himself claims 'C'est donc en qualité de commissaire général de S. M. le roi des îles Liou-Kiou que fut accepté le commissaire général de Satsouma'. The question is of course what this 'accepté' means. (Montblanc 1867: 59)

Thereupon, Tanabe and Iwashita started negotiating. Tanabe produced a map of the premises of the exhibition and de-manded that the name 'Ryūkyū' be deleted, the flag featuring the cross in a ring be removed and that the Satsuma products be exhibited under the *Hinomaru* flag, with the special mention Matsudaira Shūridaibu, the name of the lord Shimazu. Iwashita protested and retorted that the products of the fief of Satsuma could not be exhibited under the name of an individual. He demanded that they be exhibited under the name 'Gouvern-mement du Taïshiou de Satsuma'. Tanabe, unaware of the implications of the word *gouvernement*, agreed. (Takahashi says that the hapless Tanabe was undone by his Classical Chinese training. He took 'gouvernement' to be equivalent to the Chinese compound '*seifu*', which usually had an overtone of local admin-istration, and therefore could easily have a meaning equivalent to Han administration.) Lesseps thereupon prepared a memor-andum of understanding, stating that all products would be exhibited under the *Hinomaru* flag, while on one side the mention 'Gouvernement du Taïkoune' and on the other 'Gouvernement du Taïshiou de Satsouma' would be inscribed. (Takahashi: 1967: 68) Tanabe subscribed to this condition, a mistake he would later regret. The Bakufu was very displeased with the concession he had unwittingly made, called him back to Japan, and stripped him of his functions.

The following day, Parisian newspapers, such as *Le Figaro*, *Le Petit Journal*, *La Liberté* carried articles stating that Japan was a confederation not unlike Germany, and that the *Taikun* was simply the ruler of the most powerful among the confederated states. They also stated that Tanabe had recognized the existence of the Governments of Hizen (Saga) and Satsuma. (Takahashi 1967: 69) To make matters worse, *Le Temps* and *Le Figaro* reported the dinner party that de Lesseps had organised after the signing of the agreement and, wrote that Tanabe had feasted himself on the wine and made a fool of himself. (Takahashi 1967: 88) Tanabe tried to have the article retracted, but unsuc-cessfully. (Takahashi 1967: 89, 228)

The *La Liberté* of 26 April carried an article which reiterated the same idea: under the flag of the *Mikado*, 'which is the flag of the Japanese confederation, the flags of the *Taikun* and of the Lord of Satsuma were fluttering side by side. (Isomi 1989: 65) Hence, it was clear that the *Taikun* was not the emperor of Japan, but an independent ruler over his own territories, equal to but not superior to the Taishu of Satsuma and the other *daimyō kokushi*. (Takahashi 1967: 69)

The resourceful Montblanc even had a special decoration designed, inspired by the *Legion d'Honneur*. It featured a cross in

a circle in white colour, superposed over a red five-pointed star.
In between the five points of the star were written in gold the
characters *Satsuma Ryū kyū koku*. It was awarded to Napoleon
III and other dignitaries, civilian as well as military. Since
decorations are one of the perogatives of a sovereign state, it
contributed considerably to the promotion of the idea that
Satsuma was an independent state. (Takahashi 1967: 90)

MONTBLANC VISITS JAPAN

After the closure of the Paris World Exhibition, Montblanc went
to Japan for a second time in 1867. The purpose was not just a
courtesy call, as seems to be suggested by the testimony of his
brother Albéric, who says he had been invited by the Lord of
Satsuma. (Bassompierre 1953: 236) In Paris Montblanc had
concluded a contract with the Satsuma envoy Iwashita. He had
managed to open a credit line on behalf of the envoy to the
amount of 400,000 francs, to enable the latter to purchase arms
and hire naval advisors to send to Japan and help Satsuma with
setting up its own navy. To that end Montblanc had fitted out a
few retired officers and soldiers, while he himself, as Fleury
Hérard put it, had assumed the guise of a general. According to
a report by Sir Harry Parkes, the party of Montblanc numbered
between 15 and 20, but it later appeared there were only nine
of them. They were sent off to Satsuma in August 1867. Iwashita,
upon his return to Japan, told British agents that the ship
Satsuma had purchased, was the former flagship of Captain
Osborn of the Lay-Osborn Flotilla of China and that Montblanc had helped in acquiring it. (Medzini 1971: 158–9)

Montblanc himself disembarked at Nagasaki on 19 October
1867 (Keiō 03/09/23). A few retainers of Satsuma were waiting
for him in the port city. They informed him that his booklet
about Japan had been translated into Japanese. The proponents
of the Restoration had thought that he had formulated the
constitutional question Japan was facing so clearly and ade-
quately that they had adopted his analysis. (Bassompierre 1953:
236) He was accompanied by Saitō Kenjirō as his interpreter.
According to Tanabe, Saitō was later assassinated in Kagoshima.
(Tanabe 1966: 270)

From Nagasaki, Montblanc sailed for Kagoshima on board
Satsuma's newly-acquired steamer. In the course of the month
of October the count must have had an interview with the
daimyo of Satsuma, probably in Kagoshima. As a token of his

gratitude for the services rendered at the World Exhibition, the Lord Shimazu gave the count his personal sword adorned with his crest, a cross in a ring, on the tsuba. (Bassompierre 1953: 236)

Montblanc's enterprise was very embarrassing for the French envoy Léon Roches, who had been pursuing a careful policy of conciliation and cooperation with the Bakufu. When the latter got wind of Montblanc's dealings with Satsuma, it was evidently alarmed and asked Roches for an explanation, Montblanc being a French citizen. During the interview Roches had with the *Shōgun* on 24 August, he explained that the count had no connection with his government, and that there was nothing he could do about the contract the count had concluded with Satsuma. (Medzini 1971: 159)

From his side, Montblanc did everything in his power to lend his enterprise as much authority as he could. Before leaving for Japan, he informed the French Ministry of the Marine, that he was leaving for Japan to study prospects for a Japanese navy. (Medzini 1971:158) To the British Consul-General in Nagasaki, Marcus Flowers, he said that he had been promised the backing of the French government.

The British felt that their thunder was being stolen and gathered as much intelligence as possible about the Count's dealings. In Kagoshima, they learned that Montblanc's advisors would be paid for one year, and then be sent back to France. (Medzini 1971: 160) Glover and Company, the London–based company, were dismayed that the purchase of arms and the hiring of advisers had taken place without their having played any part in it. (Medzini 1971: 158) In Nagasaki, British agents learned from a French businessman, that a French trading company had undertaken to supply Satsuma and Chōshū with a warship and other arms for $200,000.

Roches did everything he could to discredit the count, especially vis-à-vis Sir Harry Parkes. He told his British colleague that the connection between Satsuma and Montblanc was a case of mutual deception, and that the French government had issued passports to the count and his party by mistake. In a report to the Ministry in Paris he wrote that he had been told that some leading figures in Satsuma considered him an intriguer and wanted the count out of their fief. (Medzini 1971:159) Even among the advisers themselves discontent seemed to breed. One of them claimed that, although he had been hired at 30,000 francs a year for three years, his contract had been annulled after half a year. He called the count 'a man of incomparable vanity, a perpetual liar'. (Medzini 1971: 160) Roches even showed this complaint to Parkes to substantiate his assessment of the man's character.

The Bakufu evidently did not like the idea of Montblanc siding with Satsuma. Upon his arrival in Nagasaki, the *bugyō*, Kawada Hiroshi, contacted Montblanc. They were old acquaintances, for Kawada had accompanied Ikeda as a *metsuke* to Paris and met the count in the French capital. (Medzini 1971: 60) Kawada tried to woo him away from the party of Satsuma by offering him a high position in the Bakufu, but the count refused. (Bassompierre 1953: 237) Some time later, after his visit to Kagoshima, Montblanc was again in Nagasaki, when an order to take him into custody was issued. According to his brother's testimony, the undauntable Montblanc went to see the *bugyō* and demanded an explanation for the order. He was accompanied by the British consul-general Marcus Flowers, because the latter was temporarily in charge of the protection of the French nationals. It was clear that the *bugyō* intended to take him into custody on the spot. When the intervention of the British diplomat turned out to be of no avail, the count pulled out a pistol, pressed it against the throat of the *bugyō*, and forced him to bring him back to his escort of Satsuma retainers who were waiting outside. (Bassompierre 1953: 237)

On 5 December (Keiō 03/11/10) Montblanc left Nagasaki and travelled to Kyoto where Lord Shimazu was staying. The *Shōgun* had already returned power to the Emperor on 9 November (Keiō 03/10/14). However, on 3 January of 1868, the armies of Satsuma and Chōshū clashed with the Bakufu troops in Toba and Fushimi. (Isomi 1989: 2) The diplomats who were following the *Shōgun* had to take refuge in the foreigners' settlement of Kōbe. During that period, Montblanc was purportedly in the neighbourhood of Kyoto with Lord Shimazu, presumably as his private councillor. De Bassompierre surmizes that he even went to Kyoto, but this is nothing more than conjecture, for in those days, Kyoto was still out of bounds to foreigners. (Bassompierre 1953: 239)

In a letter dated 3 March 1868, the new imperial government informed the French Minister in Edo, Léon Roches, that it wanted to replace the Bakufu representative in Paris, consul-general Fleury-Hérard, and appoint Montblanc in his place. (Bassompierre 1953: 240, Takahashi 1967: 211) However, Montblanc did not leave Japan until the end of the following year. In a letter dated 21 October 1869, and addressed to Max

Outrey, the successor of Roches as French Minister in Edo, the Minister of Foreign Affairs Sawa Nobuyoshi, and the Vice-minister Terashima Munenori confirmed the appointment notified in the letter of 3 March and informed the French government that until a Japanese legation was sent to Paris, Montblanc would act as consul-general and chargé d'affaires. (Dairi Kōshiken sōryōji, Bassompierre 1953: 241, Takahashi 1967: 211) In his reply of 25 October, Outrey informed his Japanese counterparts that Montblanc, being a French citizen, could not act in the capacity of official of another country without the consent of the Emperor. He added that his government would probably not object to the appointment as consul-general, but that it was unlikely that it would accept Montblanc as *chargé d'affaires* in his own country. In their reply of 12 December, Sawa and Terashima asked Outrey to convey to Fleury-Hérard the decision of his dismissal and informed him that Montblanc would replace him as *Kōmu benri shoku*. (Bassompierre 1953: *241)*

BACK TO PARIS

Montblanc left Japan at the end of December 1869. After his arrival in Paris, he presented himself to the French Ministry of Foreign Affairs in April 1870 and asked for his confirmation as consul-general and *chargé d'affaires*. The Emperor confirmed him as consul-general on 20 April. This was notified to Mont- blanc by the Ministry on 6 May. However, the Ministry added that the appointment as *chargé d'affaires* was being withheld, since the French Minister in Edo had not confirmed yet that Montblanc had been given the authority to deal with political matters. On 28 May, Outrey asked the Japanese authorities for clarification about Montblanc's status and the Japanese Ministry replied on 2 June: 'Strictly speaking, he is not a *chargé d'affaires*, but we entrust Montblanc with taking the required actions concerning problems that we assign.'

Montblanc opened a consulate in the Rue de Tivoli and hired Maeda Masana, a student from Satsuma, who happened to travel on the same ship to France, as a secretary. (Takahashi 1967: 222) Maeda stayed in Montblanc's residence while commuting to school and working at the consulate. Since there were not many matters to be expedited, Montblanc spent a good deal of time learning Japanese from Maeda Masana. He had brought a number of Japanese books back to France, and spent much time

reading them. He also translated, with the help of Maeda, part
of a *Shingaku* text, known as *Kyūō Dōwa*. (Takahashi 1967: 225)

In a letter dated 2 November 1870, Sawa informed the
French Ministry that Sameshima Naonobu had been appointed
Shōbenmushi (minister ad interim) and Montblanc had been
discharged. Here ends the public life of Count Charles de
Montblanc. After leaving public life, he continued his activities
as a Japan expert. He became chairman of the French Society
for Japanese Studies, and published articles about Japan in journals.
(Takahashi 1967: 227) He also received Japanese visitors in his
Ingelmunster château, among them Maeda Masana.

WRITINGS

In 1865 de Montblanc published a booklet entitled *Le Japon*, in
which he explained the difference between the *Mikado* and the
Shōgun, the Bakufu and the *daimyō*. It appears that, at least at the
time of writing, he still believed in the vitality of the Bakufu. He
advised the Western powers not to resort to the use of force in
Japan, and advocated a peaceful approach of persuasion in
dealing with the Bakufu.

However, in the same year, 1865, he gave a lecture for the
Société de Géographie de France, a summary of which was
published under the title 'Considérations Générales sur l'Etat
Actuel du Japon', in the Bulletin de la Société de Géographie,
(Paris, January, 1866). In this lecture de Montblanc revealed for
the first time that the Mikado was the one and only sovereign
of Japan, that under him were placed the *daimyo*, who were the
chiefs of private territories; that one of these *daimyo* was invested
with the mandate of *Shōgun*, which meant that he was
commander-in-chief of the army and had the right to administer and police the private domains of the Mikado; and that
it was this *Shōgun* or *Taikun*, whom the European diplomats had
erroneously taken to be the temporal ruler of Japan.
(Bassompierre 1953: 233)

In *Le Japon* Montblanc feels rather sympathetic towards the
Shōgun. He hopes that, by expanding trade with foreign nations,
Japan will be able to strengthen itself. All in all, he holds high
expectations of the Shogunate. However, in 1867, Montblanc is
seen acting on behalf of Satsuma to an extent that is damaging
to the honour of the Shogunate. What could the reason of that
be? The answer may be found in *Le Japon tel qu'il est*, a small
book published in 1867, and in a way a sequel to *Le Japon*.

(Montblanc 1867: 39f) This is a rather interesting piece of writing. It has a clearly political intent. First of all, he has a high idea of the Japanese and says they are different from the other Oriental peoples in that they realize the idea of progress and are not locked in lethargy as the Chinese purportedly are. He then goes on to call on the French authorities to 'aid the natural develop- ment of this nation, in its special genius and to find in it new elements of activity for ourselves, while respecting its political organization'. (Montblanc 1867: 50) He emphatically contends that the only policy the West has to follow is: 'Constantly increase our pacific action, considering the first step of our diplomacy as the beginning of a liberal policy and not the *fait accompli* of an exclusionist policy'. (Montblanc 1867: 57)

He describes the dichotomy between Emperor and *Shōgun* and says that Japan is actually a confederation of states. The Tokugawa *Shōgun* is simply the first among peers. In general he strikes a rather demeaning tone when talking about the Tokugawa, and tends to give Satsuma a prominence beyond its real power. He stresses the fact that Prince Shimazu is also king of an independent kingdom Ryūkyū. So, one may suspect that the whole book is actually a plea *pro domo*, trying to demonstrate why he has promoted the interests of Satsuma to the detriment of the Tokugawa. The drift of his argument is that the *Shōgun* has mistakenly been considered the worldly ruler of Japan, in contrast to the *Mikado*, who is supposedly the spiritual ruler. He contends that the *Shōgun* is the lord of the Kantō region and that all treaties that have been concluded have actually been done so with the state Kantō, not with Japan in its entirety. He proves his point by showing that the open ports are not really gateways to Japan as a whole, but only to the territories under the jurisdiction of the *Shōgun*. Consequently, the Western Powers are following a policy of exclusionism, making the Bakufu *a pars pro toto*. This amounts to interference in internal affairs, by imposing a unifying authority (Bakufu) on the whole of Japan, which is unwarranted, for the Bakufu does not command that authority. He calls on the readership to pursue a policy of non-intervention, 'aiding the local action and respecting its powerful autonomy'. (Montblanc 1867: 57) While this analysis may be construed as astute, at the same time it is hard to deny that it implicitly justifies treatment of the lord of Satsuma as on a par with the *Shōgun*.

In an appendix, he refers to the incident at the World Exhibition in Paris. He justifies the action taken by the com-

missioner-general of his Majesty the King of the Ryūkyū
Islands, who is none other than himself. He quotes two journal
articles that coincide with his view, one being an extract from a
note by Mermet de Cachon, (La France, Paris, 1 May 1867) who
once was the interpreter of Léon Roches. In the most un-
equivocal terms it states that the *Shōgun* is not placed above the
other *Daimyō*, that they are all equal and that every *daimyō*
receives the spiritual investiture from the *Mikado*. Each *daimyō* or
taikun – the words mean the same he remarks – has his own
government, finances, army etc. All in all, the book makes a
strong case for the independence of Satsuma. The book was put
to press around 1 May. From this it is clear that its publication
has everything to do with the row at the Exhibition between
Satsuma and the Bakufu delegation.

Medzini implies that *Le Japon*, written in 1865 and still
favourable to the Bakufu, was written after the Count's trip to
Japan the previous year. However, it is doubtful that de Montblanc made that trip. The *pro memoria*, drawn up by Albéric, the
younger brother of Montblanc, and used as a source by de
Bassompierre, does not mention anything of the kind. It is much
more likely that *Le Japon* was written in the wake of the visit of
the Ikeda mission to France. We have demonstrated that he was
still well-disposed to the Bakufu at that time. However, some-
time in 1865, he seems to have had a change of heart. This must
have had everything to do with the contacts he established with
the Satsuma mission to England. Around that time he gave his
lecture for the Geographical Society. His book, *Le Japon tel qu'il
est*, is only the consecration of his altered view.

De Montblanc's book stirred considerable debate in French
political and intellectual circles. *Le Japon, ses Institutions, ses
Produits, ses Relations avec l'Europe*, published in La Revue Con-
temporaine, (Paris, 30 June, 1867), is another article that exerted
a considerable influence, if not in Europe, at least in Japan. When
de Montblanc visited Japan for the second time in 1867, he had
frequent contacts with the samurai of Satsuma and Tosa and his
ideas were well received among the anti-Bakufu samurai. Sasaki
Takayuki recorded the sayings of the Count and collected his
notes in four volumes under the title *Kikigaki* (apparently not
preserved). Osatake Takeshi, on the other hand, relates that he
acquired a manuscript entitled *Futsujin Monburan shinsetsugaki*.
One of the entries in this manuscript bears the title *Nihon
kokutai oyobi bussan oyobi gaikoku no kōsai*. This is clearly a translation of *Le Japon, ses Institutions, ses Produits, ses Relations avec*

l'Europe. Osatake surmises that it is possibly a part of the *Kikigaki*. It has been preserved as a manuscript and Osatake reproduces in full the copy he owned. The colophon explains the circumstances in which it was translated. (Osatake 1944: 136–7) It is probable that it was this very translation that the retainers of Satsuma were referring to, when they welcomed Montblanc in the port of Nagasaki. Montblanc is credited with another article on Japan, written in 1866, but as Morimoto points out, most of his writings are variations on a few themes.

THE BAKUFU VIEW OF THE EVENTS

Now, let us have a look at the other side. Tanabe Taichi in his memoirs *Bakumatsu Gaikō Dan*, passes a harsh judgment on Count de Montblanc. He quotes Fukuchi Genichirō who describes the Count as a fortune hunter, eager to establish for himself a reputation as an expert on Japan. So, when it became known that the Bakufu wanted to participate in the World Exhibition, Montblanc established contacts with Shibata Takenaka, who was residing in Paris at the time. However, Shibata received the advice from someone that the Count's reputation in high society was dubious, and that it would be best not to mix with this kind of person. So Shibata turned a cold shoulder on him.

Montblanc was much displeased by this treatment, but would not let it at that. Just around that time, a party of samurai from Satsuma, including Niiro Nakazō and Godai Tomoatsu, happened to be in Paris. Montblanc established contacts with them. Then, calling himself the special commissioner, he sent a letter to the commissioner-general of the Exhibition, stating that the Lord of Satsuma was a vassal of the Japanese government on the one hand, but also the king of the Ryūkyūs, and to that end he had sent his trusted ministers to the French Emperor to ask for his acceptance. He also said in that letter that this participation had nothing to do with the Japanese government. Furthermore, he had a decoration made for the Lord of Satsuma King of the Ryūkyūs and advertised the matter widely in the Paris newspapers. Fukuchi Genichirō urged Shibata to publish denials in the newspapers and forewarn the French Ministry of Foreign Affairs, but he said he would wait and see. (Tanabe 1966: 253–5)

The actions of Montblanc on behalf of Satsuma do not seem to have been improvised. There are indications that everything had been carefully planned beforehand. After the Bakufu had decided to participate in the Exhibition, it issued an order in 1866 (Keiō 02/04) to the effect that those interested in participating were to send in their exhibits. Satsuma informed the Bakufu through an official at its *EdoYashiki* that it was interested. The Bakufu would charter the ship 'The Eastern Queen'. It was therefore necessary to have a list of the goods to be sent, stating their weight, volume etc. However, the Edo official of Satsuma stalled. The list was not forthcoming, he invoked all kinds of subterfuges and then stated that, since Nagasaki was much closer, the goods would be shipped from there. He mentioned that there would be about 500 boxes. When the chartered ship made its call at Nagasaki, the Satsuma officials asked the French consul to load 250 boxes out of the 506 on the chartered ship. The remainder would be shipped by the English merchant Thomas Glover. This was reported by the French consul to the Nagasaki *bugyō*.

When the ship called at Edo bay, Chevrillon, assistant of Fleury Hérard, sent to Japan for the purpose of helping the shipments to Paris, noticed that the boxes were marked Ryūkyū. He reported this to the Bakufu, but this did not particularly alarm them. After all, the Ryūkyūs were a dependent territory of Satsuma and recognized as such by the Bakufu. (Tanabe 1966: 258) It is clear, however, that Satsuma had carefully planned the action from the start. Montblanc had played a vital role in this major challenge abroad to the authority of the Shogunate, and his appointment after the Meiji Restoration to the office of consul-general, may be considered as a reward for the services he had rendered Satsuma.

NOTE

1. According to Bassompierre, (1953: 232) he was born in Paris in 1833 and died in the same city in 1894. Kokushi Daijiten, S.V. Monburan, says he was born in Belgium without specifying the place, and lists as dates 1832 to 1893. Isomi, (1989: 64) gives the same dates but says he was born in Ingelmunster. Dates given by Morimoto Hideo are 1832–1898: see Monburan, Dyupan, (1987: 198). However, Bassompierre, basing himself on information supplied by the Count's younger brother must be the most trustworthy.

BIBLIOGRAPHY

Bassompierre, Baron de, (1953) Charles de Montblanc et la Restauration Japonaise de 1868. in: *Revue Générale Belge*, volume 89, June issue, pp. 229–244.

Isomi Tatsunori, Kurosawa Funitaka, Sakurai Ryōju, (1989) *Nihon Berugî Kankeishi.* Tokyo, Hakusuisha.

Jansen, Marius, (1961), *Sakamoto Ryōma and the Meiji Restoration.* Princeton, Princeton University Press.

Kokushi Daijiten, (1989), Tokyo, Yoshikawa Kōbunkan.

Medzini, Meron, (1971), *French Policy in Japan during the Closing Years of the Tokugawa Regime.* East Asian Research Center, Cambridge, Harvard University.

Montblanc, Comte Ch. de. (1865) *Le Japon.* Paris, Imprimerie de J. Claye.

Montblanc, Comte de. (1867) *Le Japon tel qu'il est.* Paris, Arthur Bertrand, Editeur.

Monburan, Dyupan (1987) e.a. *Monburan no Nihon Kenbun Ki* – Furansujin no Bakumatsu Meiji Kan. Translated by Morimoto Hideo. Tokyo, Shin Jinbutsu Oraisha.

Nihon Shiseki Kyōkai ed. *Tokugawa Akitake Taiō Kiroku* I. Tōkyō Daigaku Shuppan, Tokyo, 1973 Nihon Shiseki Kyōkai Sōsho Nr. 146 (re-edition).

Osatake Takeshi. (1944). *Bakumatsu Gaikō Hishi Kō. Tokyo, Hōkōdō.*

Takahashi Kunitarō, (1967) *Chonmage Taishi Umi o Yuku* – Hyakunenmae no Bankokuhaku. Tokyo, Junbutsu Oraisha.

Tanabe Taichi, (1966) *Bakumatsu Gaikōdan.* vol. 2. Translated and annotated by Sakata Seiichi. Tokyo, Heibonsha. (Tōyō Bunko vol. 72).

5

Mikado – From Spiritual Emperor to Enlightened Sovereign

The image of the Emperor of Japan, 1859 – 1873, as seen by Western visitors

SEIJA JALAGIN

After 200 years of almost total seclusion Japan was forced to open up to the outside world in the 1850s. From 1859 onwards foreigners travelled to Japan in increasing numbers. First came the official representatives of Western countries, along with them sailors, merchants, soldiers, scientists and finally tourists. In Europe and America there was an eager reading audience waiting for stories of far away countries. So it became more common to publish something of one's visit to Japan than not to do it. Thus the Westerners that visited Japan in the early years of its reopening and after the Meiji Restoration (1868) produced dozens of travel books, memoirs and diaries.

In these accounts Japanese society with all its elements was widely described. As a whole the image of Japan in these accounts can be considered favourable; Westerners used to compare Japan with China and found it more civilized in almost every sense. The Emperor of Japan, the Mikado, received very much attention from the Western visitors writing on Japan. The image they created of the Emperor changed along with the political development of the country. In the period in question there can be found three phases in the image of the Emperor. During the first years, 1859–62, the Mikado was talked about as a divine Emperor, but a nonentity with no political rôle. From 1862 to 1868, the last years of the Tokugawa rule, he started to lose his divine image and get some political meaning in the eyes of the Westerners in Japan. In the early years after the Meiji Restoration the Mikado was welcomed into the group of modern Western-style sovereigns. By this time the image of the Emperor was the most positive element of the image of Japan as a whole.

During the 1850s and the first years of the 1860s Westerners in Japan lived a very secluded life. They were allowed to stay in four treaty ports, Yokohama, Nagasaki, Shimoda and Hakodate and move only in the nearby surroundings. In addition to this there was the language problem that kept foreigners effectively from closer contacts with the Japanese. Only after 1862 did the consulates start to have skilful interpreters. Acquiring accurate knowledge of Japanese society was almost impossible, at least for those other than the consular staff. When the first Western newspapers were established in Japan in 1861, foreigners could receive at least some more recent information of the country. The Nagasaki Shipping List and Advertiser was published between June and October 1861. The editor, Albert W. Hansard, moved to Yokohama and started to publish the Japan Herald in November 1861. (Fält 1990) Due to the many difficulties, the Westerners in Japan in those days mostly had to base their perceptions on their preconceptions and second on their own experiences in Japan. The expectations the Western visitors had were mainly based on old accounts, such as Engelbert Kaempfer's *The History of Japan* from the seventeenth century, C. P. Thunberg's *Resan till och uti Kejsardomet Japan 1775–1776*, Philipp Franz von Siebold's *Manners and Customs of the Japanese* from the beginning of the nineteenth century, or even the accounts of Marco Polo's travels.

This was particularly true of the image of the Emperor of Japan. Most Westerners in Japan spoke of two Emperors, the Mikado as the spiritual Emperor and the *Shōgun* as the temporal Emperor. The first American consul to Japan, Townsend Harris wrote in 1857 that 'Mikado is the only title of the Spiritual Sovereign' . . . 'who is brother to the sun and father of the moon. Ziogoon is the only title of the political ruler of Japan. It means General of the Kingdom, Lieutenant General, or Generalissimo of the whole Empire.' (Harris 1959: 371)

There was little else that the foreigners knew about the Mikado. And what they knew they had learned from old accounts, mostly Kaempfer's. For example, the English botanist Robert Fortune who stayed in Japan in 1860–61 wrote that, 'Curious stories are told about the manners and customs of the Spiritual Emperor at Miaco. (Kyoto) It is said that he is never allowed to breath the common air, nor are his feet allowed to touch the ground; he cannot wear the same garment twice, nor eat a second time from the same dish'. (Fortune 1863: 238) Bishop of Victoria in Hongkong, George Smith, who visited

Japan for a short time in 1860, had read somewhere that the spiritual Emperor led an idolatrous life with his twelve wives in the sacred capital Miaco where he was worshipped as a demigod. (Smith 1861: 289 see also Baeckström 1871: 261–2)

The Westerners repeated time after time the old stories of the mysterious spiritual Emperor but they usually did not comment on his divinity. They probably thought it was ridiculous but natural since the situation of the Emperor in Japan was pretty much the same as the Emperor in China. (Dawson 1967: 43, 48) Most of the Western visitors to Japan in those days were already familiar with China, so it was nothing new to them that the Emperor in Japan, too, was claimed to be of divine origin. Besides, this was just another peculiarity of a heathen nation. And peculiarities were eagerly searched for and written down since it was all the odd and exotic things that interested the public at home. So the writing Westerners in the Far East those days wanted to satisfy the reading public and its longing for faraway countries. (Yokoyama 1982) This way they tended to see Japan as a paradise on earth. The common Japanese people were looked upon as happy and content, primitive folk as idealized by Rousseau in the late eighteenth century. (Jalagin 1993: 79)

Since the image is born largely on the basis of an individual's own preconceptions about the object of the image, these pre-conceptions can clearly be seen in the image, particularly when there is nothing new to be added to them. This theory applies explicitly to the image of the Emperor of Japan in the early years of the reopening. Since the Mikado lived in Kyoto where neither foreigners nor ordinary Japanese were allowed to enter, proving the miraculous stories either true or false was practically impossible. The image of the Mikado was thus a very dominant element in the image of Japan as a unique and exotic country. (Jalagin 1994)

There is, however, one description of Kyoto from the early years of the reopening. The secretary of the Dutch legation, Dirk de Graeff van Polsbroek, visited Kyoto in 1858 on his way from Nagasaki to Yedo. This was a very rare occasion and due to the legendary stories written about the life of the Mikado Polsbroek's expectations were very high. But the reality turned out to be an ultimate disappointment. According to Polsbroek, the palace of the Emperor looked as humble as the residence of the governor of Ngasaki. The members of the Dutch legation came to the conclusion that the Emperor lived in prison-like conditions. The city of Miaco made an equally disappointing impression: the people looked untidy and the interpreters of the shogunate said they were lazy and rude. (Polsbroek 1987: 39–40)

One can see in Polsbroek's high expectations and disappointment the effect of his own European background. The sovereigns of Europe lived luxuriously and showed it, so if the Emperor of Japan had a humble looking palace it must mean that he had neither prestige nor wealth. A few weeks later, however, Polsbroek in an audience at the *Shōgun's* palace admired the simplicity and the modesty of the place. (Polsbroek 1987: 45–6) A more accurate picture of the life of the *Shōgun* was not at all flattering and the Westerners usually considered him a puppet in the hands of the *rōju*, the council of elders. (Polsbroeck 1987: 48, Harris 1959: 449, Smith 1861: 290–1, Fortune 1863: 238–9, de Fontblanque 1862: 21)

While the short-term visitors to Japan usually concentrated on repeating the old stories of the Mikado or passing on the rumours they had heard, the diplomats tried to find out the truth about the political position of the Emperor and the *Shōgun*. The British Minister to Japan, Sir Rutherford Alcock, noted first that the Mikado was 'the only sovereign *de jure* recognized by all Japanese from the Tycoon to the lowest beggar' . . . 'and that the Tycoon receives investiture from him as his Lieutenant or Generalissimo, *and as such only.*' (Alcock 1863: 226) By the beginning of the 1860s most of the foreign representatives were familiar with the fact that both the Mikado and the *Shōgun* were only institutional figures with no political power. (Alcock 1863: 226–7, 231–2)

In the first years of Japan's reopening the Japanese Emperor was presented as a demigod in the accounts of the Westerners, a puppet guided by others. He was considered a titular sovereign, the ruler of a heathen nation who did not have to be taken very seriously, more like a fascinating feature of a faraway country. The role of the Mikado became a topic of serious discussion after the incidents of Shimoneseki and Kagoshima in 1863 when Japan and the western powers had reached the limits of armed intercourse. The weakness of the Tokugawa shogunate was revealed by its incapability of preventing violent acts against the foreigners and its concessions to the opposing *daimyō* and the court in Kyoto. In 1866 there were two articles in the *Japan Times* written anonymously by Ernest Satow, the interpreter of the British legation, who travelled a lot in Japan and could converse fluently with the Japanese. In these articles he spoke of the Mikado as the true sovereign of Japan and urged the Western powers to get in contact with the Emperor and the *daimyō* that were on his side in order to have the Emperor ratify the treaties they had made with the shogunate. (Japan Times 16.3.1866 and 19.5.1866)

Behind these thoughts lay the commercial interests of the British, and the other Western powers, too. The Westerners had, after all, come to Japan to trade and profit. As the political stability changed, along with it changed the opinions of the Westerners. For example *The Japan Times* wrote, just two weeks after Satow's latter article, that the Mikado was a religious fanatic whom the Westerners would have to teach a lesson as they had taught the *Shōgun*. (*The Japan Times* 2.6.1866) It had been the Bakufu's decision to repeal the law forbidding Japanese to travel abroad that had made the paper sympathize so strongly with the shogunate. The paper praised the Bakufu's new policy as liberal and sensible. If support to the shogunate could promote the Westerner's own goals they would praise the Bakufu. It must be remembered that *The Japan Times* represented the interests of the Western merchants in Japan.

All in all, the divine image of the Mikado was gradually fading. In 1866 he was looked upon as the sovereign of Japan but he was seen as a serious rival to the *Shōgun* and was considered a weak recluse, not a political subject. It was easy to ignore him since he was still completely invisible, living a fairytale-like life in Kyoto. This kind of an image of the Mikado was dominant during the early weeks of the restoration at the beginning of 1868. The Westerners in Japan paid attention to the political developments, the struggle for power and the civil war.

They considered the restoration of the power from the *Shōgun* to the Mikado a *coup d'état*. They were very hopeful about the new government and regarded past developments positively since the weak shogunate had been abolished. Their attitude towards the Meiji-government was, however, dominated by their own safety in Japan. The Westerners measured the strength of the rulers by how well they could secure the position and the well-being of foreigners. The doubts the Westerners had had about the policy of the new government were partially wiped away by the Charter Oath, the edict given in the name of the Emperor, in which Western knowledge was acknowledged superior. (Black 1968: 110–11, 183, 227, Adams 1875: 79–80, 131–2)

The Westerners regarded the position of the Meiji government as weak and vulnerable. They realized that the Emperor had no more political power than he had had before and that the country was now ruled by an oligarchy of young samurai from the Western clans instead of the Tokugawa-oligarchy. But all the Westerners writing about Japan in 1868 saw the prestige of the Emperor as the strongest support to the new government. Francis Ottiwell Adams wrote in his *History of Japan* that the members of the new government 'acted in the name of the divine Mikado . . . and that for some time that Government in reality existed simply by the halo surrounding his sacred name, and that their decrees were respected and accepted by the nation simply from being issued in the name of him who, then invisible to almost all, was undoubtedly believed to be divinely descended, and was the object of blind veneration throughout Japan.' (Adams 1875: 132)

It is remarkable that Adams still used such words as divine and sacred when talking about the Emperor of Japan. This might be explained by the Westerners' habit of using the expressions created by writers of earlier centuries since the secrecy around the Mikado was to come to an end very shortly. The rapid modernization of the country by the Meiji government was welcomed with admiration and the Emperor was seen as its leading figure. (Adams 1875: 224–5; Japan Weekly Mail 31.12.1870) The Emperor who had for centuries been shut up in his palace in Kyoto was travelling from time to time to Yedo and Osaka to handle official tasks. In the spring of 1869 he moved permanently to Yedo which had been renamed Tokyo a few months earlier, and thus showed that he had taken all the power of the Tokugawa *Shōgun*. He personally received representatives of foreign countries and royals and appeared in public to all his subjects. (Adams II 1875: 128–9, 187, 196, 200–1, 292–3; Black 1968: 195–6, 381–3; Bousquet 1882: 415)

The Westerners in Japan regarded the Emperor's public appearance progressive and compared him to European monarchs. Some, however, criticized the reformation as being too fast. John Reddie Black, the Australian newspaperman, warned that the new role of the Emperor should not be adopted hastily so that 'he did not lose his deity-like character in the estimation of his subjects.' (Black 1968: 196)

It is clear that the role of the Emperor was by far the most positive element in the whole image of Japan held by the Westerners living in the country. Before the Meiji Restoration Japan had been compared to its Asian neighbours, mainly China, and found superior, Westerners now started comparing Japan with Western countries. This way Japan could in no way match the comparison. For example, Japanese women were seen as suppressed compared to Western women whereas, in the early 1860s, they had been considered free and equal companions to their husbands compared to the women in China. (Jalagin 1994)

Despite all this, the image of the Emperor turned out to become more and more favourable during the first years of Meiji. The Westerners staying in Japan wanted to prove the superiority of their own culture which Japan was rapidly adopting. So they were eager to point to any positive element in Japan's rebirth. In their favourable views of the new role of the Emperor one can also see the Westerners' detestation of despotism. Asian people were considered slavish and tolerant of despotic rule, an idea of which can be traced back to Aristotle. Montesquieu had said that there had never been freedom of spirit in Asia nor would there ever be. Thus, the Emperor adopting the Western-style costume and manners of European monarchs could be regarded as a proof of the West's successful education of a heathen country like Japan.

On the basis of the Charter Oath and the rôle played by the Mikado, Westerners expected Japan to be on its way to democracy and constitutional monarchy. Those who saw Japan as changing too rapidly, could consider the Emperor as a stabilizing element, one that represented continuity and tradition. Particularly the British were concerned about the possibility of revolution and chaos and tended to support every idea of peace in society. The desire to see Japan succeed in adopting Western civilization without any serious disturbances in society was so strong that the divinity of the Emperor was not criticized. The Westerners in Japan considered it a matter of peace in society. This is remarkable in a sense that on other questions they strongly opposed the heathen traditions of Japan.

For example, the legal system of the country was regarded as very rigid, the punishments of crimes inhuman and cruel. In the same way, the position of woman was considered suppressed. These defects were explained to be a consequence of pagan religion. All progress toward Western civilization was, according to most of the Westerners in Japan, to be achieved through Christian faith, and it was made clear that Japan could never become civilized unless it accepted Christian virtues. More than being a matter of principle or true faith, I would say that the Christian religion was presented as a solution in these issues because it would thus have contributed to the Westerners' own profits in Japan. The practise of Christianity was prohibited in Japan until 1873 and the Westerners did everything they could to contribute to it being released. The criticism against the laws was the Westerners' way of objecting to the Japanese suggestion to open up negotiations for reforming the treaties in the matter of extraterritoriality. The Westerners did not want to let their fellow countrymen be judged by the Japanese according to their severe laws.

But the favourable image of the Emperor stood above this criticism of pagan traditions. It was to the Westerners' own advantage to preserve peace in the country and thus secure the profits they were making by their trade with the Japanese. After the restoration, commercial activities had increased remarkably and the Meiji government had succeeded in stopping the violence against foreigners. The public appearance of the Emperor with European royals was seen as a sign to his subjects to be friendly towards foreigners. So the Westerners had many reasons to be thankful and favourable to the Mikado. Besides, there was no hurry in promoting Christianity in this matter since the divinity of the Emperor was expected to vanish sooner or later in the process of modernization. (Fält 1990: 72)

Behind the Westerners' image of the Emperor of Japan in the early years of the reopening had been their own preconceptions and the need to satisfy the audience at home. This had lead them to repeat the fascinating stories of the Mikado's life told by earlier visitors and thus passing these once again to the image of Japan in the West. The Mikado was once again covered with divinity and mystery. Not until the changes in the political arena had begun did the role of the Mikado become an issue of discussion among the Westerners in Japan and the divinity around him start to fade. On the eve of the restoration he was still not taken seriously which was mainly due to his invisibility and the long tradition of delegation of power in Japan. Only after the restoration and his appearing in public did the Westerners start noticing the Mikado as a subject instead of an object. The image of the Emperor could be linked with all the favourable sides of the modernization of Japan.

What, then, does this all tell us about the Westerners in Japan in those days? According to Harold Isaacs an image is born if a person is 'turned on' to receive information and if he or she is tuned to the right time. And when a person is tuned on, the image is affected by the frequency he or she is tuned to. In other words, what kind of information a person is capable or willing to receive. When the Westerners came to Japan in the late 1850s they had already some preconceptions of the country and were 'tuned on' to report what they experienced. They wanted to explore the country so little was known about and to do it so that they could respond to the needs of the reading audience back home. So westerners in Japan in the early years of the reopening were 'tuned on' to adopt information that would strengthen their idea of a paradise-like country which offered a lot of unique and exotic features to write about. This is particularly true of the image they created of the Emperor of Japan.

A few years later, the political development of the country and the insecurity the Westerners experienced in Japan had 'tuned' them on to another frequency, namely the concern for their own, mainly commercial, interests. They started to discuss the Emperor of Japan as a political matter and adopt information that would gradually erase his divine image. After the Meiji Restoration the Westerners in Japan were again 'tuned on' to another frequency. This time they wanted to witness the victory of Western civilization in Japan's modernizing process. The image of the Emperor became a very favourable one since his adopting the Western appearance and manners could be taken as proof of the superiority of Western civilization.

The image of the Emperor of Japan had thus all along reflected the hopes and aims, the preconceptions and the experiences of the Westerners in Japan. Behind the image can be revealed their general conception of the world where Western people and their civilization were considered superior to all others.

BIBLIOGRAPHY

Source Literature

Adams, Francis Ottiwell, (1875) *The History of Japan*, 2 vols. London.
Alcock, Rutherford, (1863) *The Capital of the Tycoon. A narrative of a three years residence in Japan.* 2 vols. London.
Black, John R., (1968) *Young Japan, Yokohama and Yedo 1856–79*. With an introduction by Grace Fox. 2 vols. Reprint. Tokyo.
Bousquet, (1882) Georges, *Japan I vàra dagar*. Stockholm.
Baeckström, (1871) Anton, *Ett Besök i Japan och Kina jemte bilder från vägen dit öfver Goda-Hoppsudden, Bourbon, Nya Kaledo-nien, Manilla och Kokinkina. Antechningar och minnen från en treårig tjenstgöring i franska flottan.* Stockholm.

de Fonblanque, (1862), Edward Barrington, *Nippon and Pe-che-li; or, Two Years in Japan and Northern China.* London.

Fortune, Robert, (1863) *Yedo and Peking. A Narrative of a Journey to the Capitals of Japan and China.* With notices of the natural productions, agriculture, horticulture, trade of those countries, and other things met with by the way. London.

Harris, Townsend, (1959) *The Complete Journal of Townsend Harris.* First American Consul and Minister to Japan. Introduction and notes by Mario Emilio Cosenza. Tokyo.

Kæmpfer, Engelbert; (1871) *The History of Japan. Together with a Description of the Kingdom of Siam 1690–92.* 3 vols. Reprint. New York.

van Polsbroek, Dirk de Graeff *Journaal van Jonkheer Dirk de Graeff van Polsbroek 1857–1870.* (1987) Belevenissen van een Nederlands diplomaat in het negentiende eeuwse Japan. Ingeleid en gaennoteerd Herman J. Moeshart. Assen.

Smith, George, (1861) *Ten Weeks in Japan.* London.

Newspapers

The Japan Weekly Mail 1870
The Japan Times 1866

Research Literature

Dawson, Raymond, (1967) *The Chinese Chameleon: an analysis of European conceptions of Chinese civilization.* Chatham.

Fält, Olavi K., (1990) *The Clash of Interests. The transformation of Japan in 1861–1881 in the eyes of the local Anglo-Saxon Press.* Jyväsky lä.

Isaacs, Harold R., (1970) *Sources of Images of Foreign Countries. Public Opinion and Historians. Interdisciplinary perspectives.* Edited by Melvin Small. Detroit.

Jalagin, Seija, (1993) Japanese Social Order and Its Transformation, 1859–1873, as Seen by Western Visitors. *Modulations in Tradition: Japan and Korea in a Changing World.* Edited by Jorma Kivistö, Mika Merviö, Takahashi Mutsuko and Mark Waller. Kangasala.

Jalagin, Seija (1994) Japanese woman as seen by Western visitors to Japan 1859–1873. A paper presented in the Second NEWAS Workshop in London, April 1994.

Sansom, G. B. (1987) *The Western World and Japan. A study in the interaction of European and Asiatic cultures.* Reprint. Tokyo.

Yokoyama, Toshio, (1982) *Japan in the Victorian Mind, 1850–1880; a Study of Stereotyped Images of a Nation.* D. Phil. University of Oxford. St. Antony's College.

6

The Russian Occupation of Tsushima:
a Stepping-stone to British Leadership in Japan

HERMAN J. MOESHART

INTRODUCTION

From the time of the conclusion of the treaties with Japan in 1858, the Russians had been showing themselves very little at Yokohama and Nagasaki. They had settled in Hakodate on Hokkaido and had kept so much out of sight that people generally spoke of the four treaty powers, meaning Great Britain, France, The Netherlands and the United States, forgetting about the fifth power, Russia. The settlement at Hakodate gave the Russians the much craved ice-free harbour where the Russian ships in the area could pass the winter. The settlement also fulfilled an important rôle in the Russian plans for expansion in East Asia. In 1860 a new town had been founded on the coast of the Asian continent with the ambitious name of 'Wladi-wostok' meaning Rule of the East, demonstrating the Russian imperialist intentions. The Russian expansion did not end there. Karafuto had been claimed for Russian by Neveloskoi, who regarded the island as an extension of the Amur basin. With this advance the Russians penetrated into the area of unclear nationality, consisting of Karafuto and the Kuril islands. The Japanese maintained trade relations with the peoples of Karafuto and some of the islands and had settlements in some of them without really governing the area.

THE RUSSIAN ATTACK

In March 1861 the Russian corvette *Posadnik* dropped anchor at Tsushima and the crew started to build a settlement there. Only British intervention succeeded in removing them from the island again. Though the event looks of minor importance it had a strong influence on the position of the British in Japan.

The Russian advance into the area North of Japan in the second half of the nineteenth century had alarmed the Japanese government, but not only them. It was also regarded with suspicion by the other Western nations settling in Japan in 1859. It is not surprising, therefore, that Lord Malmebury wrote in March 1859 in the letter commissioning Rutherford Alcock, British representative in Japan:

> You will take advantage of every opportunity that may present itself to obtain for Her Majesty's Government information as to Russian proceedings on the Amour and in the neighbouring countries; and you will endeavour to dissuade the Japanese Government from making any cession of territory to Russia. You must not, however, make any promise of support on the part of this country in resisting applications of that kind. (PRO 1859: FO262/1)

Nor was Alcock the only one with this kind of instruction. The Dutch Vice Consul of Kanagawa, Dirk de Graeff van Polsbroek, had also been instructed by his chief, J. H. Donker Curtius in 1859, to report each move the Russians made. In this climate of suspicion it was all the more surprising that the Russians decided to occupy Tsushima. The reasons for this decision are obscure. A letter that popped up in Hakodate in 1863 seems to offer one explanation. It is a letter dating from 29 July 1860 in which the Russian Consul in Hakodate Iosif Antonovich Goskevitch warns the Japanese government of a British occupation of Tsushima. He based himself on a conversation he had with the British Consul C. Pemberton Hodgson at Hakodate. He concluded his letter writing.

> As the English are, therefore, wonderful imposters, it is your duty, not only to take care of Tsusima, the smallest island of your empire; this must be done with the utmost watchfulness. I inform you of this danger in the most private and secret manner. (PRO 1863: FO 410/7)

Though it seems highly improbable that a British Consul would have spoken of plans like this with his Russian colleague, we must bear in mind that Hodgson was a steady drinker who lost his job because of his alcohol consumption. He might have said something like this in a state of intoxication. However, I have not found any supporting evidence for the Russian statement in documents in the Public Record Office on this matter. The

Russians might have taken the remark or rumour seriously and in order to prevent the British from doing so, occupied the island themselves at the same time obtaining an ice-free naval base.

Vice-Admiral Likatchef proposed the appropriation of the island of Tsushima in a memorandum of 21 May 1860 to the General-Admiral Great Prince Konstatin who reported it to the Tsar. On 26 July 1860 the General-Admiral wrote to Likatchef that the Russian government agreed to the desirability of obtaining a foothold on the island and left the matter in his hands. Likatchef was to avoid any diplomatic disturbance and was not to endanger harmonious relations with the Japanese government. (Fund 410, folder 2, file 2386, I am grateful for the help of Prof. dr. Julia Mikhailova in obtaining this information.)

The Russians were regarded by the Japanese as one of the strongest nations on earth. Hodgson reported a talk he had with Japanese at Hakodate about the Crimean War from which it became clear that the Russians were regarded as stronger than the British and French. (Hodgson 1861: 308–19)

THE INTERNATIONAL RESPONSE

On 13 March 1861 the Russian corvette Posadnik dropped its anchor in the fjord that bisects the island of Tsushima. The splash of the dropping anchor broke not only the peace on the island itself but the echo was heard in Edo, London, The Hague and St. Petersburg.

The attempt by a foreign nation to appropriate a Japanese island came not entirely unexpected. Rumours had been circulating among the foreign population in Japan for some months already. Even Von Siebold, acting as a counsellor to the Japanese authorities had warned the Japanese of this possibility, stating that he expected England or France to occupy a Japanese island. Being extremely pro-Russian, he had even advised the Japanese to cede part of Hokkaido to the Russians. In these rumours an island called 'Munin-shima' was frequently mentioned, probably an island belonging to the Ogasawara group. It came as a complete surprise that Tsushima had been the aim of this Russian aggression.

From the Russian point of view, the occupation of Tsushima was understandable. The island is ideally situated in the middle of the channel between Korea and Japan and a naval force based there could easily command the access to the Japan Sea and the

Russian territories North of Japan. The island itself is well suited for a military base. The mountains make it possible to establish camps or fortresses, hidden from the sea. A deep fjord affords many safe anchorages for ships. The Posadnik anchored just behind Cape Imosaki, a cape jutting forward into the fjord, hiding the ship from whatever shipping passed on the North of the island.

When the Russians anchored at Tsushima, Rutherford Alcock was travelling from Nagasaki to Edo in the company of Jan Karel de Wit, the Dutch Consul-General in Japan. When they arrived in Shimonoseki, they heard something about the trouble at Tsushima from Japanese interpreters. They were told that there had been fighting in Tsushima between Russians and Japanese. (PRO 1861:262/25) During their progress to Edo no further news had been obtained about this affair. The night after the arrival of Alcock in his legation in Edo, 5 July 1861, an attack by the Japanese took place, which pushed the Tsushima affair to the background for the moment.

The Dutch in Nagasaki had noted some unusual activity of Japanese steam ships entering and leaving the port. Mr J. P. Metman, left behind as deputy to De Wit, wrote to the Consul-General on 14 June 1861 that the *Kanko-Maru*, originally the Dutch navy ship *Soembing*, had left the port with the under-governor of Nagasaki on board. The Japanese doctor Matsumoto Ryojun had informed him that the ship went to Tushima to settle some difficulties that had arisen between the Lord of the island and the commander of a Russian ship. (ARA 1861: 260)

THE OCCUPATION OF TSUSHIMA

What happened on Tsushima? After the arrival of the *Posadnik*, the authorities on the island had immediately pointed out to the captain of the ship that it was contrary to the articles of the treaty to land at unopened harbours. Captain Birilef had declared that his ship was in need of repairs and that it was impossible to proceed to Nagasaki. A few days later, the Russians had arrested one of the crew of a Japanese boat that was rowing guard around the ship, only to give him up on the next day when the Japanese authorities asked for him. Some fighting between the Russians and Japanese broke out on 21 May when the Russians tried to pull out stakes planted in the water at the eastern entrance of the fjord. Japanese threw stones at them and the Russians answered by rifle fire. The result was that a few

Japanese were killed. The next day the Russians arrested two Japanese from the guard-house near the stakes and only gave them up the next day after a request from the authorities of the island. In the meantime, the Russians had started to build houses, constructed a road and were digging a well. The under-governor of Nagasaki, and a little later, Abe Bungo no Kami from the Ministry of Foreign Affairs, sent by ship from Edo, did not succeed in convincing Birilef that he had to leave the island.

A private conference that Alcock had with the Japanese ministers of Foreign Affairs on 14 and 15 August 1861 in the presence of Admiral Sir James Hope and Laurence Oliphant, first secretary of the legation, confirmed that the Russians had established themselves on Tsushima. This was the reason for Alcock to send Hope to Tsushima to investigate. Hope went with the *Encounter* to Nagasaki and sent the *Ringdove*, Captain Robert G. Craigie, to Tsushima with the orders to gather as much information as possible on the movements of the Posadnik and the communications of the Russians with the authorities of the island. (PRO 1861: 410/2) Captain Craigie reported the events already described above and added that the Japanese thought the repair of the *Posadnik* was a pretext as the *Posadnik* had been in the harbour of Izuhara, the capital of the island, on 18 August and had sailed around the island to return to her old station in the fjord on the 20th. This report was brought to Admiral Hope on the morning of 28 August. (PRO 1861: 410/2)

The Admiral visited the Russian camp and wrote a letter to Captain Birilef in which he told him of the commotion his stay at Tsushima had caused at Edo and asked him straight away if he would leave the island if the Japanese authorities asked him to do so under the articles of the treaty between Russia and Japan. In his answer Birilef claimed to be acting on orders of his commander, the Russian Commodore Likatchef. He claimed to have the cooperation of the authorities on the island on orders from the Edo government. About the occupation of the island he stated to have no orders to that effect. The Japanese govern-ment could contact the diplomatic agent of Russia at Hakodate if they felt distressed by the hydrographical observations he was making around the island. The Japanese ministers of Foreign Affairs had already been in touch with Mr Goshkevich, the Russian consul at Hakodate, who claimed to know nothing of the affair and had advised them to contact the Russian Commodore. (PRO 1861: 410/2)

In an extensive report written by Laurence Oliphant who returned to Europe after receiving wounds at the attack on the British legation in Edo in July of that year, the facts already revealed were described. (PRO 1861: 410/2) He added:

> Captain Barileff did not even profess that his object in remaining was to repair his ship. He had come direct from Hakodadi to Tsusima in March, with instructions to survey the island and remain there till further orders; nor do the buildings which are still in the process of erection, nor the improvements which he is carrying out, betoken any intention of evacuation.

Vice Admiral Hope went in the *Encounter* to the North in search of the Russian Commodore Likatchef. He went first to Port May, then to Olga Bay. He found Russian settlements there but no Russian ship. As Likatchef was expected in Olga Bay, Hope left a letter there informing the Commodore of his opinion that the settlement at Tsushima was a violation of the treaty with Japan and as such could not be recognized by him. (PRO 1861: 410/2)

On 19 September a meeting was held in the British Legation with Alcock, Hope and the ministers of Foreign Affairs of Japan present. The report of the Vice Admiral was made known to the Japanese ministers who were shocked at the declaration of Birilef that a high officer from Edo had authorized him to stay. The Japanese ministers asked Alcock's advice. That was exactly what Alcock had been waiting for, to teach them a lesson in international usage or law. He told them they could lodge a complaint with the Russian government at St Petersburg as there was no Russian diplomatic agent in Japan and make a similar complaint to the representatives of the other governments in Japan. Alcock offered to send their complaint by British diplomatic bag to London to have it forwarded to St Petersburg. (PRO 1861: 410/2)

The British interference with the Russian plans could serve two important goals, the improvement of British prestige in Japan, which needed some repair after the attack of 5 July, and the prevention of Russian plans for expansion of their territory in the Japanese islands. An official complaint was made by the Japanese on 4 October 1861, copies of which were sent to the foreign representatives in Japan.

On receiving the news of the Russian occupation of Tsushima in November 1861, the Dutch envoy in St Petersburg, Gevers, consulted his British colleague Lord Napier who had received the reports of Admiral Hope and Laurence Oliphant

and the letter of Birilef. Lord Napier had orders from Lord
Russell, the Foreign Secretary, to talk about the matter to the
Russian Foreign Minister, Prince Gortchakov. (ARA 1861. 112)
Gevers asked for instructions from the Dutch government. The
Dutch Minister for Foreign Affairs instructed Gevers to join
Lord Napier in talking the matter over with Prince Gortchakov.
This was surprising as the Dutch foreign policy was based on
neutrality and aloofness. The act in itself was insignificant, as
only Great Britain had enough naval power in the seas of Japan
to enforce its will upon the Russians. However, the Dutch
representative Gevers supported Lord Napier in the discussions
with Prince Gortchakov like a sloop behind the British
man-of-war. Gortchakov denied any intention to occupy the
island. He spoke of misunderstandings and supposed that the
island would already have been evacuated by Captain Birilef.
(ARA 1862: BUZA 3142)

The last remark was true. Due to the pressure on the Russians,
the *Posadnik* had left Tsushima on 19 September on orders from
Admiral Likatchef. When the news of the evacuation of the
island had been received by Lord Napier in St Petersburg he had
another meeting with Gortchakov on 24 January 1862.
According to the letter from Gevers, Gortchakov had shown
much irritation that the matter was once more referred to. He
complained about the treatment of Birilef and the language that
had been used by Admiral Hope. Lord Napier had parried this
remark by pointing to a proposal for a treaty by Earl Russell in
which both countries would refrain from expansion in the area
of the seas of Japan. Such a treaty would also make the use of
undiplomatic language by naval officers unnecessary. Gortchakov, however, refused to enter into a definite settlement. (ARA
1862: BUZA 3142)

CONCLUSION

Though the British action had caused considerable irritation in
Russian quarters it had made clear to the Russians that expansion of their control over Japanese territory would not be
tolerated by the British government. It also proved to the
Japanese that the British were more powerful than the Russians.
The Russian occupation of Tsushima had been badly timed and
the result was the opposite from what the Russians had hoped
to achieve. The Russian feeling was expressed by Commander
Konstantin Pilkin in his diary:

How we have disgraced ourselves! This means that we had not looked before leaping. It seems to me, that having once begun the matter, it was wrong to give in, as Likatchev did. (Lensen 959: 451)

Alcock could add even one more victory over the Russians to his account. He succeeded in recruiting the son of Von Siebold, who spoke fluent Japanese, for his legation. Alexander, fifteen years old, had been destined by the old Von Siebold for the Russian navy. Alcock wrote in a letter to E. Hammond, under-secretary for Foreign Affairs that he regarded gaining the boy for Britain and depriving the Russians of such a promising inter-preter a double gain. (PRO 1861: 391/1)

BIBLIOGRAPHY

ARA = Algemeen Rijksarchief (National Archives, The Hague).
PRO = Public Record Office, (Kew, London).
Lensen G. A. (1959) *The Russian Push Towards Japan* Princeton: Princeton University Press.
Pemberton Hodgson C., (1861) *A Residence at Nagasaki and Hakodate in 1850–1860, with an account of Japan generally*, London: Richard Bentley.

7

The Paradox of Progressive Conservative Leadership in Early Meiji Japan

A study of the role of Spencer's evolutionary thought in fusing progressivism with conservative objectives

ALISTAIR SWALE

INTRODUCTION

The implementation of modernization reforms following the Restoration had the potential to severely disrupt Japanese society given, first of all, the country's situation as an essentially feudal society and, secondly, Japan's vulnerable position in international affairs. The precariousness of Japan's situation was fully recognized by the Restoration leaders yet they proceeded with a programme of reform that was 'ambitious' to say the least. Their primary objective was to carry out this programme for the purpose of national salvation and if this could be achieved with the least disruption, so much the better. However, the methods conceived to attain modernization while maintaining national stability varied greatly in nature and scope(Oka 1992: 275–288).

This paper considers the responses to the challenge of modernization within that segment of the Meiji leadership whose political orientation was conservative. The term 'conservative' is notoriously difficult to define in a political context but the work of Karl Mannheim provides an eminently useful paradigm for application to the Japanese context. For him, conservatism is not mere traditionalism and reactionism but is in fact a historically variable entity produced out of a way of experiencing that which emerges in response to the process of modernization.

> Traditionalist action is almost purely reactive behaviour. Conservative action is action oriented to . . . a complex of meanings which contains different objective contents in different epochs, in different historical phases, and which is always changing (Mannheim 1986: 76).

Conservatism has its origins within traditionalism but becomes transformed through the incorporation of a degree of dynamism compatible with the kind of fluid social milieux that modernization brings about. This assertion, along with the recognition that varying expressions of conservative ideology are produced according to particular historical configurations is particularly useful when considering Meiji conservatism in the wake of the Restoration. From within a largely traditionalist orientation there gradually emerged a more dynamic mode of pursuing the traditionalist agenda. It is my contention that this dynamism achieved a rare intensity due to the specific circumstances that Japan was faced with at the time. Many are accustomed to thinking of conservatism as a largely negative movement that resists change utterly by its very nature; however, it is possible to conceive of conservatism in a somewhat more positive form. As a broad working definition for this paper, it can be characterized as a political creed that holds continuity of tradition and the maintenance of social order as the two primary objectives. From these two principles stem characteristics that conservatism is perhaps better known by. The concern for continuity of tradition is typically tied to a proclivity with *particularism* rather than *universalism*. The concern for the maintenance of social order engenders a propensity for antagonism towards radical political programmes and a scepticism with regard to the possibility of rapid progress (Mannheim 1986: 96–97).

The above points are considered to be generally representative of the fundamental political orientation within the conservative bloc of the Restoration leadership (arguably the overwhelming majority). Yet when one observes the praxis of this group two broadly different approaches emerge. One was based on a static notion of the national polity which was conceived as having origins above and beyond temporal contingencies. The emphasis was on maintaining things as they 'always had been since ancient times.' The other form of conservatism that emerges was based on a more dynamic conception of the polity, one which was seen as having a capacity for adaptation to historical circumstances. The maintenance of traditional continuity and social order were still primary objectives (and thereby an essentially conservative character remained), but there was more willingness to countenance innovative ways of pursuing the conservative agenda. In sum, the former, which we may term *formalistic* conservatism, entailed a belief that the

maintenance of national and cultural integrity was only possible
by maintaining 'inviolable' traditional institutions and customs;
the latter, which we may term *progressive* conservatism, countenanced a variety of modifications to the institutions and customs
of the polity so long as the traditional integrity of the nation was
preserved in its spiritual essence.

Formalistic conservatism found its initial inspiration in the
Kokugaku of the early Meiji period and later found a grander
expression in 'family state' ideology (Ishida 1992: 6–20). Progressive conservatism, on the other hand, was a tendency clearly
discernible among a number of conservatives from the early
eighties onwards. It arguably found its first clear ideological
enunciation in the term *Zenshin Hoshu no Shugi* (lit. 'gradualist
conservatism') which was used by Iwakura Tomomi in a document produced in 1882 to describe the approach of the Ito-led
faction to reform. Ultimately, the clearest enunciation of
progressive conservatism can be found in the *Kokusuishugi* (lit.
'national purism') of the *Seikyosha* group which produced the
journals *Nihon* and *Nihonjin* in the late eighteen-eighties. Their
espousal of a rather unorthodox mix of nationalist sentiment
and an openness regarding the need for a degree of Westeriz-
ation (Nakanome 1993: 79–84) denotes more precisely what is
meant by progressive conservatism.

Both the formalistic and progressive forms of conservatism
emerged as a response to the modernization requirements peculiar to Japan in the nineteenth century. To clarify the role of
progressive conservatism, how it came to be necessary to
develop a certain flair for institutional innovation coupled with
a form of conservative essentialism, we need to consider the
short-comings of formalistic conservatism in coming to terms
with the requirements of the modernization process, particularly with regard to the process of nation-state building.

PROGRESSIVE CONSERVATISM AND NATION-STATE BUILDING

As Ernest Gellner points out in *Nations and Nationalism*, two
basic conditions need to be fulfilled if industrialisation and
nation-state building are to proceed successfully. The first is the
establishment of a seamless state which is coextensive with a
particular territoriality. The second is the formation of a largely
homogenous culture which, besides enabling the standardization of skills as necessitated by industrial processes, also lays the
foundation for the melding of the people within a given national

territory to the state. It is important to note that technological innovation in itself is not a sufficient condition of modernity; it entails a concomitant political and cultural integration (Gellner 1983: 3–38). Also, there is not always a predestination apparent between states and the nations that come to be ascribed to them. In some cases the ascription of a nation to a particular state has to be quite consciously engineered. So it was in the case of Japan, but not all within the leadership grasped this necessity or what would be required to successfully carry it out. This point is especially significant when considering the relative strengths and weaknesses of the formalistic and progressive approaches to the process of nation-state building.

During the initial stages of the Meiji Restoration, the leadership carried out the initial steps of modernization in terms of establishing a modern state apparatus with remarkable speed and clarity of purpose. Perhaps this is not altogether surprising given that Japan had already achieved a very high degree of national integration under the *Bakuhan* system (Moriya 1990: 97–123) and that also the Satsuma and Chōshū leaders could see first-hand the enhanced military and fiscal capacity of the Western-style centralized state. However, beyond these initial steps it can be said that although the establishment of the centralized state was a relatively obvious option with clear benefits, the means of galvinizing a new nation to go with the state was a different matter.

By the end of the 1870s it had become apparent that something more sophisticated than social engineering on a purely formalistic level would be required to sustain Japan's modernization. This is evidenced by the early failed attempts to develop a new 'state religion' and revive the old *Ritsuryo* system.

There were a number of practical and perceptual shortcomings in the leadership's approach but the most fundamental one was the essentially static nature of the traditional cosmology, in particular that of Confucianism. Although officially sidelined during the early Restoration due to its association with the Bakufu and feudal thinking in general, Confucianism in both the classical and neo-Confucian forms was still firmly entrenched in the intellectual life of the time (Pyle 1969: 118–143). Both forms had inherent limitations. The classical Confucian cosmology had little scope to deal with the unfamiliar historical process of modernization. Neo-Confucianism, though somewhat more flexible, also had yet to be developed into a form that was compatible with the new social realities. At the heart of the Confucian world-view there was a notion of a set order which was constituted into dogma. In a period of extreme flux the Confucian cosmology was not viable and it would not be until the social order of post-Restoration Japan came to be more or less settled that a revitalized Confucian dogma could emerge (Ishida 1992: 21–66).

Evolutionary theory, on the other hand, countenanced social change while at the same time prescribing particular social arrangements appropriate to differing stages of human history. Intellectuals and political leaders of the period, if they were willing to forsake an utterly traditionalist and static conception of the national polity, were thereby able to reconceptualize social order within a more a fluid cosmology which nevertheless accommodated the 'Confucian' concern for a set social structure. In a period when Japan was faced with the paradoxical need to 'modernize' while maintaining some sort of national integrity, conventional formalistic conservatism was simply inadequate. Herbert Spencer, through both his evolutionary writings and personal contact with certain Japanese statesmen, provided conceptual tools and a theoretical justification for a more pro-gressive approach that did not compromise a fundamentally conservative orientation (Yamashita 1983: 56–70).

It warrants emphasizing that Spencer's popularity among conservatives did not actually constitute as significant a break with tradition as one might imagine. Spencer's division between Knowable (Science) and Unknowable (Religion) provided an amenable flexibility (Spencer 1862: 25–67). By removing the potentially disruptive Christian element of Western culture, science came packaged ready for Japanese use with 'no strings attached.' Spencer's delineation of an Unknowable spiritual realm provided generous scope for coupling a completely non-Western form of spirituality to scientific knowledge. In addition to this, Spencerian philosophy also exhibited a striking parallel with Neo-Confucian tradition. Neo-Confucianism can be described as the attempt to explain the cosmos in terms of fundamental principles (Ri) which transcend all orders of phen-omena. The architectonic nature of Spencer's philosophical under-taking is almost identical as is evidenced by the nature of the *Synthetic Philosophy*, in particular the approach of *First Principles* where he elucidates how certain fundamental physical laws apply to all levels of phenomena from the material to the super-organic (Uno 1984: 25–26 and Spencer 1862: 541). Obviously, Spencer's 'Principles' are not those of Confucius or

Mencius but, by virtue of the above characteristics, Spencer's work held the potential for an intuitive affinity which the likes of social contract theories could not.

The specific applicability of Spencerian evolutionism to the problem of nation-state building can be found in the *The Principles of Sociology*. In it Spencer laid out certain conditions that must be fulfilled for a social entity to survive and develop further. First and foremost it had to be recognized that societies develop in the same manner as organisms, and that therefore transformations of the whole occur through the gradual adaptations among the already existing constituent parts. Consequently, even if a further stage of development were conceivable it would be disastrous to attempt to effect such a vision without allowing for the essential intermediary stages to be followed through. The development of more advanced specializations in societies could only emerge through a gradual process of continuous differentiation (Spencer 1870: 435–458). In addition to the need to recognize the necessity of maintaining continuity, Spencer also emphasized the importance of maintaining the cohesiveness of the totality throughout the process. Increase in differentiation without a commensurate increase in integration would simply mean the dissolution of the totality, i.e. social disintegration (Spencer, 1870: Vol I: 457, Vol. II: 603–642 & 652). Spencer also recognized that, because industrial society entailed a great degree of *voluntary* cooperation (as opposed to the largely *compulsory* cooperation that characterizes militant societies), the integrative cement of an industrial society would be *internal* and necessitate an advanced character capable of self-imposed moral restraint. Social advance (towards industrialism) could only progress at an even pace with moral advance and he actually counselled against implementing moral strategems that were more civilized or enlightened than the actual circumstances of extant society (Spencer 1935: 100–109).

Translating these observations to the context of the Japanese process of modernization, we may see how his admonitions regarding a gradualist approach to social reform would have been relevant. Conservatives who were particularly eager to avoid a modernization programme that would entail 'wiping the slate clean' altogether had their reservations confirmed and justified. Moreover, for the conservative leadership who were finding the myriad bureaucratic developments increasingly difficult to implement and control, his framework provided a clear guide for working at social integration to maintain social order.

The historical relativization of the polity such as the Spencerian perspective would entail would not have been welcomed by formalistically-minded conservatives (a good number of them Confucianists). In the hands of progressive conservatives, however, it would prove to be of immeasurable utility as both an ideological buttress and a theoretical tool. In particular, it clarified that vital aspect of modernization, the integration of nation and state. As stated earlier, the Meiji leadership as a whole had no clear idea of how to pursue modernization beyond the centralized state and military. For the more progressive conservatives who could countenance a national polity within a broader scheme of development, Spencer's dynamic and highly pragmatic account of social evolution was in many ways instructive. An illustration of how useful Spencerian thought could be when applied to practical social issues is most apparent in the area of education reforms.

PROGRESSIVE CONSERVATISM AND EDUCATION

The education system arguably plays a central rôle in the fusing of nation and state. Besides enabling the efficient diffusion of knowledge associated with technical innovation and broadening the pool of recruitment to the bureaucratic and intellectual élite, it becomes the primary vehicle for establishing the collective consciousness of the nation (Gellner 1983: 35–38). In Japan, as the need for creating a nation of citizens who were no longer mere drudges of the state but actually identified with it was recognized, it would serve as the crucible of a new, distinctly modern form of Japanese national consciousness. As we know now, this problematic area was ultimately resolved along reactionary lines by using the education system to nurture the virtue of loyalty in all citizens as subjects of the Emperor tied into one extended familial body (Ishida 1992: 21–66). However, there were a number of tentative steps, in some cases outright about-faces, taken in the process of clarifying education's role within the broader context of the nation-state building process. It was the progressive conservatives, and chief among them Mori Arinori, who played a pivotal role in placing educational reform on the right track as far as the development of a modern national consciousness was concerned.

Mori exhibited very early on an appreciation for the internal, almost spiritual aspects of nation-building. Perhaps nothing exemplifies this more than his stand in favour of abolishing the samurai's exclusive right to bear swords. Nevertheless, although his perception of the necessity was strong, the clarification in his mind of what means were appropriate took considerable time to develop. A comprehensive *Weltanschauung*, indeed a sociology, was necessary to piece together the disparate elements of modernization. Spencer's thought proved to be of considerable utility.

MORI ARINORI AS PROGRESSIVE CONSERVATIVE

Mori Arinori, Ambassador to England from 1879 to 1884 and Minister of Education from 1885 to 1889, is a particularly significant and instructive exemplar of progressive conservative leadership. Ivan Hall in his extremely thorough monograph details Mori's political thought and actions which, although ostensibly highly conservative, were in fact tempered by a some-what paradoxical flexibility with regard to the adoption of Western models. Regarding the relation between Spencer and Mori, he states that it would be difficult to quantify or clarify the nature of that relationship even if one were to exhaustively compare the respective works of both Mori and Spencer (Hall 1973: 483–484).

It is felt on closer observation, however, that the relationship between the two was in fact quite substantial and profound. Mori's Japanese biographer indicates that while Mori was *chargé d'affaires* in Washington, he read Spencer extensively. It is also apparent that one of his more intimate acquaintances was Charles Sumner, one of the original subscribers to Spencer's *Synthetic Philosophy* in America (Duncan 1908: 100–101). More-over, the regular personal contact that was established and maintained with Spencer while in London from 1879 to 1884 was extremely significant considering Spencer's general selec-tiveness in making acquaintances. Furthermore, Mori's moral and educational thinking exhibits a structural parallelism with Spencer's that is quite striking.

Mori's connection with Spencer was first established in 1873 during a brief visit to England. However, the main develop-ments in their association occurred during Mori's time as Japanese Ambassador to England (1879–1884). Although ostensibly a career diplomat, Mori had long held a deep interest in the rôle of education in the new Japan and had been eager to participate in educational reform since his sojourn in the United States in the early seventies. It would seem that by being posted to

England Mori had been denied yet again an opportunity to get involved in the area of his primary interest. Yet not two years after he left for England, the 1881 political crisis changed the political landscape of Japan and altered his fortunes.

Following the rupture between Itō and Okuma in 1881 and the suppression of liberal activism, a constitution and the convocation of a parliamentary assembly was promised. In 1882, Itō Hirobumi visited Europe to personally investigate the various European constitutional systems with a view to formulating something appropriate to the Japanese context. Meanwhile, Mori had developed a substantial degree of contact with Herbert Spencer and a number of other leading British intellectuals at the Athenaeum Club (Yamashita 1983: 188). Mori wrote to Itō inviting him to Britain, (although as it turned out, he met him in Paris). He spoke with Itō over three days exhorting him not to underestimate the importance of augmenting constitutional reforms with a form of training that would cultivate the appropriate character among the general population. Itō was so impressed by Mori's arguments and earnestness that he soon wrote to advise him that he would soon be forming a Cabinet on the Prussian model and would make Mori the first Minister of Education (Hall 1973: 358–362).

Mori's educational thought at this time was extremely fragmentary and in terms of written material consists mainly of memoranda and the occasional speech or pamphlet. What does emerge very clearly is the use of Spencer's work, *Education: Intellectual, Moral, and Physical.* The following quote comes from an early work entitled 'On Physical Fitness':

> The chief aim of education, generally speaking, is to nourish and to develop the several faculties with which man is endowed and by so doing increase the pleasure to be gained from them. These faculties may be distinguished as three: *the intellectual, the moral and the physical* . . . [my italics]. (Mori, 1972: Vol. 1, 325–328. Translation as per Hall, 1973: 337).

A memorandum that Mori sent to Itō from London following their discussions confirms that this influence had not waned. In fact, Mori came to focus on two particular aspects, moral and physical education, which he felt were being ignored to the great peril of the realm. These later became central elements of his education policy.

Mori was eventually recalled in 1884, given a special appointment within the Education Ministry and made Minister the following year. There were two phases that we can broadly distinguish in the reforms that he undertook. The first phase of his reforms was essentially oriented toward institutional integration. The New Educational Ordinance of 1885 recentralized the education system by placing the former educational boards directly subordinate to the Ministry. Mori continued along this line to establish a nationally integrated education system for cultivating a steady supply of academic and bureaucratic élites. Tokyo University became an Imperial University directly administered by the Ministry in 1886 and guaranteed opportunities in the civil service for all graduates of the Letters and Law faculties. A number of Scientific and Professional schools which were either private or under the jurisdiction of Ministries other than the Ministry of Education were amalgamated into the University or placed under its supervision. Moreover, a meritocratic mode of recruitment through examinations was established with special preparatory High Schools strategically located throughout the country (Amano 1990: 126–130).

The second phase of reform dealt with cultural integration. Under Mori a number of reforms to standardize the curriculum and texts were introduced. Among these, one of the most significant was the promotion or moral instruction which went from being low on the list of official priorities to being first. In 1888 a new ethical handbook (the *Rinrisho*) was established to standardize instruction for graduates from the Ordinary Middle Schools. The text was completely secular in nature and its general content is broadly attributable to an influence from Spencer's *The Data of Ethics* which had been translated into Japanese in 1884 (Hall 1973: 440–443). *The Date of Ethics* follows the genesis of morality through various levels of phenomena, starting with the physical and ending with the sociological. The sections dealing with 'The Psychological View' and 'The Sociological View' clarified the relationship between morality on both the individual and social levels and led to the postulating of the main problem of ethics as the conciliation of individual and society, discussed further under the themes of 'egoism' and 'altruism'. The potential for conciliation was raised and the limitations of present realities considered. Spencer conceded that there was a necessity for a high degree of external constraint in developing moral character within less-developed, militant societies and stated that at this stage of evolution, individual interests must of necessity be subordinated to those of society. Yet ultimately this conflict was to be resolved through a conciliation of interests as humans became more suited to the community of life that society entails (Spencer 1893: Vl. I, 102–149, and 242–280).

Mori incorporated the language and motifs of *The Data of Ethics* into the *Rinrisho* with a view to establishing what he termed a 'common sense' morality. Nevertheless, his prescriptions relating to military-style physical training indicate that he regarded the Japanese at the time as requiring a degree of coercion and constraint. He even went so far as to assert most emphatically that the primary role of education was to be defined in relation to the State and to the Emperor in particular (Hall 1973: 397–440). Nevertheless, he also indicated that he expected this form of training to lead to the development of morally mature, self-regulating individuals. There was evidently a higher goal at stake. Mori wanted to produce not merely functional subjects, people who were simply 'indoctrinated', but subjects who had a degree of intellectual independence which would enable them to actively promote the good of society. This vision of moral development is in essence identical to that of Spencer (Spencer 1893: 118–124 and 133–4).

The essence of Mori's progressive conservatism emerges in an unmistakably progressive morality which modifies a conventionally conservative concern for order. His prescriptions for the present entailed a degree of external restraint and caution that any reactionary would have been satisfied with. However, his prescriptions regarding the kind of morality he intended to cultivate indicate a concern for nurturing the kernel of something that ultimately does not require and in a sense denies that constraint. Mori's moral education policy indeed exhibits a perception of the potential for dynamic change, if you like, moral evolution. Implicit in this is a rejection of the Confucian world view, both in terms of its institutional and moral prescriptions.

Nevertheless, it is important to note that Mori did not go so far as to espouse a progressive conception of morality in an abstract sense of *universal* good. He remained cognisant of the restraints of contemporary political circumstances and perceived the ultimate value of his reforms as lying in the *national* good. As Mori had pointed out to Itō in 1882, the education of the populace to develop their character was an integral part of constitutional reform. What this meant in practice was the creation of a people capable of integration into the modern nation-state. The clarity with which he perceived his educational reforms within this broader political perspective is epitomized in the following quote which is taken from a cabinet proposal of 1887:

> . . . from medieval times onward the conduct of our national affairs both civil and military, has been the concern exclusively of the samurai class. The leadership of today's movement for progress likewise rests in the hands of a very small minority. The great majority of our people probably have only the vaguest idea of what is involved in establishing a state. Looking at Europe or America, we see that in every nation people of all classes, *both men and women alike* [my italics], possess a love of country and an unshakeable [national] unity.
>
> [The population should be] taught to the very marrow of their bones to feel a fervent spirit of loyalty and patriotism, to maintain a steadfastness of character and a constancy of purpose, *to be ashamed of cowardice and to hold all servility in contempt [my italics]. (Mori 1972: 344–347. Translation as per Hall, 1973: 408).

Mori recognized the political realities of the time and did not take issue with them under the current circumstances. This was coupled with a progressive conception of morality which entails a hitherto uncountenanced degree of egalitarianism and independence. Underpinning both of these positions is a passionate concern for Japanese national interests. This signifies a degree of particularism which ultimately places Mori squarely within the compass of conservative politics, progressive though some aspects of his thought and policy may have been.

CONCLUSION

In this paper it has been argued that Japanese modernization had special requirements which could only be countenanced given a dynamic conception of social development such as is entailed in Spencerian evolutionism. Those amongst the leadership who incorporated this conception into their world view while retaining an essentially 'conservative' agenda have been referred to as progressive conservatives. Mori, as a progressive conservative, supervized a very significant phase in the development of the modern Japanese nation-state, namely the process of integration of nation and state through an education system that fostered a distinctly modern form of national consciousness. The strong influence of Spencer on this statesman and by extension the nation-state building process is undeniable. With regard to Mori's institutional reforms it has to be conceded that it is difficult to find a direct link between Spencer's sociology and specific policies, although there is substantial evidence of a logical parallelism. Nevertheless, when the influence of Spencer's ethical philosophy on Mori's moral education reforms is examined, we see in particular how Spencer's thought molded Mori's response to the needs of the times so as to draw him beyond the constraints of the Confucian world view toward a new position which nonetheless did not require an abandonment of the nationalist principle. Having said this, however, one does not want to suggest that Mori became a blind disciple of Spencer. He was too conscious of his own personal mission as a Japanese statesman to go that far. Even so, it can be argued that the principles gleaned from Spencer came to form part of the structure of Mori's thinking and were later used 'creatively' and independently of Spencer.

Unfortunately, however, Mori's career was tragically cut short. On the morning in February 1889 that the new constitution was to have been formally presented to the Japanese people by the Emperor, he was assassinated by a fanatical student. The opponents of Mori, primarily reactionary conservatives such as the Confucianist Motoda Eifu, had long characterized him as a traitorous Westernizer, and as an enemy of the Imperial throne. Despite the fact that he had done much to further the cause of conservatism in his day, the relativization of the *kokutai* (the national polity) and the secularism of the morality inherent in his textbook were construed as implying disloyalty to traditions underpinning the Imperial Court.

Ironically, the demise of Mori paralleled the demise of progressive conservatism as a whole and marked a turning point in the popularity of Spencer in Japan. After the fundamental modernizing reforms of the early Meiji period had been cemented in place and a greater degree of social stability established, there was a clear move away from the kind of progressive conservatism described above toward a more formalistic and reactionary form. Ishida's work on Meiji political thought depicts a move away from an organic conception of the national body to the notion of the 'family-state' from the 1890s (Ishida, 1992: 6–20). One cannot help but feel that this transformation was an expression of a transfer from a more fluid and dynamic form of conservatism to one which was increasingly formalistic and static. We can perhaps consider the 'national purism' (*Kokusuishugi*) of the *Seikyosha* as the last bastion of progressive conservatism (Maruyama 1987: 475–483). Yet this relatively moderate form of conservatism suffered the fate of gradually being lost amid the clamour of more reactionary forms of nationalism. The relatively Statist German evolutionism replaced Spencerian evolutionism and an uncompromising conception of the national polity was forged out of the Confucian tradition(Yamashita 1983: 157–158).

Overall, it may be concluded that Spencerian evolutionary thought came to serve as an important bridging ideology between an earlier pre-Restoration stage of Confucian dogmatism and a latter stage of Confucian dogmatism which emerged in the late 1880s. The fact that it was a transitory phase in no way means that it was not important. This importance becomes evident when considering the problems and challenges that emerged within the context of a modernizing feudal society during the early Meiji Period.

BIBLIOGRAPHY

Amano, Ikuo, (1990) *Education and Examination in Modern Japan*, Tokyo: University of Tokyo Press.

Duncan, David, (1908) *The Life and Letters of Herbert Spencer*, London: Methuen & Co..

Gellner, Ernest, (1983) *Nations and Nationalism*, London: Basil Blackwell.

Hall, Ivan P., (1973) *Mori Arinori*, Harvard: Harvard University Press.

Ishida Takeshi, (1992) (1st Reprint), *Meiji Seiji Shisōshi Kenkyū*, Tokyo: Miraisha.

Mannheim, Karl, (1986) *Conservatism: A Contribution to the Sociology of Knowledge*, D. Kettler et al (Eds), London: Routledge and Kegan Paul.

Maruyama Masao, (1987) 'Kuga Katsunan-Hito to Shisō' in *Kuga Katsunan*, Kindai Nihon Shisō Taikei (4), Ueda Michinari (Ed.), Tokyo: Chikuma Shobō.

Mori Arinori, (1972) *Mori Arinori Zenshu*, Volumes I–III, Okubo Toshiaki (Ed.), Tokyo: Senbundo Shoten.

Moriya Katsuhisa, (1990) 'Urban Networks and Information Networks' in *Tokugawa Japan: The Social and Economic Antecedents of Modern Japan*, C. Nakane and S. Oishi Eds., Tokyo: University of Tokyo Press.

Nakanome Tōru, (1993) *Seikyosha no Kenkyū*, Tokyo: Shibunkaku Shuppan.

Oka Yoshitake, (1992) 'Meiji Ishin to Sekai Josei' in *Meiji Seijishi I*, Oka Yoshitake Chosakushu, Volume I, Tokyo: Iwanami Shoten.

Pyle, Kenneth B., (1969) *The New Generation in Japan: Problems of Cultural Identity*, California: Stanford University Press.

Spencer, Herbert, (1862) *First Principles*, London: Williams and Norgate.

Spencer, Herbert, (1935) (first published in 1875), *Education; Intellectual, Moral & Physical*, London: The Thinkers Library, Walls & Co.

Spencer, Herbert, (1893) *Principles of Ethics, Volumes I & II*, London: Williams and Norgate, *The Date of Ethics* was first published in 1879 and constitutes Part I of the first volume of *The Principles of Ethics*.

Taylor, M. W., (1992) *Men Versus The State: Herbert Spencer and Late Victorian Individualism*, Oxford: Clarendon Press.

Uno Seiichi, (1984) *Jukyō Shisō, Tokyo: Kodansha.*
Yamashita Shigekazu, (1983) *Supensa to Kindai Nippon*, Tokyo: Ocha no Mizu Shobo.

8

Leaders in Change:
The Way to Official Language Reform

ANNETTE SKOVSTED HANSEN

The new international contact of the late nineteenth century not only forced a new world view upon the Japanese, but more important, it created a new world reality. US and European pressure on Japan to open its ports for trade from the mid-1850s, spurred intellectuals and politicians in Japan to argue that the strength and independence of the country depended on the creation of Japan as a nation state equal to European nations. The intellectuals emphasized the importance of the mobilization of a citizenry with the skills to support the nation, politically and militarily. They pointed to three essential factors: education, communication, and patriotism. Education would remedy the vast ignorance of Western science among the Japanese, communication would disseminate new ideas and knowledge throughout the country. Through the two it was anticipated that a sense of patriotism, as Benedict Anderson has described it, would evolve to support identification with the newly perceived nation that subordinated personal and local needs to the goals of the country as a whole. (Anderson 1991: 7) Many intellectuals emphasized the role of language as the central medium of education, communication, and patriotism, but in order to serve as a medium in the successful implementation of educational and political reforms, language itself needed to be reformed.

At the end of the Edo period numerous styles of writing existed, most of them were different blends of Chinese and Japanese syntax, writing systems, and vocabulary. The spoken language was characterized by regional differences. In the Meiji period, 1868–1912, these variations became even more numerous in the wake of individual experimentation with writing styles and new forums for communication, many of which were created by the new Meiji government through reforms on, for example: universal education (1872), the creation of a conscript army (1872) and a new nationwide postal system (1872), and the abolition of the domains of the Tokugawa Shogunate (1871).

In 1875, Fukuchi Gen'ichiro (1841–1906), the chief editor of *Tokyo Nichi Nichi Shinbun*, pointed out that the obscurity of the written language was especially unfortunate '. . . today when the government wishes to make education prosper, stresses literature, and aspires to reach a point where there are no uneducated people in the country.' (Fukuchi 1875) The year before, Nishi Amane (1829–97), a government official, had stated that because of the difficulty of the Japanese script 'the fine policies notwithstanding, the people remain as uneducated as before.' (Nishi 1874: 1–2) However, no official language reform was implemented for another 25 years.

The first official language reform was passed through the Ministry of Education in 1900. The new regulations included; a selection of one standard set of *hiragana, hentaigana* [anomalous Japanese cursive syllabary]; and restricted the number of *kanji* taught in primary school to about 1,200. The next official language reform was implemented during the US occupation on 16 November 1946 when the Cabinet approved and promulgated a list of 1,850 *tōyō kanji* [Chinese characters for current use].

This essay will take as its departure the observation that official language reforms appear to have been few, largely limited to script reform, and only launched after they had practically taken effect in reality. Therefore the issue of language reform can be seen as a significant example of the influence exerted on government policies by actors who promoted and guided change preceding official regulations. Leadership, in the realm of language and culture, can be said to have been provided by people who, in response to a new social context, influenced the usage of language with their own writing and manner of speaking.

I will identify three groups of people that played complementary roles as leaders of language change; the intellectual élite, writers of fiction, and all the Japanese who due to their increased mobility came into contact with people from other parts of Japan and created means of oral communication across regional barriers. The intellectuals conceptualised the ideas of language reform and experimented with the different scripts; the writers of fiction experimented with style, and the ordinary speakers of Japanese created variations of spoken Japanese that would later constitute the basis for a new written style.

THE INTELLECTUAL ÉLITE

The intellectuals outlined the issues of language reform. Their suggestions may be grouped under three headings: script simplification, colloquialization, and standardization. They suggested script simplification in response to the ineffectiveness of an education based on memorization of large numbers of Chinese characters. They proposed colloquialization in response to the obscurities of the written language, and standarization in response to the diverse patterns of speech which hindered communication among different regions and which was thought to delay the development of a sense of national unity.

Many intellectuals in the early Meiji period saw their rôle to be that of guiding the rest of the population towards the goal of *Bummei Kaika* [Civilization and Enlightenment]. A number of forums for discussion appeared; one of them was the Meirokusha, The Society of the Sixth Year of Meiji, established in 1874. The members published their deliberations in their journal, *Meiroku zasshi*.

In the first issue of *Meiroku Zasshi*, it was stated that the members of the Society, through their publications, hoped to help promote 'enlightenment among our countrymen.' The issues brought up in this journal ranged from the simplification and romanization of the Japanese language to observations on religious practice, and torture, including articles with titles such as 'The interrelationship between the Freedom of Peoples and the Climates of Regions.' 'Wives and Concubines,' and 'The Statesman.' These issues seem to have been chosen to illuminate various aspects of dominant themes, such as technology and democracy. It is indicative of the perception of the centrality of language in issues of reform that the two articles in the first issue were both devoted to the question of language.

The first article was Nishi Amane's 'Yōji o nite kokugo o shosuru no ron' [The Writing of Japanese with the Western Alphabet] and the second was the educator Nishimura Shigeki's (1828–1902) 'Kaika no tabi ni yotte kaimoji o hassubeki no ron' [Why the Reform of Writing Should Depend on the Level of Enlightenment]. Nishi argued for the immediate and exclusive use of the Roman alphabet in all Japanese texts, whereas Nishimura maintained that as more people became enlightened through education they would automatically come to favour language reform and not until then should language reform be implemented.

Script simplification

The idea of script simplification originated from the concern with the difficulty of learning Chinese characters. Among others, Meijima Hisoka, who later reformed the postal system, and Mozume Takami, a professor of literature at Tokyo University, discussed the disproportionately large amount of time required for learning Chinese characters, and the lack of emphasis on the content of texts read in the schools. In 1866, Maejima ventured the view that few people studied seriously because of the difficulty in learning characters:

> The few who do study zealously, spend much of the precious time and energy of their youth and still hardly learn the shape and pronunciation of the characters, and frequently the essence of the test remains obscure to them. Now exactly the time of youth which is best for comprehending the reason and truth of things is spent on the futile study of the shape and appearance of the Kanji and thus the spirit of study is broken.

He then made this calculation:

> The abolition of Chinese characters in ordinary education would shorten the time that is used solely for the purpose of learning the characters, . . . and would save children at least three years, and, for those who plan to go on to higher levels of study, five to eight years. If the time saved this way were to be spent in the study of Western science, . . . it would be an inestimable advantage. (Maejima 1866; repr. Yamamoto 1978: 128)

This was a simple calculation that represented a way to achieve the goal of students acquiring knowledge of science and technology earlier in their schooling. By eliminating the cause of the disproportionately time-consuming study of the written language, students would be able to read about scientific ideas after only a few years of reading practice.

Many advocates of script simplification argued for the abolition of the Chinese characters, but they did not agree on the ideal substitute. Nishi Amane asserted that the Roman alphabet was the key:

I have pondered the fact that the Europeans now lead the world. If one considers this from the point of view of reason, their race has achieved greatness by piling up the lesser results of their minute observations. They view even the vastness of the universe in terms of the falling apple. They guide legions by beginning with the training of but one soldier. They depend on nothing more than the expanding power of steam to send ships across the four seas. Their transmission of electricity to the four continents is derived from observing a humble kite. And similarly nothing has contributed more to their world preeminence in science, the arts, and letters than the twenty-six letters of the 'ABC.' (Nishi 1874: 9)

Although this was a powerful argument, other intellectuals asserted that an indigenous script would be more suitable. Some suggested *hiragana*, others *katakana*, another syllabary, and others maintained that a mixture of standardized Chinese characters and *hiragana*, *kanamajiribun*, was the best option. (Shimizu 1874: 9, Nishimura 1874: 4)

Colloquialization

The advocates to colloquialization emphasized intelligibility as an important argument for the use of spoken language as the basis for a new written style; because in the '*bummei*', [en-lightened] era of Meiji even scholarship should be intelligible to every one, 'even women and children.' In the editorial of the first issue of *Yomiuri shinbun*, 2 November 1874, the editor declared that the newspaper ' . . . will be written in a style close to speech, because it is the intention to write about matters in a way so anyone can understand in order to educate women and children'. Thus the idea of a broad readership encompassing all members of the nation, and the role of the newspaper as an educator and guide, had been presented from the very begin-ning. The opening sentence was borrowed from *gesaku* literature where specific mention of women and children was made to emphasize that the desired readership included everyone, even the less educated. The editor was aware that language had a role in making this possible.

Another argument for colloquialization was that it was the basis for being able to stir the emotions of the readers. Shimizu Usaburō, the owner of a book-store and printing company, argued that:

There naturally should be no departure from the spoken language. If the written form differs from the spoken language, reading the material will not produce feelings of joy, anger, sorrow, and happiness. And education loses its appeal when these emotions are not stimulated.

Shimizu used some examples of Japanese literary tradition to support his argument:

Even women and children are readily moved to sorrow and laughter by reading such works as the *Inaka Genji*, the *Jiraiya monogatari*, the *Hizakurige*, the *Hasshojin*, the *Gidayubon*, and the *Jōruribon*, because they were written in a language that is the same as the spoken tongue. (Shimizu 1874: 8–9)

These works consisted largely of dialogue written in a style resembling that of the contemporary colloquial language and were especially popular among urban commoners.

Mozume Takami expressed his conviction that enlightenment of children in the schools would be a natural consequence of colloquialization. Mozume described in 1886 how children at the time memorized long passages of the Chinese classics but were unable to understand the content of these passages until the teacher explained it. However, with a curriculum including practical learning, he assessed that: 'The children will gain knowledge, if only the texts are written in a way so that they can understand them.' 'Today,' he wrote, 'when the Japanese speak, it is with their own mouths, living mouths, but [when they write] it is with the hands of dead men . . . . [because] If you look at the works of the brush, the old parts are the creation of a thousand years, and the new parts that of five hundred years ago.' (Mozume 1886 (1935): 132) Mozume expressed his opinion of the inadequacy of a written language which had not renewed itself in response to centuries of historical and social changes.

Standardization

In addition to education, communication on a national scale was a practical concern of the debates from 1866. According to many debaters, for all citizens 'to understand each other,' the citizens faced the problem of the many existing patterns of speech, the obscurity of learned writings, and new influences from abroad 'corrupting' the language; all of which combined made communication difficult.

In 1875, Nambu Yoshikazu (1840–1917), a scholar and advo-

cate of the exclusive use of the Roman alphabet, predicted that
if the Japanese language was not reformed and standardized, it
would no longer be intelligible in the future:

> The language of this sublime imperial state is becoming con-
> fused and chaotic due to the high degree of Chinese influence
> as well as to the changes brought through languages such as
> English, German, and French and will in the future reach a point
> where it can no longer be understood. Is that not unbearably
> sad! (Nambu 1875)

One pure indigenous language did not exist, he argued, and
only the containment of unselective borrowing would secure
the survival of an intelligible national language.

The way to strengthen the Japanese language, according to
Nambu, would be to first make it easier by writing it with
Roman letters, and then to translate and write works of interest
in Japanese so it would become commonly used and studied.
This in turn would create the basis for a common knowledge
and usage of words so that people could in fact communicate
without difficulty.

In the classical tradition one unified written style existed, but
this was the style and script the advocates of language reform
wanted to simplify. Therefore, they argued, new codifications
and a standarization of new language usage and script were
needed to facilitate broad education and communication
among all Japanese citizens.

Many regarded the ideal language reform as a combination of
script simplification, colloquialization, and standardization. In
his petition to the shogun in 1866, Maejima Hisoka outlined
the above issues of language reform and their interdependence.
(Maejima 1866: 135) Some of the same issues had already been
mentioned in various sources during the previous century, but
had not gained official recognition. (Sakai 1992)

These aspects of language reform were debated in the abstract
throughout the 1870s, but in the 1880s the intellectuals began
experimenting with their suggestions. It seems, however, that
they forgot their own original insistence that the three were
interdependent, because when they began to experiment they
split into groups that advocated different scripts, but forgot to
change style along with it. This resulted in long unintelligible
articles in the old obscure style with classical grammar, but with
no Chinese characters to provide the meanings of words.

THE WRITERS OF PROSE LITERATURE

At the same time that movements for the simplification of the script in the 1880s were leaving the concern for colloquialization behind, colloquialization became a main issue in the creation of a new literary genre, the modern novel. The large number of translations during the early Meiji period made those who translated Western literature into Japanese acutely aware of the existence of written styles of a very different nature than those in the Japanese tradition. Writing in literary Japanese, they encountered numerous problems when they tried to create the same effect they found in the literature of the West. The translators identified these problems as due to the characteristics of the Japanese language, which, they stated, lacked the precise and concrete vocabulary of Western languages, and relied on vague and allusive expressions. Furthermore, the restrictions of Japanese honorific language left writers no opportunity for neutrality in personal relations. Many years of experimentation and frustration lay ahead before writers found a satisfactory medium for their stories.

The goal of a new literary movement, the *Genbun'itchi* movement, was to create a literary style based on the style of the spoken language. The term '*genbun'itchi*, [Making One of the Spoken and Written] was used by Shinda Kohei in 1885 in an article in *Tokyo gakushikaiin zasshi*, but is often said to have been coined by Mozume Takami in his article of that name in 1886. As a professor of literature at Tokyo University, Mozume exerted much influence in the popularization of the term. (Shinda 1885; Mozume 1886)

Tagusari Tsunaki developed a Japanese shorthand, a technique to transcribe an oral statement as fast as it was made. This technique was introduced to the public in 1882 and proved significant for the development of a *genbun'itchi* style. Shorthand made it possible to transcribe contemporary speech, and writers could consult these transcriptions in creating their own style. The colloquial speech of the Edo period found in the writings of Saikaku and others was already dated, and therefore was unsatisfactory as a model. In 1884 *Botan doro* [The Peony Garden] a piece recited by the *yose* [storytelling] performer San'yutei Enchō (1839–1900) was transcribed and published by stenographers educated at Tagusari Tsunaki's shorthand school. To the astonishment of the readers they could now read the story in Enchō's own words without actually being at the performance.

The principal concern of the *Genbun'itchi* movement was the verb form used at the end of sentences. The verb-endings used in the classical style required the writers to either speak up or down to their readers. Some of the colloquial forms considered by different members of the movement to replace the literary forms were 'de gozaimasu' (from Edo samurai women's speech), 'desu' (polite or formal), 'da' (informal), and 'de aru' (impersonal).

Futabatei Shimei (1864–1909) was a translator of Russian literature and the author of *Ukigumo*, the first Japanese novel written in a style close to the style of the spoken language, using the 'da'-form of the verbs. *Ukigumo* was published 1887–89. Futabetei's translation of Turgenev's *The Rendezvous* into the *genbun'itchi* style, *Aibiki*, in 1888 met with skepticism and criticism from established writers. Many young writers and poets, on the other hand, praised it for its ability to engage the reader emotionally. This supported Shimizu's claim ten years earlier that the colloquial was more apt to stir emotions.

In an article written in 1909, Kambara Ariake (1876–1952), a leading symbolist poet, recalled his reaction to *Aibiki*, when it first appeared in 1888.

> Futabatei's *genbun'itchi* style with its masterly use of colloquial language – that unique style – sounded so fresh its echoes seemed to go on endlessly whispering in my ears. A nameless joy filled me. I was so moved that something deep down within me almost wanted to shut it out . . . . When I read the passages describing the forest, I could visualize the scene before my eyes. The changeable sky of late autumn, the light of the sun piercing through the forest, the rain lightly falling – it was as if I was looking at a scene in the country through which I had walked just the day before. I could hear the arrogant, cold, rough voice of the man, and the pleading, forlorn voice of the girl. The experience was all the more magical perhaps because I could not understand why I was so deeply moved. My reaction to the story filled my whole being; it was like music. Reading *Aibiki* was a completely new experience in my life. (Kambara II 1953–54: 194–95)

This enthusiasm for Futabatei's translation suggests a great contrast with the experience of reading traditional texts. Writers who translated or experimented with the writing of Western style fiction needed colloquialization for creative purposes. However, because the writers were for the most part trained in the classical tradition, they first had to unlearn their trade before they could master the new style.

Moreover, many authors who had perfected their skills in the old literary style found the attempts at creating a new colloquialized style hopelessly vulgar and ugly. Ozaki Kōyō (1867–1903), a writer who wrote in a beautiful literary style, criticized the attempts of Futabatei and others at colloquialization for their lack of beauty. Later Kōyō himself experimented with the colloquial style, in world such as *Aobudō* [Green Grapes] which was published in September 1895 and *Tajō takon* [Many Feelings, Many Sorrows] which was published serially in 1896. (Keene 1971: 171) In these two works Kōyō used the 'de aru' – form of the verbs, but in 1897 he abandoned the *genbun'itchi* style again in his last novel, *Konjiki yasha* [The Demon Gold], convinced that true literature needed to be written in a more elegant style. The successes of *Aobudō* and *Tajō takon*, however, inspired the subsequent predominance of the 'de aru' – form within the *Genbun'itchi* movement. (Twine 1991: 154)

The advocates of colloquialization were confident that the greater comprehensibility of the spoken language could be transferred to written texts by applying the style of the spoken language to the written. The spoken style reflected historical and social change and was therefore more adept at expressing current issues. There was, however, one problem, namely the absence of a unified spoken language and style. Different 'dialects' were spoken throughout the country and it was not practicable to employ them all as the basis for a new written style. One standard inevitably had to be chosen and here the third group of leaders, the people who spoke the language in settings where various 'dialects' were represented, came into play.

THE SPOKEN MODEL

Traditionally, it has been stated that the *Yamanote* 'dialect' of Tokyo was chosen as the model for the Japanese standard language today. Though this is not incorrect, I will in the following indicate how exactly this 'dialect' was the most hybrid 'dialect' in Japan because of the influence its users had exerted and continued to exert on it.

Both the linguists Yaeko Satō Habein and Kay Genenz have argued that the *Yamanote* 'dialect' of Tokyo was influenced by patterns of speech from outside of Tokyo, and that this influence took place throughout the Edo period and continued in the Meiji period. Habein described how the Tokugawa family itself as well as 'those who came to serve their local lords brought their own speech patterns from all over Japan' to Edo (Habein 1984: 86–7), first because of the *Sankin Kōtai* system established by the Tokugawa shogunate which required all the major retainers to have alternate residency in their respective provinces and in the capital, and later because of the urbanization that followed industrialization.

Kay Genenz wrote that the *Yamanote* 'dialect' which he denied as the 'spoken language of educated people in Tokyo' was not a pure 'dialect' of Tokyo, because of strong influences from the Kinki area around Kyoto and Osaka. As evidence he mentioned the large number of honorifics which were not used in other 'dialects' of the Kantō area; at the same time typical phonetic characteristics of the surrounding 'dialects', such as the fusion of diphthongs, were absent in the *Yamonote* 'dialect'. (Genenz 1989: 65) Bruno Lewin described the *Yamanote* 'dialect' as progressive. (Lewin 1989: 165) It was the idiom of educated city-dwellers, continually modified by influx from other parts of the country and by modernization as it also depended on official reforms. Political reforms in early Meiji, such as the abolition of the domains in 1871, that allowed all Japanese a new mobility, resulting in rapid urbanization, and the establishment of the new conscript army in 1872, increased contact among people and fuelled awareness of 'dialect' differences.

In 'Hanashi no kotoba' from the 1930s, Yanagita Kunio described the popular awareness of the sharp differences in speech around the country in the Edo period and he documented contact among people speaking distinct 'dialects'. Contact had occurred in various contexts. Ise pilgrimages brought the pilgrims through the country and into contact with people along the way, and at times the result was even intermarriage. (Yanagita repr. 1963: 521–7) Travelling merchants and wandering monks brought and received news in different 'dialects' as they passed through the country. The *Sankin Kōtai* system of alternate attendance and residency meant that large groups of samurai, servants, and lords travelled through the country back and forth to the capital from their home province. They would communicate with the merchants and inn keepers along the highways.

The Danish linguist Otto Jespersen pointed out that increased interaction inspires an automatic exchange and polishing of 'dialects' into a more uniform and shared speech form. (Jespersen, 1925: 63–73) In Japan, these spontaneous compromises made in order to communicate, notwithstanding the regional differences in speech patterns, were referred to as *kyōtsūgo* [common languages]. Whereas *kyōtsūgo* developed spontaneously during the Edo and Meiji periods as a practical response to contact among users of various speech patterns, the aspiration of linguists and other intellectuals for a standard language in the 1890s and later were deliberate attempts towards ideological ends. Speakers created *kyōtsūgo* through constant adjustments to changing circumstances in order to make communication successful. Intellectuals were simultaneously discussing the optimal adjustments of language to the new reality to be created through government policies and advocated the adoption of one standard language, *hyōjungo*. I will on the basis of the above venture the conclusion that there was a connection between *kyōtsūgo* and *hyōjungo*, and that again on the joint efforts of many people communicating in spite of regional differences in their speech. Colloquialization together with script simplification can be seen as a reflection as well as a result of a democratisation of access to knowledge and thus power and influence.

CONCLUSION

The 1870s and 1880s saw an increase in interaction between people from different regions, which made the need for a common language evident to many. Further the expansion of Japanese interests beyond its traditional borders supported a development of identification with the nation and a call for a unified national language. In comparison with political and educational reforms and the visions of the intellectuals of the 1870s, the language reforms decreed by the Japanese government have been few and late. This might have been because the conditions for these changes were not present in the early Meiji period; there was not a consensus as to what the ideal reform would be; intellectuals experienced tension between attachment to the written style in which they were trained and their conviction that Japan as a nation state needed a reformed official language; and as the experiments with different possibilities suggested, even if the theories were sophisticated, the initial application of those theories lacked comprehensibility. In other words, it took time to coordinate a simplification of script with finding the appropriate standard spoken form in which to write. This process took place in an informal setting before the results came to be the foundation for official language reforms.

The government did initially not propose language reforms, but the other reforms of the time greatly influenced language usage and stimulated a debate on language reform. The intellectuals who participated in the debate were predominantly supportive of the efforts of the government to create a Japanese nation, but insisted that the success of other reforms depended on the creation of a language that could meet the needs of a new nation state. It can be argued that only their efforts in conceptualizing the issues of language reform, the experimentations of the writers with new written forms, the creation of hybrid languages in public spaces made it possible for the government to later implement language reforms.

Intellectuals in Japan have traditionally formed a locus of politics apart from, but intersected with, a political leadership, that listened to and depended upon them for advice. In the Meiji period many of the intellectuals became part of the political leadership during the 1880s and 1890s. The language debate, however, did not occur within the government sphere before the turn of the century, but was a private initiative in support of the attempts made by the government to create a nation state. Prose writers had not earlier enjoyed prestige, but became instrumental in the development of a new written style. As for the more general public, its influence on the formation of hybrid languages was a spontaneous and necessary response to changed social circumstances where communication and information transfer had become paramount for the survival of the nation as well as for the individual within it.

BIBLIOGRAPHY

Anderson, Benedict, (1991) *Imagined Communities: Reflections on the Origin and Spread of Nationalism* revised edition, London and New York: Verso.

Fukuchi Gen'ichirō, (29 August 1875) 'Bunron' [Discourse on Writing] , in *Tokyo Nichi Nichi Shinbun* editorial.

Genenz, Kay, (1989) 'Dialekte', in Bruno Lewin, ed., *Sprache und Schrift Japans*, Leiden: E. J. Brill, 63–97.

Habein, Yaeko Satō, (1984) *The History of the Japanese Written Language* Tokyo: University of Tokyo Press.

Jespersen, Otto, (1925) 'Mankind, Nation and Individual from a Linguistic Point of View', 1–221 in *Instituttet for sammenlingnende kulturforskning Serie A* Forelesninger IV, Oslo: H. Aschenhoug & Co. (W. Nygaard).

Kambara Ariake, (1909) 'Aibiki ni tsuite' [Concerning Aibiki], *Futabatei Shimei Zenshū* Tokyo, 1953–54.

Keene, Donald, (1971) 'The Sino-Japanese War 1894–95 and Its Cultural

Effects in Japan', Donald H. Shively ed., *Tradition and Modernization in Japanese Culture* Princeton, New Jersey: Princeton University Press, 121–175.

Lewin, Bruno, (1989) 'Gegenwartssprache', Bruno Lewin (ed.) *Sprache und Schrift Japans* Leiden: E. J. Brill, 162–184.

Maejima Hisoka, (1866) 'Kanji no gohaishi no gi', (The Abolition of Kanji), 127–136 reprinted in Yamamoto Masahide, 1978, *Kindai buntai Keisei shiryō shusei*, Tokyo: Ofusha.

Mozume Takami, (1886) 'Genbun'itchi', in *Mozume Takami Zenshū*, Mozume Takami zenshū hensankai, Tokyo, 132–37.

Nambu Yoshikazu, (January 1875) 'Shu kokugo ron' [Concerning the Study of Our Language] in *Yoyoshadan*, 7.

Nishi Amane, (March 1874) 'Yoji o nite kokugo o shosuru no ron' (The Writing of Japanese with the Western Alphabet), in *Meiroku Zasshi* 1, 1–2.

Nishimura Shigeki, (March 1874) 'Kaika no tabi ni yotte Kaimoji o Hassubeki no ron' (Why the Reform of Writing Should Depend on the Level of Enlightenment), *Meiroku Zasshi* 1, 3–4.

Ryan, Marleigh, (1967) *Japan's First Modern Novel: Ukigumo of Futabatei Shimei*, New York: Columbia University Press.

Sakai Naoki, (1992) *Voices of the Past: The Status of Language in Eighteenth-century Japanese Discourse*, Ithaca, New York: Cornell University Press.

Shimizu Usaburō, (May 1874) 'Hiragana no setsu' [The Hiragana Theory], *Meiroku Zasshi* 7, pp. 8–9.

Shinda Kohei, (November 1885) 'Bunshoron o yomu' [Reading the Debate on Style] in *Tokyo Gakushikaiin Zasshi* Vol.7, No.1.

Thränhardt, Anna Maria, (1976) *Schriftreform-Diskussion in Japan zwischen 1867 und 1890* Helmut Buske Verlag, Hamburg.

Twine, Nanette, (Autumn 1978) 'The Genbun'itchi Movement: It's Origin, Development, and Conclusion', *Monumenta Nipponica*, Vol. 33, No. 3, 333–56.

Twine, Nanette, (1991) *Language and the Modern State: The Reform of Written Japanese* London and New York: Routledge.

Yanagita Kunio, (1963) 'Hanashi no hanashi', *Yanagita Kunio Shū*, Vol. 19., Tokyo: Chikuma shōbō, 521–27.

9

The Meiji Élite and Western Culture

SELÇUK ESENBEL

Studies of modern Japan have tended to emphasize the 'Japanization' of Western culture and its minimal impact at a personal level as modernization overtook the structural and institutional construction of modern society on the basis of nascent institutions and values. It has been suggested that the continuation of a Japanese way of life in the private realm helped 'placate' the psychological stresses suffered during 'modernization' by being able to be 'Japanese' at home. (Hanley 1986: 447–462).

The modernizationist view curiously agrees with the prewar idea of Japanese national education and popular literature of being Western at the work-place and Japanese at home as an ideal of national identity. Both views assume, from different angles, that the 'restriction' of Westernization to the public sphere ensured the preservation of the nascent qualities in the private realm of the Japanese person. This was through Japanese pragmatism towards Western culture that combined *Wa*, or Japanese, and *Yō* or Western cultural elements in a flexible formula of eclecticism to serve as the basis for modern Japanese national identity in a bi-cultural civilization. The nationalist version was the *wakonyōsai*: Japanese spirit balanced with Western know-how. While there was a wide range in the interpretation of the idea of Western civilization balanced with Eastern ethics as a desirable national identity, the formula has been assumed to have assured a pragmatic adaptation of the individual to sufficient Westernization in scientific and material culture without unhealthy deep-set Western influences. (Gluck 1985: 3–6, 284) Hence, the Japanese were able to modernize without the social instability or the psychological stresses of modernization and even avoid revolution.

The narrative of this paper takes issue with the modernizationist interpretations of Japanese pragmatism towards Western culture, especially the notion that Japanese eclecticism was based upon the flexibility of splitting their public and private realism into a 'separate but equal' Western and Japanese cultural identities, or that this formula avoided the stresses of modernity at least for those who had an intimate proximity to Western culture in their everyday lives.

The study of the Meiji Japanese 'élite' of the nineteenth century is important at this point for they had a 'head start' position in the internalization of Western cultural forms. (Lebra 1993:82–84, 188, 190) After the collapse of the Tokugawa feudal order and the inception of a new regime with the Meiji Restoration the adoption of Western civilization went through a first phase of enthusiastic adoption followed by a second phase around the turn of the century of nationalist criticism that strove to restrict the normative Westernization of individuals. Throughout this process, the Meiji élite continued to be pioneers in the adoption and rejection of Western cultural styles for personal as well as public purposes of civilization and enlightenment and economic prosperity and military strengthening, the main slogans of the Meiji government.

This paper ventures to understand the meaning of Western culture for the self-perception of particularly the Meiji élite individual by focusing on an analysis of attire, household environment, and manners and ethics. Nineteenth-century thought in Europe and Asia abounds in discussions of Ethics, Propriety, and Civilization. Compared to today, this was a time when dress and ceremony carried more importance in the everyday life of an individual in the position of élite leadership. They reflected immediately at a personal level one's individual perceptions of suitable culture, social status, political purposes, and in the case of Japan the self-perception of modernity for the individual. In this way, one can hope to decipher the complex layers of meanings that Western culture carried which have not been explained to a full extent by the modernizationist or the nationalist *Wa/Yō* formula.

THE CIVILIZING PROCESS AND THE MODERN INDIVIDUAL
OF NORBERT ELIAS AND THE MEIJI ÉLITE

When seen at a personal level, Western culture in Japan which
has had a history of more than a hundred years since the Meiji
Restoration, seems to have infiltrated into deep waters as it has
been meaningful to many in Japan as the cultural symbol of the
psychological self-perception of the modern individual in contemporary times. Norbert Elias' treatment of the history of the
individual in the West is a comparable starting point for the
discussion of the Meiji experience. Elias saw the emergence of
the perception of the modern individual in Western Europe in
a historic context of societal conditions that helps the comparative analysis of a cultural environment such as that of Meiji
Japan where the modern individual, for reasons of tradition and
ideology, continued to be seen in the light of his or her societal-
Confucian context of human relations. (Elias 1978; 1982; 1991)

For Elias, the environmental story of the modern individual
since the middle ages is through the civilizing process of this
personality through the history of medieval manners of court
culture to the public manners of *civilité* for modern society that
ensured the control of aggressive instincts, the development of a
sense of sexual modesty and shame. (Elias 1978: 51–53)
Politically the transition entailed the increase in the social and
political control of the state in the direct discharge of impulses
and individual violence. This was reinforced with the emphasis
that sport, festivals and dance gained in modern society.
Economically, the perception of such a self-restrained individual
was integral to the requirement of a sophisticated market
economy and the increasing importance of social and economic
integration. (Elias 1982: 229–295) This is the historical background to the emergence of the self-perception of the modern
individual that Elias terms 'the civilizing process'.

The socio-psychological aspect of the argument is perhaps
the most interesting as Elias traced through memoirs and
personal accounts the gradual emergence in Western Europe of
the image of the modern individual as a rational being which
interacts with an inseparable emotive side during this transition.
While this is defined as a mental self-perception of the separation of the rational and emotive in the modern mind of the
individual, for Elias these perceptions have a societal context in
that the consciousness of an autonomous self was necessary to

function in the complexity of class relations in capitalism and state formation. (Elias 1991: 8–9, 27–34; 1978: 261)

Yet, in Elias's typology, the Western European individual is not in reality free of family and society as claimed by the ideology of individualism. The 'modern person' is an individual who has developed a perception of independence but he/she is still dependent upon a social network. This individual has had to face in reality the stress and tension felt due to the inseparability of the rational and emotive sides mentally and an interdependency with others socially, and has had to find a modicum of balance within this ambivalent state of affairs.

It is this acknowledgement of 'the interdependency of the individual to a social network and the stress and tension due to the inseparability of the rational and the emotive' part of the argument that is particularly appealing for a comparison with the Meiji experience. From the Meiji period to this day, Japanese modern individuals have been sensitized to the tensions and social dependencies that were engendered by modernity for reasons of bi-culturality. Given similar although not identical conditions in the history of the modern Western European individual, Elias's studies inspire the question; Do the same cultural components create a similar self-perception of the modern individual vis à vis collectivity even in an initially alien cultural environment such as that of Meiji Japan?

DRESS AND GROOMING

The Japanese use of native and Western costume has carried an important symbolic message to reinforce the pragmatism argument of modern/Western at work in the public realm versus being more Japanese at home in the private real. A 1930s book on modern Japan aptly defines these images as European at work with Western attire/Asiatic at home with a kimono. (Lajtha 1936: 46) The history of Western dress in the Meiji period shows that the Meiji élite's experimentation with Western attire resulted in the eclectic use of Japanese and Western forms for similar functions, or for different ones that had a rich hierarchy of political, social, personal meanings that would defy the dualistic simplicity of the modernist argument for the public.

The primary meaning of Western attire for the Meiji élite was political. With the 1872 *Dajōkan* order for the adoption of Western dress and hair-styles by the Meiji bureaucratic élite, Western attire became crucial as an image in order to represent the policy of civilization and enlightenment and to impress the Westerners that Japan was civilized enough to warrant treaty revision in order to gain the status of equality with the Western nations. This was an exercise to revise the 1858 series of international treaties with the West that had compromised Japanese sovereignty. Prime Minister Itō Hirobumi and the Foreign Minister Inoue Kowashi were at the forefront of the Westernization policy for the upper class élite who were to have direct interaction with Westerners. (Chamberlain 1985: 43, 63, 122–126; Seidensticker 1983: 33, 96, 97; Tsuda 1991: 76, 268, 289, 291)

In many ways, the experiment with Westernization was also theatrical, and the members of the élite women who were dressed in their Western finery were the 'actors and actresses.' For the Meiji élite, the style of dress represented the political meaning at an individual level of the patriotic cause. The Rokumeikan, the Deer Cry Pavilion, which was established as a ball room entertainment club for Tokyo society in 1884 was to be the stage. When Westerners criticized what they thought was the ungainly sight of having dainty Japanese women wearing Western dresses in contrast to the much more becoming styles of the traditional kimono, Prime Minister Itō is said to have laughed and commented that all of this is for politics: in kimono Japanese women look like puppet dolls whereas he felt in Western dress they looked modern and educated, like their Western sisters. (Tomita 1984: 150).

A second aspect of the symbolic meaning of Western culture in dress was the interaction with Westerners on this and other matters of Westernization. Beneath the garb of traditional virtue, the woman's kimono, the Tokugawa kimono was modified during the Meiji era due to Japanese and Western concerns of modern propriety that it be shortened and wrapped around more tightly to eliminate the erotic quality to the upper class kimono of Tokugawa women. In this 'suppressed' form, the kimono could now serve as a suitable modern traditionalist attire for the new middle-class image of the Meiji public. (Chamberlain 1985: 122–126).

Class and gender roles also dictated different expectations of attire for individuals. While the general female population of Meiji Japan continued to wear the kimono that also befitted their role as the bastion of tradition and family virtue expected by the authorities, the Meiji élite women had to uphold a Western-style public image which represented modern education, Westernization of social life, and advancement of

women's position in society. Tsuda Ume, the pioneer of women's
education who had been brought up in the United States, is a
particularly astute observer of the association between policy
and dress during this period. (Tsuda 1991). She complains that,
with the demise of the Westernizers such as Mori Arinori,
briefly in the 1890s, a new court dress inspired by the Heian
costumes of the ancient Japanese court of the tenth century
became mandatory. But in a few years, Western gowns again
became the norm for the aristocratic women. (Tsuda 1991: 268,
289, 291).

For the élite, Japanese and Western attire had very specific
meanings in the public images of ideology and were not flexible
choices of Japaneseness in private at home versus Westerners in
public at work. While the general public seemed vastly freer in
their eclectic combinations of *Wa* and *Yo* culture in dress, the
more one moved up the social ladder the more cultural cate-
gories of dress were dictated by rigorous ideological concerns.
Lebra notes that the families of the Meiji aristocracy had to
provide in their dowry a *junihitoe* which was a Japanese court
dress, a European-style robe decolleté, and a tiara, each used for
Japanese or Western-style ceremonies. (Lebra 1993: 230) Tsuda
Ume refers often to her stressful experience of having to change
and shift her dress from one style to another, Western to Japanese
because of the nature of the public occasion or when enter-
taining at home. (Tsuda 1991: 63, 289)

For the politically engaged, the public image of ideological
stance strictly dictated the choice of dress. Members of the Meiji
opposition confronted the completely Western outfit, the so-
called *hakama*, male kimono, which in this case did not represent
a relaxed Japanese sense at home. The political stance of the
opposition had a wide spectrum. Fukuzawa Yukichi, the famous
liberal and pro-Western educator, intellectual of Meiji Japan,
usually preferred the *hakama*. On him, it was the symbol of his
liberal stance, refusal of joining the oligarchy in morning coat
grooming, and a symbol of him as an independent thinker.
(Fukuzawa Yukichi 1960) On the other hand, for Tokutomi
Soho, liberal journalist, nationalist, Asianist intellectual and
ideologue of Meiji and Taisho Japan, who was typical of the
politically ambitious nationalists of the second Meiji generation
with strong Asianist/Japaneseness tendencies, the same *hakama*
symbolized a Japanese nationalist reaction, and the criticism of
the *haikara* weak-kneed oligarchic leadership in foreign affairs.
(Pierson 1980: 228–230)

WESTERN CULTURE IN THE HOME INTERIOR

The standard modernizationist argument notes that most Japanese experienced the transition from Tokugawa to Meiji Japan in small, traditional Japanese-style households due to practicality and poverty that reinforced the Japaneseness of home life. While this description suffices for the general public, again the situation was very different for élite families who lived in beautiful Western-style mansions in Tokyo such as the Iwasaki mansion, built by one of the pioneer entrepreneurs of the Meiji industrial establishment and the founder of the Mitsubishi concern. (Seidensticker 1983: 245)

The élite homes had a great number of rooms which represented multi-cultural functions and meaning in addition to the usual multi-functional quality of the traditional Japanese rooms. Tsuda Ume's memoirs reflect the home life of many Tokyo élite families including that of Count Itō, and reveal that the family members relaxed in the inner sanctum of private life in the inner rooms of the house, the *okunoma* area which was constructed in Japanese style and decorated in an informal hodge-podge manner combining Western and Japanese components in a liberal fashion. (Tsuda 1991: 22, 116, 311; Lebra 1993: 22, 116, 311) In addition, there were the formal Western-style rooms and the formal Japanese-style rooms for public entertainment. (Lebra 1993; Seidensticker 1983; Tsuda 1991)

The accounts of the three types of rooms, the private inner rooms of 'pure' Western and Japanese styles represent an almost perfect image of the Meiji civilizing mission: Pure Westernist policies of reform counterbalanced with Pure Japanese public images of national ideology, and finally the 'real world' where there was a mixture of the Japanese and Western with no cultural consistency. In this eclectic way of life of the élite, the outer public Western façade was not reinforced by a pure nascent Japanese inner being, both were formal images for the public.

Seen from the perspective of Elias' description of the self-perception of the modern individual, the Meiji accounts of élite lives suggests it was in the *okunoma* of mixed cultural elements that individuals allowed for themselves the expression of their emotive sides in a free and relaxed manner. It was in the culturally 'impure' and undefined realm that the modern self-image was at liberty. On the other hand, the Meiji 'public' image of civilization split into 'pure' Western and Japanese compartments, both constituting a dual cultural definition of rationality in the public realm.

MEIJI ETIQUETTE AND ETHICS

Nothing brings out the personal problem of the rational and the emotive in a cultural context more clearly than the Meiji dictates on public propriety, manners, and etiquette. The Meiji authorities dictated new forms of public propriety to make Japan acceptable as a civilized nation to the nineteenth century self-centred Westerner. As a result, the Japanese individual had to enter into new constraints of public modesty, proper dress, censorship of the traditional expressions of sexuality and eroticism which had been previously accepted by Tokugawa society. The razing of phallic statues in the countryside, the requirement that male workers wear shirts within the city boundaries of Tokyo were but some of the many new constraints on public behaviour that were geared towards the adoption of nineteenth-century Western norms for Meiji public culture, in this case of squeamishness about nakedness and sexual express-iveness. (Chamberlain 1985: 258–62, 423; Seidensticker 1983: 42–45, 92)

Furthermore, in line with the early Meiji vision of civiliz-ation and enlightenment, the incorporation of Western manners and rules of propriety into the modern etiquette of Meiji became an important means with which to achieve the idea of *civilité* or civilized behaviour for the middle class aspirations and values of the nineteenth-century Japanese. In the Japanese case, the formation of the 'modern' rational self-perception was ac-companied by the adjustment of the culture of controlling sexual expression, nakedness, and public behaviour in the public culture. Thus, Meiji Japan acquired a Western cultural com-ponent additional to the traditional Japanese cultural framework for rational public bahaviour.

Historically, etiquette, or *reigi*, had carried a central import-ance in the socialization of the Japanese person into society. The rules of etiquette, derived from the Confucian tradition of China were adapted by the court aristocracy and the samurai warrior class rulers during the Tokugawa feudal order. Specific rules of conduct such as the three levels of seated bows re-inforced physical behaviour and gestures that expressed the virtues of filial piety, loyalty, obedience, harmony, reciprocity and the like in the ideal social hierarchy between superiors and inferiors adhered to by the feudal culture of Japan. (Kōdansha Encyclopedia of Japan 1983: Vol. 2, 232–234, Vol. 6, 68).

The Meiji texts are frequently titled *Meiji Reigi* or *Sahō*, represent striking examples of the *Wa* and *Yō* duality ideal of Meiji cultural eclecticism. The new Meiji etiquette was idealized as a fairly uniform standard of public behaviour for the nation which would replace the distinct class-based manners of the feudal heritage. Similar to the development of *civilité* in Europe for the modern public, Meiji etiquette texts are the adaptation of the Tokugawa manners to establish the public manners of the Japanese nation. The Ogasawara school, known for its subdued style and elegance, published numerous books on the subject that included an etiquette book for standing and bowing, the familiar three-tiered Japanese bow of today, which were necessary for the first time in Meiji Japan with the Western-style architecture and standing culture. (Ogasawara 1882: 8–12.) A ladies' etiquette book for the Meiji bride contains the picture of a kimono-clad Meiji woman who shows how to bow while standing next to a European chair – the solution to a Meiji problem. (Matoba 1899: 66.)

The Meiji etiquette works divided the text between the *Wa* and the *Yō* components of manners. But, in books meant for the general public, the emphasis was on Japanese manners. Unlike European etiquette books which tend to emphasize proper public behaviour, Meiji books differ for they focus on the special forms of modified traditional manners for the individual among family, relatives, friends, and superiors. These were gestures that were reflective of an ideal Confucian order of loyalty and filial piety in family and society as encouraged by Meiji modernity. (Norihashi and Shinoda 1881)

In general, Western manners received lesser coverage and were kept to a discussion of the handshake, proper eating manners (drinking soup quietly as the Japanese custom of slurping was considered offensive by Westerners), the use of knives and forks, the introduction of the *meishi*, the proverbial name card, instruction of appropriate attire for various occasions. The individual is encouraged to adjust his/her behaviour according to the norms of the Westerners during the brief encounters they were sure to have in this contemporary age.

As in the case of dress and home life, class and gender rôles differed in the world of Meiji etiquette. The élite men and women who were cut out to play a visible rôle in representing Westernized Japan were expected to be masters of European high protocol. A Tokyo Nichi Nichi Shimbun writer who was critical of excessive Western styles at the Rokumeikan balls still complemented contemporary élite women as so much better at salon interaction than men thereby serving the patriotic purpose of helping international relations. (Tomita 1984: 168)

While the etiquette books for the upper classes have a cosmo-politan air that stresses conviviality and good breeding, the books of the general public discuss Western manners as a political instrument of power. After the Russo-Japanese War when the surprising Japanese victory appears to have incited nationalist feelings, one book warns, Japan may win a lot of battles, but she will be doomed to lose all by her lack of knowledge of etiquette for the West uses it as a tool in war and competition. (Miyamoto 1906) Even more, Western manners like dress were seen dispensible by some. One book mentions that there are recent opinions that claim it is no longer necessary to imitate the manners of those round-eyed and red-haired foreigners. (*Meiji reishiki* 1899: 2)

The dilemma that remains unanswered in this fascinating body of literature on etiquette and manners is where the issue of morality and ethics fits with respect to Western manners for the authors and the Meiji readers. The books do not express a choice in this respect. The *Wa* and *Yō* duality in manners determined that ethical values be operative primarily in the *Wa* world of etiquette in a Japanese moral and social setting. The *Yō* etiquette, while necessary for the public image of the civilizing process and part of the rational self-perception of the individual, remained outside the Confucian realm of civic and individual morality. The Meiji attitude towards the use of Western-culture in etiquette reveals the quagmire in the pattern of *Wa Yō* eclecticism that shows the limits of the pragmatic solution. The problem was always not so simple and humorous as Chamberlain noted as having to give way to your wife only when she was in Western dress, but invites the profound issue of how to envision a stage of universal individual and civic morality in the Western form, for only the Japanese etiquette forms demanded moral dictates from the Meiji individual. (Chamberlain 1985: 500)

THE MEIJI CIVILIZING PROCESS AND THE MODERN INDIVIDUAL

The Meiji élites' use of Western culture close to their person in dress and home and manners represents one solution to the problem of multi-cultural existence in an eclectic pattern of the *Wa* and *Yō* elements as the definition of modernity. Given the above complex account, one suspects that the individual in a Meiji élite environment could not enjoy the benefits of a simplistic formula of being Western at work and Japanese at home despite the ideological stance that was advocated for the masses in order to avoid the stresses and tensions of modernization.

The élite's intimacy with Western culture at work and at home was also marked with thorns. Even after the Meiji era, members of the Japanese aristocracy continued to feel the psychological pangs of mental and emotional Westernization due to their proximity to a Western style of cosmopolitan life-style. They were expected to be symbols of the Imperial institution, yet also be completely Westernized mentally, a difficult task indeed. (Lebra 1993: 82–83, 190) Certainly, to be Japanese at home was not the source of security and emotional comfort. After all, for the élite, to be pure Japanese in the Meiji sense entailed a formal public image of rationality which was just as stress-filled as trying to be Western.

The Meiji dictum appears to be that those lower in the social scale in terms of political power were expected to have less intimacy with Western culture unlike the élite who were expected to master it because of their head start position of leadership. This different level of intimacy could be politically explosive in later generations as social change and political participation brought the general public who lacked the Meiji élite's cosmopolitan solutions to bi-culturality to hold more power after replacing the firm hold of the Meiji élite.

Whatever its problems, however, the above narrative also indicates that the emergence of the self-perception of the modern individual in Meiji Japan required Western culture as the means with which to create a public culture even if it sometimes meant adjustment to peculiar Western fears and prejudices. The self-perception of the rational public world acquired a Western identity in addition to the Japanese one, if one were to be modern. And the inner rooms where the emotive realm of the private self could express itself were no longer pure Japanese but hybrid mixtures of the Western and Japanese elements. The personal Westernization of this bi-cultural context of the civilizing process must have burdened those Japanese individuals with the challenge to handle the complex psychological 'double' tensions of the process.

Nor is it surprising to see the dark side of this double tension dilemma of modernity. Many Japanese intellectuals who have had an intimate knowledge of Western culture and experienced its psychological consequences have written modern Japanese novels on this theme. It is not without coincidence that such intellectuals as Yukio Mishima have rationalized the anguish of their suicides as the anguish of civilization from the encounter of Japanese cultural identity with Western civilization.

In sum, Western culture has had a deep-set influence in the formation of the perception of the modern individual within Japanese society. The above narrative defies the dualistic category of *Wa* and *Yō* at least as defined in the general modernizationist approach of the past. The history of Western culture in dress, homelife, public behaviour, and manners, in an initially alien environment as Japanese society appears to have been a crucial component in the civilizing process that brought about the perception of the modern Japanese individual, albeit with special traumas and cultural compositions that has made this individual different from the one defined by Elias for Western Europe. It is not so much the pragmatic Japanization of western culture that seems to have ensured the ability of the modern individual to handle the so-called stresses of modernization. At least this is so for the members of the Meiji élite who were intensely involved with Western culture compared to the rest of the population. The pragmatic Japanization approach was not possible in view of the highly rigid and inflexible political and social symbolism associated with Western culture. Under such circumstances, it was rather the ability of the modern Japanese individual to face the inherent tensions between a bi-cultural world of rationality and emotive sensibilities that brings this historical experience closer to that of Western Europe. In this sense, the history of Western culture outside of the historic cultural geography of the West is an authentic component in the history of Japanese society.

BIBLIOGRAPHY

Chamberlain, Basil Hall, (reprint 1985 orig. 1904) *Japanese Things* Tokyo: Charles E Tuttle and Co.
Elias, Norbert, (1982) *State Formation and Civilization: The Civilizing Process* (Cambridge: Basil Blackwell), Vol. 2.
Elias, Norbert, (1978) *The History of Manners: The Civilizing Process* New York: Urizen Books, Vol. 1.
Elias, Norbert, (1991) *The Society of Individuals* Cambridge: Basil Blackwell.

Gluck, Carol (1985) *Japan's Modern Myths: Ideology in the Late Meiji Period* Princeton: Princeton University Press.

Hanley, Susan, (1986) 'Material Culture: Stability in Transition' in Marius B. Jansen and Gilbert Rozman, eds, *Japan in Transition From Tokugawa to Meiji* Princeton: Princeton University Press.

Kodansha Encyclopedia of Japan (1983) Tokyo: Kodansha Vol. 2.

Lajtha, Edgar, (1936) *La Vie Au Japan* Paris: Payot.

Lebra, Takie Sugiyama (1993) *Above the Clouds: Status Culture of the Modern Japanese Nobility* Berkeley: University of California.

Matoba, Seinosuka, (1899) *Meiji Reishiki* Osaka: Shobundo.

Miyamoto, Keisen, (1906) *Seiyo danjo kosaiho* Tokyo: Hakubunkan.

Norihashi, Gyokusan, and Shinoda, Shōsaku, (1881), *Ogasawara shōrei taizen* Osaka: Heijokaku.

Ogasawara, Seimu, Mizuno, Tadao, (1882) *Ogasawara shinsen tatsu reishiki* Tokyo: Genshado.

Seidensticker, Edward, (1983) *Low City, High City* New York: Alfred A. Knopf.

Tomita, Hitoshi, (1984) *Rokumeikan: Nise seiyōka no seikai* Tokyo: Hakusuisha.

Tsuda, Ume, Yoshiko Furuki, ed., (1991) *The Attic Letters: Ume Tsuda's Correspondence to Her American Mother* New York: Weatherhill.

10

The 'Unique' Character of the Emperor: The Main Leader of Modern Japan?

The Japanese Emperor's position in the Meiji Constitution

EWA PALASZ RUTKOWSKA

Following the Meiji Restoration, after about seven hundred years of the military rule of the shogunate (Bakufu), the Emperor, at least theoretically, took over power in Japan. The leaders of the Restoration, samurai from mainly four feudal domains (han), Satsuma, Chōshū, Tosa and Hizen, became the creators of the new political system of the country. First of all, they emphasized the continuity of the Imperial Dynasty as well as the legitimate Japan monarch's descent from Heaven by reference to the oldest Japanese sources, the *Kojiki (712)* and the *Nihon shoki* (720). According to them the Imperial dynastic line had been derived directly from the great-great-grandson of Amaterasu-Ōmikami, the main Goddess of the shintoistic pantheon, the legendary first Emperor, Kinmu, who was supposed to have started his reign over the land later called Japan, in 660 BC. The Emperor's 'divinity' was also emphasized in the 'Constitution of the Empire of Japan '(DaiNihon-teikoku-kenpō)' (Ito 1906), called also the 'Meiji Constitution' (Meiji-kenpō), promulgated in 1889. It became the legal base of Japan's political system and the Emperor system (*tennōsei*), because it precisely determined the monarch's position.

Was the Emperor's position in the modern Japanese State really 'unique', as some Japanese researchers mantain (Minobe 1918; Ishii 1950; Bito 1990: 5–30) and had no features in common with the positions of monarchs of the European constitutional monarchies in the eighteenth and nineteenth centuries?

In order to answer this question I decided to draw a comparison of positions of some chosen monarchs, defined in the constitutions valid in their countries at the time under consideration. But my present aim is not the analysis of particular systems, looking for the principles putting order in the political systems, requiring a comprehensive knowledge of both the history of state and law as well as the law itself. I would simply like to outline the problem, to present what might be a kind of introduction for further research.

It is necessary to add here that, although the number of publications concerning the Emperor and his position in modern Japan increased distinctly within the last few years, particularly after the death in 1989 of the last 'divine' Emperor, Hirohito, there is still a lack of comparative study regarding the *tennōsei*. In my opinion, the filling of this gap is a special task and duty of non-Japanese researchers of Japanese culture and history. And therefore I absolutely agree with George Sansom, who wrote, that we, Westerners

> . . . cannot hope to approach the standard of scholarship of Japanese specialists in historical research or in the interpretation of their national culture. The Western student must always be handicapped by linguistic and other difficulties, because his early education and environment deprive him of advantages which the Japanese student naturally enjoys. But the Western student has some compensating advantages, and of course the chief of these is his familiarity with his own culture. For just as the history of an individual is of little importance unless it is related to the history of the nation, though it is interesting to the members of that nation, is not significant until it is brought into relationship with the history of their nations. It is by comparison, by resemblances and contrasts, that history enables us to draw some inferences . . . about the principles and the prejudices that govern the behaviour of men, in so far as the behaviour of men can be analyzed and predicted.
>
> It is in comparative studies . . . that . . . Westerners can make some useful contribution to the work of their Japanese colleagues. (Sansom 1981:13)

Thus, the object of my present comparative study will be the Meiji Constitution, the Polish Constitution of 2 May 1791 (Konstytucje polskie 1990: 13–18), the first European democratic one, as well as the Constitution of Prussia of 1850 (Konstytuca Pruska 1850), which was the base for the creation of the Meiji Constitution. Besides I will sporadically refer to the German Empire's Constitution of 1871 and the so-called 'flexible' Constitution of England, where as is generally known, there is no single constitutional act, but a collection of laws, called common law.

The Constitution of Prussia, as is generally known, became the main pattern for the authors of Meiji Constitution. Itō Hirobumi (1841–1909) chose it among several European ones in the course of his travels to Europe in 1882–1883, following consultations with such German specialists as Professor of Law, Rudolph Gneist (1816–1895) and Professor of Social Sciences and Administration Lorenz von Stein (1815–1890). And therefore among those working on the final draft of the Japanese Constitution apart from Japanese: Itō Hirobumi, Itō Miyoji (1857–1934), Inoue Kowashi (1844–1895) and Kaneko Kentarō (1853–1942) there were also two Germans: Albert Mosse (1846–1925), Gneist's student, invited to Japan specially for that purpose and Hermann Roesler (1834–1894), adviser to the Japanese Ministry of Foreign Affairs. (Akita 1971: 118–24)

The Constitution of Prussia, compared with that of other European countries, emphasized most strongly the monarch's position and therefore was the most appropriate to Japan, aiming at putting the Emperor, above all in the state and thereby at preserving the '*kokutai*', national polity, national character. At the same time, the Prussian Constitution had several features in common with some other European constitutions of those days.

Now, it is worth recalling the situation, which enabled the transformation of the absolute monarchies into constitutional ones in Europe. In the second half of the eighteenth century the industrial revolution created crises within the hitherto dominant feudal structures and their institutions as well as the requirement for new laws, social doctrines and political structures. The Age of Enlightenment came. In accordance with the political and social ideas of Locke (1632–1704), Montesquieu (1689–1755), Rousseau (1712–1778) the most distinctive features of that time were the conception of the liberal state and the system of divided powers (legislative, executive and judicial). It was not easy to put theory into practice everywhere, it often required time, sometimes even blood, such as during the French Revolution. Notwithstanding, the situation in France exerted influence on the course of events in Poland, it was Poland where on 3 May, 1791 a democratic constitution was promulgated; the first in Europe and the second in the world, following the American Constitution of 1790.

One of the reasons, why I decided to choose the Polish Constitution for this comparative study is that the 3 May Constitution was the first written European constitution of the Enlightenment era, which regulated the principles of the constitutional monarchy. A second reason is that the Constitution was not only the first, but also the last modern constitution of the sovereign Polish Monarchy, totally given shape and promulgated by Poles. Although it was valid only until January 1793, that is to say until the Second Partition of Poland, followed in 1795 by the Third Partition, the abdication of the last Polish King, Stanislav August Poniatowski (on the throne: 1764–1795) and in consequence by the disappearance of the Polish Monarchy from the map of Europe, it went down in national tradition as a symbol of aspirations for sovereignty of the state and of activities driving at the internal consolidation.

Each of the three constitutions of the three monarchies, which had very different histories and cultures, were worked out and put into life in very different social and political situations. First of all, each of them reflected the specific character of the country. But it does not mean, that it is hard to find any features in common. We should remember that all of them were worked out in accordance with the Enlightenment idea of the monarchic system.

The creators of the modern political system in Japan, ashamed of Japan's backwardness compared to Europe and America caused by over two hundred and fifty years of state isolation, wanted, in particular in the first decade of the Meiji era (1868–1912), to avail themselves exclusively of the verified European and American patterns. However, they soon realized, that they had to find such a constitutional formula, in which Western standards would be consistent with the Japanese tradition. (Okubo 1988 Vol. 7: 291–321) Lorenz von Stein also mentioned it during the lectures given to Itō Hirobumi. He warned against inconsiderate adaptation of the constitution of another country. (Komatsuroku 1940 Vol. 2: 291–321) His argumentation was consistent with an idea very popular earlier, that is to say during the days of creation of the 3 May Constitution and the Prussian Constitution. It was the idea of the profound relativism of Montesquieu who exerted such a significant influence on the Enlightenment ideology. Montesquieu wrote in his greatest work *L'Esprit des Lois* (The Spirit of Laws) as follows:

> Better is it to say, that the government most conformable to nature is that which best agrees with the humour and disposition of the people in whose favour it is established . . . [Laws] should be in relation to the climate of each country, to the quality of its soil, to its situation and extent, to the principal occupation of the natives whether husbandmen, huntsmen, or

shepherds: they should have relation to the degree of liberty which the constitution will bear; to the religion of the inhabitants, to their inclinations, riches, numbers commerce, manners and customs. (Montesquieu 1952: 3)

Thus he recognized that the laws good for one nation could be wrong or worthless for others existing in different conditions. Owing to the fact that the idea of relativism was also taken into consideration in Japan, the new Constitution was not only modern but also suited the specificity of Japanese tradition. But on the other hand, it was not entirely different from other constitutions. The highest purpose of the Meiji Constitution was to emphasize the Emperor's role. This was for several reasons. One of them was the necessity of the realization of the Meiji Restoration slogans: *sonnō*, reverence for the Emperor and *ōsei-fukko*, restoration of the Emperor Rule. The restoration of the strong Emperor rule was supposed to prevent the 'usurping power' (*hafu*), which would be exercised by somebody other than the Emperor. (Itō 1929: 22) The Bakufu was considered to be such a power, but in the modern state it would be replaced with other 'bakufu-like bodies' (*bakufuteiki-sonzai*), like political parties, which might govern not on behalf of the nation, but of a social group. Besides, during those days of chaos and transformation an element consolidating the whole nation was necessary. This element could only be the Emperor, who – in accordance with the *kokutai* idea – was the head of the great Japanese family. The consciousness of unity was to facilitate the introduction of reforms and transform the country from a feudal state into a constitutional monarch. Therefore, a determination of the Emperor's position in the first chapter of the Constitution was extremely important. The nation consolidating role, which the Emperor was supposed to play in Japan, in Poland was attributed to the Roman Catholic religion, and was, as in earlier ages, the main and dominant one.

All constitutions emphasized what was permanent and unchangeable. In Poland it was religion. In Japan the Emperor descended from the line of Emperors unbroken for ages eternal (*bansei-ikkei-tennō*). In Prussia, however, it was the territory of the country, which had to be defended like a holy and unchangeable thing, like the cradle of statehood. In Prussia religion was not able to fulfil the consolidating role, because the Constitution assured the freedom of religion. (Konstitucja Pruska 1850: 5–6)

In all the constitutions compared here the first chapters concerned the most important element to each nation, the consolidating element. The composition of the constitutions' chapters shows clearly the hierarchy of importance of problems for each of the countries. Only in the Meiji Constitution was the position of the Emperor treated in Chapter I. In the 3 May Constitution the King's position was described in Chapter VII and in the Prussian Constitution in Chapter III.

Furthermore, only in the Meiji Constitution Article 1 read:

'The Great Empire of Japan shall be reigned and governed by a line of Emperors unbroken for ages eternal.'

In the Polish Constitution the principle '*rex regnat sed non gubernat*' (the King reigns but does not rule), patterned after British constitutionalism, was assumed as a base to determine the King's position in the country. It was emphasized that the King 'is not an absolute monarch, but the father and head of the people', but next to that it was added, that: 'we entrust to the King and His Council the highest power of executing the laws'. (Konstitucja Polski 1990: 15–16) This way the Polish Constitution took away the highest power from the King himself and transferred it, although in a limited way, to the King's Council, called Straz Praw (Council of Inspection translated also as Guardians of the Laws). It consisted of the King, Primate, President of the Commission of National Education and five Ministers. The hereditary Prince could assist at the sessions but he could not vote therein. The Marshall of the Diet had the right to sit in this Council as well, but 'without taking any share in its resolves'. (Konstytucja Polski: 1990: 15–16; Ajnenkiel 1983: 70) The King presided over the Council for life.

On the other hand, in Japan, as was stated in Article 4 of the Constitution, the Emperor was not only 'the Head of the Empire' (*kuni-no genshu*) but he was also 'combining in Him- self the rights of sovereignty and exercised them according to the provisions of the . . . Constitution'. Here, as in Prussia, where only the King had executive power (Art.45), the entire and indivisible executive power was handed over to the Emperor.

The interdependence between monarch and Japanese ministers was explained in detail in Article 55. Each minister of state was individually responsible to the Emperor. Besides, each minister, as an adviser of the Emperor, took on responsibility for the decision of the supreme power, signing under the monarch's seal. Article 55 reads:

The respective Ministers of State shall give their advice (*hohitsu*) to the Emperor and be responsible for it. All Laws as well as Imperial Ordinances of whatever kind, that relate to the affairs of the State, require the countersignature of a Minister of State.

The so-called principle of countersignature, according to which a minister had to bear responsibility for the decisions of the supreme executive power, was valid in the majority of European countries, including Prussia and Poland. The first time it was officially drawn up as a principle of modern constitutionalism was in Poland, in the 3 May Constitution:

Every resolution of this Council (the Council of Inspection) shall be issued under the King's signature, countersigned by one of the Ministers sitting therein and thus signed, shall be obeyed by all executive departments. (Konstytucja Polski 1990: 16)

This principle originated from English impeachment, which gave the opportunity to accuse a minister of putting a seal under the abusively formulated royal act. This unwritten law was vested in England to the House of Commons. The first time the principle of countersignature was written down was in Poland and then in France. The Ministers of State in all these countries were obliged to give advice to the monarchs and by counter-signature take upon themselves responsibility.

Therefore I cannot agree with those Japanese scholars, who, like Ishi Ryōsuke, maintain, that 'indirect Emperor's rule (*tennō-fushinsei*), which means the lack of Emperor's responsibility, 'is an exceptional feature of Japanese Emperor's system'. (Ishii 1950: 224; Bito 1990: 25–6) The author of the so-called 'the indirect Emperor's rule theory' (*tennō-fushinseisetsu*) was Minobe Tatsukichi. (Minobe 1918: 91–3; Bito 1990: 25) He derived it from an analysis of the Meiji Constitution, especially Article 55, concerning countersignature and Article 3, which stated:

'The Emperor is sacred and inviolable'.

I am not going to polemicize with the great Japanese specialists of law and constitutional systems, considering that my knowledge in this field is more limited, but I think it should also be mentioned that in several European constitutions, besides dispensing monarchs from the responsibility, the special, superhuman or divine monarch's position was also emphasized.

The 3 May Constitution read as follows:

'The King's person is sacred and inviolable; as no act can proceed immediately from him, he cannot be in any matter responsible to the nation'. (Konstytucje Polskie 1990:16)

The source of such designation was naturally different to that in the Meiji Constitution. In Japan, the Emperors were supposed to descend directly from Heaven. In Christian countries this 'sacredness' derived from the medieval theological motivation of absolute royal power, interpreting position and power of the sovereign by God's law and power deriving from God. During a coronation a King took some special holy orders from the church dignitaries that emphasized not only the special monarch position but also his nearness to God through the close connection with the church. Thanks to that, the sovereign was not responsible to his subjects, but only to God. The consequence of this principle was the legal inequality of people. In the course of the political and social transformations of the Enlightenment era, when the principles of equality of people and social sovereignty became common and important, this theological motivation was rejected.

But due to the predominant religion, the word 'sacred' as a qualification of monarchy remained in a majority of cases. Traditionally, he was still the 'Lord's Anointed' and the unique person in the country. So neither 'sacredness' nor 'inviolability' connected also with 'lack of responsibility' of a monarch were peculiar to the Emperor system. We can find them also in European monarchic systems, although they sometimes had a different value, resulting from the specific circumstances of the country.

Moreover, the monarchs of the countries under discussion appointed and dismissed ministers, higher civil and military officers and also they were entitled to order amnesty, pardon or commutation of punishments and rehabilitation. (Itō 1929: 23–4) However, only the Emperor determined the organization of the different branches of the administration and salaries of all civil and military officers (Art. 10). Only in Japan was the monarch given supreme executive power containing also power concerning state organization. But he, like other non–absolute sovereigns, was supposed to exercise this power according to the provisions of the Constitution (Art.4). Constitutions were the most important legal acts determining not only the monarch's position but also the organization and structure of the monarchies. Moreover, the Emperor, like the Kings of Poland

and Prussia, like a majority of constitutional monarchs, had the supreme command of the Army and Navy (Art., 11)

> This is a principle, Hermann Roesler wrote – universally acknowledged in all the constitutions, republican as well as monarchical. So in Prussia and Belgium, in France and in the United States, the Chief of the State is uniformly declared the Chief Commander of armed forces . . . . The principle has two important consequences:
>
> 1. unity of the military command in one single person;
> 2. unity of the civil and military power in one person.
>
> No well-organized government can exist without the united supreme disposition of the armed forces, to execute the laws, to maintain peace, and to resist foreign invasion and oppressions. (Siemens 1962: 39)

But comparing the Emperor with the King of Prussia, who had also supreme command of the army (Art.46), the role of the Polish King as the Supreme Commander was limited only to war (Konstitucja Polskie, 1990: 16), probably derived from a fear of loss of national sovereignty in the case of a King's malfeasance. For this reason the king was 'expressly forbidden . . . to declare war; to conclude definitively any treaty, or any diplomatic act' (Konstitucja Polskie 1990: 15), while the Emperor (Art.13), again like the King of Prussia (P. C. Art.48), was entitled to 'declare war, make peace and conclude treaties'. We can see here how history and experiences deriving from it influenced the constitutions.

Now I would like to discuss briefly the monarch's position concerning legislative power. Was the Emperor's position in this field also 'unique'? Certainly, it differed from the position of the Polish King as a result of quite different political, social and historical conditions at the time when the Constitutions of Poland and Japan were given shape.

According to hitherto Polish political practice as well as the political idea of Rousseau, it was accepted that the Seym, the Polish parliament, would be an exponent of sovereign national will. The Seym, after the King had been curtailed of the privilege of being 'the independent house' with the rights of a house, it was to be divided only into two Houses, the House of Nuncios or Deputies and the House of Senate. The Constitution read:

> The former being the representative and central point of su-
> preme national authority, shall possess the pre-eminence in the

Legislature; therefore, all bills are to decided first in this House.
. . . under the presidency of the King, who shall have but one
vote, and the casting voice in case of parity. (Konstytucja Polskie,
1990: 14–15)

Besides, in Poland the executive power could not assume the
right of making laws or of their interpretation. (Konstytucja
Polskie 1990: 15) On the other hand, in Japan the Emperor
exercised legislative power with the consent of the Imperial
Diet (Art.5) In other words, the legislative power was handed
over to the Emperor which was in line with the idea of
concentrating the whole sovereign power in the hand of one
person. But it had to be limited by the 'consent of the Imperial
Diet', because it was necessary to keep to the basic principles of
the Enlightenment monarchy:

It is the most important limit – Roesler wrote – because the law
was the highest and the most general form of rule of human
conduct in the State. (Siemens 1962: 26)

Although it was written down that: 'every law requires the
consent of the Imperial Diet' (M. C. Art.37) it was added, that:
'the Emperor gives sanction to laws and orders them to be
promulgated and executed' (M. C. Art.6). In Prussia, the legislative power was executed by the King and two houses of the
Parliament together, passing each bill required the consent of
the King and the Houses (Art.62). Furthermore, the Emperor,
like the King of Prussia

. . . in consequence of an urgent necessity to maintain public
safety or to avert public calamities, issues, when the Imperial
Diet was not sitting, Imperial Ordinances in the place of law.
   Such Imperial Ordinances are to be laid before the Imperial
Diet at its next session, and when the Diet does not approve the
said Ordinances, the Government shall declare them to be
invalid for the future. (Art.8).

All of the three monarchs had the right of legislative initiative,
convoked parliament as well as opened, closed and prorogued it
and the laws were promulgated on their behalf and with their
signatures. (Itō 1929: 11, 13; Konstytucja Polskie 1990: 15, 16;
Konstytvcje Pruska: 12,64)

   As we can see from the above very general comparison, the
Emperor's position was neither unique nor completely different
from the position of other monarchs, for example those discussed here: the King of Poland and the King of Prussia. Despite

cultural disparities differentiating the states, we can find several features in common concerning their sovereigns' positions, which were determined by their particular Constitutions.

Naturally, one can also find differences, but there is no possibility to create the most important legal act without a consideration of the specificity of the country. Constitutions were supposed to reform and improve the country, but not create it from the beginning as a Utopian State, timeless, where tradition, history, habits would be condemned.

It is natural that practice does not always correspond with theory. But I decided to discuss only the theory, omitting entirely the practice. The aim of my deliberations was to compare the positions of sovereigns only and exclusively on the basis of the constitutions, the fundamental legal acts of their countries, not to analyze their roles, which they played in real political life. As time went by, the history, political, social, economic conditions of the country changed and therefore the monarchs fulfilled their duties more or less in conformity with the letter of the law, interpreting the constitution otherwise than its authors. Moreover, in such a comparison of position and role it would be difficult to be precise about clearly common features and differences due to the number of elements to be taken into consideration. Despite the several monographs, which reflect upon the role that the chosen monarchs played in their epochs, there is still a lack of definitive conclusions. We do know, how difficult, even for Japanese specialists, it is to devise a common opinion concerning the real role the Shōwa Emperor has played in the political life of Japan.

Although the majority of Polish historians recognized the Constitution of 3 May as very democratic for its time and strongly in keeping with the spirit of the Enlightenment era, there are also some researchers, who reckon that despite the fact that the Constitution was promulgated, all political power was still concentrated in the King's hands. Although the democratic Constitution of Prussia was valid from 1850, some Polish specialists maintain that it was only theory, because in practice the old principles of absolute monarchy were still in operation and therefore, in several monographs, Prussia at the end of the nineteen century is described as an example of absolute monarchy.

Thus, the position of the Emperor was not unique and it is easy to find several features in common with the position of other sovereigns. The source of these common features was the political idea of the Enlightenment era, which was the basis for the authors of the constitutions discussed here. One might argue that too many years separate not only the Constitution of Japan, but also the Constitution of Prussia from the time of the great transformations in Europe. However, one has to remember that those reforms, which could be carried out in Poland owing to the suitable political conditions at the end of eighteenth century, could not take place in Prussia and Japan until the beginning of the second half of nineteenth century because of the situation in those two countries. Even so, the general Enlightenment ideas like national, social sovereignty and the division of power were the same. They were just the same principles, which through the Constitution of Prussia – the Japanese Meiji reformers borrowed during their work when drawing up the Constitution or new Empire of Japan.

BIBLIOGRAPHY

Akita George, (1971) *Meiji Rikkensei to Itō Hirobumi* Tokyo: Tokyo Daigaku Shuppankai.
Bitō Masahide, (1990) 'Nihonshijō ni okeru Kindai Tennōsei', *Shisō*, 8, 5–30.
Ishii Ryōsuke, (1950) *Tennō: Tennō Tōchi no Shiteki Kaimei, Tokyo: Kōbundō*.
Itō Hirobumi, (1929) *Itō Hirobumi Hiroki* Tokyo: Shunshūsha.
Itō Hirobumi, (1978) *Commentaries on the Constitution of the Empire of Japan*, Tokyo: Chuō Daigaku 1906 reprinted by Greenwood Press.
Kaneko Kentarō, (1940) *Itō Hirobumi-den*, Vol 2, Tokyo: Komatsuroku.
Konstytucja Pruska, Przyjeta Przez Króla Pruskeigo I Obiedwie Izby, (Constitution of Prussia) (1850) Posnan.
Miller O., (1972) *Minobe Tatsukichi: Interpreter of the Constitution of Japan* California: University of California Press.
Minobe Tatsukichi, (1918) *Kempō Kōwa*, Tokyo.
Montesquieu Charles (1952) *The Spirit of Laws* Great Books of the Western World, 38, Chicago: Encyclopedia Britannica.
Ōkubo Toshiaki, (1988) 'Meiji Kempō no Seitei to Kokutairon', in *Ōkubo Toshiaki Tekishi Chosakushū* (Selected Works of Ōkubo Toshiaki) Vol. 7, Tokyo: Yoshikawa Kōbunkan.
Sansom George, (1981) *Japan in World History*, Tokyo: Tuttle.
Siemens Johannes, (1962) 'Hermann Roesler's Commentaries on the Meiji Constitution', *Monumenta Nipponica* 1, 4.
Ustawa rzadowa z dnia 3 maja 179lr, (Constitution of 3 May, 1791) in *Konstytucje Polskie* (Polish Constitutions), (1990) Warsawa: Przemiany, 13–18.

11

The Imperial House Law of 1889 and its Meaning for the Position of the Tennō in the Meiji State.*

ERNST LOKOWANDT

AIMS AND METHODS

This paper tries to contribute to the understanding of the position of the *Tennō* within or rather, vis-a-vis the *Meiji* state (meaning here the Japanese state between 1889 and 1945). In those times, the *Tennō* had at least three functions: He was the sacrosanct foundation of the state (cf. Preamble and Art.1 of the *Meiji* Constitution, henceforth MC), he was the sovereign ruler within this state (cf. Art.4 MC) and thirdly, as an analysis of the interplay of the highest organs of state would show, he was at the same time a part of the executive – as opposed to the legislative – power (Lokowandt 1992: 12–13). This understanding of the role of the *Tennō* having been gained mostly through an analysis of the legal norms governing the organs of state under the *Meiji* Constitution, it should be useful to complement it through an analysis of the norms governing the interna of the Imperial Household.

The Imperial House Law was promulgated at the same time as the constitution and the attendant laws on state organization like the Imperial Ordinance Concerning the House of Peers, the Law of the Houses, the Law of Election, and the Law of Finance. All these legal norms were formulated by the same men and formed parts of one big parcel by which the state was to be basically reformed. Thus, the norms of the Imperial House Law certainly are not in conflict with those of the constitution – but it is still worthwhile to study them in order to get a complementary view of the Emperor, the Imperial House and in fact of the whole system. Through the study of the Imperial

---

* This paper is to be published also in Japanese, in Tomisaka Kirisutokyō Sentā (ed.), *Kindai Tennōsei no Seiritsu to Sono Kinō*, Shinkyō Shuppansha, Tokyo.

House Law we will attempt to get an additional glimpse of the position and functions of the *Tennō*, as they were established by the legal order of the *Meiji* state, i.e. by the men who created this order. The Imperial House Law – as any legal norm – was the crystallization, the objectification of the subjective wishes and wills of the men who wrote it. Therefore, and as it was binding law, unlike the motives of its authors, it makes more sense to study the completed norms of the Imperial House Law than the wishes and motives of Itō Hirobumi, Inoue Kowashi, Yanagiwara Sakimitsu and whoever else may have been involved in its compilation.

In this paper, the Imperial House Law will be looked at under two aspects: one is in comparison with contemporary European house laws, especially those of Prussia, Bavaria and Hanover. For the purposes of this paper, however, it suffices simply to show that a certain provision of the Japanese house law has or has not an equivalent in any European house law or constitution. It is not necessary and, given the unsystematic way in which information on nearly every country in Europe and beyond had been gathered in the Japan of those days, it also would be near to impossible to try to show which provision in the Imperial House Law had been influenced by which European model.

The second aspect is a comparison with Japanese tradition. The Imperial House Law will be put before two coordinates: comparison with Europe and comparison with tradition. In this way it is hoped that the individual characteristics, the aims and motives of the house law – and of the whole legal system, as far as it relates to the position and the functions of the *Tennō* – will be demonstrated all the more clearly.

THE RELATION BETWEEN THE CONSTITUTION AND IMPERIAL HOUSE LAW

The Constitution and Imperial House Law were promulgated on the same day. The former 'is a collection of the fundamental rules of the State, and lays down clear definitions of the relations that ought to mutually exist between the Sovereign and His people' (*Ito* 1889: III). The latter 'is the house law which the Imperial House has given itself' (*Itō* 1940: 133). Both were considered independent of each other and of equal rank. Art. 74 of the *Meiji* Constitution stated: 'No modification of the Imperial House Law shall be required to be submitted to the deliberation of the Imperial Diet. No provision of the present

Constitution can be modified by the Imperial House Law.'[2] The independence of the Imperial House Law from the constitution and its equal – if not higher – rank showed in the other provisions of the constitution. For example Art.2: 'The Imperial Throne shall be succeeded to by Imperial male descendants, according to the provisions of the Imperial House Law' and Art.17: 'A Regency shall be instituted in conformity with the provisions of the Imperial House Law . . . '. These articles excluded two basic concerns from the sphere of the state and treated them as matters of the Imperial House: the determination of the regular and that of a provisional ruler of the Empire. Not only this. Even the calendar followed the provisions of the Imperial House Law, as Art. 12 stated: 'Upon an ascension to the Throne, a new era shall be inaugurated, . . . '. More down to earth, 'The expenditures of the Imperial House of all kinds shall be defrayed out of the National Treasury at a certain fixed amount' (Imperial House Law [henceforth HL] Art.47) and these expenditures 'shall not require the consent [. . .] of the Imperial Diet, except in case an increase thereof is found necessary')Art.66 MC). Thus, as long as the Imperial Court did not seek a raise in income, the Diet was precluded from trying to exert financial pressure.

Still more note-worthy in regard of the relation between constitution and house law was Art.48 HL: 'The estimates and audit of accounts of the expenditures of the Imperial House and all other rules of the kind, shall be regulated by the Finance Regulations of the Imperial House.' The finances of the Court, even though borne to a great part by the state, were removed from all and any state regulation and even from the control by the Board of Audit, and these exemptions were effected by a provision of the Imperial House Law, not the constitution.

The status of the Imperial House Law as independent of and equal to the constitution was very much in contrast to the situation in Europe, where everywhere the house law was subordinate to the constitution. To give but one example, the King of Bavaria states in the preface to the Königliches Familien-Statut (house law) of 1819 that 'As the constitution of our Empire from 26 May 1818 necessitates in some substantial parts changes of the Family Law publicized on 18 January 1816', he has promulgated a new one. And in Fünfter Titel §1 (which deals with succession) of same house law, it is stated that in case of succession to the throne, the provisions of the constitution shall be followed. House laws in Europe were dependent on and subordinate to the constitution.[3]

In this context it may be noted that in later times the immensely influential Minobe Tatsukichi attempted to change the constitution via reinterpretation. In his commentary to Art.2 MC and else he argues that regulations concerning succession etc. are no interna of the Imperial House but are genuine matters of the state which have been delegated by the constitution to the Imperial House Law. Consequently, the constitution is superior to the Imperial House Law. Unfortunately, he continues, the people who have compiled the Imperial House Law did not understand this and thus have caused grave confusion. In arguing his case, Minobe also mentions the European house laws which are all incorporated in their respective constitution and derive their authority from them. (Minobe 1934:110–111,108–109).The great adversary of Minobe, Uesugi Shinkichi agrees that the regulations concerning succession are no private matter of the Imperial House. But, he contends that the *Tennō* has essentially no private side, and he thus can describe the Imperial House Law and the Constitution as two parallel basic laws of the state (Uesugi, 1925: 253–257).

Both authors agree that the main objective in instituting a parallel house law with wide-ranging competencies was to deny the parliament and thus the people the right to discuss and decide matters of the Imperial House, Minobe disagreeing, Uesugi agreeing with this policy. The Imperial House Law as the expression of – and an instrument to further – the policy of separating Court and Government (*kyūchū/fuchū no betsu*).This policy, the most prominent expression of which, besides the parallel promulgation of Constitution and Imperial House Law, had been the position of the Minister of the Imperial House outside the cabinet[4] from 1885 onwards, seems to have been firmly in place already by 1878.[5] But the separation of Court and government gained in importance from 1881 onwards,[6] when the establishment of a parliament was promised for 1890. The ruling class was afraid of the parliament as it was to be elected by the people. It was feared that the government would come under the influence of the parliament and political parties and so it was safest to separate the Court as completely as possible from the government, in order to ensure that its independence and its dignity would never be jeopardized. For this reason, the Imperial House Law as not countersigned by the Prime Minister. And to make things completely clear, Art.62 HL decreed 'When in the future it shall become necessary either to amend or make additions to the present Law, the matter shall be decided by the Emperor, with the advice of the Imperial Family Council and with that of the Privy Council.' – and without any involvement of Parliament.

SUCCESSION TO THE THRONE

The succession to the throne was by male descendants in the male line, from the eldest son to the eldest grandson, then to the second son and to his eldest son etc. This was in rough correspondence to the contemporary European order of succession, with the exception that in Europe female succession was normally not absolutely excluded. In the United Kingdom female succession was provided for – and in fact had happened quite a few times – if there were no direct male descendants. In Bavaria, female succession could only take place, if there was neither any male royal prince at all nor a male descendant in another German governing house with which a contract on mutual succession had been concluded (Verfassungsurkunde für das Königreich Bayern [1818], Titel II §5 and Königliches Familien-Statut [1819], Fünfter Titel §2). In Prussia female succession was not provided for, but it would have been possible to change the constitution accordingly, should need arise (Schulze Bd.3, 1883:625).

The exclusion of female members of the Imperial House from succession was in approximate accordance with Japanese tradition, too. Of course there have been some female Tennō in Japanese history, eight in all, of whom two became Tennō twice but apart from two Tennō in the Edo period, all of them ruled in the Nara period and before. And as most of these Tennō were standing in for an infant Crown Prince, they may be regarded as a kind of historical accidents. Still, they were precedents and so it is no surprise that in the first draft of the Imperial House Law from 1886 female succession was accepted in case there were no Princes in the Imperial House (Inada Vol.2, 1987: 958). The reasons against female succession were often rather down to earth ones. One, being put forth in a public discussion of 1882 which was later published in a newspaper – and which still later was fully endorsed by Inoue Kowashi – was the apprehension that in Japan with its traditional male dominance the consort of a female Tennō might be perceived as superior to her, which would be damaging to the dignity of the Tennō (Tōyama, 1989: 279). Another reason, pointed out by Inoue Kowashi in his critique of the first draft of the Imperial House Law, was the contradiction in refusing on the one hand women suffrage, and accepting on the other hand a woman as sovereign (Inada Vol.2, 1987:961). It can be concluded that the denial of female succession was half natural and half accidental and is thus of but limited value for an understanding of the special character of the *Tennō* and the Imperial House in the *Meiji* state.

Of more importance is the fact of the regulation of succession itself. This was of course in full accordance with the contemporary European constitutions and house laws. But it was at divergence from the Japanese tradition. The order of succession was anything but uniform, with, up to *Meiji Tennō*, in only 60 out of 121 cases a son – not necessarily the eldest – succeeding his father (*Nihon Gakushiin* Vol.3, 1979:127). The reason for putting this into an order was probably to prevent infighting and intrigues within the imperial House as well as the exertion of influence from outside, thus protecting the order, integrity and authority of the Imperial House.

A rather perplexing aspect of the order of succession is the provision that legitimate children (*chakushi*) have precedence over illegitimate ones (*shoshi*), or, in the official translation of Art. 4 HL, descendants 'of full blood shall have precedence over descendants of half blood.' The illegitimate descendants were not excluded completely, however. If there was no direct legitimate heir, the order of succession went to the illegitimate ones. Thus an illegitimate grandson of the last *Tennō* had precedence over a legitimate younger brother of the last *Tennō*.

This was completely different to the order of things in Europe, where illegitimate children as well as their descendants were absolutely excluded from succession. This could not be overcome even by a later legitimation by marriage or by royal dispensation (cf. Zachariä, 1853: 312–314 and Seydel, 1896: 191). Besides, in Europe the marriage had to be legally valid, concluded according to the house law, with a partner of equal birth and with the consent of the monarch. The latter two requirements were not identical, as the monarch could give his consent to a marriage with a partner of lower aristocratic birth as well. Yet their offspring would be excluded from succession.

Of course in Europe marriage was a holy sacrament and consequently illegitimacy had quite a different meaning from Japan, in whose tradition there was neither holiness in marriage nor monogamy. So the perplexing aspect is not so much that illegitimate children could succeed to the throne, than that there was a differentiation between 'legitimate' and 'illegitimate' at all. Itō Hirobumi in his commentary to Art.4 HL gives as a reason only the precedent of *Jimmu Tennō*, who passed over an older illegitimate son in favour of a younger legitimate one. In absence of monogamy, 'legitimate' meant, since the Chinese inspired *Taihō Ritsuryō* of 701 the eldest son – later sons – of the first wife, 'illegitimate' meant children of second and further wives, and those by other women (cf. the entry *chakushi* in *Kokushi Daijiten*Vol.9, 1988: 452–453). According to the same *Ritsuryō* the *Tennō* was supposed to have one main consort plus two plus three plus four more wives of three different ranks, altogether ten consorts (cf. the entry *kōgō* in *Kokushi Daijiten* Vol.5, 1985: 333–334). In later times the numbers, names, background, all changed, there were elevations in rank and also, from *Ichijō Tennō* (980 – 1011) onwards, there have been many *Tennō* with two first consorts (Yokoo, 1987: 59). Incidentally, the now common expression Imperial Family (*Tennō-ke*) was coined only in the Shōwa period. Up to the Taishō period the *Tennō* had no family (Yokoo, 1987: 53). It is small wonder then, that at times the differentiation between legitimate and illegitimate children has been unclear. Incidentally, out of 60 sons and three daughters, who up to Meiji *Tennō* followed their father on the throne, 27 are officially listed as illegitimate (*Nihon Gakushiin* Vol.3, 1979: 129 and 131–135).

The question arises then, why the differentiation between legitimate and illegitimate has been included into the Imperial House Law. One may assume that the objective was to strengthen the order in the Imperial House and thus to enhance Imperial authority. It was in keeping with tradition and it corresponded to the emphasis laid on the purity of blood in those days. Still, there probably was also the factor of inter-national reputation. According to regulations to be observed on the birth of an Imperial illegitimate child from 1877, the fact of the birth was to be communicated immediately to the members of the Imperial House and ministers of state, and also to the people. There were to be festivities. But foreign monarchs and the foreign diplomatic corps were not to be informed (*Kunaichō* Vol.4, 1970: 265–266). In this context it should also be noted that the Imperial House Law did not regulate all aspects of the Imperial House. It was an official document and real interna were not included. According to Ottmar von Mohl, who from 1887 to 1889 served as adviser to the Imperial Court, there were in his time five official second-wives of the *Tennō*, whose selec-tion, ranks, sequence of service in the inner chambers etc. were regulated (Mohl 1904: 46–48). There is no word on them in the Imperial House Law.

The aforementioned aspect of purity of blood was the rationale for restricting the potential consorts of male members of the Imperial House to members of the House and of 'certain noble families specially approved by Imperial Order' (Art.39 HL). In former drafts of the law they were restricted to the two highest ranks of (albeit mostly new) nobility, and only in the last deliberation in the Privy Council (*Sūmitsuin*) was this relaxed to all ranks of nobility. The arguments of Itō Hirobumi against relaxation were that the [blood] lineage (*kettō*) of the heir to the throne might be corrupted, as in practice the noble families did not sufficiently pay attention to lineage and family rank in selecting their partners in marriage. Also, the dignity of the Imperial House might be prejudiced, if marriage with daughters of the general nobility were to be allowed.[7]

The arguments of blood and dignity of the House were in complete conformity with contemporary European praxis, where the condition of equal birth (Ebenbürtigkeit) was of absolute importance. According to the house law of Hanover (Königliches Hausgesetz für das Königreich Hannover [1836], Drittes Capitel §2), marriages of equal birth were defined as those with members of other sovereign houses or with members of houses which formerly had been subject to the Emperor alone but had lost this status in or after 1806. Prussia was a little more strict. There only princely houses which were governing at present (inclusive of new royalty like the Bonapartes or Bernadottes) were 'equal', or ones who in times of the old Empire had been subject to the Emperor alone and had been governing a territory. In case of a foreign princely house, it had to be Christian too (Schulze Vol.3 1883: 615–616). As in Japan the Imperial House did not accept international marriages, the concept of equal birth was precluded. The alternative was, to restrict the number of families from whom Imperial consorts would be accepted.

Incidentally, 'Marriages of the members of the Imperial Family [were] subject to the sanction of the Emperor' (HL Art.40). The same provision can be found in probably all European house laws. The difference being, that in Europe marriages without royal consent were possible and provided for in the house laws. There were sanctions concerning rank and titles, right of succession, property rights etc. of consort and children (e.g. the Bavarian Königliches Familien-Statut [1819], Zweiter Titel§3) yet the marriage was – naturally in the Christian context – still valid. As mentioned before, an unequal marriage with royal consent was possible, too, albeit also with sanctions concerning the rights of succession. Both cases were obviously unthinkable in Japan and therefore not provided for in the House Law.

Concerning the aspect of blood, there are two more facts to be mentioned. One was the prohibition of adoption (HL Art.42). That was a natural measure and there was also a precedent in the house law of Bavaria (Königliches Familien-Statut [1819], Zweiter Titel §5). Still, as this prohibition diverged from tradition, it is worth mentioning. For example, *Arisugawa no Miya Takahito Shinnō* was adopted (*yūshi*) by the former Emperor *Kōkaku* (great grandfather of *Meiji Tennō*), and his son *Arisugawa no Miya Taruhito Shinnō* was adopted by *Ninkō Tennō*), the grandfather of Meiji Tennō (*Kokushi Daijiten* Vol.9, 1988:70 and 317). But, as these two examples suggest, adoptions in the Imperial House seem to have been undertaken only between members of the House.

The other memorable fact was the deletion in the draft of the clause giving the consorts of Imperial Princes the title Imperial Princess or Princess (*Naishinnō* or *Joō*, according to the number of generations between their consort and his Imperial ancestor), as these titles should be used only by female Imperial descendants (Inada Vol.2, 1987:1016). This was in discrepancy with Art.30 HL which listed the members of the Imperial Family starting with the Grand Empress Dowager, the Empress Dowager and the Empress – all three but consorts of Emperors – and mentioned only in the fourth place the Crown Prince, then his consort, and so on. Also, Art.17 and 18 HL laid down the styles of address not only for the Emperor, but also for the Grand Empress Dowager, the Empress Dowager and the Empress as Majesty (*Heika*), and for the other members of the House as Highness (*Denka*), again without any differentiation between members by blood and members by marriage. It was in accordance however with Art.44 HL, which, although it excluded female members of the Imperial Family who had married a subject from the House, let them retain their title of Imperial Princess all the same. The undilutable dignity of the Imperial Family, the great weight of blood lineage are stressed here in an a rather strange way.

THE ADVISORY ORGANS OF THE COURT

The administration of the Court was in the hands of the Ministry of the Imperial House (*Kunaishō*). Apart from the aforementioned position of the minister outside the cabinet –

and the ministry outside the state structure – there is nothing special about this organ in the context of this paper. Besides the Ministry of the Imperial House, there was the Privy Council (*Sūmitsuin*) and the Imperial Family Council (*Kōzoku Kaigi*). Of other organs of the court, the Lord Keeper of the Privy Seal (*Naidaijin*) is mentioned only once in the Imperial House Law, as one of those having to take part in the deliberations of the Family Council. The Court Councillors (*Kyūchū-komonkan*) are mentioned not at all.

The Privy Council was established on 30 April 1888, broadly modelled after the Bavarian Staatsrat, although the latter had broader competences (cf. Seydel, 1896: 499–504). It was the highest consultative organ of the *Tennō* and held its deliberations in his presence. The ministers of state were created members of the Privy Council. The male Imperial Princes of age had the right to take part in the deliberations, but usually refrained. The first tasks of the Privy Council were deliberating the drafts of the constitution and of the Imperial House Law. The Privy Council was included into the constitution, too (Art.56): 'The Privy Councillors shall [. . .] deliberate upon important matters of State, when they have been consulted by the Emperor.' The Privy Council was thus an organ of the state, but it had important functions in matters of the Court, too. In this respect it was different from the Bavarian Staatsrat; at least there is no mention of the Staatsrat in the Bavarian house law of 1819.

The Imperial Family Council was an organ of the Court, with no competences in matters of state. It was based on Art.55 and 56 HL. Its members were 'the male members of the Imperial Family, who have reached the age of majority.' Besides, the 'Lord Keeper of the Privy Seal, the President of the Privy Council, the Minister of the Imperial Household, the Minister of State for Justice and the President of the Court of Cassation shall be ordered to take part in the deliberations of the Council' (Art.55 HL). In Bavaria, the family council included also the high functionaries of the Court (Kronbeamte) and the ministers of state as regular members (Königliches Familien-Statut [1819], Zehnter Titel §4), in Hanover the family council was composed of all members of the family of full age and ministers of state (Königliches Hausgesetz für das Königreich Hannover [1836], Sechstes Capitel §2).

The advice of both imperial Family Council and Privy Council was a condition in order to change the succession to the throne (Art.9 HL), to institute a regency in case the *Tennō* 'is

prevented by some permanent cause from personally governing'
(Art.19 HL), and to change the order of the regency in case of
disability of the regent or the regent-to-be (Art.25 HL). The
advice was a condition, too, for the regent to appoint a guardian
(Art.27 HL) in case the Emperor was a minor, or to remove the
guardian from his post (Art.29 HL). Amendments and additions
to the House Law were also subject to the advice of the two
organs (Art.62 HL). The Privy Council alone had to give its
advice on including landed and other property into the Imperial
Hereditary Estates (Art.46 HL). The Imperial Family Council
alone had to give its advice (Art.54 HL) if 'a member of the
Imperial Family has committed an act derogatory to his (or her)
dignity, or when he has exhibited disloyalty to the Imperial
House' and was to be punished 'by order of the Emperor'
(Art.52 HL), or if 'a member of the Imperial Family acts in a way
tending to the squandering of his (or her) property' and was to
be 'prohibited from administering his property' (Art.53 HL).

It is easy to understand that in these last two cases only the
Family Council was consulted. These were internal matters of
the Imperial Family and in this context it would have been
improper to have mere subjects participate in meting out disci-
plinary punishment and similar measures against a member of
the Imperial Family. In Bavaria however, things were different.
The King could convene the family council in order to decide
important personal matters of members of the Royal family
(Königliches Familien-Statut [1819], Zehnter Titel §4). The
family council had to decide according to the legal situation,
although the King had the right to sanction (or to refuse) the
finding (Königliches Familien-Statut [1819], Zehnter Titel §8).
This stress on the rule of law set quite a different accent to Japan,
and so it appears only natural that in Bavaria subjects were
allowed to take part in the deliberations of the family council as
regular members, while in Japan they served only in a consultative capacity.

The key to understanding the clauses concerning the requirement of advice by Family Council and Privy Council in
cases of changing the order of succession to the throne, of
instituting a regency, of changing the order of regency, etc. might
be Art.62 HL which makes the advice of the two organs a
condition of changing the Imperial House Law. At first glance
this appears to correspond to the principle that a change of
vested rights requires the consent of those who are affected by
the change, in this case the members of the Imperial Family.

Concerning house laws, this view was widely held in Germany (cf. Heffter, 1871: 87). Consequently, in the preface to the Bavarian house law of 1819 the advance consent of the male members of the Royal family is mentioned, and the house law of Hanover decreees that no stipulation of this house law concerning the succession to the throne and its order may be changed without the consent of all male members of the family, including those of minor age, who are entitled to succession (Zweites Capitel §3).

However, there is no mention of the consent of the male members of the Imperial Family to the promulgation of the Imperial House Law. The supposition of an acknowledgement of any vested interests appears thus to be rather thin. Besides, there were diverging views in Germany too. It should be noted here that the two preceding Bavarian house laws of 1808 and 1816 not only do not mention any consent of the potential heirs to the promulgation of these laws in their prefaces or otherwise, in the last paragraphs of the house law of 1808 the King even stresses his sovereign right to abolish former laws and treaties and to promulgate this new one. Some contemporary authors also stress that with the demise of the old Empire and the newly attained sovereignty, the members of the Royal family have become subjects of the King and consequently treaties between the King and them – or the necessity to obtain their consent – have become obsolete. The state no longer was the object matter of the ruling family, but the state, personified in the King, regulates with his law the family of the ruler (Seydel 1896: 203).

The Imperial House Law, too, was promulgated unilaterally, with the advice of the Privy Council only and without any contractual elements. The advice of Family Council and Privy Council on changes to the Imperial House Law – and probably on the other aforementioned subject matters as well – thus can only have had the following reasons: First, of course, to get the best possible decisions. Second, to exempt the *Tennō* from any responsibility. This is also to be seen in Art. 41 HL: 'The Imperial writs sanctioning the marriages of members of the Imperial Family, shall bear the countersignature of the Minister of the Imperial Household.' A provision, incidentally which had precedents in Bavaria as well as in Hanover (Königliches Familien-Statut [1819], Zweiter Titel §2 and Königliches Hausgesetz für das Königreich Hannover [1836], Drittes Capitel §5) and which also corresponded to the countersignature in matters of state required in Art. 55 MC.

The third reason is the most important one: To preclude any

external influences on the *Tennō* – like those of the Fujiwara family in olden times – as well as internal influences via intrigues or concentration of power within the Court, as it is always easier to influence one man than an assembly of men, much less two assemblies. In this context mention should be made of Art. 23 HL, according to which 'A female member of the Imperial Family to assume the Regency, shall be exclusively one who has no consort.' Also the prohibition of Art. 28 HL for the Regent or any of his descendants to become guardian of a *Tennō* of minor age, as well as the protection of the guardian against a removal by the Regent in Art. 29 HL via the pre-requisite of the advice of Family Council and Privy Council can only be interpreted as a precautionary measure. This view is confirmed by the commentary of Itō Hirobumi to the said articles. In Germany, by the way, the Regent was precluded from becoming also guardian to a King in Hanover (Königliches Hausgesetz für das Königreich Hannover [1836], Sechstes Capital §2), but it was possible without any problems in Prussia and elsewhere (Schulze Bol. 3, 1883: 626). And lastly, that an abdication of the *Tennō* was not provided for should also be seen as a measure to prevent manipulation of the occupant of the throne and to protect the position and the dignity of *Tennō* and Court.

CONCLUSION

Upon the ascension to the throne, the new *Tennō* 'shall acquire the Divine Treasures of the Imperial Ancestors [*sosō no shinki*]' *(Art. 10 HL)*, and 'The ceremonies of Coronation [*sokui no gi*] shall be performed and a Grand Coronation Banquet (*Daijōsai*) shall be held at Kyoto' (Art. 11 HL). All three ceremonies mentioned in these two articles, especially, despite its English translation, the last one, are of religious character. An oath on the constitution is requested neither here nor in the constitution. This contrasts with Europe, where, naturally, coronation cere-monies in religious forms are also performed, but where the oath on the constitution is a common requirement in constitutional monarchies. In Prussia the King and the Regent had to swear in presence of both chambers of parliament to keep the constitu-tion and to govern in accordance with constitution and laws (Verfassung-surkunde für Preußischen Staat [1850], Art. 54 and Art. 58). In Bavaria, not only the King and the Regent, but all Royal Princes as well had to perform, on reaching majority, an oath on the constitution (Verfassungsurkunde für das Königreich Bayern [1818], Titel 10 §1. Titel 2 §16 and Titel 10 §3)

Here again, it is made quite clear that the *Tennō* derives his right to rule from his divine ancestors alone, and that the People have no right to hold him accountable. Of course, the fiction of the *Meiji* Constitution that the Monarch was the bearer of sovereignty, and that only in executing this sovereignty was he bound, by his own free will, to follow the constitution, was a common artifice in probably all contemporary constitutional monarchies except the UK. Still, there is a difference. In Europe the monarch was not only bound to keep the constitution, he was bound to swear to keep it, and to swear it in the presence of representatives of the people. In Japan, however, there was no such necessity. Instead, the ceremonies on ascension to the throne conveyed nothing but the divine rights of the *Tennō*.

The governing circles did everything they could to assure the continued order, dignity and authority of the Imperial House. The regulation of succession, the stress laid on blood lineage (abolition of adoptions and differentiation in the titles of the female members of the Imperial Family), the exemption of the *Tennō* from responsibility and the preclusion of internal and external intrigues and exertion of influence have been mentioned.

The governing circles also did everything they could to protect the Court from any influences from parliament and political parties, in short from the people. Their main means in doing so was the parallel promulgation of constitution and Imperial House Law, as generally the separation of Imperial Court and government. In their endeavour to protect the *Tennō* from politics, they even went so far as to do without the usual countersignature in enacting the Imperial House Law, and to publish it only unofficially. The last two measures however, were both not continued when the Imperial House Law was amended in 1907.

One important measure to strengthen the Imperial House was to increase its finances. In contrast to the European house laws which dealt extensively with property and finances of the house, the monarch, the princes and princesses, even of the widows, the Imperial House Law was almost silent on these subjects, stating not much more than that 'The expenditures of the Imperial House of all kinds shall be defrayed out of the National Treasury at a certain fixed amount' (Art.47 HL), and that 'The property, annual expenses and all other rules concerning the members of the Imperial Family, shall be specially determined' (Art.61 HL). This was done with the Imperial Decree on the Property of the Imperial House (*Kōshitsu Zaisan-rei*) of 1910.

The Imperial House Law keeps nearly silent on the subject, but as a matter of fact the fortune of the Imperial House was increased on a grand scale. The most important proponent of this policy was Iwakura Tomomi, who in 1882, then Minister to the Right (*Udaijin*, the third highest function of state), proposed in a memorandum to the government to increase the fortune of the Imperial House by transferring state property and by other means to such a degree that it would be approximately as big as all private property combined. If need arises, it should be made big enough to bear the expenses for the Army and Navy. The reason was – of course – the approaching constitution and National Assembly. He argued that the constitution is but a law, a text, a flower and that it could, as the French example showed, easily be overthrown. To protect the authority of the constitution it was necessary to put its substance, that is the Imperial House on a firm basis and provide it with a large fortune. If this was done, it would not matter if the Parliament would turn radical one day (cited in Tōyama, 1989–260). Naturally, it was not possible to increase the fortune of the Imperial House on the scale proposed by Iwakura. Still, the Imperial House was provided with an immense fortune, and above all the motivation of Iwakura which was widely shared at the times, deserves attention. The Imperial House was to be protected at all costs.

Different from Europe, where a Crown Prince or Monarch may relinquish the throne or may abdicate, where a member of the Royal house may accept the sanctions and marry against the norms of the house law – as did Edward VIII of Great Britain – such things are impossible in Japan. There the *Tennō* and to a lesser degree the other members of the Imperial Family are public persons and only public persons.[8] The *Tennō* promulgated the constitution and the Imperial House Law as two parallel *public* laws.[9] This is possible only, when the *Tennō* is not just the sovereign ruler, but the basis, the foundation of the state. The *Tennō*, too, had a dual character. But this dualism was not public and private, nor was it the dualism between divine rights and people's rights, but it was the dualism of public court and public state.[10] The link between these two spheres was, besides himself, the Privy Council, which was an advisory organ in matters of court as in matters of state. The Imperial Family was detached from the outside world. Not only was it not possible to enter it as a full member, but great-great-great-grandsons and below of an Emperor who had, on Imperial command or by their own wish, left the Imperial House and become members of the nobility, were not allowed to return to their original status.[11] Once a subject, ever a subject.

The dual character of the *Tennō* as head of the Court and head of the state was not an equal one. Court and state were not on the same level. Despite Art.74 MC and despite the official interpretation of constitution and Imperial House Law as being independent of each other and of equal rank: The Imperial House Law as the basis of the constitution, the state was founded on the Imperial Family.

NOTES

1. Translations of articles of the Meiji Constitution and of the Imperial House Law are here as below by Itō Meyoji (Ito, 1889), all other translations by the author.

2. According to Inada, Vol. 2, 1987: 976 Roesler had recommended following the model of the constitution of Hanover and include into the constitution a clause to the effect that the house law does not need the approval of parliament, but that the constitution cannot be changed by the house law, either. This is exactly the contents of Art. 74 MC. However, until the demise of the kingdom of Hanover in 1866 there had been three constitutions as well as some revisions and it is not clear to which constitution Roesler refers. It has not been possible to confirm the provision mentioned by (or attributed to?) Roesler: The short constitution of 1918 – in fact only a constitution of parliament of Hanover – (Hannoversche Gesetz-Sammlung 1819: 135–139) does not mention the house law at all. The constitution of 1833 (Hannoversche Gesetz-Sammlung 1833: 286–331) mentions the house law in §26), but not a mutual independence of house law and constitution. §26 proscribes even that inasfar as the order of succession to the throne is concerned, the house law may not be changed without the consent of parliament. Furthermore, the constitution contains in §11–25 very detailed provision on the succession to the throne, on the regency, and on the education of a King of minor age. In the constitution of 1840 (Huber Vol. 1, 1978: 305–322, extensive excerpts only) the King is mentioned in the preface the consent of parliament to the provisions of the constitution, and in the First Chapter §12 the succession to the throne is regulated in detail. Both facts would indicate the superiority of the constitution.

3. This seems to have been different from the European usage. At least in Bavaria, the function of Minister of the Royal House could be conferred concurrently on any of the ministers of state. (Verfassungsurkunde für das Königreich Bayern vom 26. Mai 1818, Titel 11 §12).

4. Cf. Yamazaki, 1959: 166. A request by a group of advisors of the *Tennō* to be allowed to participate in the council of government had been refused in reference to this principle.

5. 'The Grand Outline of the Constitution' (*daikōryō*) by Iwakura Tomomi from 1881 stipulated that 'The law of succession to the Throne is a legacy of the Heavenly Imperial Ancestors. It is to be included in a separate charter of the Imperial House and should not be included in the constitution of the Empire.' (Inada Vol. 1, 1987: 490).

6. Inada Vol. 2, 1987: 1017. At first the original draft had been approved with 13 out of 25 votes (ibid.: 1018), however at a later stage of deliberations the text was changed from 'the first two ranks of nobility' to just 'nobility', as the condition of special approval by Imperial Order was now considered to be safeguard enough.

7. Cf. the chapter '*Tennō ni shi [watakushi] nashi*' in *Kōshitsu-hō Kenkyūkai*, 1987: 200–211.

8. This is different from Europe, where the house laws were subordinate to the respective constitution and of half public, half private character.

9. This dualism of two public spheres is one of the reasons, why the *Tennō* – in contrast to Europe – could not develop a private side. In Europe the monarchs were of a threefold character. They were head of state, half public and half private head of their respective house, and private man. In Japan, where the *Tennō* was constrained on the one side by his role of public head of state and on the other side by his role of equally public head of the Imperial House, there was no 'bridge', no 'exit' to private life.

10. Amendment of the Imperial House Law (*Kōshitsu Tenpan Zōho*) of 1907, Art. 1 and Art. 6. The way of thinking was the same in the original Imperial House Law. Otherwise it would not have been necessary, in order to secure heirs to the throne, to preclude Princes of the fifth, sixth and more generation from leaving the Imperial House. This was made possibly only through the amendation of 1907, when their number had grown too big.

11. The Meiji Constitution was not once changed or amended, while the Imperial House Law of 1889 was amended twice: in 1907 and in 1918. The fact that only the Imperial House Law has been amended shows that the governing circles held the concurrence of the text of the house law with reality to be important, whereas they could tolerate discrepancies between reality and the text of the constitution. The immutability of the constitution may be regarded as a sign of heightened respect for the constitution, or of disregard. Accordingly, the constitution may be considered as of higher or of lower rank. Seen under a different category, however, it is clear that the Imperial House Law was judged to be the more important of the two legal norms.

BIBLIOGRAPHY

'Grundgesetz des Königreichs [Hannover] (1883) pp.286–331, in *Hannoversche Gesetz-Sammlung 1833*

Heffter, August Wilhelm, (1871) *Die Sonderrechte der souveränen und der mediatisirten vormals reichsständischen Häuser Deutschlands*, Berlin: E. H. Schroeder.

Huber, Ernst Rudolf, (1988) *Deutsche Verfassungsgeschichte seit 1789*, Bd. 2, Stuttgart/Berlin/Köln/Mainz, 3rd edition Kohlhammer.

Huber, Ernst Rudolf (Hrsg.), (1978) *Dokumente zur deutschen Verfassungsgeschichte*, Bd. 1, 3rd edition Stuttgart/Berlin/Köln/Mainz, Kohlhammer.

Inada Masatsugu, (1987) *Meiji Kenpō Seiritsu-shi* Vol. 1 and 2, 4th printing Tokyo, Yūhikaku.

Ishii Ryōsuke, (1988) 'Chakushi', p. 452, in *Kokushi Daijiten*, Vol. 9, Yoshikawa Tokyo, Kōbunkan.

Itō Hirobumi, (1889), *Commentaries on the Constitution of the Empire of Japan*, translated by Itō Miyoji, Tokyo, Igirisu-Hōritsu Gakkō.

Itō Hirobumi, (1940) *Teikoku Kenpō, Kōshitsu Tenpan-Gige*, 19th edition Tokyo, Maruzen.

'Königlich Baierisches Familiengesetz von 1808', pp. 312–321, in Schulze, Hermann (Hrsg.), (1862) *Die Hausgesetze der regierenden deutschen Fürstenhäuser*, Bd. 1, Jena, Gustav Fischer.

'Königliches Familiengesetz [von Bayern] von 1816', pp. 322–337, in Schulze, Hermann (Hrsg.), (1862) *Die Hausgesetze der regierenden deutschen Fürstenhäuser*, Jena, Bd. 1, Gustav Fischer.

'Königliches Familien-Statut [von Bayern] vom 5. August 1819', pp. 337–347, in Schulze, Hermann (Hrsg.), 1862, *Die Hausgesetze der regierenden deutschen Fürstenhäuser*, Bd. 1, Jena, Gustav Fischer.

'Königliches Hausgesetz für das Königreich Hannover [1836]', pp. 490–507, in Schulze, Hermann (Hrsg.), (1862) *Die Hausgesetze der regierenden deutschen Fürstenhäuser*, Bd.1, Jena, Gustav Fischer.

Kōshitsu-hō Kenkyūkai (Ed.), (1987) *Genkō Kōshitsu-hō no Hihanteki Kenkyū*, Tokyo, Jinja Shinpōsha.

'Kōshitsu Tenpan', pp. 131–185, in Itō Hirobumi, (1940) *Teikoku Kenpō, Kōshitsu Tenpan-Gige*, 19th edition Tokyo, Maruzen.

'Kōshitsu Tenpan Zōho', pp. 187–192, in Itō Hirobumi, (1940) *Teikoku Kenpō, Kōshitsu Tenpan-Gige*, 19th edition Tokyo, Maruzen.

Kunaichō (Ed.), (1970) *Meiji Tennō-ki*, Vol. 4 Tokyo, Yoshikawa Kōbunkan.

'Landesverfassungsgesetz für das Königreich Hannover vom 6. August 1840', pp. 305–322, in Huber, Ernst Rudolf (Hrsg.), (1978) *Dokumente zur deutschen Verfassungsgeschichte*, Bd. 1, 3rd edition Stuttgart/Berlin/Köln/Mainz, Kohlhammer.

Lokowandt, Ernst, (1992) 'Zur Struktur der japanischen Staatsführung: Meiji-Staat und heute', pp. 3–30, in *Münchner japanischer Anzeiger*, Nr. 4.

Minobe Tatsukichi, (1934) *Chikujō Kenpō-seigi*, 10th printing Tokyo, Yūhikaku.

Mohl, Ottmar von, (1904) *Am japanischen Hofe*, Berlin, Dietrich Reimer.

Morimatsu Toshio, (1988) 'Taruhito Shinnō', p. 317, in *Kokushi Daijiten*, Vol. 9 Tokyo, Yoshikawa Kōbunkan.

Nihon Gakushiin (Ed), (1979), *Teishitsu Seido-shi*, Vol. 3, reprint Tokyo, Yoshikawa Kōbunkan.

'Patent, die Verfassung der allgemeinen Stände-Versammlung des Königreichs [Hannover] betreffend (1819) pp. 135–139, in *Hannoversche Gesetz-Sammlung 1819*.

Schulze, Hermann (Hrsg.), (1862 and 1883) *Die Hausgesetze der regierenden deutschen Fürstenhäuser*, Bd. 1 and Bd. 3 Jena, Gustav Fischer.

Schulze, Hermann, 'Die Zollernschen Hausgesetze, Einleitung', pp. 539–643, in Schulze, Hermann (Hrsg.), (1883) *Die Hausgesetze der regierenden deutschen Fürstenhäuser*, Bd. 3, Jena, Gustav Fischer.

Seydel, Max von, (1896) *Bayerisches Staatsrecht*, Bd. 1, 2nd edition Freiburg/Leipzig, J. C. B. Mohr.

Takebe Toshio, (1988) 'Takahito Shinnō', p. 70, in *Kokushi Daijiten*, Vol. 9, Tokyo, Yoshikawa Kōbunkan.

Tōyama Shigeki, (1989) *Tennō to Kazoku, Nihon Kindai-shisō Taikei*, Vol. 2, 3rd printing Tokyo, Iwanami.

Uesugi Shinkichi, (1925) *Shinkō Kenpō-jutsugi*, revised 4th edition Tokyo, Yūhikaku.

'Verfassungsurkunde für das Königreich Bayern vom 26. Mai 1919', pp. 155–171, in Huber, Ernst Rudolf (Hrsg.), (1978) *Dokumente zur deutschen Verfassungsge-schichte*, Bd. 1, 3rd edition Stuttgart/Berlin/ Köln/Mainz, Kohlhammer.

'Verfassungsurkunde für den Preußischen Staat vom 31. Januar 1850', pp. 501–514, in Huber, Ernst Rudolf (Hrsg.), (1978) *Dokument sur deutschen Verfassungsgeschichte*, Bd. 1, 3rd edition Stuttgart/Berlin/Köln/Mainz Kohlhammer.

Yamazaki Tanshō (1959) *Tennōsei no Kenkyū*, Teikoku Chihō-gyōsei Gakkai, Tokyo

Yokoo Yutaka, (1987) *Rekidai Tennō to Kōgōtachi*, Tokyo, Kashiwa Shobō.

Yoneda Yūsuke, (1985) 'Kōgō' pp. 333–334, in *Kokushi Daijiten*, Vol. 5, Tokyo, Yoshikawa Kōbunkan.

Zachariä, Heinrich Albert, (1853) *Deutsches Staats- und Bundesrecht*, Erster Theil, 2nd edition Göttingen, Vandenhoech und Ruprecht.

12

The Leadership of Admiral Katō Tomosaburō

IAN NISH

Katō Tomosaburō (1861–1923) was one of the three leaders of the Imperial Japanese Navy who stands alongside Admirals Yamamoto and Togo but has tended to be dwarfed by them. He was born in Aki domain in present day Hiroshima, the son of a Satsuma samurai. He passed out of the Japanese naval academy (*kaigun Heigakko*) in 1880 second in the class to (Admiral) Shimamura Hayao (1858–1923) who was to dog his steps throughout his naval career. The navy he joined was still of a modest size. He was sent to Britain in 1891 as an ordnance supervision officer and travelled back to Japan with the cruiser *Tsukuba* which had been built in British yards. At the time of the Russo-Japanese War, he reached the rank of rear-admiral (*Kaigun shosho*) and served as chief of staff to Admiral Togo, being present at the battle of Tsushima. After the war, he became naval vice-minister in 1906 and commander of the Kure base three years later. Katō was appointed commander of the First Fleet as rear-admiral in 1913. His first senior post in government was as navy minister in Okuma's second cabinet in 1915.

Katō came to prominence as the navy was making its case for a larger share of the national budget. Responding to the rumours of an American-Japanese war which were circulating in the 1900's, it made a claim for the creation of a Big Navy in line with the army's demands for two extra divisions. When the navy at last tasted political success with the setting up of the cabinet of Admiral Yamamoto Gonnohyoei (Gombei) in February 1913, it was hoped to steer funds the navy's way. But the cabinet had not been in office for a year when a major international scandal over shipbuilding contracts, the Siemens affair, broke. There was a motion of no confidence in the Diet because of the allegations of bribery of Japanese admirals and as a result stout opposition to any claim for increased naval estimates. The scandal caused the resignation of the cabinet and injured the reputation of the navy but does not seem to have harmed Katō. (Ikeda 1988: 20–6)

When Katō became navy minister in August 1915, Japan had been at war with Germany for one year and her fleet had been active not merely at Tsingtao and Singapore but also in the South Pacific and Indian Oceans. Some members of the navy were anxious to erase the ill-reputation which it had acquired as the consequence of the Siemens affair by expanding their operation sphere globally. Katō continued to serve under the Terauchi and Hara cabinets, for seven years in all, most of which were years of comparative prosperity for Japan. (Hirama 1986: 30–1)

Katō inherited the decision of the Defence Conference (*Bōmu Kaigi*) which had been set up in June 1914 in order to ensure some continuity in service budgeting despite the frequent changes in cabinets. It had ruled in July 1914 that the navy should have as its objective the completion of an 8–8 fleet but that this was unattainable for the present for financial reasons. It should therefore be the navy's plan to aim for an 8–4 fleet and move towards an 8–8 fleet when the country's resources permitted it. Katō himself presented a memorandum on 15 October 1918 advancing the plans for an 8–6 fleet and using the argument that the remit of the fleet from 1917 onwards was extending to the western Indian Ocean and to the Mediterranean where it was engaged in joint operations (*Kyōdō sakusen*) with its allies. (1966: 407–30) Moreover, it seemed likely that Japan would fall heir to some at least of Germany's islands in the Pacific as a result of the peace settlement; and this would place a burden on the existing fleet. It was against this background that Baron Katō reiterated his case budget after budget for an expansion of the fleet, during which he acquired a reputation as the main advocate for a Big Navy. It was Kato's main achievement during this period of his career to take the Japanese navy gradually towards the status of a major world navy.

Japan's wartime prosperity ended abruptly in 1919 and gave rise to anxieties in the navy. The steel on which her shipbuilding programmes depended was not available in the quantities she asked for because of America's own domestic building programme. There were serious strikes in 1920 at the Yawata Steelworks and at the Kawasaki dockyard. (Young 1928: 169) The fact that the world's navies were moving over to oil as the source of energy was worrying for Japan because of her lack of oil resources. Naval observers who were sent to European waters during the war came back with doubts about the validity of Big Navy arguments. All these factors planted doubts within the naval hierarchy about the wisdom of the naval expansion plans.

Whatever these doubts and dismays, the 8–8 programme was approved by the Diet in June and July 1920 after lengthy debates. It had been necessary for Katō in the process to woo the political parties and seek compromises with the army. But this was thrown into the melting-pot when Japan received on 11 July 1921 President Harding's invitation to an international naval conference at Washington with a clear implication that all the participants would be under pressure to limit the size of their fleets. Japan replied that she would be pleased to participate in a conference on naval limitation though it showed itself less willing to discuss publicly Pacific and Far Eastern problems about which she had reservations. Naval committees were immediately set up to consider Japan's national interest.

Prime Minister Hara on 24 August asked Katō to become the senior Japanese plenipotentiary. This was a surprise in Japan and a matter of bewilderment in the United States which would have preferred representation by civilians. But Hara who was a superb tactician knew Katō well and was friendly towards him. He presumably had the idea that any solution that was reached at Washington could only be sold to the Japanese navy if the most senior figure from the fleet was present at the deliberations. Already basic divisions were appearing within the naval hierarchy over the merits of a Big Navy. Katō himself was changing his views; and it was essential that there should be a fundamental review before the conference itself. The instructions to the delegation formulated by the *Gaikō Chōsakai* and cabinet and despatched to the delegates on 14 October reflected these new views. The portion on naval limitation read as follows:

'For the sake of Japan's security and world peace, Japan's naval strength must be kept in line with the strength which other powers can employ, at least in eastern seas. As for the naval strength that Japan will claim on the occasion of the present disarmament negotiations, the 8–8 fleet will be the standard; but to the extent that the United States and Britain will maintain a ratio which is in conformity with the above-mentioned idea and no great changes emerge in the future situation in the

Pacific, it is not the case that we shall persist in the programme which is being pursued at present and we are not averse to reducing it in accordance with circumstances. We should propose the abolition or limitation of fortification of islands in the Pacific and at least strive for the setting up of a treaty preserving the status quo.' (Nihon Kokusai Seiji Gakkai 1963: 22)

In addition, Japan wanted the naval issue to be resolved first. Her instructions were remarkably non-committal and broad-minded, considering the long struggle for the 8–8 programme.

Civilians and civilian politicians had their own views to offer. One contemporary writer observed: 'It was with a certain relief that Japan looked forward to a halt in the feverish preparations for war.' Before the conference began in November Katō assured the public that Japan had never entertained the idea of maintaining a navy equal to those of America or Britain. (Young 1928: 255)

On his arrival in Washington, Katō discovered from the secretary of state's initial speech to the conference on 12 November that limitation was to be the order of the day. He approached the problem, we are told, looking for compromise from a broad perspective. On 14 November he responded, accepting the American plan in principle and saying that Japan was ready to proceed with determination towards a sweeping reduction in her naval armament. That did not prevent much dissension within his delegation and much intense technical debating among the naval staffs in Washington. On 12 December at a three-sided meeting Japan accepted the ratio of 5:5:3 for battleships and, when Japan's determination to retain the new battleship *Mutsu* had been accepted, a draft treaty was agreed three days later.

At Washington Katō was one of the triumvirate who made the critical decisions on naval matters. He had a role equal to that of Secretary of State Charles Evans Hughes or A. J. Balfour. This may have modified his philosophy about the Imperial Japanese Navy even more. From the Shoreham Hotel, on 27 December, Katō sent a message through his attaché, Capt Hori Teikichi, to the navy vice-minister in Tokyo, Admiral Ide Kenji, which reflected on events:

Since the recent world war it would appear that the feelings among civilian politicians about security have generally been the same around the world. That is to say, defence is not something which can be made by soldiers alone. It is difficult to achieve one's objectives if one does not operate on the basis of total mobilization of the state. Thus, while one can on the one hand arrange for munitions, one cannot put them to practical use unless one can exploit the industrial power of the people, encourage trade and maximize the national strength. One has to admit frankly that, if one has no money, one cannot make war . . . . Even if we assume that our munitions are equal to those of America, we can no longer make war on the small amount of money that we could afford at the time of the war with Russia. If we consider where funds might be obtained, there is no other country apart from the US which could supply a loan to Japan. If America is to be the enemy, the means of raising funds is restricted and Japan would have to build up her military finance by herself . . . . we can only conclude that a war with America is to be avoided. (1963 Vol. 7: 3–7)

But criticisms of Katō's thinking came at two levels. The Big Navy group within his delegation in Washington contained some of the most dissatisfied. There were also political enemies in Japan who were making difficulties. So long as Hara was acting as navy minister, Katō was relatively safe. But Prime Minister Takahashi who took over after Hara's assassination at Tokyo station on 4 November had neither the power nor the inclination to interfere with their criticisms. So, when Katō arrived back in Japan, his reception could only be described as cold. But he could console himself that he had by persuasion within his Washington team managed to carry the day with his programme of naval limitation provided the safeguards over the *Mutsu* and Pacific fortifications were incorporated.

But Takahashi's days as prime minister of a Seiyukai cabinet were numbered. He resigned on 6 June 1922. The Elder Statesmen called on Admiral Katō, somewhat surprisingly, as his successor. He was a man who had won golden opinions at home and abroad for his successful conduct of his mandate at Washington. Because of Shidehara's illness and Prince Tokugawa's attendance on a largely ornamental basis, Katō had had to bear the burden not just of the naval talks but also of the sessions on China and far eastern problems. His image had changed from that of the unrepentant expansionist to that of the sober international statesman. Among foreigners he earned the reputation of being an advocate of disarmament. Admiral Yamanashi later recalled that Katō looked upon the invitation to Washington as a 'gift from the gods' that would extricate him from the multiple difficulties surrounding the construction of the 8–8 fleet. The paradox was that he was not universally popular in the navy –

or the army for that matter. Indeed, the disagreements that had surfaced before the conference had worsened considerably. Nonetheless he was able to obtain the cooperation of the Seiyukai party and with that assurance accepted office on 12 June. (Dingman 1976: 280) Of course the implementation of the Washington treaties was the vital issue to be faced, and there was good reason to leave it to be resolved by one who had been involved in the negotiation.

On 5 August the Prince Regent acting for the ailing emperor gave his sanction to the Washington treaties after the proper ratification procedures. On 24 June the new government had already announced the withdrawal of its troops from Siberia which was largely completed in October. Early in July Katō who was himself acting as navy minister published a plan for naval retrenchment, involving the decommissioning of 11 warships and reducing the numbers of sailors by 12,000. The so-called Yamanashi plan for the army reduced it by over 60,000 troops. In December, Japanese troops were evacuated from Tsingtao as a result of agreement with China, though Japan refused to accede to China's request for the return of Dairen and Ryojun. It cannot be imagined that such a large agenda should go through without problems and disagreements but it was passed remarkably smoothly. Under Katō's leadership a remarkable slate of reforms had been carried through. He died from stomach cancer on 24 August 1923 and was posthumously created a viscount and promoted to be admiral of the fleet. (Young 1928: 294)

There is a remarkable agreement among outside observers about Katō's personality. Speaking of an earlier part of his career, Sir Claude MacDonald who was the senior British representative in Tokyo from 1900 till 1913 wrote that Katō was a very silent and reserved man but was said to be one of the cleverest men in the navy. (Nish Vol. 9 1989: 73) Professor Ikeda writes that on the surface he was cautious and calm but 'under the calmness a bold personality was lurking.' (Ikeda 1988: 127) The same features impressed observers at the time of the Washington conference. General Piggott who saw him often at Washington recorded: 'Though a man of few words, he was reported to be one of the most widely read of all officers in the navy'. (Piggott 1950: 140) An American journalist, Mark Sullivan, similarly wrote: 'In appearance, as well as intellectually, Baron Kato was one of the most impressive men in Washington'. (Sullivan 1922: 240) Ichihashi Yamato who was secretary to Katō at the time of the conference, is, however, not uncritical, describing him as too honest and too simple a diplomat. On another occasion, he wrote about later events in January 1922: ' . . . for the first time one could see the lack of clearness in his expression. The writer called his attention to that fact more than once, and he gracefully admitted it . . . . Nevertheless, by tact and patience he was able to win both his opponents at home and his colleagues at the conference'. (Yamato 1928: 90) Yet he seems to have combined the attributes of a thinker with those of a practical man of affairs.

Why do I think that Katō was a good leader? I am not alone in this. Professor Asada has written that Katō was 'a figure of towering prestige and unquestioned leadership' (Asada 1973: 228), while Professor Dingman's conclusion is that 'Kato was a brilliant, energetic, perhaps even politically ambitious man'. (Dingman 1976: 191) Katō was flexible. He was prepared to change tack, to jettison his earlier beliefs in a Big Navy and accept the realities of the international situation after 1918, namely the dominance of Washington in the Pacific area. From being Japan's Big Navy admiral, he won fame as a pacifist at Washington. Katō's career was therefore something of a paradox. Doubtless each of these images was exaggerated in certain respects. His 'conversion' was probably a gradual and reluctant one without a dramatic volte-face. But he readily faced the fact that the Japanese economy was weak and that Japan could not yet afford to indulge in naval building competitively with the United States. He therefore favoured a diplomatic attempt to seek good relations with the United States. Throughout this he displayed leadership qualities which may have been founded on Satsuma loyalties. During the 1910s he had carried the navy with him in aiming at naval expansion. After the Washington Conference his hold over the navy was by no means so complete but he was able to implement the measures to which he had agreed as plenipotentiary at Washington. In doing this, he faced unpopularity among his naval colleagues so his actions required courage and persuasiveness. Among Japanese statesmen he was one who combined a keen sense of his country's national interest with an awareness of its international responsibilities.

BIBLIOGRAPHY

Asada Sadao, (1973) 'The Japanese Navy and the United States' in D. Borg and S. Okamoto, *Pearl Harbour as History*, New York: Columbia University Press.

Dingman R., (1976) *Power in the Pacific: Origins of Naval Arms Limitation, 1914–22*, Chicago: University of Chicago Press.

Hirama Yoichi, (1986) 'Dai ichiji sekai taisen e no sanka to kaigun', *Gunji Shigaku*, 22.

Ikeda Kiyoshi, (1988) *Nihon Kaigun* 2 Vols., Tokyo: Asahi Sonorama.

Nish I. H. (ed.) (1989) *British Documents on Foreign Affairs* Part 1, Series E, Asia, Vol. 9, Maryland: University Publications of America.

Piggott F. S. G., (1950) *Broken Thread*, Aldershot: Gale & Polden.

Sullivan M., (1922) *The Great Adventure at Washington*, New York: Doubleday, Page & Co.

Yamato Ichihashi, (1928) *The Washington Conference and After*, Stanford: University Press.

Young A. Morgan, (1928) *Japan under Taisho Tenno*, London: Allen & Unwin.

Navy Ministry (1966) *Yamamoto Gombei to Kaigun* Tokyo: Hara Shobo.

Foreign Ministry (1955) *Nihon Gaikō Nempyō narabi ni Shuyō Bunsho*, Tokyo: Kokusai Rengo Kyokai.

Nihon Kokusai Seiji Gakkai (1963) *Taiheiyō Sensō e no Michi*, 7 vols. Tokyo: Asahi Shimbunsha.

13

Anarchist Communism and Leadership: the Case of Iwasa Sakutarō

JOHN CRUMP

Iwasa Sakutarō (1879–1967) possessed many of the qualities which make for a successful Japanese politician. First, he was long-lived, being 87 at the time when he died. Second, he enjoyed robust health throughout his long life and retained his vitality almost to the end. Third, he was highly educated by the standards of his day, having graduated from Tōkyō Law College (*Tōkyō Hōgakuin* – the forerunner of Chūō University) in 1898. Fourth, he came from an affluent background, being the son of a wealthy farmer. Fifth, he was well-connected; as a young man he lodged with and was tutored by some of the leading scholars of the time, whose houses were frequented by powerful members of the Meiji élite, such as Yamagata Aritomo. (Noguchi 1931: 161) Sixth, he was naturally gregarious, thriving on human contact and being a skilled conversationalist. Seventh, as a young man he was ambitious and had a keen desire to become a politician in order to improve Japanese society. Eighth, without making any special effort, he inspired respect from those around him, so much so that from the age of 25 or 26 he was already known as Iwasa Rō (literally, 'the aged Iwasa'), a respectful term which Japanese are inclined to employ when referring to venerable scholars or elder statesmen. (Museifushugi Undō 10 April 1967: 3) Finally, he had a breadth of international experience which was unusual for the time, having spent thirteen years in the USA between 1901 and 1914.

Many Japanese politicians have achieved success with far fewer attributes than these. For a single individual to have possessed so many advantages indicates an unusual convergence of good fortune and talent in the case of the young Iwasa. Yet

155

possession of these advantages was to bring anything but success for him. As his life unfolded, it became a long history of setbacks, persecution and frustration, all connected with the fact that the road which Iwasa chose to walk was the path of anarchist communism. If one analyses the reasons for Iwasa's lack of worldly success, one can see that the roots of this were twofold. On the one hand, anarchist communism threatened all the foundations on which the modern Japanese state rested. It rejected the capitalist system of producing and distributing wealth; it opposed militarization internally and imperialist expansion externally; and it challenged status and hierarchy within society, symbolized above all by the existence of the Emperor. With goals such as these, which subverted the very bases of the existing system, Iwasa and his comrades brought down on their heads the unbridled hostility of the state. On the other hand, although being advantageously placed for launching himself into a career as a political leader, Iwasa refused to play the game by the rules of conventional leadership. He made no promises to people, neither sought nor offered patronage, had no interest in acquiring power and did not pursue personal advantage.

Despite this, it would be quite wrong to imagine that Iwasa rejected leadership in any shape or form. As we shall see, he regarded the anarchist communists as an intellectual vanguard and believed that they had an exemplary function to fulfil as challengers of authority. What he was at pains to emphasise, however, was that undertaking such roles held no promise of either fame or material reward for the anarchist communists. On the contrary, by questioning the dominant values of society and challenging the existing power structures, anarchist communists exposed themselves to ridicule, danger and often thankless toil. Iwasa's own life provided ample evidence of this. To take just one example, even in his sixties and seventies, at a time of life when conventional politicians would be devoting their energy to wheeling and dealing in the backrooms of the Diet or in the luxurious surroundings provided by expensive restaurants and hotels, Iwasa was still walking the streets, with a signboard slung round his neck, selling unpopular journals. (Museifushugi Undō 10 April 1967: 3) It was his engaging in activity such as this, which was so conspicuously at odds with the conventions of mainstream politics, that enables us to say that Iwasa was an anarchist communist leader who refused to lead in any sense that the word is conventionally understood.

Nevertheless, this paper will also take the opportunity to

question the residual form of leadership which Iwasa did attri-
bute to anarchist communists. Iwasa understood perfectly well
that anarchist communism was an alternative form of society
which, by virtue of abolishing the state and holding wealth
communally, would eradicate leadership. In such a society, decisions would be taken as a community and no one would be
provided with either the power or the wealth to impose their
will on others. Even with this clear perception, however, the
question remained how to get from society as it was presently
organized to a society exhibiting these features. Opposed
though they were to existing society, its practices and its values,
Iwasa and his comrades remained products of it themselves and
therefore could not jettison entirely all the assumptions on
which it rested. Particularly for someone of Iwasa's generation,
born only twelve years into the Meiji era, the heroic exploits of
the Meiji Restoration of 1868 had a lingering influence, despite
the fact that he was conscious of the Restoration's shortcomings
as a revolutionary transformation. Undoubtedly, the Meiji
Restoration was one of the sources from which Iwasa's self-
image of anarchist communists as a heroic and self-sacrificing
minority derived.

In addition, Iwasa was well aware of the extent to which the
mass of the people had had their courage and independence
sapped by oppression and insecurity. Understandably perhaps,
Iwasa and most of his comrades reacted to the social order they
opposed by concluding, somewhat paradoxically, that the way to
bring about an alternative, leaderless society was to rely on the
(albeit highly unconventional) leading role of the minority of
anarchist communists. Seeing the problem in this way imposed
on the anarchist communists the arduous responsibility of
bringing new ideas to ordinary working men and women and
the risky tactics of galvanizing the masses into rebellion by
engaging as a minority in acts of defiance against the state and
confrontation with the capitalists. Had Iwasa and his comrades
rejected this strategy of assigning a particular leading role to
themselves as anarchist communists, in their eyes the effect
would have been to have put back the prospect of revolution by
many years, since it was obvious that most people were currently
socialized into accepting capitalism and lacked the determination to confront those who exercised power. With the benefit
of hindsight, however, we can see that such a rethinking of the
relationship between anarchist communists and the masses
would have had the advantage of realism, since the revolution

which inspired Iwasa throughout his adult life has remained a remote prospect even several decades after his death.

Had Iwasa and his fellow anarchist communists realized that the revolution to which they were committed lay far ahead in an indeterminate future, it would have had an effect on their perception of themselves and their self-assigned rôle. Less of their energy would have been poured into ephemeral activism, allowing more of their time and effort to be redirected towards research into the nature of an anarchist communist society and the means to achieve it. In this regard, it was incongruous that, despite his talents, Iwasa published only three works throughout his long life, some of them mere pamphlets and all essentially collections of articles written for immediate purposes in agitational journals. These were *Workers and the Masses* (*Rōdōsha to Taishū*) (1925), *Anarchists Answer Like This* (*Museifushugisha wa Kaku Kotau*) (1927) and *Random Thoughts on Revolution* (*Kakumei Dansō*) (1931). To these can be added the autobiographical essays which were republished posthumously under the title *One Anarchist's Recollections* (*Ichi Anakisuto no Omoide*).

Erasing the distinction between the anarchist communists and the masses would not have deprived the former of any rôle at all. As part of the masses, they would still have been free to put forward their views and argue for the type of society they wished to achieve. Nevertheless, by eliminating any special anarchist communist responsibility for the outcome of events, it would have been brought home that only determined action by self-organized masses who are intent on freeing themselves can bring about a free society based on mass self-organization. In other words, the contradiction implicit in the proposition that achieving a society without leadership depends on the leading rôle of a minority of anarchist communists would have been eliminated and a greater degree of consistency achieved between the means of struggle employed and the ends to which that struggle was directed.

FORMATIVE INFLUENCES

Iwasa was born in 1879 in a farming hamlet in Chiba Prefecture. His father was a land-owning farmer who acted as the headman of a group of five villages. (Museifu Shimbun 15 March 1956:2) His grandfather had been headman, too, and had strongly encouraged communal production and cooperative practices within the area for which he was responsible. Under Iwasa's grandfather, the paddy fields were farmed communally and the hill land was owned in common by the villagers. As a result, the community had the character of a 'half-communist village' (*han kyōsan mura*). Iwasa came under the influence of his grandfather during his childhood and for the rest of his life he perceived anarchist communism not as an ideal project waiting to be tested, but as a form of social organization which comes naturally to local communities, providing the state does not interfere. (Noguchi 1931: 161)

Iwasa received a traditional form of primary education and learnt Chinese characters (*kanji*) by means of the rote reading of the late Edo text *The Unofficial History of Japan* (*Nihon Gaishi*) by Rai Sanyō. In addition to absorbing Chinese characters by reading such books, young Iwasa was evidently highly receptive to the heroic stories in which they abounded. At one point in *The Unofficial History of Japan*, Taira no Masakado surveys Kyōto from Mount Hiei and expresses his determination to rule Japan from there. Reading this, Iwasa is said to have pounded his desk and shouted: 'This is it; this is it! I am going to hold society [*tenka* – literally 'all under heaven'] in the palm of my hand.' As a result, the village children henceforth gave Iwasa the nickname '*Masakado*'. (Museifu Shimbun 25 September 1955: 1) Similarly, Iwasa further astounded his teacher when, in an essay written at the age of 13, he declared his intention to become one day the ruler of Japan. (Museifu Shimbun 25 September 1955: 1) Obviously, it would not do to make too much of these childish flights of fancy, but they do give an indication of the extent to which Iwasa was inspired by the heroism which permeated his reading primers.

Nevertheless, Iwasa was far from being putty in the hands of his teachers. Much of the formal education to which he was exposed struck him as uninteresting and he therefore dropped out of middle school. Eventually, he progressed to Tōkyō Law College, but only to conclude that the lessons there, too, were uninspiring and that there was little point in continuing. Only his mother's tears, who feared that the family's reputation would not survive her son dropping out for a second time, persuaded Iwasa to press on to graduation in 1898. (Museifu Shimbun 25 September 1955: 1) Like many other young intellectuals of this period, Iwasa was exposed to Christian ideas and for a time took lodgings in the house of a Christian convert. However, he did not himself become a Christian, on the grounds that 'Jesus was a person. Buddha and Confucius were persons. And I am a person too'. (Museifu Shimbun 25 September 1955: 1) What these various episodes indicate are Iwasa's independent spirit and his own perennial reluctance to follow leaders, either secular or divine.

As was mentioned previously, Iwasa was fired with political ambition at this stage of his life and realized that, in order to make an impact on society, he would need to acquire knowledge and equip himself with learning. He therefore decided to prepare himself for enrolment in Tōkyō Imperial University and took up further studies under Yamai Kanroku, who was a disciple of Yasui Sokken, a major Confucian scholar during the final years of Tokugawa power (the *Bakumatsu* period). (Museifu Shimbun 25 September 1955: 1) With the same overall purpose in mind, Iwasa lodged in the houses of a number of politicians and scholars, but the experience proved to be disillusioning. Such houses were frequented by 'the great and the good' of Meiji society and, observed at close quarters, Iwasa saw little to admire or emulate in their behaviour. (Noguchi 1931: 161) One strong influence acting on Iwasa at this stage of his life was a book he read at about the time he graduated in 1898. Known in Japanese translation as *The Secret Fraternity* (*Himitsu Kessha*), this was a study of late nineteenth-century anarchism written by a French priest whose name was rendered 'Rigiyoru' in *katakana* syllabary. It is said that it was via this book that Iwasa first came to know about anarchism and that it was influential in finally dissuading him from following a conventional career in the law or in politics. (Museifushugi Undō 10 April 1967: 1)

THE AMERICAN YEARS

Iwasa left Japan for the USA in 1901 and remained there until 1914. It was during his extended stay in America that he became an anarchist communist and, as with many others, it was the impact of the Russo-Japanese War (1904–5) that particularly radicalized his political views. The Japanese government had refused to allow the famous novelist Jack London into Japan as a war correspondent on the grounds that he was an 'anarchist' and Iwasa shared the platform with London at a public meeting held in San Francisco to protest against this. (Museifu Shimbun 25 September 1955: 1) Following the war, the most famous socialist in Japan, Kōtoku Shūsui, arrived in the USA in December 1905 and spent the next six months in California. During his time in America Kōtoku's ideas also moved in an anarchist communist direction, which drew Kōtoku and Iwasa together, although Iwasa was never reticent about criticizing as 'stupid' the ideas of even celebrities like Kōtoku when the occasion demanded it. (Iwasa 1982:145) Iwasa became a member of the Social Revolutionary Party (*Shakai Kakumei Tō*) which Kōtoku organized in California in June 1906 shortly before his return to Japan. The Social Revolutionary Party's programme stated:

> Our party seeks to destroy the present economic and industrial competitive system and, by placing all land and capital under the common ownership of the whole people, to eradicate all vestiges of poverty.
>
> Our party seeks to overhaul the current class system, which depends on superstition and convention, and to secure equal freedom and rights for all people.
>
> Our party seeks to eliminate national bias and racial prejudice and to realise genuine world peace for all people everywhere.
>
> Our party recognises that, in order to attain the objectives given above, it is necessary to unite and cooperate with comrades throughout the world and to bring about a great social revolution. (Hikari 20 July 1906: 7)

The name adopted by the Social Revolutionary Party indicates the influence of the terrorist-inclined Russian Social Revolutionaries (SRs) on those who formed it and this impression was strengthened when the journal *Revolution* (*Kakumei*) was issued in the Party's name from December 1906. Iwasa was one of the key people involved in writing and producing *Revolution*.Taking its lead from the SRs, *Revolution* advocated violent social revolution, declaring that:

> The sole means is the bomb. The means whereby the revolution can be funded too is the bomb. The means to destroy the bourgeois class is the bomb. (Suzuki 1964: 467)

The handful of Japanese revolutionaries in California lacked the resources to sustain either the Social Revolutionary Party or the journal *Revolution* for long, but they created a major incident when they marked the Meiji Emperor's birthday on 3 November 1907 by issuing an 'Open Letter to Mutsuhito the Emperor of Japan from Anarchists-Terrorists'. With bravado that verged on the reckless, the 'Open Letter' proclaimed:

Mutsuhito, poor Mutsuhito! Your life is almost at an end. The
bombs are all around you and are on the point of exploding. It
is goodbye for you. (Suzuki 1964: Supplement)

In view of the subsequent execution in 1911 of Kōtoku Shūsui
and others who were involved in the High Treason Incident
(*Taigyaku Jiken*), there were perhaps good reasons why Iwasa
steadfastly denied over the years any involvement in the production of the 1907 'Open Letter', but it was nevertheless
widely believed that he was one of those responsible for its
publication. (Crump 1983: 210) What Iwasa never made any
attempt to hide was his support for Kōtoku and the others
implicated in the High Treason Incident. This was clearly expressed in another 'Open Letter', this time unambiguously
signed by Iwasa and which he addressed 'To the Japanese
Emperor and Senior Statesmen' in November 1910. (Iwasa
1982: 174–9) When news of the execution of Kōtoku and his
comrades in January 1911 reached Iwasa in the USA, it had a
traumatic effect. The shock of losing such a respected comrade
was so severe for a sensitive man like Iwasa (who was then 31)
that he immediately became impotent. (Suzuki 1964: 534–5)

HOUSE ARREST

What eventually induced Iwasa to take the considerable risk of
returning to Japan was a message received from his younger
brother, telling him that his mother was ill. He arrived back at
the family home in June 1914 and for the next five years was
placed under house arrest. The hamlet where Iwasa had grown
up and to which he now returned was a tiny rural community
comprised of only about 50 farmhouses, but three police sub-
stations were erected to house the officers who were assigned to
keep him under constant surveillance. (Museifu Shimbun 15
February 1956: 2) With characteristic wit, Iwasa referred to the
police buildings as 'dog kennels' ('dogs' was widely used
anarchist slang for the police) and he needed all his reserves of
fortitude and humour to survive the years of isolation that now
ensued. Iwasa was not formally prohibited from receiving
visitors, but it required great courage for anyone to call on him.
Not only were any visitors likely to bring upon themselves
intense surveillance (with its attendant consequences, such as
loss of jobs) but they also ran the risk of gratuitous violence
from the police. Many years later, Yamada Seiichi recalled calling

on Iwasa in the latter half of the Taishō period (1912–26) and being beaten up by the 'special police' (*tokkō*) simply because the mood took them to do so:

> Without any reason I was surrounded by several 'special police' and knocked about like the ball in a game of volleyball. It was that sort of era. (Museifushugi Undo 10 April 1967: 2)

ARCHETYPAL PURE ANARCHIST

After Iwasa died, it was said about him that 'the road which Iwasa *Rō* [the aged Iwasa] walked, extending through the Meiji [1868–1912], Taishō [1912–26] and pre-war and post-war Shōwa [1926–89] eras, was the history of the Japanese anarchist movement itself' (Museifushugi Undō 10 April 1967: 2) That this was so is illustrated by the way in which Iwasa's personal circumstances fluctuated in harmony with the ups and downs of the anarchist movement as a whole. In 1919 Iwasa was able to shake off the restrictions of house arrest and head for Tōkyō. This reflected the anarchist movement's emergence from its 'winter period', during which it had forcibly been kept dormant by the state ever since the High Treason Incident. An upsurge in rank-and-file militancy, brought about by the economic conditions following the First World War, created a situation beyond the state's ability to control and those like Iwasa were quick to seize the opportunities that presented.

From 1919 Iwasa threw himself into the burgeoning movement and life became a whirl of attending meetings, writing articles, distributing journals and, least conspicuous but probably most important of all, spreading the word through chats with individuals or informal discussions. This last form of activity was something at which Iwasa excelled. In 1931 Noguchi Yoshiaki published a volume of biographical sketches of all the prominent militants in the proletarian movement. The entry on Iwasa included a passage which read:

> His special feature could be said to lie in the fact that, together with being a founder of anarchism in Japan, he excels in the underground movement. What I mean by that is that he has the knack of informal conversation. He has travelled the country on one journey after another, having talks with comrades [in one place after another]. He gathers comrades around him by the attractiveness of his personality and the skill of his conversation. (Noguchi 1931: 162)

Iwasa joined the Labour Movement (*Rōdō Undō*) group, which from October 1919 published the journal of the same name. This was a group which included Ōsugi Sakae, Itō Noe, Mochizuki Kei, Wada Kyūtarō, Mizunuma Tatsuo and Kondō Kenji, all of whom played important roles in the development of Japanese anarchism and several of whom paid with their lives for their prominence in the movement. What distinguished Iwasa from other anarchists like Ōsugi was that, while they were deeply influenced by syndicalism, his vision of a new society and the means to achieve it were rooted in the theoretical principles of anarchist communism as defined by Kropotkin. It was this feature of Iwasa's thought that caused the term 'pure anarchist' to be applied to him from an early stage. As Noguchi also wrote about him:

> It is said that he was the sole pure anarchist in Japan. In other words, there was none of the deficiencies of the type found in Ōsugi or Kōtoku. (Noguchi 1931: 161)

In September 1920 an attempt was made to form an umbrella organization which would encompass all shades of opinion claiming allegiance to socialism. This was the Japanese Socialist League (*Nihon Shakaishugi Dōmei*). It published the journal *Socialism* (*Shakaishugi*) and Iwasa was named as its editor. However, both attempts by the Socialist League to hold major conferences (attended by several thousand participants) in December 1920 and May 1921 were disrupted by the police and Iwasa was given a six months prison sentence when the organisation was banned and its journal prohibited. At this juncture Iwasa was even more popular than Ōsugi among the anarchists, although the latter's martyrdom in 1923 subsequently elevated his status to a prime position.

After Ōsugi was murdered by the military police in the chaos accompanying the Great Kantō Earthquake, Iwasa's 'pure anarchism' gradually became the dominant current within the Japanese anarchist movement. 'Pure anarchism' was not a term regularly employed by Iwasa and his comrades. They believed that their ideas represented authentic anarchism and hence that it was sufficient to refer to their doctrine simply as 'anarchism' or, when they wanted to be more specific, 'anarchist communism'. They were anarchists because they opposed state power and communists because they believed that the form of social organization which comes naturally to humans is one based on communal solidarity and mutual aid. Thus, echoing Kropotkin, they argued that 'Anarchy leads to Communism, and Communism to Anarchy'. (Kropotkin 1972: 61) It was their anarchist syndicalist opponents who sneeringly dubbed this doctrine 'pure anarchism', in an effort to ridicule what they regarded as the holier-than-thou attitude of, if not Iwasa, at least many of his young supporters. What caused the name to stick was that it certainly conveyed the intention of Iwasa and others to eliminate from anarchism extraneous elements, such as syndicalism.

The theories of 'pure anarchism' were mainly formulated by two people – Iwasa and Hatta Shūzō, with Hatta playing the more important role in this respect. Not only did Hatta write more profusely than Iwasa, but he was also a more systematic and innovative thinker, whose writings ranged over a wide area of economic, sociological and philosophical investigation. Indeed, Hatta was widely regarded among the 'pure anarchists' as 'the greatest theoretician of anarchist communism in Japan'. (Hatta 1981: 309) Nevertheless, despite being somewhat overshadowed by Hatta as a writer, Iwasa did make original contributions to the theories of 'pure anarchism'. Iwasa's role in this regard will be exemplified by reference to his 'labour union mountain bandit theory'. Before examining this, however, it is worth stressing that Iwasa's popularity within the anarchist movement and the high regard in which he was held did not derive from a reputation for bookish learning. Even on paper, Iwasa adopted an unadorned and chatty style of writing, but it was above all through the spoken word, and in his everyday dealings with his comrades, that he built up support for his ideas and came to exert influence on theoretical questions. Although it was natural that Iwasa's negative evaluation of labour unions should have provoked criticism from anarchist syndicalists, given their entirely different assessment of the efficacy of union organisation, such was Iwasa's rapport with rank and file workers that many responded positively to his denunciation of the very movement which was supposed to represent their interests. As his fellow anarchist, Kawamoto Kenji, commented:

> Bearing in mind the situation of workers, who usually have no opportunity to read books and are not endowed with knowledge, Iwasa Rō adopted the frame of mind of the workers and explained anarchism in a friendly fashion so that it was easily understood and could be simply grasped. Yet what stood out about his approach was that at its core was a superlative and well thought out theory of anarchism. (Museifushugi Undō 10 April 1967: 2)

In his 'labour union mountain bandit theory', Iwasa distinguished between the 'labour movement' and the 'mass workers' movement'. By 'labour movement' Iwasa meant the union movement of a minority of urban, male workers who occupied a relatively advantageous position within the working class. According to Iwasa, what characterized this movement was its incorporation into capitalism as a labour aristocracy and its reformist concern with maintaining its privileges relative to the rest of the working class. The analogy of a gang of mountain bandits was introduced to convey the relationship which, Iwasa argued, existed between the capitalists and this 'labour movement'. Just as squabbles might occur between a bandit chief and his henchmen, with the latter harbouring the ambition to lead the gang themselves, so the 'labour movement' was likely to clash with the capitalist class. Yet, to continue with the analogy, just as whoever might seize the leadership of a gang of mountain bandits would have no influence on their pillaging relationship with the surrounding villages, so whichever side emerged victorious from the class struggle between the capitalists and the 'labour movement' would leave the basically exploitative nature of society unaffected. By way of contrast, Iwasa insisted that the 'mass workers' movement' encompassed the vast majority of working men and women, both in the towns and in the countryside. It did not depend on union organization, since, whether 'organized' or not, what defined the working masses as a 'movement' were their common experiences of exploitation and oppression. Likewise, since the working masses had no privileges to maintain within capitalism, the logic of their disadvantaged position would lead them to seek revolutionary solutions to their problems. (Crump 1993: III ff)

Iwasa's 'labour union mountain bandit theory' lent itself well to 'pure anarchist' criticism of syndicalism. The importance which anarchist syndicalists attached to the union form of organization, their essentially urbanized and industrial vision of an alternative society, and their ambition to take over the capitalist means of production and maintain them so that they could be used for different purposes, were all cited as evidence that (like the Bolsheviks) they intended to substitute themselves for the capitalists but not fundamentally to eradicate capitalism. It was maintained that syndicalism would leave intact capitalism's division of labour, its privileging of production relative to consumption, its centralization of power and its advantaging of the towns over the countryside. Such theoretical arguments lay behind the rising tension between 'pure anarchists' and anarchist syndicalists which was such a marked feature of Japanese anarchism in the latter half of the 1920s.

In 1926 two nationwide anarchist federations were formed which each had several thousand members and were thus larger than any previous organizations the anarchists had set up. The Black Youth League (*Kokushoku Seinen Renmei*, or *Kokuren* for short) was founded in January 1926 as a group of young militants in the Kantō area, but it soon expanded into a nationwide federation with members in all age groups. Four months later, the All-Japan Libertarian Federation of Labour Unions (*Zenkoku Rōdō Kumiai Jiyū Rengōkai*, or *Zenkoku Jiren* for short) held its founding conference on 24 May 1926. Starting with 8,400 members, it reached a peak membership of 16,300 in 1931. (Crump 1993: 69 ff) Within the space of two years, the anarchist syndicalists were driven out of *Kokuren* and *Zenkoku Jiren* by the 'pure anarchist' majority in these federations, the final split occurring at the latter organization's reconvened second conference on 17–18 March 1928. Iwasa was absent from this conference and hence played no direct part in the split between 'pure anarchists' and anarchist syndicalists. This was because in 1927 he had been invited by some Chinese anarchists to take part in their activities in Fukien and Shanghai. Responding to this invitation, Iwasa was away from Japan for two years, during which he participated in the armed struggle prosecuted by the anarchists in Fukien and taught at the Labour University in Shanghai. (Museifushugi Undō 10 April 1967: 1)

Since Iwasa did not return to Japan until November 1929, he was not directly involved in the confrontations between 'pure anarchists' and anarchist syndicalists which led to their organizational separation over the next six years, but his influence was nevertheless felt due to the 'labour union mountain bandit theory'. After the anarchist syndicalists withdrew from its ranks in March 1928, *Zenkoku Jiren* remained a federation of labour unions, but its activity was in marked contrast to that castigated by Iwasa as typical of the 'labour movement'. *Zenkoku Jiren* continually sought to direct the attention of the workers beyond immediate struggles over wages and working conditions to the ultimate battle to establish a new society. Similarly, although *Zenkoku Jiren*'s members were mostly industrial workers in the big cities, its aim was to dissolve both existing industries and urban centres in order to replace them with a network of autonomous communes, each of which would be a balanced amalgam of fields, factories and workshops, as Kropotkin had put it. (Kropotkin 1974)

From 1931 anarchism in Japan was increasingly put on the defensive as, following the Manchurian Incident in September of that year, militarization and repression intensified. As the state's vice closed on the anarchist movement, particularly some of the younger activists were inclined to grasp at illusionary solutions to the dilemma which faced them. One such illusion was the belief that Bolshevik organizational methods would provide a defence against the state's intention to crush the anarchists. This was the line of thought that lay behind the ill-fated attempt by Aizawa Hisao and others to launch the Anarchist Communist Party of Japan (*Nihon Museifu Kyōsantō*) in 1934. (Crump 1993: 180 ff) Iwasa was scornful of the idea that Bolshevik methods could be made to serve anarchist ends, denouncing such illusions as 'complete rubbish'. (Crump 1993: 183) In this respect his assessment proved correct, since the Anarchist Communist Party's conspiratorial methods led to the destruction of the entire anarchist movement in 1935–6 as the state unleashed a wave of terror.

Although Iwasa was perceptive with regard to the contradictions inherent in anarchists resorting to Bolshevik organizational methods, this was a difficult time for all anarchists and he did not avoid committing mistakes of his own. In February 1937 an essay entitled *Outline of the Theory of the State (Kokka Ron Taikō)* was published over his name. In this essay Iwasa appeared to be offering an olive branch to the advocates of nationalism and statism. For example, at one point he posed the rhetorical question: 'isn't it only our unique Great Japanese Empire which is a naturally generated state and the others which are all artificially constructed states, no matter whether they are monarchical or democratic?' (Iwasa 1974: 337) Some anarchists, such as Ōshima Eizaburō, denied that Iwasa was the author of *Outline of the Theory of the State*, arguing that it was a forgery perpetrated by the 'special police' and rightists. (Iwasa 1982: 180; Iwasa 1984: 44) However, a more likely explanation is that the reason Iwasa wrote *Outline of the Theory of the State* was that he was trying to create some ideological space within which anarchism could survive, despite the prevailing climate of hysterical nationalism. If this was his intention, he did not succeed. From 1936 organized anarchist activity became impossible. After a failed attempt to make a living by opening a café (*yakitoriya*) in Tōkyō in 1935, Iwasa returned to his native village and eked out an existence by growing his own food during the years of the Second World War. (Yomiuri Shimbun 29 December 1935: 7)

POSTWAR YEARS

Iwasa was already an old man of 66 when the war ended, but he nevertheless threw himself into the efforts to relaunch the anarchist movement. The Japanese Anarchist Federation (*Nihon Anakisuto Renmei*) was formed in May 1946 and Iwasa was elected chairman of its National Committee. Throughout all the trials and tribulations brought about by his political beliefs, Iwasa was always deeply conscious of what he regarded as 'the honour of being an anarchist communist', (Kakumei Shisō 16 June 1951) but he neither sought nor received either honour or rewards for occupying one of the 'top' posts in the Japanese Anarchist Federation. He was well known for advising others 'you mustn't go about thinking of yourselves as important [*erai*]' and, in that respect, he led by example. (Museifushugi Undō 10 April 1967: 3) The job of chairing the National Committee was unpaid and arduous, involving endless organizational work and much travelling across the length and breadth of Japan. On these journeys Iwasa thought nothing of regularly hanging placards round his neck to advertise anarchist journals, for as he explained: 'Since I'm an old person and can't be as active as I might, I want to be of some use to the movement by selling newspapers with a signboard slung round my body. (Museifushugi Undō 10 April 1967: 3) His lack of affectation was also revealed by the fact that, when he was not away on propaganda trips, he lived with his wife, Fumie, in a converted country temple (*yamadera*) growing potatoes and pumpkins for food. (Museifushugi Undō 10 April 1967: 1)

Despite the best efforts of Iwasa and his comrades, the anarchist movement was unable to attain the sizeable proportions it had achieved in pre-war days. This had less to do with any deficiencies on the part of the anarchists than it had with the altered circumstances in which they now operated. In the early post-war years Japanese society was politically polarized between the Left and the Right, with the anarchists targeted from both sides. They were discriminated against on account of the policy of 'anticommunism' which both the American Occupation authorities and the Japanese government pursued (not a few anarchists were victims of the 'red purge', for example) (Hagiwara

1969: 192) while in the unions and elsewhere anarchists were frequently obstructed and all but silenced by the control exercised by Communist Party and other officials. In addition, first land reform and then rapid economic growth changed Japanese society in ways that were disadvantageous to anarchism. In pre-war days the 'pure anarchists' in particular had seen the tenant farmers as the core of any potential movement for achieving anarchist communism. However, post-war land reform eliminated both landlords and tenants as significant social groups and created instead a politically conservative class of land-owning, small farmers who were incorporated into the networks supporting the Liberal Democratic Party and its fore-runners. Similarly, high economic growth uprooted people from their long-established village communities and deposited them as factory-fodder and office-fodder in anomic, urban con-glomerations where only the crass pursuit of consumerism offered any compensation for the vanished solidarity and mutual aid on which rural life had depended.

The expectations triggered by the end of the war had induced anarchists of all persuasions to sink their differences and from 1946 to cooperate under the umbrella of the Japanese Anarchist Federation. However, as changing social conditions brought difficulties and frustration, so the old tensions between anarchist syndicalists and 'pure anarchists' resurfaced. In May 1950 an Anarcho-Syndicalist Group (*Anaruko Sanjikarisuto Gurūpu*) was formed and in June 1951 the Japanese Anarchist Club (*Nihon Anakisuto Kurabu*) was organised. The latter was essentially anarchist communist in its orientation and at its centre were Iwasa Sakutarō and other veterans of the pre-war 'pure anarchist' wing of the movement. From September 1951 the Japanese Anarchist Club started to publish the journal *Anarchist Club* (*Anakisuto Kurabu*) and, passing through various changes of name to first *Anarchist News* (*Museifu Shimbun*) and later *Anarchist Movement* (*Museifushugi Undō*), this continued to be published until March 1980, long after Iwasa had died in February 1967. For as long as it existed, the Japanese Anarchist Club and its journal adhered to the theory and practice of anarchist communism which was grounded in Kropotkin's writings of the 1880s and 1890s, had first been introduced to Japan by Kōtoku in the 1900s, and which had been adapted and refined to meet Japanese conditions by Hatta, Iwasa and others in the 1920s and 1930s. That this doctrine has survived into the 1980s and 1990s, in a period when each successive phase of capitalism has taken Japan further away from everything that anarchist communists regard as important, is testimony in part to the lasting influence of Iwasa's intellectual and, above all, moral stature.

When Iwasa died in 1967 his comrades tried, individually and collectively, to summarize the essence of the man and his thought. In a commemorative issue of *Anarchist Movement,* his comrades eulogised Iwasa as someone who had 'spent his whole life as a warrior fighting humankind's battle without end' and Ōshima Eizaburō spoke for many when he declared 'a giant has fallen'. (Museifushugi Undō 10 April 1967: 4–5) Yet, at the same time that they recognized Iwasa's heroic proportions, none of them overlooked the childlike simplicity, honesty and integrity which had characterized him and which had worked to make him a figure of affection rather than of awe. Thus, while Yamaga Taiji remembered the 'Comrade Iwasa Sakutarō whom all of us who called ourselves anarchists held in esteem as high as the mountains and the stars', Mochizuki Kei recalled that 'Iwasa had a gentle personality which inspired love and affection from everybody'. (Museifushugi Undō 10 April 1967: 1, 4) Even political opponents, such as Yamakawa Kikue, recollected Iwasa as an 'eternal youth', on account of his ready laugh and general disposition, while others who had met him only once or twice still called to mind a man who epitomized 'the very model of what an anarchist should be'. (Museifushugi Undō 10 April 1967: 2–3)

CONCLUSION

Clearly, the Iwasa Sakutarō who has been described in this article was far removed from the conventional type of political leader. Although the article started by listing various qualities which Iwasa possessed that make for a successful Japanese politician, he refused to use those attributes for achieving political success. In that sense, Iwasa rejected leadership and this squared with his egalitarian and communal vision of what an anarchist com- munist society should be. Yet, as was made clear earlier, in another sense Iwasa was not opposed to leadership, since he believed that it was a minority of anarchist communists who would supply the intellectual spark and courageous audacity for the revolution. According to Iwasa, this minority was to be intimately connected with the mass of the people. Indeed, the minority would arise out of the masses, would enjoy no power or privileges separate from the masses and, far from being famous, would be composed of essentially 'anonymous people' (*mumei no hitobito*) who, in this sense, too, would be indistinguishable from the masses. Nevertheless, having laid down all these provisos and qualifications, Iwasa still insisted that the role of the minority of anarchist communists was crucial:

> Whatever the period, whatever the world of that time, these people equipped with initiatives and proposals are a minority. Furthermore, this minority are anonymous people (*mumei no hitobito*)! In the era of revolution which is coming, they will certainly be a minority and they will equally be anonymous. (Iwasa 1982: 137)

Why, in Iwasa's estimation, was this minority of anarchist communists so important? Essentially, the answer was that he believed they would think through, refine, and articulate in more systematic and therefore attractive form, the inchoate aspirations of the masses, who were assumed to be incapable of doing so themselves. Iwasa wrote:

> If this minority of anonymous people can make their ideas, in other words their initiatives and plans, coincide with the hopes and demands of the masses, and if without any sinister designs they are inspired by great ideals, the masses will not desert them. (Iwasa 1982: 138)

To this he added, in a passage which conveyed both his basic assumptions and the influences acting on him:

> The people with initiatives and plans are the wind. The masses are just like the grass. The grass will bend with the wind. (Iwasa 1982: 138)

The parallel here with Confucius' teaching in the *Analects* is striking. Confucius is reported as having said:

> In administering your government, what need is there for you to kill? Just desire the good yourself and the common people will be good. The virtue of the gentleman is like wind; the virtue of the small person is like grass. Let the wind blow over the grass and it is sure to bend. (Confucius 1979: xii, 19)

Out of this Confucian prescription for good government, Iwasa excised government itself and its attendant implications, such as a naturally hierarchical social order. What he retained was the basic division between a minority of 'gentlemen' (in his case, the anarchist communist revolutionaries) and the majority of 'small persons' (in his case, the masses of working men and women) at least for the duration of the revolutionary process which was expected to bring about anarchist communism. The drawbacks of this approach were twofold. First, it relied on the revolutionary minority not harbouring 'any sinister designs'. That Iwasa himself was free of such self-serving ambitions seems obvious enough from the foregoing account, but the same cannot be said of numerous other revolutionaries who, at different times and places, have appointed themselves to lead the masses to the promised land. Requiring the masses to trust the good intentions of their leaders is a strategy fraught with peril, as history has repeatedly shown. Second, as was mentioned earlier, there is a fundamental contradiction in relying on leaders (even anarchist communist leaders) to achieve the leaderless condition of anarchist communism. For that reason, Iwasa should have recognized that Confucianism is not adaptable for anarchist communist purposes. To stick to the Confucian metaphor, for anarchist communism to come about, it would take more than the wind to bend the grass. Wind and grass would have to become one; the masses would have to be anarchist communists. In Iwasa's day, this no doubt seemed virtually as improbable as it would have been 2,500 years earlier in the time of Confucius himself, since society remained composed very largely of ignorant peasants, with little education, a narrow range of experience and poorly developed conceptual powers. In the light of this, the post-war development of capitalism in Japan has brought mixed blessings. While it has destroyed so many of the rural communities which seemed in Iwasa's day to offer themselves for conversion into the communes favoured by anarchist communists, it has created a highly educated and accomplished population who are demonstrably far removed from the condition described by Confucius: 'the common people can be made to follow a path but not to understand it'. (Confucius 1979: viii, 9) Capitalist development has undermined the need for leadership and this should be particularly apparent to those, like anarchist communists, who wish to transcend capitalism.

BIBLIOGRAPHY

Confucius (1979) (translated by D. C. Lau) *The Analects* Harmondsworth: Penguin. (*Shōjin* has been amended to 'small person' in quotations from this source.)

Crump, J. (1983) *The Origins of Socialist Thought in Japan* Beckenham: Croom Helm.
Crump, J. (1993) *Hatta Shūzō and Pure Anarchism in Interwar Japan* Basingstoke: Macmillan.
Hagiwara, S. (1969) *Nihon Anakizumu Rōdō Undō Shi* Tōkyō: Gendai Shichō Sha.
Hatta, S. (1981) *Zenshū* Tōkyō: Kokushoku Sensen Sha.
Hikari (Meiji Shakaishugi Shiryō Shū no. 2) Tōkyō: Meiji Bunken Shiryō Kankōkai, 1960)
Iwasa, S. (1974) 'Kokka Ron Taikō', *Shisō Geppō* no. 34 Tōkyō: Shihōshō Keijikyoku Shisōbu; republished 1974.
Iwasa, S. (1982) *Kakumei Dansō* Tōkyō: Kokushoku Sensen Sha.
Iwasa, S. (1984) *Museifushugisha wa Kotaeru* Tōkyō: Kokushoku Sensen Sha.
Kropotkin, P. (1972) *The Conquest of Bread* New York: New York University Press.
Kropotkin, P. (1974) *Fields, Factories and Workshops* London: Allen & Unwin.
Nihon Anakisuto Kurabu Kikanshi Tōkyō: Kokushoku Sensen Sha, 1991.
Noguchi, Y. (1931) *Musan Undō Sō Tōshi Den* Tōkyō: Shakai Shisō Kenkyūjo. Reproduced in Iwasa (1982).
Suzuki, M. (1964) *Zaibei Shakaishugisha Museifushugisha Enkaku* Tōkyō: Kashiwa Shobō.

14

Strong Leaders: The Charismatic Founders of Japanese Utopian Communities[1]

CHRISTOPH BRUMANN

Leadership, the theme of this volume, is difficult to locate in the conventional pictures painted of Japanese society. Somewhat overstated, there are no leaders in Japan, there are only groups, and these, small and consensus-oriented as they are presumed to be, do not need a strong personality at the top in order to function smoothly. This is expressed clearly in one of the few general treatments of Japanese leadership, a section of Nakan Chies *Japanese Society* (1970: 63–80). Nakane presents what one is tempted to call the 'theory of the weak leaders.'

According to her, Japanese leaders (or superiors or directors; Nakane shifts between these terms) do not have to excel in objective qualities such as intelligence, efficiency, or merit. They will often reach their position automatically by way of the seniority system. In order to stay there and operate effectively what they need most are intimate personal ties to their subordinates. 'Consequently, Nakane states, 'it may be that Japanese soil cannot grow a charismatic leader, or, to put it in other words, a leader may exercise his charisma only through immediate personal relations (1970: 70–71). This makes leaders and subordinates mutually dependent. Leaders must always be ready to listen to their subordinates advice and to acknowledge the importance of their support; at the least, they must be given compensation for their lack of opportunity to rise to the top themselves, since they are often no less qualified by objective standards. In effect, the domains of activity of leaders and subordinates overlap to a large extent. Probably the best metaphor for what Nakane has in mind is a concave mirror. Leaders simply bundle what comes up to them via vertical and concatenated *oyabun-koban* relationships and cast it back into the group, focusing but not distorting too much. They must be careful to be weak rather than overwhelming.

UTOPIAN COMMUNITIES IN JAPAN

In this paper, I shall assess the validity of Nakanes statements with regard to the charismatic founders and leaders of four Japanese utopian communities. I define such communities (also called communal groups, communitarian groups, or communes) as groups formed by not exclusively kin-related men and women who live and work together and share their property on idealistic grounds. This is almost always done with a utopian purpose: the explicit wish is to create a model for a better society that is often expected to be adopted globally after having been successfully implemented on a small scale. Well-known examples include the kibbutzim in Israel, the Hutterite colonies in North America, the Findhorn Community in Scotland and historical cases such as Brook Farm, New Harmony, Oneida Community and the Shakers in the nineteenth-century United States.

Modern Japan has been the site of a fair number of such experiments, although this is not widely known, either among the general public or by Japan specialists.[2] Most of these communities were founded independently, and religious as well as secular motivations stand behind them. When compared to utopian communities in Western countries, the Japanese communes distinguish themselves not so much by their number but by their longevity: the oldest, *Ittō-en*, dates back to 1913, which makes it only a little younger than the first kibbutz. The second oldest, *Atarashiki mura*, was founded in 1918; it is the best known because of its connection with novelist Mushakōji Saneatsu and the Shirakaba writers. While these groups and several others are in decline today, another group initiated in 1958, *Yamagishi-kai*, has grown to one of the most vital communal movements in the world. It is now a federation of about 40 settlements, with more than 2000 inhabitants throughout Japan and several branches in Asian, North American and European countries.

Eight of the nine utopian communities I came in contact with have been founded and guided by a charismatic leader.[3] It is fitting, therefore, to ask whether the common social form also entails commonalities among the leaders, and, furthermore, whether these conform to Nakane's picture of Japanese leadership. Before pursuing this question, I will present brief biographical sketches of four of the communes leaders, Nishida Tenkō, Ozaki Masutarō, Yaoi Nisshō, and Fukuzato Niwa.

THE FOUR LEADERS

Nishida Tenkō

Nishida Tenkō was born in 1872 in Nagahama (Shiga Prefecture).[4] The son of a wealthy paper and cloth merchant, he followed in the family business at age 19. He left this occupation only two years later to take over the leadership of an agricultural colonization project in Hokkaidō, moving there together with some one hundred peasant families. At that time, this was the only legal way to avoid conscription for the impending war against Russia. Soon, however, Nishida found himself in an inextricable double bind. He had invested his money into the project and felt responsible towards the other investors, but at the same time he lived and worked with the pioneers and shared their joys and sorrows. Both parties to the project, capital and labour, wanted the best conditions for themselves, and Nishida felt torn apart by their incompatible demands. After six years, he cut off his middle finger, wrote a letter of resignation to the investors with his blood and left the colony.

Little has been written about the next few years of his life. Throughout this time he was searching for a way to avoid the competitiveness of the human struggle for existence. For a while, he stayed as a Zen monk in Nanzenji temple in Kyoto. In 1905, he read Lev Tolstois autobiographical essay, *My Religion* and was deeply impressed by this description of a life crisis overcome with the help of a strengthened Christian belief. The sentence, 'Die if you want to live, especially moved him. He decided to take it literally and expire from his old life by leaving his wife and two sons behind and trusting his destiny to Heaven. Alone in a small temple, he was determined to fast and die of hunger if there were no other way to begin a new existence.

In the third night of his fast, he heard a crying baby, followed by silence. He pictured a mother nursing her child and realized in this the ideal state of human existence. The mother gave to the child what nature had provided for, and the happiness of both was not affected by any competitiveness. Being content with natures free blessings could end human conflicts. The next day, Nishida left the temple. He went to the house of an acquaintance where he started to do all kinds of menial work, declining all food offers and asking only for the rice baked to the bottom of the pot that usually would be washed away. During the following years, he led a nomadic life, moving from house to house and offering his services free of charge. He came to be considered as a madman by his relatives but was admired by others, who eventually assembled and started to share his way of life. (Nishida 1971: 76–92; 1183: 45–58)

In 1913, the small group was given a house in Kyoto as a present and thereby became a sedentary commune, named *Ittō-en* ('Garden of the One light). In 1919, Nishida introduced *Rokuman Gyōgan* ('60,000 Prayers), i.e. free toilet cleaning in the households of strangers. For him and his followers this was an exercise in humility and the most effective way to world peace. After Nishida published his bestselling book *Zange no seikatsu* ('Life of Repentance) two years later, the group became famous, and membership rose sharply in a short time. In 1928 the group moved to its present location in the outskirts of Kyoto, which had been given as a donation by one of Nishidas admirers.

Ittō-en has had up to 350 members but now is down to 135. It adheres to a self-fashioned religion that venerates *o-hikari* ('the light), an abstract divinity equated with nature and the essence of all religions. Buddhist ingredients are most prominent, but Christian elements have also been incorporated. The commune constitutes a village in itself and operates several companies; agricultural research, construction and printing are most important. The members receive a little pocket money, but other than this all property is held in common, in keeping with Nishida's tenet of *fu-bunpai* ('no distribution), which in his eyes circumvents the antagonism of capital and labour.

Nishida was unpretentious in his relations with the members and was affectionately addressed as '*Tennō-san* by them, which was his adopted first name. He was often active outside the community, engaging mostly in free service, but also spending time on lecture tours and in a six-year term as a member of *Sangiin* (the upper house of Japans parliament) immediately after World War II. Nishida always wore a black traditional garment, lived with his second wife in a three-mat room and claimed never to have acted according to his own will, faithfully responding to the requests of others instead. Each New Years Eve, he left the community to return to what he called his real home, the wayside. Delegates of the community would find him cleaning the precincts of Heian Shrine the next day and beg him to come back into the commune for another year.

Although much administrative authority must have been delegated to other members, Nishida nevertheless was the undisputed ruler of the community and stood behind all important decisions. Life-size sculptures were erected even during his lifetime, and he did not mind appearing adorned with the regalia of a Buddhist abbot on solemn occasions. When he died in 1968, he left a gap that – as his successor, his grandson, is the first to acknowledge – is difficult to fill. *Ittō-en* has decided to immortalize its founder rather than take a progressive course. Thus, now the visitor may stroll through a museum presenting Nishida and his achievements and choose among many books written by and about him but will rarely witness members rendering free service any longer.

Ozaki Masutarō

Ozaki Masutarō was born in 1900 in the Yamato plains near Sakurai (Nara Prefecture). (Plath 1969, Sugihara 1973) As the younger son of a peasant family he was trained as a missionary of Tenri-kyō and afterward worked as such in Osaka. Soon, however, he was troubled by doubts, mainly about the missionaries practice of living on the contributions of the believers. In addition, his daughter fell seriously ill and remained mentally handicapped, a tragic event for which the Tenri religion offered him no consolation.

In 1936, Ozaki resigned from his office and returned to a peasants life in his home village. Convinced of Tenri-kyō's shortcomings, he caused a scandal by destroying the wooden altars of Tenri believers and burning them to heat his bathing water. In addition, Ozakis overly outspoken personal criticism caused a break with an old friend, the most influential farmer of the village. Soon Ozaki was ostracized (*mura hachibu*), together with four families that were loyal to him. The other villagers did not speak with them any more and excluded them from the indispensable reciprocal support in agriculture.

Under these circumstances, the outcasts drew together and in a purportedly unplanned way came to live communally over the next years. They concentrated their houses in one location and shared their land, working power, livestock, harvest and finally also clothes and bathing water. Ozaki knew how to get around obstacles; when he learned that the family fathers gave preferential treatment to their own ox at feeding time, he decided to sell all the oxen and buy new ones, now as common property.

Ill treatment by the other villagers did not subside, however, and in 1943 the group started to emigrate to Manchuria to evade it. Within two years, Japan had lost the war, and the emigrants were forced to return. Back in the old village, the group, which had absorbed several wartime refugees, lost some of its already scarce holdings in the land reform. To survive, the members tried *tatami* manufacture. After many frustrating experiences, the group became successful at this – in fact, it became the largest maker of *tatami* in Japan. Buying rice straw from their neighbours as raw material made the outcasts respectable again, and Ozaki was even elected village headman (*kuchō*). The group now enjoyed an affluent life-style, but not satisfied with luxury alone, it started to take in mentally-handicapped adults as members in 1966. At present, these comprise about three-quarters of the 180 members. Treating them as nearly as possible like anybody else is the one proclaimed principle the group follows; other than that it is not bound to any creed or ideology. As suggested by its name *Shinkyō dōjin* ('People of the Same State of Mind/Heart), or *Shinkyō* for short, emotional compatibility is seen to be holding the commune together.

According to the members, Ozaki was the benevolent dictator of the commune throughout its existence. He consulted with a childhood friend and with his common-law second wife, both of them founding members, but others in the group were more likely to be presented with established facts, preferably very early in the morning at spontaneous meetings for which Ozaki had awoken them. They emphasize that this seemed most natural to them, for they had complete trust in Ozaki and were never disappointed. Opposition resulted from the decision to take in handicapped members, but Ozaki prevailed and a few of the rebellious members left the commune. Although it must have been foreseeable, it came as a severe shock to the members when Ozaki became bed-ridden in 1992 and died a year later. They realize that they will have to implement more democratic procedures now, but in the face of growing age and dwindling numbers the future seems uncertain.

Yaoi Nisshō

The third leader, Yaoi Nisshō, was born into a landowners family near Nara in 1911. (Ueno 1985; Tsushima 1973) From his female ancestors he had inherited a special sensitivity for the supernatural which made itself felt for the first time when he was 15 years old. Much against his own will at first, he felt compelled to act according to the orders given him by beings of the spiritual world (*reikai*). After graduating from the Imperial University in Tokyo (*Teikoku daigaku*), he worked as a *kendō* teacher in Nara. When World War II broke out, he escaped the draft because of a presumed mortal illness; thereafter he felt obliged to give something in return for having been spared. Once again in Tokyo, he moved into a suspected haunted house to open an orphanage. He aroused the suspicion of the secret police because of his contacts with dissident general Ishihara Kanji and because of his lectures questioning the legitimacy of the imperial house. After the spirits warned him that Tokyo would be bombed soon, Yaoi returned to Nara and started to till his familys fields.

On 15 August 1945, Yaoi listened to the radio broadcast of the emperors capitulation speech. With gloomy thoughts, he went to a nearby Shintō shrine. There, a spirit addressed him and ordered him to found a religion; soon afterwards, Yaoi, started to preach in the streets of Osaka. Former convicts, the homeless and war orphans assembled around him; he took all to his house in the countryside. When his family complained, he removed himself from the household headship and, together with his charge, moved to the present site of the commune – an undeveloped strip of land owned by his family. The group built a house and started to clear and farm the land, suffering from stark poverty in the beginning. Up to 60 persons assembled around Yaoi. In time, they came to call their settlement *Ō-yamato ajisai mura* ('Great Yamato Hydrangea Villaga). Since many orphans had joined, a welfare institution was founded in 1956 which brought in financial support from the prefectural government. In the following years, an old peoples home and an institution for the mentally handicapped were added; today, these are the mainstays of the communitys income. Ordinary business enterprises in printing and construction have also been started. In the 1980s, nearly all the buildings on the ground were rebuilt, and a large hospital and a worship hall are the latest additions.

Most of the people living and/or working in *Ō-yamato ajisai*

mura do not share their property. This is restricted to a circle of
about 30 persons including Yaoi and his wife. Although they
pool their salaries, families live in separate households and do
not live very differently from ordinary Japanese, cooking and
cleaning for themselves. I was assured that their communal
arrangement is only for convenience sake and that it will likely
fade out with the deaths of the present members. Other people
also live in the small village; they are mainly those descendants
of commune members who prefer to keep their finances separate.

Yaoi Nisshō, still healthy and vivacious in 1993, is the founder
and head of the religious corporation *Ō-yamato-kyō* ('Great
Yamato Religion). It lacks a well-defined dogma and organizational structure and can best be described as a folk version of
shintō with a strong shamanistic element. Yaoi regularly contacts
shintō gods, animal spirits or the souls of deceased, often on
behalf of sick or spirit-possessed clients and aided by several
women who serve as media. Yaoi also is on close terms with the
spirits of many prominent historical figures such as Shōtoku
Taishi, Nichiren, Oda Nogunaga and Emperor Meiji. Most
important among these is Empress Kōmyō, who in the eighth
century built houses for the poor and hospitals where she
nursed leprosy patients herself. Yaoi believes that the empress
used to live at the site of the community and explains his welfare
commitment as being commanded by her.

Subscribing to Yaoi's peculiar beliefs, however, has never been
a prerequisite for joining the commune, and many members are
not interested in spirit religion. Not a few of them came in great
distress and look up to Yaoi as a benevolent and highly charismatic father figure who has always responded generously to the
requests of the needy. Yaoi says that the name of the commune
was selected by Empress Kōmyō. The hydrangea (*ajisai*), with its
multicoloured petals as diverse as the villages members, is a
symbol for the spirit of tolerance to be realised in the village.

Fukuzato Niwa

The only female commune leader I learned about is Fukuzato
Niwa. (Fukuzato 1986; Veno 1988) She was born in a rural area
of Miyazaki Prefecture in 1919. As the youngest of ten children,
she was educated by an aunt in Osaka and suffered especially
from being separated from her mother. She had a successful
rehearsal for the Takarazuka revue theatre, but her family withheld notice of this from her. At the age of 16, she eloped to

Taiwan, then a Japanese colony. There, she came to know Fukuzato Toshio, a colonial administration official and unconventional free-thinker whom she married a year later. After returning to Japan she became the mother of two children.

In quick succession, however, her husband and her son died, leaving her a widow in her early twenties with a fatherless daughter. Instead of staying with her husbands family, she preferred to start out on a professional career of her own. Whether as an insurance agent, coffee-shop manager, journalist or jewellery saleswoman, she became remarkably successful within months, but lost interest in her job equally fast and switched to some other occupation. She constantly felt a lack of purpose in life.

This continued for over a decade, until in 1957 she came in contact with Yamagishi-kai, the largest Japanese communal movement (mentioned above). In one of its introductory psychodynamic courses, the sentence 'I am nobodys property (*watashi wa dare no mono de mo nai*) occurred and it struck her deeply. She joined the organization, and a year later, when the first communes were founded, she started to live with the groups charismatic leader Yamagishi Miyozō.

In 1961, Fukuzato Niwa was again bereft by Yamagishis untimely death. She held a cautious position in the ensuing leadership struggle, maintaining that Yamagishis philosophy still needed further refinement before being presented to the world. The majority, however, considered it complete and voted for immediate expansion. Consequently, Fukuzato left Yamagishi-kai in 1964 to form her own commune of 80 members.

Now, her luck failed her and the group went bankrupt because of business ventures she has proposed. She was hospitalized at the same time because of cancer which was to continuously recur. A few of the members stayed with her, worked off the debts and formed a new commune in 1970, named *Fukuzato tetsugaku jikkenjō* ('Fukuzato Philosophy Laboratory). They soon opened a roadside restaurant which has sustained them ever since. Fukuzato Niwa died in 1984. Her daughter Miwako followed in her position – less dominating than her mother but the acknowledged leader of the small and virtually unchanged group of 27 persons.

Members reminiscences focus on Fukuzato Niwas psychic strength and commanding presence. Her heroic struggle against cancer is much admired. It seems likely that it often removed her from the practical affairs of the commune, yet when she was well, she took a powerful lead in the many mutual-improvement meetings and freely rebuked the faults of other members. She did not spare herself, however. When punishing her daughter and grand-daughter for some egotistic offense, she made them stand outside the house with a cardboard sign specifying their sin hung around their necks, but in spite of her weakened condition she also stood, facing and watching them. Fukuzato Niwa also was the chief ideologue of the group; printed lectures of hers and a book she dictated on her death-bed (Fukuzato, 1986) were recommended to me as the best expressions of the groups secular faith. Her connection to the late Yamagishi Miyozō adds to her charismatic appeal and is regarded as a guarantee that her interpretation of his philosophy is superior to rival versions.

COMMON FEATURES OF THE FOUR LEADERS

The four leaders biographies are unconventional and colourful, especially when set against the background of a society where individuals often follow very predictable pathways through life. Despite idiosyncracies, however, the leaders careers and rôles share some features which I will attempt to expound.

All four of them lived inconspicuous lives until they were in their thirties; Ozaki and Nishida were in leadership positions. Applying conventional standards, Nishida, Ozaki and Fukuzato seem to have been successful. (It is unclear whether professional success was important to Yaoi since he could rely on his familys property.) All four leaders, however, felt uneasy about their activities. Nishida and Ozaki came to perceive a sense of insufficiency that did not so much result from an objective lack of competence for their tasks but rather from the strict moral judgement they applied to themselves. This made it impossible for Nishida to compromise when satisfying both sides of the pioneer venture was impossible, or, for the missionary Ozaki, to live off of other people's largesse. The decision to break with the old life did not come suddenly but rather after a prolonged crisis in their lives, with a dramatic climax in Nishida's fast in the temple. The crisis was less pronounced in the two other cases but still present. Fukuzatos business career was accompanied by persistent uneasiness. Yaoi struggled with the spirits demands on him for a long time and often had to consent against his own will.

The leaders' eventual break with their old lives was swift and complete. It was accentuated by sudden dramatic (endogenous or exogenous) revelations and spectacular and controversial action, with the leaders losing no time in concretely demonstrating their new callings. Nishida had a liberating vision in the temple and turned to a homeless life of service. Ozaki quit the missionary service, crushed altars and alienated his fellow villagers. Yaoi, commanded by the spirits, preached in the streets and took care of the needy, estranging his family. Fukuzatos break-through experience was induced by the Yamagishi followers, but she also immediately became active, immersing herself in the organisation and rising to become one of its most influential members. Old partners were left behind: Nishida, Ozaki and Fukuzato lost their spouses by divorce or death but found new ones in their utopian ventures. Yaois wife stayed with him, but not the rest of his family. Moreover, the leaders developed habits that would be regarded as eccentric by most of their countrypeople. Mishidas wore somewhat monkish-looking, unconventional clothes; Yaoi sports a long white beard and often wears traditional garments; and Fukuzato donned dresses and accessories more appropriate for a film star than for an elderly Japanese lady. Ozaki also failed to conform to standard expectations by addressing the communes visitors in an unusually outspoken way very different from what social etiquette normally requires.

While many elements of these careers are common ingredients of charismatic leadership everywhere and while to some extent the biographies may have been teleologically refashioned, the particular stress on action in all of them is peculiar. Radical action stands at the beginning of the new life, and when in time a following gathered around the charismatic leaders, these were again trusted and admired for what they did and not only for what they preached. Ozaki worked fervently and untiringly with the other members. Nishida led the life of repentance he demanded and always emphasized that his religion required selfless deeds. Yaoi was generous in helping many destitute people, regardless of whether they shared his religious convictions or not. Fukuzato showed resolve and self-discipline when fighting her disease and admonishing erring members, while still showing them that she cared for them. Teachings and actual conduct were in accord in all four cases, and it is safe to assume that this sincerity, more than any other feature, made up the leaders charisma in the eyes of their followers.

The leaders of Japanese communes not discussed here are very similar in this regard, but charismatic leaders in other areas of Japanese society often differ. The founders and leaders of the many new religions (*shinkō shūkyō* or *shin-shūkyō*) usually are venerated for their spiritual or magical powers, often being mouthpieces for deities that deliver messages through them rather than being leaders making independent decisions. Yaois divine revelations and his function as counsellor and healer come closest to this pattern, but he and the other religious leader Nishida are very critical of the tight organization and the centrality of fund-raising activities that characterize many of the conventional new religions. Selfless action of *shin-shūkyō* leaders, in contrast to Nishida and Yaoi, often restricts itself to acquiring divine blessing for the believers; leaders enjoy substantial privileges and are very much removed from the rank and file. Moreover, while Yaoi maintains close relations to the supernatural, neither he nor Nishida raise the claims to divinity that are so common among new religions leaders (Hori, 1968: 224 fn. 9, 228–9; Thomsen, 1963: 86) who frequently declare themselves either receptacles for divine beings or even living gods (*ikigami*).

To some extent, this difference can be explained by the requirements of utopian communities which are far smaller than most new religions and demand a more total involvement by their adherents. Since the members live in close quarters with their leaders, any gap between ideal and reality will be noticed immediately. But even under such conditions, the leaders of some North American and European communes became kings rather than saints, often according themselves all kinds of material, social, and sexual prerogatives. Well-known examples are John Humphrey Noyes of Oneida Community in New York State (1844–1881, see Carden, 1971; Thomas, 1977) and Otto Mühl of AAO (short for Aktionsanalytische Organisation) centering on the Friedrichshof in Austria (1968–1990, see Martin, 1990). In contrast, the privileges enjoyed by the Japanese communes leaders can be termed modest at best.

The loyalty of the followers is not restricted to the leaders lifetimes. Fukuzato and Nishida are posthumously honoured with publications; Nishida even with a museum. None of the four leaders has been replaced by a comparable figure. Ozaki and Yaoi will very likely have no single successor. Nishida's grandson and Fukuzatos daughter have followed in their charismatic ancestors footsteps, but both willingly concede that they cannot measure up to them. Thus, loyalty to the founder is expressed both through the humbleness of the successor and the genetic continuity he or she embodies. Moreover, none of the communes has turned away from the founders ideals. An ageing and/or declining membership seems to be preferable to betraying the founders vision by introducing ideological changes. It is interesting that Yamagishi-kai succeeded in evolving beyond the founders shadow and started its growth period not earlier than almost a decade after his untimely death. Perhaps Yamagishi Miyozō's early death, only three years after the first communes had been started in 1958, helped in this regard. Yamagishis followers had had enough time to absorb his philosophy but had not yet become totally dependent on his leadership in practical matters. Not surprisingly, the founder plays only a minor rôle in the self-representation of Yamagishi-kai today.

WEAK LEADERSHIP REASSESSED

It is obvious that the four commune leaders considered here are not 'weak in Nakanes sense. Their geniality in everyday social interaction is praised by their followers, and it is likely that their charisma was, to a large extent, built on personal relationships with the members – according to Nakane the only way to actualize it in Japan. But Ozakis and Nishidas communes were large enough to make it difficult for the leaders to maintain intimate, *oyabun-kobun* ('patron-client)-style relationships with each member. In all four cases, more than social competence was involved: the leaders practical examples and sincerity were what attracted their followers. In their eyes, the leaders were powerful and colourful personalities true to their ideals and not just focal points in a social network.

This is not to deny that there is indeed a lot of 'weak leadership in Japan. The weak frontman is an established pattern in party politics, and the emperors have for centuries been honoured but excluded from real decision-making. In conventional walks of life, such as the work groups in companies Nakane seems to have in mind most of the time, superiors often try hard to find the least controversial solution. This tendency is certainly more pronounced than in many Western societies.

Nonetheless, weak leadership is not the all-encompassing paradigm Nakane sees in it. When breaking away from existing conditions as in times of change, strong leaders, often distinguished by radical and courageous action, may be more effective and are by no means uncommon in the Japanese past and present. Even if they fail, their memory is often honoured, as is the case with the popular tragic heroes of Japanese history (Morris, 1982). While established institutions in Japan may be even more inimical to the actualisation of personal charisma than elsewhere, starting something new (be it companies, Buddhist sects or dictators dynasties) seems to require all the more of that quality. New social theoretical formulations of leadership in Japan should take the strong pattern into account and would, like many other aspects of Japanese social life, benefit greatly from additional empirical research.

NOTES

1. I thank my colleagues Joachim Görlich and Hartmut Lang for their helpful comments on an earlier version.
2. But see the studies by Thomsen (1963: 221–234), Plath (1966, 1967, 1969), Davis (1974) and Plath's translation of the commune Shinkyō's autobiography (Sugihara and Plath 1969). Nonscientific overviews of Japanese utopian communities have also appeared (Fairfield 1972; Kusakari et al. 1977; *Asahigurafu* 1979). In previous work I describe the actual conditions of some of the communes and analyse their position in relation to the Japanese mainstream (Brumann 1992) and alternative culture (Brumann in press).
3. I conducted fieldwork in Japan during two-month stays in 1990 and 1993. It was supported by the Kölner Gymnasial- und Stiftungsfonds and by the William Weiss Stiftung, both Cologne. In all the communes I was received with cordial hospitality for which I am most grateful.
4. For details on Nishida and Ittō-en, see Kurokawa (1959), Thomsen (1963: 221–234), Byles (1965: 131–134, 160–174, 183–192), Davis (1974), Nishida (1971, 1983), and the overviews cited in Note 2. As with the following communes, I also make use of unpublished material I received and of the extensive interviews I conducted with members during my visits.

BIBLIOGRAPHY

Asahigurafu (ed.), (1979) *Nippon komyūn* Tokyo: Asahi Shinbunsha.
Brumann, Christoph, (1992), 'Kommunitäre Gruppen in Japan: Alternative Mikrogesellschaften als Kultureller Speigel, *Zeitschrift für Ethnologie*, Vol. 117, (119–138).
Brumann, Christoph, (in press), 'Alternativkultur in Japan, in *Lexikon der Japanischen Alltagskultur*, ed. by Peter Pörtner, Stuttgart: Kröner.
Bules, Marie Beuzeville, (1965), *Paths to Inner Calm*, London: Allen & Unwin.
Carden, Maren Lockwood, (1971), *Oneida: Utopian Community to Modern Corporation*, Balitmore: Johns Hopkins University Press.
Davis, Winston, (1974), 'Ittō-en: The Myths and Rituals of Liminality,

History of Religions, Vol. 14 (Part 1) (282–321) and in *History of Religions*, Vol. 15 (Part 2) (1–33).

Fairfield, Richard, (1972), *Communes, Japan*, San Francisco: Alternatives Foundation.

Fukuzato Niwa, (1986), *Zenjin kōfuku no dōhyō* [*Sign-posts toward Happiness for All Humanity*], Kōsei: (Japan): Fukuzato tetsugaku jikkenjō.

Hori, Ichirō, *Folk Religion in Japan: Continuity and Change*, (1968), Chicago: University of Chicago Press.

Kurokawa, Colbert N., *What is Itto-en? Its Theory and Practice*, (1959), Kyoto: Ittō-en.

Kusakari, Zenzo, Michael M. Steinbach and Moshe Matsuba, (1977), *The Communes of Japan: The Kibbutz on the Other Side of the World*, Imaichi Nihon Kyōdōtai Kyōkai [Japanese Commune Association],.

Martin, Carmelo, (1990), 'El final de la utopia: La antigua comuna austriaca de La Gomera defenestra a su fundador y abandona el sexo y la filosofia libertaria, in *El Pais Domongo*, 30 September 1990 (10–11).

Morris, Ivan, (1982), *The Nobility of Failure: Tragic Heroes in the History of Japan*, Tokyo: Tuttle.

Nakane, Chie, (1970), *Japanese Society*, London: Houghton Mifflin.

Nishida Tenkō, (1983), *Life of Ittoen: A New Road to Ancient Truth* (*Revised Japanese Edition*), Kyoto: Ittoen Publishing House.

Plath, David W., (1966), 'The Fate of Utopia: Adaptive Tactics in Four Japanese Groups, in *American Anthropologist*, Vol 68, (1152–1162).

Plath, David W., (1967), 'Utopian Rhetoric: Conversion and Conversation in a Japanese Cult, in *Proceedings of the 1966 Annual Spring Meeting of the American Ethnological Society*, ed. by June Helm, American Ethnological Society, Seattle & London, (96–108).

Plath, David W., (1969), 'Modernization and Its Discontents: Japans Little Utopias, in *Journal of Asian and African Studies*, Vol. 4 (1–17).

Sugihara Yoshie, (1978) *Ai no aru mura* [*A Village of Love*], Tokyo: Shunjūsha.

Sugihara, Yoshie and David W. Plath, (1969), *Sensei and His People: The Building of a Japanese Commune*, Berkeley: University of California Press.

Thomas, Robert D., (1977), *The Man Who Would Be Perfect*, Philadelphia: University of Pennsylvania Press.

Thomsen, Harry, (1963), *The New Religions of Japan*, Rutland, Vt. & Tokyo: Tuttle.

Tsushima Hideo, (1973), 'Gendai no kyūseishu-tachi (8): Yaoi Nisshō [Saviours of Our Time, part 8: Yaoi Nisshō], in *Gendai Ekonomisuto*, Vol. 9, (116–123).

Ueno Masahito, 1985, 'Ō-yamato ajisai mura, in *Gekkan Kyōdōtai*, No. 229 (Part 1) (1–5) in *Gekkan Kyōdōtai, No. 231 (Part 2) (1–5) in Gekkan Kyōdōtai*, No. 233 (Part 3) (1–5).

Ueno Masahito, 1988, *Fukuzato tetsugaku jikkenjō*, Nihon kyōdōtai kyōkai [Japanese Commune Association], no place.

15

The Spy Activities of Diplomat Terasaki Hidenari in the USA and his Rôle in Japanese-American Relations

GERHARD KREBS

JAPANESE INTELLIGENCE IN AMERICA

Diplomat Terasaki Hidenari belonged to the staff of the Japanese Embassy in Washington in the months preceding the attack on Pearl Harbor. Since he cooperated with Ambassador Nomura Kichisaburō and Special Ambassador Kurusu Saburō in the Japanese-American talks at that time, had an American wife (Gwendoleen Harold, usually called 'Gwen', whom he had married during his Washington Embassy days in 1931), and worked as go-between the Imperial Court and the GHQ in the early years of the allied occupation of Japan, he has the image of a peace-lover working for US-Japan understanding.

Soon after the end of World War II, however, an American navy intelligence officer, Ellis M. Zacharias, claimed that Terasaki had been the leader of the Japanese intelligence network in North as well as South America in the period before the outbreak of the Pacific War. Zacharias' book, published in 1946, was based on the author's experience and knowledge. It was, however, not backed up by the release of documents which could have proven his statements. (Zacharias 1946) But, Terasaki's name was mentioned in the papers on the Congressional investigation on the Pearl Harbor attack, published in the same year, where he was called head of Japanese espionage for the Western Hemisphere. Since the released papers included only very few documents in connection with Terasaki's activities, (U.S. Congress 1946 Vol. 9: 4201–2; Vol. 12:227, 234) doubts about his involvement in spy activities remained until the bulk of intercepted Japanese telegrams related to the case were declassified in 1978. They are included in the so-called *magic documents*, but only a small portion is included in the printed edition *Magic Background of Pearl Harbor*, published in 1978, and none are to be found in the *Magic Summaries* available on microfilm.

The GHQ documents of the occupation period in Japan, declassified only in 1982, contain even a proposal to ban Terasaki from public service, since he was seen to have been responsible for Japan's spy activities in the USA during the months immediately before the outbreak of the Pacific War. (Asai 1988:15)

In Japan, all documents relating to intelligence activities were destroyed at the end of the war, either as the result of American bombing or they were burned intentionally. Apparently, for most Japanese historians, the subject 'Terasaki as spy' is taboo; it seems that until recently only a single scholar has made thorough use of the *Magic* material proving Terasaki's intelligence activities, published in a not very widely distributed journal. (Asai 1988)

Terasaki's assignment to Washington was dated 20 October 1940. On 10 December, Foreign Minister Matsuoka wired the Washington Embassy that together with the assignment of Ambassador Nomura he wished to formulate a definite plan for Japan's propaganda and information-gathering work by seeking the cooperation of Japanese bank and business officials in the US. (Magic Background I: A–73) This telegram was decoded only a month-and-a-half later and, being a warning, seems to have accelerated the decoding and translation work henceforth.

On 30 January 1941, Matsuoka wired the Washington Embassy, that in view of the critical situation in recent relations between the two countries and taking into consideration the small amount of funds at their disposal, Japan had decided to deemphasize propaganda for the time being, and instead, to strengthen the intelligence work. (Magic Background I: A–76) The Embassy was instructed to establish an intelligence organization which would maintain liaison with private and semi-official intelligence organs. The focus of their investigations was to determine the total strength of the US. The investigations were to be divided into three general classifications: political, economic, and military. The Embassy was furthermore instructed to make a survey of all persons or organizations which either openly or secretly opposed participation in the war. It should utilize US citizens of foreign extraction and aliens (other than Japanese), communists, Afro-Americans, labour union members, and anti-Semites, in carrying out the investigations. These men, moreover, should have access to governmental establishments, (laboratories?), governmental organizations of various characters, factories, and transportation facilities. The Embassy should also use 'second generation' (*nisei*) Japanese and Japanese resident nationals. In the event of US participation in the war, the Japanese intelligence set-up was to be moved to Mexico, making that country the nerve center of Tokyo's intelligence network. For that purpose, the Embassy was instructed to set up facilities for a US-Mexico international intelligence route. This network which would cover Brazil, Argentina, Chile and Peru would also be centred in Mexico. In addition, Japan should cooperate with the German and Italian intelligence organs in the US. This phase had been discussed with the Germans and Italians in Tokyo, and it had been approved. The Embassy was asked to get the details from Secretary Terasaki when he assumed his duties there. (Magic Background I: A–76–7)

Now, the role Terasaki was supposed to play became clear to the embassy as well as to the American decoders.[1] He arrived in Washington on March 29, 1941, working as Secretary Second Class and from August onward as Secretary First Class until the outbreak of the Pacific War. It was a great exception for a Japanese diplomat to be assigned to the home country of his wife. It gave him easy access to American society. He retained, moreover, contacts with his friends from his student days at Brown University and frequently visited the meetings of the University Club. (SRDJ: 11. 811–3)

Ellis Zacharias, the already mentioned US naval intelligence officer, maintains that in 1941 the Japanese not only intensified their spy activities but also gave them a completely new dimension. Intelligence-gathering rôles were changed and assigned to different personalities. It was no longer confined to the Japanese Navy to conduct offensive intelligence against the US. The activities were now broadened into total espionage, seeking military and naval, as well as political data. The Japanese required a different network for this enlarged organization – a network that expanded far beyond the former confines of Naval Intelligence. So they decided to base it on their diplomatic guise within the sacrosanct confines of the Japanese Embassy in Washington. The man chosen for this responsible position was Terasaki, Japan's master spy in the Western Hemisphere. Working under him was a vast network of spies, based in the various Japanese consulates situated at strategic points. Terasaki plunged into building up his network and establishing a system. (Zacharias 1946: 199f)

The *Magic* documents declassified in 1978 proved the statements of Captain Zacharias. On 15 February 1941, the day after Ambassador Nomura assumed his duties, just before Terasaki's arrival in Washington, the Japanese embassy received a catalogue of detailed points to be investigated. Among them were the strengthening or supplementing of military preparations on the Pacific Coast and the Hawaii area; amount and type of stores and supplies; alterations to air parts; ship and plane movements; whether or not any troops were being dispatched to the South Pacific by transports; general outlooks on Alaska and the Aleutian Islands, with emphasis on plane movements and shipments of military supplies to those localities. (Magic Background I: A–82)

On 6 March, 1941 Matsuoka wired that Secretary . . . was receiving instructions in Japan for intelligence work which he was to take up on his return. He would provide detailed explanations upon arrival in Washington. (SRDJ: 10.331) The name of the secretary was obliterated before declassification, but in connection with other documents it is probable, that it was Terasaki. Two days earlier an intelligence conference was held in Tokyo with Terasaki as participant. (SRDJ: 11.812) Less than two weeks later, a telegram was sent to Washington by Prime Minister Konoe who was also in charge of the Foreign Ministry during Matsuoka's visit to Europe. The embassy was informed that Terasaki was assigned to direct the information and propaganda activities in the USA. The embassy was instructed to have him convene or visit officials concerned whenever he deemed it necessary. If Terasaki considered it necessary he had permission to travel to Central and South America to contact Japanese representatives in charge of information in those countries. To carry out his duties sufficient funds were to be granted him. The embassy was asked to give him every assistance. (SRDJ: 10.441) The salary Terasaki got was unusually high compared with the low position of a mere first secretary. He was fifth in rank at the Embassy, but third in payment. (SRDJ: 16.452)

On 1 April, immediately after Terasaki's arrival in Washington, Tokyo sent further instructions for intelligence work: in the event of war it was expected that the American labour unions would become a major political factor in hindering unity in the United States. In this telegram, as in others, the name of the addressee at the Japanese Embassy was obliterated before declassification, but it can be assumed that it was Terasaki. He was now instructed to get in touch with the leaders of labour unions, the Communist Party, the Socialist Party, and other anti-Roosevelt movements in the near future. At the same time he was asked to study the possibility of using persons such as Oyama Ikuo, a self-exiled Japanese Socialist residing in the USA. (SRDJ: 14.703–4) It is not clear what intentions the Japanese Foreign Ministry had. It may have tried to make use of Oyama's patriotic feelings, which could have been stronger than his Socialist leanings. It took several months before Terasaki managed to contact Oyama who showed no aggressive attitude against the Japanese government. He recommended that Japan avoid war with the USA and develop her national resources, so that she could profit from the golden opportunity offered by America, Germany, Britain and the USSR consuming their national resources in a long, drawn-out war. (SRDJ: 15. 486–7)

On 24 April, the Japanese Foreign Ministry demanded a report from its Washington embassy on the progress of setting up the intelligence organization. (SRDJ: 14. 161) The contents of this telegram were transmitted to all Japanese consulates in North America. The consulate in Vancouver answered that it had recruited an Irish spy with Communist Party affiliations. It was intended to send this man in the near future to seaports in British Columbia and to Yukon, inasmuch as the progress of the US-Canada joint defence plans and the question of air connection with Alaska deserved Japan's attention. (SRDJ: 14. 162)

Los Angeles, where a large colony of Japanese immigrants existed, reported that in connection with the efforts to gather intelligence material its consulate had decided to use white as well as black people, through Japanese people who could be trusted completely. (It not only would be very difficult to hire US experts for this work at the present time, but the expenses would be exceedingly high.) With regard to airplane manufacturing plants and other military establishments in other parts of America, it was planned to establish very close relations with various organizations and in strict secrecy have them keep these military establishments under close surveillance. Through such means they could expect to obtain accurate and detailed intelligence reports. Contacts with absolutely reliable Japanese in the San Pedro and San Diego area had already been established. They would keep a close watch on all shipments of airplanes and other war materials, and report the amounts and destinations of such shipments. To intensify intelligence activities within the army, they would also nurture contacts with enlisted *nisei* (second generation Japanese). They had furthermore connections with *nisei* working in the aircraft industry for intelligence purposes. With regard to the navy, they were co-operating with the Japanese Naval Attaché's office, and would submit reports as accurately and as speedily as possible. Information would be gathered on military movements, labour disputes, communist activities and anti-Jewish movements. They had moreover established connections with very influential Afro-Americans to keep them informed with regard to the negro movement. (SRDJ: 11. 769) The consulate in Seattle answered it would gain information on the military by using *nisei* reservists. (Magic Background I: A–99–100) The evidence that Terasaki directed an extensive network among second-generation workers in airplane plants may have had an influence on the US government decision to intern the *nisei* population in midwestern camps after the outbreak of the war. (Costello 1981: 613; Asai 1988: 23)

Nomura sent an account of Terasaki's activities on 19 May, reporting that the secretary had held talks with the consulate general in New York. Among the results was the conclusion that Roosevelt's dictatorial attitude was becoming more pronounced and the US administration was leaning towards an all-out war. Nomura reported furthermore that the duties of an intelligence officer were becoming increasingly difficult due to strengthened surveillance. Since the embassy wished to make Washington and New York one unit under a unified policy, Terasaki would be sent to New York regularly. His title was now that of 'press attaché'. (SRDJ: 11. 811–2)

It appears that in the higher circles of the US administration there were some people 'in close touch with the president and his wife' who, consciously or unconsciously, were considered valuable sources of intelligence by Japan. For example, in a report transmitted by Nomura in his telegram of 19 May, Terasaki identified his Brown University classmates, W. of the State Department's European Section and Senator G., as sources. (SRDJ: 11. 812–3) The American codebreakers had added in footnotes the names of the persons Terasaki was reporting on, but they were obliterated before declassification. Finally, Terasaki asked for an increase in funds for his intelligence activities (SRDJ: 11. 813).

Although Terasaki was working hard, Foreign Minister Matsuoka apparently was not content as his telegram of 11 June 1941 shows. He asked if it were possible to contact black American agitators and leaders and to train negroes (as fifth columnists). (Magic Background II: A–129) Nomura answered that while it might be possible to use Afro-Americans to slacken the progress of the United States' plans for national defence efforts and the economy as well as for sabotage, black Americans were poorly organized. Therefore Japan cannot expect very great results. (Magic Background II: A–719)

In mid-July Terasaki went to Central and South America for a period of six weeks. His instructions for this mission had been sent from Tokyo on 10 July. One of the reasons to increase Japan's intelligence activities were the closing of German and Italian Consulates and the breaking of their espionage net. It was assumed that Japanese intelligence activities in the Americas and suitable liaison were now essential. So Terasaki was asked to go to Mexico to confer with the Japanese Minister there, in order to realize Tokyo's plans in a concrete fashion. It was envisaged to have three routes to Mexico from the USA, consisting of Laredo, Ciudad Juarez and Mexicali. The last place in particular was seen as a convenient point for Japan on the west coast. In case Japan would need more personnel, it could be provided by the Ministry in Mexico City. It was further planned to establish a Chile route from Mexico by way of Manzanillo and a Brazil route by way of Vera Cruz. Various officials in the USA and Mexico would work out all the details of their own espionage nets, correlate them, and develop a concrete plan for making contacts and exchanges on the border. To succeed in this objective, ways and means for keeping in contact through telegraphy, telephones, memoranda, and by word of mouth would be decided upon and put into effect. These routes were to be established by the day of evil – i.e. the outbreak of an American–Japanese war – and, while all was calm, nothing must be done that would jeopardize their security; therefore, Terasaki was asked at present to investigate only the feasibility of these channels. Because of its geographical position, Mexico was Japan's main point for intelligence work in Brazil, Argentina, and Chile, as well as in the USA. Therefore, before thinking of relying too much on Brazil, Argentina, and Chile, Tokyo would try to concentrate on Mexico. The other three bases were different. In case the USA joined the war, they would inevitably come under her control, but as long as Mexico did not officially join the war, Japan could continue its intelligence schemes there. Paralleling these plans Terasaki was instructed to work out a plan for establishing a liaison net with Brazil, Argentina, and Chile. (SRDJ: 13. 413)

The US Naval Intelligence knew that Terasaki was a specially trained secret service agent, that he had a number of specially trained men with him and that his chief concern during the summer was to set up an espionage establishment in Latin America. (Hearings 33: 860) The British intelligence organization in the USA concluded, too, that Japan's embassy and the consulates had developed into centres of spy activities. Among other sources they had one in the Argentine Foreign Ministry from which they learned in the middle of 1941 that the Japanese, in the event of hostilities with the United States, were preparing to transfer their espionage headquarters in the Western Hemisphere to Argentina. The government in Buenos Aires, however, refused to accredit two Japanese diplomats who had been scheduled to be moved from the Washington Embassy to Argentina. Among them was Hirasawa Kazushige, who belonged to the staff of the Japanese consulate in New York. Under some pretext, he had been arrested by British authorities in Barbados while on his way to South America, and was then flown to Trinidad where spy material in his possession was confiscated. (Farago 1967: 219–20; Hyde 1977: 233–4; Hata 1981:193)

In Mexico City, Terasaki and Consul Itō, who accompanied the former to Mexico but not to the other Latin American countries, held consultations with Minister Miura resulting in a pessimistic report on 22 July: it was believed best not to regard Mexico, as heretofore, as the main base of intelligence in comparison with Brazil, Argentine and Chile. Mexico's connections with the USA were so close that it would follow an American entrance into war, if not formally at least practically. Chile or Brazil were perhaps better suited as main bases for relaying intelligence home. (SRDJ 13. 453–4)

On 22 August 1941, Terasaki sent a telegram from Santiago de Chile reporting the results of his conference with the Japanese Ministers to Brazil, Argentina, Chile and other Latin American countries. The participants proposed an intelligence set-up in Latin America to secure intelligence data on public opinion in the USA, and on her military and diplomatic situation. The method to accomplish this should be roughly as follows: Spies should be set up inside the United States to supply secret intelligence. Their duty was to collect and evaluate information obtained from the offices and personnel of American ministries in Latin America, from individuals and government offices of their host countries, as well as from the offices of third powers there. (SRDJ: 14.862–3)

Terasaki emphasized that in the organization and early operation of an intelligence network, it was advisable to use experienced
operators. But unfortunately Japan had few such specialists. It
could not place great confidence in spies attracted purely by
pecuniary interests, and habitually rendering service to others,
because of their possible infidelity. Inside the USA all Japanese
activities would be under strict observation of the American
authorities, while letters and wires from the members of the
intelligence network would have to pass through rigid
censorship. (SRDJ: 14.864)

After Terasaki's return to the United States, the Japanese
legation in Santiago sent a long report on the possible methods
of intelligence gathering. Among their recommendations was
the advice to make indirect use of the Spanish and Portuguese
language correspondents. Should the German and Italian diplomatic officers be ordered out of a country before the Japanese,
Japan should make arrangements to take over their informants.
They should not be limited to Latin Americans, but the
informants should also include those who resided in Spain and
Portugal.[2] (SRDJ: 15.097–8)

Japan feared very much that the USA would enter the
European war so that Tokyo would have to fulfil its obligations
according to the terms of the Tripartite Pact. On 6 September
1941, Ambassador Nomura cabled for permission to have
Terasaki go on an official mission to Chicago in order to make
secret contacts with members of the 'America First' Committee,
an influential organization which propagated the maintenance
of US neutrality. The most prominent member was Charles
Lindbergh. The contacts with the committee were established
and continued at least until late October 1941. Terasaki even
succeeded to come into indirect contact with Lindbergh providing him with Japan's interpretation of the reasons for the
tensions in the Far East. (SRDJ: 14.649; 16.279)

At the same time, Terasaki participated in the efforts to reach
an understanding in the Japanese-American talks held in
Washington since the spring 1941. So did his brother, Terasaki
Tarō, in Tokyo, as director of the America Bureau in the Foreign
Ministry until October 1941. (Terasaki 1982) On one of his last
days in office Terasaki Tarō telephoned Minister Wakasugi of the
Japanese Embassy in Washington. In their coded conversation
they used Hidenari's daughter's name *Mariko* as a code word
meaning *US attitude towards Japan*. (SRDJ: 15.718; Terasaki 199: 3)

In mid-November, Ambassador Nomura cabled from

Washington that he would send the unnecessary staff home or dismiss them. But the intelligence staff would not be sent back to Japan. Rather, he planned to arrange the transfer of Secretary Terasaki and Clerk Yamamoto to South America. Those returning to Japan would go in one of the evacuee ships, while those transferring to South America would leave immediately for their posts. (SRDJ: 16: 732) Terasaki himself was assigned to Brazil. (Hata 1981: 157) On 29 November, he sent a cable to the Japanese legation in Rio de Janeiro asking for the addresses of two foreign subscribers of American newspapers and magazines. (SRDJ: 17.157) Apparently, he tried to establish contacts for his intelligence work after moving to Brazil.

On 3 December, the Washington Embassy asked the Foreign Ministry in Tokyo to postpone Terasaki's departure to sail on the 19th because he was in the midst of intelligence work. (Hearings 12: 227) Japan's Foreign Ministry, however, on 5 December, repeated its instruction to have Terasaki and other staff members leave the country by plane within the next couple of days.[3] (Hearings 12: 234) Special Ambassador Kurusu Saburo, however, replied that with regard to the importance of the intelligence set-up and in view of the present condition of the Japanese-US negotiations, it would be most desirable to have Terasaki, who would be extremely difficult to replace suddenly due to certain circumstances, remain in Washington until the end of the negotiations. (Hearings 9: 4202)

Kurusu had a reason to keep Terasaki in Washington. Several days before, the young diplomat, in cooperation with Kurusu, had contacted Dr E. Stanley Jones, a well-known Methodist leader and missionary of long experience in the Far East to transmit a new proposal to President Roosevelt. The core of the plan was to have the President send a direct message over the head of Prime Minister Tōjō to the Emperor of Japan appealing for peace. On 3 December 1941, Jones was granted an audience with Roosevelt, who hesitated since he did not want to hurt the Japanese at the embassy in Washington by going over their heads to the Emperor. But when assured that the suggestion came from the embassy itself the president agreed. The cable would be sent not to the Japanese Foreign Ministry, but to US-Ambassador Joseph Grew in Tokyo who had the right of audience to the head of a state. So a long telegram was cabled to Grew on 5 December. (Terasaki 1973: 65–9; Morgenstern 1947: 100–3) It arrived at noon of the 7th local time in Tokyo, but was delayed by the telegraph office apparently acting under the instruction of the military. Ambassador Grew therefore got the telegram only in the late evening and had an interview with Foreign Minister Tōgō shortly after midnight. Tōgō promised to make efforts to arrange an audience with the Emperor. When Grew returned to the embassy the Japanese attack on Pearl Harbor had already begun.

On the evening before the outbreak of war, the Japanese Embassy in Washington had given Terasaki a farewell party in the Mayflower Hotel. The diplomats, however, then knew nothing about the impending attack. Their participation in the party is said to have been responsible for the delay in decoding and typing of the final Japanese note which announced the discontinuance of the Washington talks so that it was handed over to Secretary of State Cordell Hull only after the opening of hostilities. (Tokuoka 1986: 226; ;Pritchard 1981: 26.210)

At the end of the month, Ambassador Nomura cabled that his staff with families were living all together in the embassy, and that Terasaki's family including his American wife had joined them there. (SRDJ: 18.326) In August 1942, Terasaki Hidenari, his wife Gwen and daughter Mariko, having left the USA on an exchange vessel, reached Japan where they spent the war years. (Terasaki 1973: 99–100) Hidenari worked in the foreign ministry until December 1944 when he retired.

TERASAKI'S POST-WAR CAREER

With the American occupation in Japan starting in September 1945, Terasaki gradually regained important positions. In the USA the public and many important politicians opposed a lenient peace with Japan claiming that Hirohito should be tried as a war criminal. The accusations in other countries against the Emperor were even stronger, particularly in the USSR and Australia. In contrast to this mood, General Douglas MacArthur, Supreme Commander for the Allied Powers in Japan, was planning to ensure a smooth administration by utilizing the Japanese people's continuing faith in the Emperor and thereby reducing US troops in Japan. So he decided not to accuse Hirohito of responsibility for the war. His determination was even strengthened during the famous first meeting he had with the *tennō* on 27 September 1945, when Hirohito declared that he offered himself to the judgement of the allied powers as the one to bear sole responsibility for every political and military decision made and action taken by the Japanese people in the conduct of war, thereby making a strong impression on MacArthur. (MacArthur 1964: 287–8)

In the following month, Terasaki was reactivated for Japan's foreign service. On 16 October 1945, Washington instructed MacArthur to collect immediately all obtainable evidence to prove Hirohito's guilt in connection with Japan's violation of international law. In contrast to this instruction, however, General Headquarters struggled apparently to provide evidence for the *tennō's* innocence. On 26 October, Cabinet Secretary Tsugita Daizaburō was informed that Brigade General Bonner Fellers, who was working under MacArthur, had indicated that the Emperor's responsibility for the Pearl Harbor attack was the most important and critical question for the USA. The Japanese side gained the impression that MacArthur and Fellers, having sympathies for Hirohito, tried to find exculpatory answers. So the official version was created which claimed that since the Meiji era the Emperor had always sanctioned all decisions made by the government and the Supreme Command. Only in ending the Pacific War had he made a decision by himself, as requested by the Prime Minister, since the cabinet and the military command were deadlocked. (Tsugita 1991: 118–9)

In January 1946, Terasaki was asked by Foreign Minister Yoshida Shigeru to function as 'spokesman' (*goyōgakari*) of the Emperor for liaison reasons with MacArthur's General Headquarters and to devote himself to protecting the emperor system. (Terasaki 1991: 189, 192) So in the next month he became an official in the Imperial Household Ministry. Apparently, the Japanese government's intention was to make use of Terasaki's excellent English language ability and his family background to gain goodwill from the American side. The facts of his spy activities had not been revealed by the USA at that time. During his liaison work with the General Headquarters, Terasaki soon discovered that Brigade General Bonner Fellers was a distant relative of his wife Gwen. From that time on, they had frequent private contacts. (Terasaki 1973: 206–7) In his capacity as a liaison person, Terasaki also functioned as the interpreter during the five meetings between the Emperor and MacArthur. (Awaya 1985: 41)

On 6 March, Brigade General Fellers visited Admiral Yonai Mitsumasa, former Prime Minister and longtime Navy Minister, known for his pro-American leanings and a respected person in Japan. Fellers informed him what the GHQ was planning for Japan's future: the Emperor would play a rôle of cooperator with the occupation authorities and the *tennō* system would continue. Fellers further explained that in the USA and other allied nations, however, the Emperor was viewed widely as a war criminal so that many people were demanding a trial for him. Among those voices was Secretary of State Byrnes' top advisor (Benjamin V.) Cohen. Further, the USSR aiming at world revolution, regarded the *tennō* system and MacArthur's existence as a great obstacle. As a policy against such demands, Fellers asked if the Japanese side could provide some proofs for the innocence of the Emperor. This time, immediately before the opening of the Tokyo trial, would be a good opportunity to put all responsibility on former Prime Minister Tōjō Hideki's shoulders. One could claim, for example, that the Emperor in the conferences before the outbreak of war opposed the opening of hostilities, but was forced to sanction the decision. Yonai fully agreed to make Tōjō as well as former Navy Minister Shimada Shigetarō responsible for the war thereby whitewashing the Emperor. Fellers later informed Terasaki about the talk with Yonai and let him know that from the standpoint of MacArthur it would be extremely disadvantageous to prosecute the Emperor. Terasaki also had an audience with the Emperor during this time. (Takada 1993: 235–243; Terasaki 1991: 201–2, 203)

Hirohito's advisers now made preparations for the explanations demanded by the American side. A certain delay was due to an illness of the Emperor. On 18 March, a series of reports by the Emperor in front of his entourage began stretching over several weeks into April of that year. Five of Hirohito's aides helped him to make a record as preparation to questions MacArthur and his headquarters might ask about the key events during Hirohito's reign until 1945. Since MacArthur had not yet formally communicated to the court his decision to exempt Hirohito from trial for war crimes, the Emperor's explanations had a strongly apologetic character. (Hatano 1991: 27–8) One of the participants was Terasaki who later wrote out in pencil certain portions of the longer stenographic transcript. This so called 'Emperor's monologue' (*dokuhakuroku*) of the key events during his reign until 1945 were found only after Hirohito's death and were published in the December issue of *Bungei Shunjū* in 1990. In this publication, however, it was not mentioned that MacArthur and his headquarters had been the instigators of the '*dokuhakuroku*' in order to keep Hirohito away from a military trial and to use him for the recreation of a stable and anti-communist Japan.

Other than his contacts with Brigade General Fellers, Terasaki had also a special relationship with Roy Leonard Morgan, an FBI agent he had known ever since his internment immediately following the Japanese attack in December 1941. In late January 1946, the American agent arrived in Tokyo to serve as chief of the Investigative Division of the International Prosecution Section and hence was in frequent contact with Terasaki. During their meetings, the Japanese diplomat gave him the names of prominent Japanese politicians and military men who in his opinion were responsible for the war, thereby influencing the selection of defendants for the military tribunal under preparation at that time. (Awaya 1991: 125–147) Admiral Yonai, too, had had an interview with Morgan the day before he had met Bonner Fellers. (Takada 1993: 236)

TERASAKI'S IMAGE IN JAPAN

The Japanese-American Terasaki family was in an ideal situation to contribute to the reconciliation of their two nations after the war. Hidenari died in 1951 at the age of only 50 years. His wife Gwen moved with her daughter to the USA, where she published her memoirs in 1957 under the title *Bridge to the Sun*. A Japanese translation followed. Under the title *Mariko* the family story was treated in a popular book written by Yanagida Kunio in 1980, and a TV-melodrama was furthermore based on it. Thus was born the Terasaki myth demonstrating the absolute necessity of good Japanese-American relations. In all these years there was no attempt to uncover Terasaki's intelligence work which could have thrown a shadow on his efforts for peace and understanding thereby damaging his image. Neither the Japanese nor the American side could have had an interest in such a development. Perhaps the late declassification in 1978 of the *Magic* material in connection with Terasaki has to be seen in this light. At least the numerous obliterations are an attempt to hide the identity of the persons involved, including Terasaki.

The aversion of Japanese historians to deal with Terasaki's spy activities (Awaya 1985: 41; 1991: 131–2) and the indignation met from Japanese scholars when these activities are mentioned, apparently results from the conviction that his spy work would contradict the former diplomat's struggle for peace and understanding. In the opinion of the author of this study, however, the search for peace and spy activities do not exclude each other at all. As an example, Allen Dulles' efforts in Switzerland during

World War II can serve: While operating a very effective
intelligence network for the OSS he negotiated a separate
surrender of the German troops in Italy and held talks with
Japanese officers and civilians on concluding peace in Asia. In
Germany, Admiral Canaris was the head of the military spy
organization *Abwehr* and became one of the most prominent
members of the opposition movement against Hitler. The best
example, however, that the combination of a diplomacy
oriented towards peace and spy activities are compatible might
be Terasaki Hidenari himself. Apparently, his spy colleague from
the American side, Roy Morgan, understood this best: both had
very good relations which could even be called friendship.

NOTES

1. Zacharias in correspondence with Asai confirmed that code breaking
persons in the United States concerned with counterintelligence already
before Terasaki's arrival knew the true reason of his mission (Asai 1988: 17).
2. During the war an intelligence network in the United States was working
for Japan, operated by a Spanish nationalist using Spanish spies and brought into
existence with German assistance. It is not possible to check if Terasaki's
activities have been one of the sources from which this idea developed. One can
prove, however, that a proposal similar to the idea realized in Madrid, came
from the Japanese Legation in Buenos Aires which had belonged to Terasaki's
area of operation in 1941: to use the Spanish Embassy in Washington by the
good offices of Germany to gather intelligence.
3. American intelligence officers knew within one day after the telegrams
had been exchanged between Tokyo and the Washington Embassy, that the
diplomat would be sent abroad, and a little later that the destination would
be South America. In connection with another order, that of destroying the
code books, they concluded that time was running out and the crisis was fast
approaching (*Hearings 9*: 4201–2, 4577; *Part 33*: 860).

BIBLIOGRAPHY

Asai N., (1988) 'Nichi-Bei kaizen zenya ni okeru Terasaki Hidenari no
    yakuwari' (Terasaki's role on the eve of outbreak of war between Japan
    and the USA), *Kōbe Gaidai Ronsō*, 39, 7, 15–34.
Awaya Kentarō, (1991) 'Tokyo Saiban to Tennō Dokuhaku (The Tokyo
    War Crimes Tribunal and the Emperor's Monologue), in Fujiwara A.
    et al., *Tettei Kenshō. Shōwa Tennō Dokuhakuroku* (A Thorough Study of
    Emperor Showa's Monologue), Tokyo: Otsuki Shoten.
Costello J., (1981) *The Pacific War* London: Collins.
Department of Defence, USA, (1978) *The 'Magic' Background of Pearl Harbor*.
    4 volumes. Washington: Government Printing Office.
Farago L., (1967) *The Broken Seal: 'Operation Magic' and the Secret Road to
    Pearl Harbor*, New York: Random House.
Hata Ikuhiko, (1981) *Senzenki Nihon Kanryōsei no Seido, Soshiki, Jinji*

(System, Organisation and Personnel of the Bureaucracy in Prewar Japan), Tokyo: Tokyo Shuppankai.

Hatano Sumio, (1991) 'Shōwa Tennō 'Dokuhakuroku' no gyakusetsu' (The paradox of the Showa Emperor's 'Monologue Protocols' *Shokun*, 23, 1, 26–37.

Krebs G., (1988) 'Japanese-Spanish Relations, 1936–1945', *Transactions of the Asiatic Society of Japan* Fourth Series, 3, 21–52.

MacArthur D., (1964) *Reminiscences*. New York: McGraw Hill Book Co.

Montgomery-Hyde H., (1977) *Room 3603: The Story of the British Intelligence Centre in New York During World War II* New York: Ballantine Books.

Morgenstern George, (1947) *Pearl Harbor – The Story of the Secret War*, New York: Devin-Adair Co.

National Archives Washington, Record Group 457, Cited as SRDJ.

Pritchard R.J., and Magbanua Zaide S. eds. (1981) *The Tokyo War Crimes Trial* (The Complete Transcripts of the Proceedings of the International Military Tribunal for the Far East in 22 Volumes), New York and London: Garland Publishing.

Takada Makiko, (1993) *Yonai Mitsumasa no tegami* (The letters of Yonai Mitsumasa) Tokyo: Hara Shobō.

Terasaki Gwen, (1973) *Bridge to the Sun* Tokyo: Tuttle.

Terasaki Tarō, (1982) *Reimei: Nihon Gaikō Kaisoroku* (Dawn: Memoirs of Japanese Diplomacy), Tokyo: Chuō Kōron Jigyoshuppan.

Terasaki-Miller Mariko, (1991) Shōwa Tennō dokuhakuroku – Terasaki Hidenari goyogakari nikki (Monologue of the Showa Tenno – spokesman Terasaki Hidenari's diary), Tokyo: Bungei Shunjū.

Tokuoka Takao, 'Dare ga junigatsu yoka o kokujoku no hi ni shita ka', (Who made 8 December the day of infamy?) *Bungei Shinjū*, January 1986, 210–231.

Tsugita Daizaburō, (1991) *Tsugita Daizaburō Nikki*, Ed. Ota Kenichi et al., Tokyo: Sayo Shinbunsha.

US Congress, (1946) *Joint Committee on the Investigation of the Pearl Harbor Attack* 39 volumes. Washington: Government Printing Office.

Zacharias, E.M., (1946) *Secret Missions: the story of an intelligence officer* New York: G. P. Putnam's Sons.

16

The Principal Japanese Communist Leaders in the View of US Officials, 1944–1946

HENRY OINAS-KUKKONEN

The best-known of all Japanese communist leaders has been in the news in the last few years. Nosaka Sanzō, often said to have been one of the founders of the Japanese Communist Party in 1922, was expelled from the party and stripped of the title of honorary chairman in 1992. A letter from him had been found in the Soviet Communist Party archives in which he falsely accused another Japanese communist, Yamamoto Kenzō, of being a spy who had stayed in the Soviet Union and had subsequently been executed. Nosaka died in November 1993 at the age of 101. US officials[1] had been aware of Nosaka during the Second World War, and when it ended and the occupation began they also placed other Japanese communist leaders, particularly Tokuda Kyūichi and Shiga Yoshio, under closer surveillance. By the end of the first year of occupation a certain view existed regarding these communist leaders. US officials reckoned that the main communist leaders were largely pursuing their own interests, but what kind of personalities were they? What type of ideological line did they support within the communist movement? Was it possible to cooperate with them? Were they able to seize power in Japan?

NOSAKA SANZŌ: A MODERATE, SENSIBLE AND TALENTED LEADER

During the Second World War, the Japanese Communist Party, or *Kyōsantō*, was repressed by the government. Its leaders were imprisoned or in exile and its members driven underground. US officials contacted exiled Japanese communists in Yanan, where the Chinese communists had their headquarters, and it was there that they met the most important Japanese communist leader of the time, Nosaka Sanzō, who used the pseudonym Susumu Okano, in connection with efforts to cooperate with elements opposed to the Japanese government. (Colbert 1952: 61; Swearingen & Langer 1968: 79)

Because the United States was attempting to win the war against Japan as fast as possible and with as few losses as possible, they hoped for a decisive contribution from the Chinese. In June 1944, Vice-President Henry Wallace persuaded Jiang Jieshi, leader of Nationalist China, to allow a sixteen-member US Military Observer Group to travel to the Chinese communist headquarters in order to merge their operations into a common anti-Japanese front. The United States Embassy in Chongquing had a number of young Foreign Service officers who were especially keen supporters of cooperation with the Chinese communists, and similar ideas on a combined operation were also fostered by Japanese communists in Yanan. (Emmerson 1978: 152, 179; Rose 1976: 9–18; Harries 1987: 13)

John K. Emmerson, the second secretary at the embassy, had the idea of enlarging the anti-Japanese front by uniting all anti-war, anti-facist, anti-militarist, pro-democracy groups under the same banner. Accordingly, he interviewed a Japanese author called Kaji Wataru, exiled in Chongquing, who was the leader of an anti-Japanese league called Hansen Dōmei. This had been established in 1939, served the central government of China and was in cooperation with the US Office of War Information, its purpose being to indoctrinate Japanese prisoners-of-war and conduct psychological warfare against Japan. (CUSSDCF: 5.879; Amerasia Papers: 1386–8; Emmerson 1978: 178, 180, 225, 230; Takomae 1987: 343; Colbert 1952: 59; Ranelagh 1986: 64)

In summer 1944, the government of the United States sent its Military Observer Group to Yanan, where they met also Nosaka Sanzō. A US observer, John S. Service, indicated in August that he was not ready to make a full report on him or to give an opinion on him, (The Amerasia Papers I: 762; Emmerson 1978: 179) but one of the observers, F. McCracken Fisher, head of the Office of War Information in China, submitted a brief biographical sketch of Nosaka in September, including largely personal details, his date and place of birth, for example, the most important events in his life and information about his education. Nosaka had been born into a poor merchant family in Hagi in the prefecture of Yamaguchi in 1892, was a graduate of Keiō University in Tokyo, had studied at the London School of Economics, was a member of the original Japanese Communist Party established in 1922, and had succeeded Katayama Sen as the key Japanese member of the Comintern. (The Amerasia Papers II; 1103–5) Nosaka had recounted some things about himself, but had said that he had come to Yanan in 1943 although he had in fact done so in 1940. (Emmerson 1978: 193; Emmerson 1972: 565; Nishi 1982: 96; Colbert 1952: 60; Swearingen & Langer 1968: 73–4, 114)

Further, more evaluative information was to be obtained in October, when Emmerson, an expert on Japan, came to Yanan. There had been a branch of Hansen Dōmei there since 1940, but the communists had replaced it in 1944 by establishing the Japanese People's Emancipation League, or *Nippon Jinmin Kaihō Renmei*, to indoctrinate Japanese prisoners-of-war. Emmerson was sent to Yanan on 22 October, along with Koji Ariyoshi from the Office of War Information as his aide, to interrogate Japanese prisoners-of-war. Since it was his task to investigate the Japanese in Yanan, he met a number of Japanese communists and had many discussions with the leader of the *Nippon Jinmin Kaihō Renmei*, Nosaka, concerning the future of Japan and its Communist Party.[2] (Emmerson 1978: 180–201; Emmerson 1972: 565; Colbert 63, 330)

Emmerson tried to estimate the capabilities of the Japanese Communist Party, and of course evaluate the personality, views and skills of its leader, Nosaka. John K. Emmerson regarded Nosaka as a quiet, scholarly person with whom it was possible to have friendly discussions. He might have regarded him as scholarly because of his academic background, but it is also a fact that Emmerson used his library in Yanan. (FCJ 1–C–43: 16; Emmerson 1978: 184–191)

Emmerson later described Nosaka in his memoirs as 'a small man, then fifty-two years old, neatly dressed in his homespun Yenan uniform, kindly and soft-spoken, with clear, penetrating eyes'. (Emmerson 1978: 190) He was of the opinion then, and even later, that Nosaka was highly talented, but this was not only his view. Nearly a year later, in 1946, for example, Kenneth Colgrove, an American professor of Political Science who had visited Japan and Korea, expressed to President Truman his regret that the cleverest man in Japan was Nosaka. (Emmerson 1978: 284) Many US officials, including George Atcheson Jr., Political Adviser to the Supreme Commander for the Allied Powers, saw his proposals to be sensible and were surprised. It must be remembered, however, that many of Nosaka's ideas were consistent with the State Department's post-surrender directives and goals. They had many notions of liberties and civil rights in common, e.g. the freedom of speech. Emmerson later stated in his memoirs that 'Nosaka's programme, as described to us in 1944, sounded like a paraphrase of the American Bill of Rights'. (Emmerson 1978: 200, 203; Emmerson 1972: 567).

Nosaka was seen as a moderate communist leader because he proposed an initial period of democracy or democratic capitalism, would eventually lead to its own downfall and the establishment of socialism in Japan, a country which was not at that moment ready for immediate socialism. He had modified the Comintern Thesis for Japan set out in 1932 in a more moderate direction. Since Nosaka believed that Japan would not go any further than democracy in his lifetime, Emmerson saw him as a 'gradualist', for whom communism was the goal, not violent revolution. (Emmerson 1978: 199–200; Emmerson 1972: 565; Takamae 1987: 343; Langer 1972: 49)

In the opinion of Emmerson, Nosaka's words carried considerable weight, because the other major Japanese communist leaders were either dead or in prison, while Nosaka had been doing organizational work among the Japanese with considerable success in an atmosphere that had probably reinforced his party spirit. Nosaka had emphasized to the US observers the special nature of the Communist Party, its usefulness and its preparedness for the democratization of Japan after the war. He demanded that all political prisoners in Japan should be liberated, and he wanted cooperation between Japanese communists and the United States in anti-Japanese warfare, promising the Allied Forces the full support of the Japanese Communist Party. (America Papers II: 1232; Emmerson 1978: 180–198, Colbert 1952: 61–2; Swearingen & Langer 1968: 79, 81) As he stated in the Seventh Congress of the Chinese Communist Party in April 1945, the programme of the Japanese Communist Party would not be in conflict with interests of the United States in Japan or in Asia. (Pohl 1976: 34, 51)

In Emmerson's opinion, the communists could ;have formed the basis for a democratic post-war government, which the United States might even have had to rely on. (The Amerasia Papers II: 1224, 1388) It may be that this idea of broad representation was induced by Nosaka's idea of *Nippon Jinmin Kaihō Renmei* taking part in the government. (CUSSDF: 5.879) At any rate, Emmerson wrote later in his memoirs that he was 'No doubt influenced by the crisp air and contagious zeal of Yenan'. (Emmerson 1978: 201) It is interesting to note that it was the evaluation given of their leader, Nosaka, that determined how the communists as a group were evaluated.

Emmerson emphasized that one must not fear the Communists in the case of Japan. Instead they should be utilized in political warfare inside and outside the country. He thought that this could be done, and that they would try to help the United States. (Amerasia Papers II: 1224–5: CUSSDF: 1.2) This view may be a result of Nosaka's statements and of the fact that he broadcast radio programmes to Japan with the cooperation of the Office of War Information encouraging an end to the war against the United States. (Baerwald 1965: 199–200) Furthermore, the Chinese communists were favourably disposed towards the United States at that time, and Emmerson had had friendly discussions with Nosaka. (Emmerson 1978: 184–190) One reason could have been the fact that the communists had been illegal in Japan for many years and many of them had been imprisoned, so that they would enthusiastically accept liberation. Exploitation of the Japanese communists could strengthen the prestige of the United States, and the Communists might be helpful in reconstructing Japan. (Amerasia Papers II: 1224–5; Emmerson 1978: 203)

On the other hand, Emmerson regarded them as too weak to seize power on account of the crippling actions of the Japanese police and the fact that the party's pre-war membership had not exceeded 1000. (Emmerson 1972: 569) The communist underground movement was acting in a disorganized manner in Japan and did not have any appreciable impact on society. Emmerson nevertheless considered the Japanese communists important, since they were the sole underground group known to be active in Japan. They could be used inside the country as agents for spreading defeatism, gathering intelligence information, undertaking sabotage and making preparations for an invasion. Emmerson calculated that the Japanese communists would be content after the war if, for the first time in their history, they were allowed to act legally. (Emmerson 1978: 201, 205)

Emmerson regarded the Japanese communists as allies of the United States, which would mean that the United States and the Soviet Union were operating side by side against the Axis Powers, and former ideological disputes would be put aside. (Amerasia Papers II: 1219–25; Takamae 1987: 344)

The State-War-Navy Coordination Committee, which was

the major US organ to decide on the occupation of Japan, and reached a position in which the President directly accepted its recommendations, considered Emmerson's views on 5 July 1945. If his plan had been accepted, however, connections with the communists would have become too intimate. Other obstacles also appeared, e.g. it proved too difficult to find a widely enough known Japanese opposition leader. Even though Emmerson's plan was not implemented, the work of organizing anti-war operations continued. Furthermore, the information that had been collected had a major impact on US policy towards the communists in post-war Japan. Nosaka was not regarded as sufficiently well known in Japan, although he did achieve fame after his return. (Emmerson 1978:224–5; Takamae 1987, 343–4; Paterson 1988: 36, 37; Barton 1967: 18, 22) Nosaka was known to US officials as 'Moscow's man', who had up-to-date contacts with the Soviets, although he was naturally also seen as having close contacts with the Chinese communists.

Service was fairly sure that some kind of contact existed between the Chinese communists and Soviets, because there had been Chinese communists in Moscow and there was a radio transmitter in Yanan, although no Soviet weapons had arrived, but in his opinion Nosaka had no close contacts with the Soviet Union at that moment. (Amerasia Papers II, 1444–6; Emmerson 1978: 152–179) Davies reckoned that the leaders of *Nippon Jinmin Kaihō Renmei* were potential leaders of post-war Japan, and believed that the Soviet Union would attempt to influence Japan and to use this group as a channel. (FRUS 1969: 931)

Nosaka returned to Japan in January 1946, where he became a member of party's Bureau, Secretariat and Central Committee, Chief of Propaganda and Investigation and principal of the party school and was elected a member of the Diet in the April of that year. (CUSSDCF: 914, 916) US Officials estimated that Nosaka would restrain the policies of the other communists, (FRUS 1946: 114) and this was indeed what happened. Nosaka's moderate ideas were adopted as the policy of the Japanese Communist Party, a policy which was well illustrated by his statement that the intention was to make the party 'lovable'. (CUSSDCF: 1.812)

Nosaka was seen as a moderate, sensible, talented leader, because he supported the idea of a gradual change to socialism, could act as an organizer in difficult circumstances, had a scholarly background, behaved quietly and seemed not to be in close contact with the Soviets at that time. It seemed that US officials could even cooperate with him, but there were other reasons why this was not done, mainly that he was not very well known in Japan and that contacts with the communists would have become too close.

TOKUDA KYŪICHI AND SHIGA YOSHIO: AGGRESSIVE, ORTHODOX FIGHTERS

While Nosaka was the most prominent Japanese communist leader to be found in Yanan, China, another centre of communist leadership existed in Japan itself. (OSS 1945: 11.1) When the war against Japan ended and the occupation began on 2 September 1945, an opportunity arose to evaluate this second centre. Many communist leaders had died in prison during the war, but the surviving political prisoners, including communists, were released in October. The most important communist leaders still in Japan, Tokuda Kyūichi and Shiga Yoshio, were investigated and evaluated by US officials, who pondered over the possibility of utilizing them in the political arena of occupied Japan, since they were planning to change the political structure in Japan and to democratize it.

The Supreme Commander for the Allied Powers, General Douglas MacArthur, requested that his Political Adviser, George Atcheson Jr., on 3 October 1945 investigate the Japanese political parties, their backgrounds, their leading personalities and their objectives. This would enable US officials to foreshadow political trends and structures in Japan, and would also affect political life, in that the adviser was to make whatever recommendations he deemed necessary. Atcheson delegated this investigation task to John K. Emmerson, who thereby became a US occupation official having constant contacts with the Japanese communists. (CUSSDCF: 1.218, 1.216; Emmerson 1978: 260–1; Reischauer 1984: 7)

On the other hand, the US Army's Civil Intelligence Section, led by Brigadier General Elliott R. Thorpe, was given the task of organizing the release of Japanese political prisoners, and he delegated the work of organizing the investigations and releasing the prisoners to E. Herbert Norman, with certain State Department officials from the Office of the Political Adviser to the Supreme Commander for the Allied Powers as his aides. John K. Emmerson had assisted counter-intelligence to compile a list of war criminals, and he now began to work together with his friend Norman on the task of investigating and releasing the political prisoners. (Emmerson 1978: 253–8; Thorpe 1969: 193, 221–3)

Emmerson and Norman visited political prisoners in Fuchū prison on 5 October, and it was there and at the headquarters of the Allied Powers two days later that they interrogated the communist leaders Tokuda and Shiga. They soon realized that these were the most prominent communist leaders in Japan at that time, in addition to Nosaka, who was in Yanan. No new leaders had emerged from the underground movement. (Emmerson 1978:258–61; Wildes 1954:269; Sheldon 1965:133; CUSSDCF: 1.223, 312)

Some biographical information on Tokuda and Shiga had already been received from the US Military Observers in Yanan. It was known about Shiga that he had been born at Hagi in the prefecture of Yamaguchi in 1901, had graduated from Tokyo University, had been an activist in the student movement, a volunteer in military service for one year and editor of a magazine called *The Marxist*, and that at that time was working as an editor of communist publications. Tokuda was known to have been born in Okinawa in 1894, to have graduated from Middle School but to have discontinued High School because of lack of funds, after which he had been a primary school teacher. He had attended the Comintern Conference in Russia in 1922 and had been given orders to organize a Japanese Communist Party. He had later been in Russia and had had contacts with the Comintern in 1926 and 1927, but had been arrested in 1928. He was known to control the party funds. (Amerasia Papers II: 1224, 1234–5; OSS 1945: 11.1)

The face-to-face meetings nevertheless gave more revealing pictures of these leaders. Emmerson later wrote in his memoirs that Tokuda was a professional revolutionary, 'a rough, fiery, dynamic spellbinder, the direct opposite of the quiet Nosaka', while Shiga was 'less flamboyant and more intellectual'. This view could have partly been due to the fact that Shiga had introduced Emmerson to some Japanese literature, and partly because he was better educated and was quieter in his behaviour. (Emmerson 1978: 257–62)

It is highly illustrative that the Communist Party in Japan was regarded as a vigorous, well disciplined, aggressive group, largely on the basis of the impressions gained from the liberated leaders Tokuda and Shiga. Vigour and discipline were probably seen in the fact that these liberated leaders had immediately set about organizing their party, and aggressiveness partly because the

communists made harsh attacks on other party leaders and on
the Emperor. (CUSSDCF: 1.215–7, 223, 313) US officials were
amazed at their fighting spirit, since the Interim Research and
Intelligence Section of the State Department had assumed from
press articles that those who had been imprisoned would have
lost their former zeal. (Emmerson 1978: 203; Emmerson 1972:
567) It was also surprising that Tokuda seemed to be remarkably
well-informed about Japanese political events and personalities
in spite of his imprisonment. A US official in the Political
Adviser's Office, Robert A. Feary, thought that Tokuda and Shiga
were capable leaders and that the party would be vociferous
under their leadership. But Emmerson regarded the other Communist leaders as falling far short of Nosaka in their talents and
was convinced that Tokuda and Shiga could not 'shoulder the
entire responsibility', if the Japanese Communist Party were to
progress rapidly. (CUSSDCF: 1.223, 338, 339, 313; FRUS 1946
VIII, 338–9, Emmerson 1978: 284).

Tokuda and Shiga represented an older political line than
Nosaka, and they diverged markedly from the latter's views on
the question of the Emperor, advocating abolition of throne
whereas Nosaka maintained that the Japanese people should
decide the future of the Emperor. Atcheson thought that Tokuda
and Shiga were brutally honest but too theoretical when supporting the detention of the Emperor. While viewing Nosaka's
moderate proposals as sensible, he regarded those of Shiga and
Tokuda as concrete and uncompromising. (Emmerson 1978:
203; 1972: 567) One State Department report named them as
political rivals to Nosaka and looked on the latter as being in a
position of advantage over them. Tokuda and Shiga had been
imprisoned for the period 1928–45 and still followed the orthodox international communist line after their release. (OSS 1945:
11.1, 2; CUSSDCF: 1.902)

Upon gaining their freedom Tokuda and Shiga were indeed
highly conspicuous and vociferous, acting as the party's spokesmen even though their position was not formalized until
December, when the Fourth Congress of the Japanese Communist Party was held. Their prominence was evident
immediately after their release, as they at once issued a manifesto
'*Jinmin ni uttō*', an Appeal to the People. (CUSSDCF: 1.811;
Emmerson 1978: 567–8) Tokuda was elected General Secretary,
chairman of the Political Organization Committee and a
member of the Political Bureau and Committee at the Fourth
Congress, and became a member of the Diet in the elections of

1946. Shiga was chairman of publications, editor of *Akahata* and a member of the political bureau, Secretariat and Central Committee after December 1945 and was elected to the House of Representatives in 1946. (CUSSDCF: 1.673–4 914–6) Nosaka returned from China in January 1946, and the Fifth Congress of the Japanese Communist Party was held immediately. He persuaded Tokuda and Shiga to adopt his moderate policy, and the three became the leading personalities in the Japanese Communist Party. (FCJ 1946: 1–C–43: 16; CUSSDCF: 1.902)

Although US officials regarded Tokuda and Shiga as vociferous, vigorous, aggressive, concrete, orthodox Communist leaders, Nosaka had engaged their support for the idea of a 'lovable' communist Party. The Political Adviser to the Supreme Commander for the Allied Powers, George Atcheson Jr., wrote to President Truman that the Japanese communists had resisted the wartime government, were in support of the Allied Powers and the Potsdam Declaration, were 'democratic' and wished to avoid a class war. They could not seize power. He thus declared that on these grounds they could be tolerated. (FRUS 1946 VIII, 89) The wartime idea of cooperation would not succeed, but coexistence was possible.

NOTES

1. In this article this term includes US Military Observers in Yanan 1944–45 and US Occupation authorities, who were mainly State Department Officials located in the Office of Political Adviser to the Supreme Commander for the Allied Powers.

2. Mainly due to these discussions, Emmerson, while in Yanan, wrote a study 'The Japanese Communist Party', January 5, 1945 (The Amerasia Papers, Volume II) Emmerson, Thread, pp. 180, 181, 190, 197, 201, 426 reference to p. 201; Emmerson, Party, p. 565 n. 6; Colbert, pp. 63, 330.

BIBLIOGRAPHY

US State Department Confidential Files *Japan: Internal Affairs 1945–1949* Fredrick Md.: University Publications of America. Cited as CUSSDCF.

US Senate, Committee on the Judiciary, Senate Internal Security Subcommittee, *The Amerasia Papers: a clue to the catastrophe of China*, Volume II, Washington 1970. Cited as The Amerasia Papers.

Foreign Relations of the US 1945 Volume VI, The British Commonwealth, The Far East, Washington 1969. Cited as FRUS.

Framing the Constitution of Japan: Primary Sources in English 1944–49, Congress Information Service, Bethesda Md. (1989). Cited as FCJ.

OSS/State Department Intelligence and Research Reports, Part II. *Post war*

Japan, Korea and Southeast Asia (1945–1949). Frederick, Md.: University Publications of America. Cited as OSS.

Baerwald H.H., (1965) 'The Japanese Communist Party and its Rivals', in *The Communist Revolution in Asia* ed. R.A. Scalapino, New Jersey: Prentice Hall.

Borton H., (1967) *American Presurrender Planning for Post-war Japan*, New York: Occasional Papers of the East Asian Institute, Columbia University.

Ciamporcero A.F., (1980) *The State-War-Navy Co-ordinating Committee and the Beginning of the Cold War* Ph D. State University of New York at Albany.

Colbert Evelyn S., (1952) *The Left Wing in Japanese Politics* New York: International Secretariat, Institute of Pacific Relations.

Emmerson J.K., (1972) The Japanese Communist Party after Fifty Years, *Asian Survey* Vol. xxiii, 7.

Emmerson J.K., (1978) *The Japanese Thread: a Life in the Foreign Service*, New York: Holt, Rinehart and Winston.

Harries M & S., (1987) *Sheathing the Sword* London: Hamish Hamilton.

Langer P., (1972) *Communism in Japan: A case of naturalisation*, California: Stanford University Press.

Nishi T., (1982) *Unconditional Democracy: Education and Politics in Occupied Japan, 1945–52* California: Stanford University Press.

Paterson T.G., (1988) *Meeting the Communist Threat: Truman to Reagan*, New York: Oxford University Press.

Pohl, M., (1976) *Die Kommunistische Partei Japans: Ein Weg Ohne Peking und Moskau* Hamburg: Verbund Stiftung Deutsches Obersee-Institut.

Ranelagh J., (1986) *The Agency: the rise and decline of the CIA*, New York: Simon & Schuster.

Rose L.A., (1976) *Roots of Tragedy: the United States and the Struggle for Asia, 1945–53*, Westport: Greenwood Press.

Sheldon W., (1965) *The Honorable Conquerors: the occupation of Japan 1945–52*, New York: MacMillan.

Swearingen R, and Langer P., (1968) *Red Flag in Japan*, New York: Greenwood Press.

Takamae E., (1987) 'Early Post-war Reformist Parties', in *Democratising Japan*, ed. R. E. Ward and Y. Sakamoto, Honolulu: University of Hawaii.

Wildes H.E., (1954) *Typhoon in Tokyo: the Occupation of Japan 1945–52*, New York: MacMillan.

17

Douglas MacArthur and the Occupation of Japan: British Perceptions and Reactions

PETER LOWE

Douglas MacArthur was a figure of deep controversy in his lifetime and remains as controversial today. Unquestionably, MacArthur possessed potent leadership qualities and exerted extensive influence in East Asia in the later stages of the war against Japan and in the occupation of Japan. His military record was impressive over a prolonged period in the US army, culminating in his direction of the South-West Pacific Command between 1942 and 1945. As a personality MacArthur was charismatic, assertive, and noted for his theatrical gifts and conduct: all who met him remarked on his dramatic character and capacity for stage management. He was a man of vision and outstanding ability, yet simultaneously flawed. MacArthur did not welcome views contrary to his own and liked to be surrounded by sycophants who would demonstrate appropriate deference and strengthen his confidence in his commanding talent.

His political sympathies within American domestic politics were located in the right wing of the Republican party yet here, too, MacArthur was idiosyncratic. Many of the decisions he took in Japan were very different to those one might have expected a man of his political persuasion to have taken and they gave rise to considerable criticism from right-wing circles in the United States. The answer to this paradox is that MacArthur took his responsibilities within Japan with intense seriousness: he grasped the profound challenges facing him and he was determined to succeed, since this would be the concluding and, perhaps, most constructive phase of his career – unless he moved from the Dai-Ichi building to the White House. Sir Alvary Gascoigne, the head of the British liaison mission in Tokyo for most of MacArthur's term as SCAP, rightly referred to MacArthur's 'crusading' approach in Tokyo. (PRO Fo 371/92521/S) MacArthur was dominated by an intoxicating sense of mission. The intention of this paper is to assess British perceptions and reactions to MacArthur's leadership. These will be pursued under the headings of the political, social, economic, and strategic themes of the occupation.

In the political sphere the Labour government of Clement Attlee hoped originally to exercise a larger rôle in determining the future administration of Japan but this prospect was dashed by the determination of MacArthur, and the Truman administration, to minimize the contribution of allied countries to the evolution of the occupation notwithstanding the fact that it was formally an *allied* occupation. (Buckley 1982) Despite the doubts of some officials and commentators, MacArthur believed that it was imperative to retain the monarchy and the person of the individual Emperor. Whatever the arguments regarding the Shōwa Emperor's actions before and during the Pacific War, MacArthur held that he must be retained and deployed to lend credence and to support the reforming policies he aimed to implement. (MacArthur 1965: 323, 329–30) British politicians and officials concurred through grounds of pragmatism: it was thought that a British tutor should be involved in the education of Crown Prince Akihito but this was prevented by MacArthur, who had no intention of permitting the British to extend their influence. (PRO: 1951 FO 371/92521/5) The British understood that the Emperor favoured the idea of employing a British tutor but it was to no avail. The vital importance of constitutional reform was grasped fully. The Meiji constitution was far too conservative and ambiguous a document and had to be replaced. MacArthur compelled the Japanese government to accept a new democratic constitution in which the contradictory features of the Meiji constitution were replaced by a full commitment to parliamentary democracy. Naturally, Japanese politicians built on the foundations developed, somewhat precariously, in the pre-war era but MacArthur secured a more liberal constitution than would have emerged from the Japanese government. MacArthur wished to consolidate democracy on the basis obtaining in the USA or in Britain which implied alternating government between left and right or, more accurately, between centre left and centre right. Despite his conservative inclinations, MacArthur respected the socialist leader, Katayama Tetsu, when he assumed office at the head of a coalition government in 1947. (James 1985: 312–3) It is likely that SCAP's sympathy was strengthened by the fact that Katayama was a Christian, since MacArthur wished to encourage Christianity in Japan.

British officials welcomed MacArthur's drive for democratization but were less sanguine than he was as to longer-term prospects. However, MacArthur himself was careful to describe his approach in qualified terms. In February 1948 Lord Killearn, a distinguished diplomat with considerable experience of East Asia and then serving as high commissioner in South-East Asia, visited Tokyo. He met MacArthur and Gascoigne recorded the salient points in a telegram to London. After reviewing international relations with reference to the Soviet Union, they turned to domestic features. Killearn inquired as to the functioning of SCAP and MacArthur's aims. Gascoigne reported:

> The General described the situation most lucidly in terms similar to those which he has used with me before. He made a point, however, of stressing that his administration could not claim to have 'democratised' Japan. Every effort, he said, had been made to clear away the old feudalistic obstacles to democracy, and to make it possible for each Japanese individual to play his or her part in the life of the country. There had been considerable criticism of MacArthur by journalists and others that he has claimed to have actually converted the Japanese to democracy; I would stress that he does not himself claim this, although, of course, there are some 'galloping Colonels' in his administration who do make propaganda on these lines. (PRO: FO 371/699 12/2023/ 237)

MacArthur remained consistent in his opinion. Almost three years later Gascoigne accompanied another prominent visitor, the Japanologist and retired diplomat, Sir George Sansom, to see MacArthur. Sansom provided a brief resumé of the meeting in which he assessed shrewdly the strengths and weaknesses of the general. He was undoubtedly impressive and was imbued with profound faith in the justice of his actions. However, he was prepared to adjust facts to fit in with his preconceptions and was weakened by vanity. Sansom recorded MacArthur as stating:

> He said (what he has said before) that he did not believe in Occupations, and thought it was high time that the Occupation of Japan came to an end. He did *not*, he said, suppose that the Japanese had become democrats. The Occupation had merely provided the apparatus which the Japanese could use if they desired. He thought that there would be a good deal of change after the peace treaties were made, but he did not believe the

Japanese would revert to unqualified militarism. They could not, even if they wished, so long as the Allied Powers could use economic pressure. But in any case, he believed that there was, since 1945, a growth in the feeling for freedom among the Japanese people and this was bound to play a part in domestic politics in Japan in the future. (PRO: FO 371/92521/3)

British officials doubted the longer-term prospects for democratization. In December 1948, Gascoigne was dismissive of SCAP's achievements, describing the effect of democracy on the Japanese mind as 'almost nil': of course, the Japanese paid lip-service to democratic aims, since it was not wise to take a different view, but Gascoigne was sceptical of the degree of genuine commitment. (PRO: FO 371/76178/7527) In his concluding survey, at the end of his term of office in February 1951, Gascoigne sought to report in a balanced manner upon the achievements and failings of SCAP. Gascoigne viewed the monarchy as a key aspect in stable government. Most Japanese revered the monarchy and deeply respected the Emperor. Once the occupation ended, it was possible that reverence for the Emperor 'might conceivably translate itself into a demand for the restoration of the sacerdotal monarchy if little is done in the meantime to foster the idea of the Emperor as a genuinely popular monarch in a dignified and fatherly relationship to his people'. (PRO:FO 371/92521/5) Britain could have assisted in furthering this objective but MacArthur was determined to handle the situation himself.

The outstanding Japanese politician of the era was Yoshida Shigeru. An able diplomat in the pre-war period, Yoshida emerged as an ambitious and adroit leader of conservative forces. He opposed the new constitution and regarded various SCAP initiatives as too radical. But Yoshida was a realist and concluded that he must work with the Americans, while seeking to modify their policies in the directions he desired. (Dower 1979) Ironically, MacArthur preferred the left-wing Katayama Tetsu to the right-wing Yoshida Shigeru. MacArthur deemed Yoshida too slippery and perhaps indolent. F.S. Tomlinson of the Foreign Office rather patronisingly observed that Yoshida was 'able in his own way' but did not appear 'particularly well qualified' to deal with the problems facing him. (PRO: FO 371/76179/2420) Gascoigne commented in a final despatch that Yoshida was clever in evading responsibility on crucial issues by referring them back to SCAP:

Successive Prime Ministers, and especially Mr Shigeru Yoshida of the Liberal Party, who served as Ambassador in London from 1936 to 1939, have made the most of the necessity to refer matters of substance to the Supreme Commander for his decision, thus escaping responsibility and criticisms from their political opponents. This continual process whereby the Japanese Governments could lean back upon the Occupation in all moments of political difficulty has undoubtedly proved most deleterious to the political initiative of the men in power, who were losing their sense of responsibility. (PRO FO 371/92521/5)

At the close of MacArthur's term in April 1951, it would be accurate to state that MacArthur was confident that the occupation had placed Japanese politics upon a secure foundation which would obviate a recurrence of a bellicose foreign policy. The Foreign Office was less confident and feared that some of the old traits could reappear in the later 1950s.

In the social sphere MacArthur believed, in 1945–6, that encouraging trade unions would do much to change the balance in Japanese society away from excessive bias in favour of capitalism and the state obtaining previously. Trade unions were legalized fully for the first time and the Japanese Communist Party was permitted to operate without hindrance. MacArthur wished to see unions developing on the American pattern which meant, in essence, concentrating on economic objectives and eschewing political activities. American trade unionists were imported to assist.

The Labour government in Britain was keen to see moderate trade unionism triumph: the Ministry of Labour sent two labour advisers to assist the liaison mission in pursuing labour issues in discussions with SCAP. They were E. Ganz Wilson and George F.C. Matthews. However, sections of the labour movement in Japan did not act with the disciplined moderation MacArthur expected and friction between the unions and SCAP developed, stimulated by communists. MacArthur was determined not to tolerate a challenge from workers in the public sector. The British government shared anxiety over communist activities, since it was combating these in Britain itself but the right to take industrial action had to be respected. MacArthur adopted a policy of cracking down on militant unions and was subject to criticism from some in the United States for being soft on communism. Britain did not approve of the National Public Service Law as drafted and protested in August 1948. This incensed MacArthur and he gave vent to his wrath in a meeting with Gascoigne. Usually their discussions were amicable but this was an exception:

> My interview with the Supreme Commander was the most painful one I have yet had with him during my duty in Japan. The mere mention by me of National Public Service draft legislation and of our opinion thereon caused him to shout at me without stopping for one and three-quarters hours. (PRO FO 371/69823/12111)

MacArthur was irate at the fact that British criticisms echoed certain of those emanating from Moscow and this was described by MacArthur as a 'betrayal of trust'. Gascoigne denied any British intention of supporting the Soviet Union. MacArthur also made clear his annoyance with Australia because of the radical line adopted by the ambitious minister of external affairs, Dr Herbert Evatt, and the Australian representative in Tokyo, Patrick Shaw. (PRO FO 371/69823/1211) Gascoigne loyally adhered to Bevin's policy of fostering responsible trade union-ism in his discussions with MacArthur and Yoshida. He applauded MacArthur's decision to purge the entire central committee of the JCP in June 1950, just before the start of the Korean war:

> Happily, the Supreme Commander has recently taken what, in my opinion, was a very wise step: he has made two strong moves against the Communist Party by purging the whole of the party's Central Committee and the executive staff of its press organ. . . Furthermore he is prepared to make additional moves if necessary against the Communists. Indeed, it may become necessary for him to outlaw the party itself, and I am convinced that he will do this if he considers that the situation warrants it. (PRO FO 371/83831/93)

Gascoigne viewed SCAP's policies towards the trade unions as only partially successful: Japanese unions were still 'immature'. (PRO FO 371/92521/5)

MacArthur followed an enlightened policy towards the status and role of women in Japanese society. He attached importance to this in his memoirs. (MacArthur 1965: 349–50) This has to be seen in the light of his determination to eliminate militarism: greater influence for women could moderate the macho char-acteristics of Japanese society. Thus women received the vote and were encouraged vigorously to participate in national and local politics. The role of women had already been changing in consequence of the social and economic repercussions of the Pacific War: these had compelled women to play a bigger part in the functioning of families and of the economy. (Havens 1975: Hunter 1992) The initiatives of SCAP were welcomed by Gascoigne, if in terms reminding us that he was not an untypical member of the Foreign Office:

Heretofore the Japanese woman has been treated as the servant (almost the slave) of the male. It has been the object of the competent department of MacArthur's Headquarters to try to instil into the mentality of the Japanese male the necessity in our modern age, for Japanese women to be on an equal footing and to have equal rights with men. . . Instead of looking forward only to married life and the necessity of bearing as many children as possible, the young Japanese girl of to-day can in fact lead an independent life, and be of use to her country in many ways other than in the home. The emancipation of women must necessarily operate slowly; the older generation of Japanese men undoubtedly resent the freedom which is being given to the opposite sex, and their personal attitude towards women has changed very little during the past 4½ years. Thus in the case of the middle-aged and elderly people, the wife nearly always conforms to the feudal practice of waiting upon all the man's needs and gratifying his every whim and fancy. (PRO FO 371/92521/5)

Gascoigne was correct in discerning that the initial pace of change in advancing women's rights had slowed amidst the 'reverse course' from 1947–8. Japanese attitudes remained conservative but MacArthur had given an impetus to further change which would assume greater significance a generation after the occupation ended.

Education was crucial in transforming attitudes. The former emphasis on State Shintoism, militarism, and Japan's unique position, in expansionist terms, within Asia must be ended. MacArthur acted resolutely to undermine State Shintoism through advancing renunciation of divinity by the Emperor in 1946 and in pushing through the new constitution. He was less skilled in anticipating that Christianity might develop and offer a better foundation for a moderate, pacific approach than Shinto or militant Buddhism. The school structure and system were transformed on the American pattern. Co-education was encouraged, although this affected only ten per cent of schools by 1951, according to Gascoigne. (PRO FO 371/92521/5) Reactionary teachers were purged and textbooks revised; progress in the latter task was slowed by lack of paper and Gascoigne regarded this as 'particularly unfortunate'. He observed:

The process of purging the teachers, revising the text books and reorganising the curricula has been a long and difficult one; it is not at all certain even to-day that it has been successful. All that I can say here is that great efforts have been made to arrange for Japanese education on democratic lines and that this process is still continuing. (PRO FO 371/92521/5)

MacArthur was less successful in the economic sphere than in other directions and the successful revival of the economy resulted from the combination of intervention from Washington against his wishes, accentuated subsequently by the effects of the Korean War in stimulating economic growth. To be fair to MacArthur, he lacked economic expertise and the initial policy at the beginning of the occupation was to remove Japan's capacity to provide an economic base for renewed militarism and to purge the *zaibatsu*. The occupation was subsidized heavily by the American taxpayer, as John Foster Dulles liked to remind the British during his negotiations over a peace treaty in 1950–1. The Republican party controlled Congress in 1946–8 and calls for reductions in expenditure by the Truman administration were vocal. Ironically, MacArthur himself became embroiled in arguments when he allowed his name to be entered as a candi- date in certain of the primary election campaigns in 1948. MacArthur was a right-wing Republican, if of idiosyncratic bent, and he was irate at being denounced for favouring 'socialistic' policies in the running of the economy in Japan: he denounced his critics as a mixture of the ignorant and those representing vested business interests in the USA. When he met Lord Killearn early in 1948, MacArthur defined his attitude on economic questions:

> Turning to Japan's economy, MacArthur explained that what he wanted was to bring about suitable conditions for 'free com-petitive enterprise'. He stressed that his economic pattern for Japan was similar to the economic regime obtaining in the United Kingdom before 1939. He was not in favour of 'nation-alised' economy, nor, of course, was he in favour of the economy of the country being run in a centralised fashion by the large private combines of the past (the Zaibatsu). Japanese firms should be encouraged to trade freely and with as little inter-ference from the State as possible. Under present conditions, he explained, there were reasons why there must be integrated controls throughout Japan's economy, which would be necessary until peace had been signed and normal trading had been resumed. (PRO FO 371/69912/2023)

Developing signs of dissatisfaction in Washington with MacArthur's handling of the economy caused anxiety in London. The Foreign Office recognized that a more coordinated approach to economic issues was required but were apprehensive that those advocating a new policy might ride roughshod over America's allies and go too far by way of stimulating economic growth. Two of the influential Americans involved were George Kennan, head of the policy planning staff in the State Department, and General Draper. Gascoigne spoke to Kennan on 11 March 1948 to ascertain how the latter saw his mission. Kennan explained that he had come to Tokyo to familiarize himself with planning for East Asia. The surrender terms had been fulfilled and a phase of 'marking time' had been reached:

> During this period it might be desirable, while maintaining the present regime of occupation, to give Japanese more freedom in their own house so as to prepare them for the future when they would be on their own. I asked him what exactly he implied by this but he did not give me any specific examples; he made it quite clear, however, that he did not envisage an over-all change in the present mechanism of occupation and that he was only thinking of effecting such modifications in the said mechanism as might make the Japanese rely more upon themselves and less upon America. For instance he thought they should be informed of the total economic help which they might expect to obtain from the United States and be made to realize that over and above that they must shift for themselves. (PRO FO 371/69885/4043)

Gascoigne was impressed with Kennan's ability, appreciating that he was one of the key figures in developing the broad strategy of the Truman administration as the Cold War evolved. Kennan agreed that Britain must be consulted fully. Gascoigne believed that economic and strategic purposes were blending as American policy developed:

> Big business in America has entered upon the scene and there are probably influential persons in the State Department and out of it who feel it might be more in America's interests to delay making peace with Japan and thus get her firmly implanted within American orbit. Russia's recent policy of expansion no doubt also looms largely in the American picture and I feel that there are many in the States who probably hesitate to push on a peace conference which they fear might result in Japan being left wide open to Russian designs. (PRO FO 371/69885/4043)

Pressure from Washington increased in 1949. Joseph Dodge

visited Japan in April 1949 to assess the economic situation and he criticized MacArthur's direction of the occupation: he castigated his social reforms as 'uneconomic, impracticable, and dangerous'. (PRO FO 371/76182/6475) He favoured replacing MacArthur with a civilian body closely supervized from Washington. MacArthur was compelled to accept that he had lost control of the Japanese economy but Truman drew back from the immense challenge of dismissing MacArthur (only in March–April 1951 did Truman face up to this problem and then because of Korea, not Japan). Draper and Dodge desired stability in the economy and the serious threat of inflation was defeated as a consequence of firm action implemented in 1949 to control the budget and to eliminate subsidies. The Attlee government agreed, in 1948–9, that the economy should be revived with the aim of achieving the standard of living attained in 1930–4.

The USA was moving towards a more liberal and lenient policy towards Japan and this was significantly in advance of the approach advocated in Britain. Kennan was told in March 1948 that reparations should be demanded which should incorporate industrial assets, shipping, and ship-building capacities; gold deposits and other external assets should be used. (PRO FO 371/69885/4213) Specific causes for concern were the textile industry, shipping, and the potteries. The Lancashire textile industry was particularly energetic in conveying its alarm at a time when one of the periodic endeavours to revive the ailing industry was underway. Representations came from employers, trade unions and MPs. Raymond Streat, the able chairman of the British Cotton Board, feared low-cost Japanese competition. Streat attempted to advance cooperation with the American textile industry but this did not develop as he had hoped originally. In May 1950, Streat went to Japan and saw MacArthur. He congratulated MacArthur diplomatically on his success in heading the occupation: Streat emphasized that Japan should not entertain ambitions beyond its fair share in world cotton competition. Streat was impressed with MacArthur's mastering of his brief:

> He proceeded to speak with extreme lucidity and the liveliest expression on his face. He is an uncommonly good talker and easy indeed to listen to. He knew all the figures of spindlege pre-war and post-war and most of the figures of Japanese trade. He said that before the war Japan had built up a large international textile trade, part of which in his view, was legitimate and part illegitimate. Insofar as they provided cheap goods of

low quality for the coolies of eastern countries, who could not
afford anything better they performed a service to the world and
created for themselves a trade which conformed to their opportunities and resources. That was the legitimate half. Insofar as
they intruded on the very different trade in superior goods
which Britain and Germany and USA could make better than
they could and for which these and other countries had established
legitimate mark and insofar as this intrusion was achieved by
methods of subsidy and selling at less than cost it was an
illegitimate trade and very disruptive in world trading circles.
(LOWE 1986: 76)

Streat was dubious of MacArthur's distinction between 'legitimate' and 'illegitimate' trade. It would be accurate to state that
Streat was impressed deeply with MacArthur as a stage manager,
which was the usual reaction of those who met him in Tokyo,
but he was unconvinced that the economic recovery of Japan
would suit British economic interests.

The Labour government recognized that it would be impracticable to include restrictions on specific Japanese industries
in a peace treaty but the Foreign Office, Treasury, and Board of
Trade wanted action taken outside the framework of a treaty.
American policy proceeded more rapidly towards generous
treatment of Japan. This was a logical extension of the policy
followed by MacArthur and Gascoigne remarked, in mid-June
1950, that American policy was so easy-going that a crisis would
arise unless a peace treaty was concluded speedily:

> . . . the period of drift in our treatment of Japan which started
> some two years ago, is now reaching a critical stage, and I feel
> that if it should continue for much longer we may arrive at a
> point when either the Japanese will virtually be the masters of
> the occupation or the occupation will have to take very stern
> steps against the Japanese, which would indeed be a retrograde
> step. . . (PRO FO 371/83831/93)

From the summer of 1950 John Foster Dulles dominated discussions over a peace treaty, as he showed great energy and
vigour in securing a generous treaty in 1951.

MacArthur's original intention – and one that he reiterated
at regular intervals – was that Japan should become the 'Switzerland of the Far East and Pacific'. He wished to see a permanent
renunciation of militarism and regarded article 9 of the constitution
as sacrosanct. However, his comparison always involved
ambiguity, since Switzerland while refraining from war for a
lengthy period, has been prepared to defend itself tenaciously

via a 'citizen army'. (Lowe 1986: 77) Repercussions of the
deterioration in relations between the Soviet Union and the
West plus the victory of the Chinese communists, intensified
anxiety over Japan. In February 1948 MacArthur told Lord
Killearn that the western frontier of the USA had moved to
comprise a line extending through the Mariannas, Ryukyu, and
Bonin islands. He distinguished between Soviet expansion in
Asia, connoting China and Korea, which was 'a mainland affair'
and Soviet expansion to Japan and neighbouring islands which
could not succeed because of American air control in the
Pacific. If the Soviet Union ever threatened Japan directly, the
USA would respond immediately. (PRO FO 371/69912/2023)

The Pentagon believed in 1948–50 that Japan should be more
fully integrated into the Western defence structure: the generals
in Washington thought that MacArthur was too sanguine or
complacent in his rhetoric about Japan as an Asiatic Switzerland.
Accordingly, they opposed MacArthur's advocacy of an early
peace treaty, which was endorsed by Britain. For his part
MacArthur regarded the military men in Washington as obsessed
with European issues and ignorant of Asia. MacArthur was not
worried especially over the Soviet menace. He felt that the
whole of the Korean peninsula would fall into the communist
orbit within a few years, by which he meant Soviet orbit: this
did not alarm him, probably because he had seen it as inevitable
since 1947, if not earlier. MacArthur was alarmed at the victory
of the communists in China, for this raised the possibility of a
reunited and hostile China under dynamic new leadership,
adjacent to Japan. He believed passionately that Taiwan must not
be allowed to fall. (Foreign Relations of US 1949, VII, 2: 891–4)

In the main, British leaders and officials agreed with MacArthur
except in relation to Taiwan. The British outlook was affected by
the trauma of 1942 symbolized in the humiliating surrender of
Singapore and by the sadistic treatment of prisoners-of-war. In
addition, Commonwealth aspects had to be kept in mind: Australia
and New Zealand feared a revival of Japanese militarism more
than the threat of communism. Britain wished to defuse problems with Communist China through extending recognition to
Mao Tse-tung's regime in January 1950. Attlee and Bevin
aspired to drive a wedge between the Soviet Union and China
through fostering Western links with Peking. This initiative was
too bold for the USA: the Truman administration was ex-
coriated by Republicans for having 'lost' China and hysteria
over communism assumed dangerous proportions. A serious

divergence between Britain and the USA occurred over recognition, which continued to cause difficulties during the Korean War. (Lowe 1993: 211–26) The Foreign Office appreciated that inexorable pressures were pushing the USA towards encouraging a measure of rearmament in Japan before the outbreak of the Korean war. MacArthur apparently permitted certain former Japanese army officers to go to Taiwan from 1947 to advise the Kuomintang government: these included a prominent general. (PRO: FO 371/75770/10G)

The advent of the Korean War rendered it more urgent to produce a peace treaty and to ensure that Japan regained sovereignty upon a harmonious basis. The USA had vacillated over a treaty, largely because of disagreements between the State Department and the Pentagon, since the latter wished to ensure that American troops remained in Japan. President Truman acted to achieve a solution through appointing Dulles. Gascoigne reflected, in his concluding despatch, on the character of an impending treaty:

> There can be no question at this stage of our imposing a restrictive treaty on Japan. We shall have to rely upon our ability to control her by limiting, if that should be necessary, the importation of her vitally needed raw materials. Japan's future security must in the end, I feel sure, be provided by her own strength of arms. Her rearmament, which presents us to-day with complex political and economic problems, political because several of the allied nations concerned and notably Australia and New Zealand, will be likely to object, economic because Japan cannot under present conditions afford to re-arm herself without outside assistance, must come and come soon. For one thing, we cannot afford to use allied troops (American) to continue to guard Japan in a time of world crisis. Furthermore, as I see it, Japanese armies may well, in the not distant future, be needed to assist the allies to maintain the balance of power in this part of the world. (PRO FO 371/92521/5)

The problems to which Gascoigne alluded were handled by Dulles as satisfactorily as was possible which involved Japanese consent to American forces remaining on Japanese soil and the creation of the ANZUS treaties to afford sufficient guarantees to Australia and New Zealand. As regards MacArthur's achievements, Gascoigne concluded that SCAP had created the basis for a successful democratic system but:

> American Occupation officials have spoken too long and too loudly about the concrete and positive success of their democratic

campaign. In their great enthusiasm they have, many of them, made themselves believe that Japan is already firmly fixed within the democratic fold, and that the teachings which they have been at such pains to disseminate in this country for the past five years have taken firm and permanent root. The occupation has undoubtedly done extremely good work, but it is patently obvious that democracy, as we know it, cannot be imposed upon a people during a time of occupation; the democratic way of life can only be attained by years of patience and practice. (PRO FO 371/92521/5)

Thus, Gascoigne's conclusion, shared by colleagues in Whitehall, was that MacArthur had achieved a great deal in leading Japan to a new and more stable future but that extravagant claims were forthcoming on the extent of the achievement. Once the Japanese regained freedom from occupation constraints, it was probable that a swing to the right would occur. Gascoigne thought that there was a reasonable chance that Japan would 'settle down under a government which, although it may not be termed democratic, as we understand the use of that word, will exercise a degree of liberalism such as was implemented in this country in the 1920s'. (PRO FO 371/92521/5) However, this depended upon the international situation with communism being contained and with steady progress being made economically in Japan.

Only the coming generation could demonstrate how successful MacArthur's direction of the occupation proved. From the perspective of the 1990s, MacArthur was more successful than Gascoigne and British officials thought. The constitution survived without fundamental change; political stability existed, if with a distinct bias towards conservatism. Japan pursued a quiescent foreign policy and accepted American protection in defence policy. The economy grew to proportions undreamed of in 1951. Of course, many other Americans contributed to the development of the occupation and those pressing the 'reverse course' from 1947–8 deserve their share of credit for establishing the foundation of a more successful economic policy. The British perception of MacArthur's direction of affairs was positive, despite occasional disputes: he had worked hard and achieved as much as could be expected. This was in strong contrast to the British disapproval of MacArthur's leadership of UN operations in Korea: here he was seen as highly dangerous and British pressure contributed to Truman's decision to remove MacArthur in April 1951. (Lowe 1990: 624–53; 1994: 279–94,

340–2) In retrospect, Douglas MacArthur was the right man for the tasks of reconstructing Japan in the most constructive phase of his lengthy career.

BIBLIOGRAPHY

PRO = Public Record Office, Kew, London.

Buckley R.W., (1982) *Occupation Diplomacy: Britain, the United States and Japan* Cambridge: Cambridge University Press.
Clayton James D., (1970–85) *The Years of MacArthur* Boston.
Dower J.W., (1979) *Empire and Aftermath: Yoshida Shigeru and the Japanese Experience 1878–1954*, Cambridge, Mass.: Harvard University Press.
Foreign Relations of the United States (1949) Vol. 7, Part 2.
Havens T.H., (1975) 'Women and War in Japan, 1937–1945' *American Historical Review* 80, 4.
Hunter J., (1992) 'Women in the Japanese Labour Force' in T.G. Fraser and P. Lowe, *Conflict and Amity in East Asia: Essays in Honour of Ian Nish* Basingstoke: Macmillan, 59–76.
Lowe P., (1986) *The Origins of the Korean War* London: Longman.
Lowe P., (1990) An Ally and a Recalcitrant General: Great Britain, Douglas MacArthur and the Korean War, 1950–1 *English Historical Review*, CV, 624–653.
Lowe P., (1993) 'Hopes Frustrated: the impact of the Korean War upon Britain's Relations with Communist China, 1950–1953', in T.G. Fraser and K Jeffrey (eds.) *Men, Women and War Historical Studies XVIII*, 211–26.
Lowe P., (1994) 'Sir Alvary Gascoigne in Japan, 1946–1951', in Ian Nish (ed.) *Britain and Japan: Biographical Portraits* Folkestone: Japan Library, 279–94, 340–2.
MacArthur D., (1964) *Reminiscences*. New York: McGraw Hill Book Co.
Schaller M., (1989) *Douglas MacArthur: the Far Eastern General*, Oxford: Oxford University Press.

18

The Image of the Emperor Shōwa as a Symbol of National Aspirations

OLAVI K. FÄLT   *Translated by Malcolm Hicks*

The aim of this paper is to seek an answer to the question of what national aspirations the Japanese press projected as symbolized in the image of the Emperor Shōwa in 1945–1960, the years following the Second World War, i.e. the period of occupation and reconstruction. The sources employed for this are the issues of the English-language newspapers *The Japan Times* and *The Mainichi* and the Japanese-language *Asahi Shimbun, Mainichi Shimbun* and *Yomiuri Shimbun* published on the Emperor's birthday, 29 April, and *Kigensetsu*, 11 February.

THE YEARS OF OCCUPATION – RISE OF A NEW IMPERIAL IMAGE

When the Second World War ended in unconditional surrender for Japan this brought a fundamental change in the position of the Emperor. Acceding to the demands of the American occupation authorities, he was obliged to issue a rescript in January 1946 denying his divine nature, and when the constitution of 1947 was promulgated it contained an official definition of his new status. The Emperor was to be a symbol of the unity of the state and the nation, accorded this position by the free will of the people, who exercised supreme power. Thus all the actions of state which the Emperor performed were to be approved; by the government and the government was to be held responsible for them. (Brown 1955: 240–50)

Throughout the Second World War, the press had made use of the Emperor above all as a symbol of the fighting spirit of Japan, (Fält 1993: 93–106) and the adoption of this new approach did not come at once, for the tone of the newspapers at *Kigensetsu* and the Imperial Birthday in 1946 was still virtually the same as before. Thus, the *Nippon Times* (*The Japan Times*) sought to raise the nation's morale on the occasion of these festivals, and just as appeals had been made to the people during the war to continue the struggle in spite of all the setbacks, efforts were now made to stimulate confidence in the future and in national reconstruction. (*Nippon Times*: 11.2.1946)

The same spirit was also manifest on the Emperor's birthday in the spring, when the papers harked back to former times in telling of the honour afforded to the Emperor by all his people. Again, his status was exploited in the spirit of the traditional world-view in order to overcome the current difficulties, by emphasizing how the emotional bonds between a gracious ruler and his faithful people shaped the nation into a united family which was able to withstand the essential changes which had to be made in the country without any dangerous conflicts or tensions. (*Nippon Times*: 29.4.1946)

The crucial moment of change was the adoption of the new constitution and the decree by the occupying authorities on 5 July 1948 that *Kigensetsu* should be removed from the list of national feast-days and that the name of the Imperial Birthday should be changed from *Tenchōsetsu*, which referred to a special birthday, to *Tennō tanjōbi*, implying simply an ordinary birthday. The aim of the authorities was evidently to reduce the atmosphere of extreme reverence that surrounded the Emperor. (Woodward 1972: 142–7)

In addition to the official changes, a new element was introduced into the Emperor's birthday in 1948 by the opening of the area of the Imperial Palace to the public for the first time, and a further new feature was that the Emperor himself appeared on the roof of the palace to wave his hat in acknowledgement of the '*Banzai*' greetings shouted by the people. (*Nippon Times* 30.4.1948) This event can be interpreted as a conscious attempt to popularize the Imperial throne and bring the Emperor closer to the people in a manner in which the previous emphasis on the bond between the ruler and his people and their common destiny were replaced by a demonstration of personal interest and initiative on the part of the people.

During the later part of the occupation the image of the Emperor conveyed by the press was both very neutral and highly consistent. With only slight exaggeration, one could say that the bureaucratic conformity with which the image and information was communicated by the press resembled the situation during the war, a state of affairs brought about not only by the standard publicity material issued to the newspapers but also most of all by the circumstances of the occupation and the resulting mood of caution.

THE DECADE OF RECONSTRUCTION – THE EMPEROR AS A SOURCE OF INSPIRATION

The image seeks a form

The end of the occupation on 28 April 1952 meant a new situation for the development of the image of the Emperor and the symbolic use made of it. It was now possible to approach the question of his status from a national standpoint, free of the restrictions, seen or unseen, directly imposed or indirectly occasioned by the occupying powers. This became evident from the comments made on the termination of the occupation itself. All the papers carried the same picture of the Emperor and Empress, and those published in Japanese also contained long articles discussing the Emperor from various points of view.

The image conveyed by the *Asahi Shimbun* resembled that projected during the war, that of a ruler working to the utmost on behalf of his people. Now he was encouraging them in the work of reconstruction, attempting to share their burden with them. (*Asahi Shimbun* 28.4.1952) Almost the only differences, in fact, were that where appeals had previously been made to the image of the Emperor in order to promote the war effort, the appeal was now directed at the reconstruction effort, and that the image was no longer in the same sense a superhuman one.

The attitude adopted by the *Yomiuri Shimbun* was somewhat different. It projected the Emperor as an entirely human personality, with all his fears and uncertainties, and his sense of dependence on General Douglas MacArthur which had developed during the occupation. No attempt was made by this paper even indirectly to appeal to his image in connection with the reconstruction work, the paper being content to record the Emperor's own efforts in the same direction. (*Yomiuri Shimbun* 28.4.1952)

The image projected by the *Mainichi Shimbun*, on the other hand, was substantially similar to that of the *Asahi Shimbun*, in that it was exploited to encourage the people in the task of reconstructing their country. The paper was particularly anxious to emphasize the work done by the Emperor for the good of the whole nation during the occupation even though he had no formal political power. Also, contrary to the other papers, the *Mainichi Shimbun* did not even allude to any matter that might detract from his image, e.g. the demands made for his abdication at various points during the occupation years. (*Mainichi Shimbun* 28.4.1952)

It is extremely interesting to note that the English-language newspapers, intended for foreigners, did not carry any articles about the Emperor on Independence Day, only the same pictures as those published in Japanese. In other words, the nature of their readership was such that they would not concern themselves with what was an internal matter for Japan but were content to discuss independence from the viewpoint of the Japanese state and the international community. In this sense the image of the Emperor projected by the papers published in Japanese was both more intimate and more national in tone than that in the English-language ones, where it was cool and external. For foreigners the Emperor was an institution with a certain constitutional status, while for the Japanese he was, under the new interpretation, a person, a human Emperor, but still, with all his weaknesses, a figurehead whose image could be exploited for such purposes as advancing the rebuilding of the nation after the war. It is also possible that the attitude adopted by the English-language press may have been an attempt to avoid creating any impression that the Emperor occupied a special position in Japanese thinking.

The Imperial Birthday of 1953 was the first to be celebrated with the traditional ceremonies since the war, as the *Nippon Times* put it. The occasion had been kept to very modest proportions throughout the occupation, but now, on the first anniversary of the restoration of independence, all the rites and ceremonies that had existed before the war were being revived. The image of the Emperor contained in the papers spoke once more of his close relationship with the people, but with the added elements of his paternal feelings, evidently connected with Crown Prince's journey to Europe, and his scientific career, with references to his latest biological research, to be published in June of that year. (*Nippon Times* 29.4.1953, 30.4.1953; *The Mainichi* 30.4.1953; *Mainichi Shimbun Yukan* 28.4.1953: *Yomiuri Shimbun* 28.4.1953)

The emphasis placed on the Emperor's role as a father may point not only to an effort at softening his image and presenting more of his human side but also to his position as a symbol of national unity as viewed from the traditional Confucian perspective, i.e. that as well as being a father to his son, the Emperor was a father to the whole nation and cared for it in the same way.

The discussion of the Emperor's research interests was aimed at generating fresh respect for him as a person, and above all at encouraging the people in their reconstruction work and the creation of a new, affluent Japan. Certain fields of international cooperation existed in which the Japanese were able to compete freely with the Western nations and in which they could expect to be successful, and one of these was scientific research, in which the Emperor set an excellent example.

The *Mainichi Shimbun* went further than the others in conveying an impression of the Emperor as an eminent scientist and in stressing his closeness to the people, even going so far as to employ the metaphor of fusion, '*hitotsu ni toke atta*' (*Mainichi Shimbun Yulcan* 29.4.1953) This image had much in common with that which had prevailed during the war, in which the relation between the Emperor and the people had been regarded as some kind of bond of destiny.

Comparison of the papers published in Japanese and English shows very clearly that the former dealt in much greater detail with the ceremonies and other events connected with the Emperor's birthday, as these were naturally of greater importance to the Japanese themselves than to foreigners. (*The Mainichi* 29.4.1954; 30.4.1954; *Mainichi Shimbun* 29.4.1954)

Scientist, father and servant of the nation

The Emperor's scientific rôle was again the chief element in the image communicated by the press on the occasion of his 54th birthday, in 1955. The *Nippon Times* reported that his third scientific publication was to appear on his birthday, concerned with marine biology and containing details of 37 species of manatee, of which the Emperor himself had discovered 13. He was described as one of the most significant marine biologists in the world. *The Mainichi* similarly presented the Emperor as a researcher and indicated that the majority of his time was spent in the biological laboratory at the Imperial Palace. (*Nippon Times* 29.4.1954; *The Mainichi*, 29.4.1955)

In the same manner as the English–language papers, the *Asahi Shimbun* conveyed an image of the Emperor as a scientist, introducing his latest publication and his plans for further works in the future, while the *Mainichi Shimbun* recounted the course of his research work from the collection of samples from a ship to the publication stage, and the *Yomiuri Shimbun* wrote of his scientific career, stretching back to 1925, and emphasized the world-wide reputation that he had acquired in his field. (*Asahi Shimbun Yukan* 28.4.1955: *Mainichi Shimbun* 28.4.1955; *Yomiuri Shimbun* 28.4.1955)

The national day of commemoration, *Kigensetsu*, which had been prohibited by the occupation authorities eight years earlier, was discussed prominently in all the papers studied here in February 1956. There had admittedly been some references made to it in previous years, but now it seemed to be afforded very much more attention as an item of news. (*The Mainichi* 12.2.1955) The explanation for this must be sought in the general mentality of the times, for as noted by Kōsaka Masataka, the Japanese appeared to be instilled with a new vigour towards the end of the decade. (*Kōsaka* 1982:59–65) The country established diplomatic relations with the Soviet Union in October 1956 and became a member of the United Nations at the end of that year. Could it have been that this increased endeavour and restored self-respect were reflected in a heightened interest in the popular national day of commemoration, *Kigensetsu*, both in government circles and among the general public? In any case, the celebration of this day in a more visible form and the reporting of it in the news may be regarded as an indication of a recovery of the traditional Emperor-centred world-view after defeat in the war, even though the festival is not directly connected with the Emperor as such.

The *Nippon Times* gave wide coverage to the event, with a three-column picture on its front page and a reference in the caption to a parade of 3000 people demanding restoration of the national day, while *The Mainichi* noted that the festival was being celebrated on a wide scale for the first time since its prohibition by General MacArthur. (*Nippon Times* 12.2.1956; *The Mainichi* 12.2.1956) The *Asahi Shimbun* similarly went over the history of Foundation Day from its prohibition onwards and reported that Shintō circles, the political right wing and the conservatives were all calling for its restoration as a national feast-day. (*Asahi Shimbun* 11.2.1956)

It was evident that the national traditions associated with the Emperor had become an issue of the moment once more, for the old customs were also in evidence on the occasion of his

birthday. The *Nippon Times* drew particular attention to the fact
that the same ceremonies that had taken place before the war
were now being enacted all over the country, ceremonies in
which the Emperor was treated as a god. The paper was highly
critical of such commemorations, and pointed out that the
essential thing at that moment was to recall how wonderfully
the Imperial family had responded to the altered needs of the
nation when some circles had called for a restoration of the
pre-war *Tenchōsetsu*. This had stirred up bitter memories of the
objectionable conformity of opinions and their subordination
to the will of the brash element in the population who had
seized absolute power for themselves in the name of the
Emperor. The paper noted that this may have fitted in with some
people's plans, but the Emperor and the people knew better.
(*Nippon Times* 29.4.1956)

It was in precisely these turns of phrase that the *Nippon Times*
had, in an embarrassingly repetitious fashion, alluded to the
authority of the Emperor year after year throughout the 1920s
and 1930s to defend democracy against the threat of totali-
tarianism. Now the Emperor was again being invoked as a
symbol of democracy.

The Japanese-language newspapers, on the other hand, did
not comment on the celebrations other than observing at most
that certain attitudes existed that could be interpreted as critical
and mentioning cautiously that *Tenchōsetsu* was a celebration of
a divine emperor whereas *Tanjōbi* celebrated a human emperor
(*Asahi Shimbun* 29.4.1956; *Yomiuri Shimbun* 29.4.1956) The
reason why the Japanese-language papers did not contain the
same criticism as the *Nippon Times* may lie in their more
cautious attitude, as the subject was a delicate one on account of
the powerful emotions involved. It was very much easier for the
English-language papers to discuss such things, as they had a
predominantly foreign readership.

The above speculation that the increased interest in the
traditional *Kigensetsu* celebrations may have reflected a revival of
national self-confidence and endeavour receives support from
an article that appeared on 10 February 1957 in *The Japan Times*,
which had abandoned the name *Nippon Times* and reverted to
its former title. The paper noted that increasing support was
being shown for the notion that Japan should have a patriotic
day of its own, this idea having arisen out of a growing feeling
that the country had finally regained its international reputation
by having successfully completed the task of reconstruction and

having gained membership of the United Nations. The Japanese had regained much of their self-esteem and had even begun to feel proud of their country. This new mood was perfectly in order, as was the related idea of a national day. On the other hand, the paper maintained that this did not mean the revival of *Kigensetsu*, the feast of 11 February, as in addition to its lack of historical authenticity, it carried so many extremist military and nationalistic overtones. It was necessary to find another national day which took place on a different date and commemorated some other event. (*The Japan Times* 10.2.1957)

Celebration in which demands were made for the reinstating of *Kigensetsu* no longer commanded so much attention in the newspapers by the end of the period studied here, i.e. in 1960, possibly on account of the fact that the LDP government had abandoned its parliamentary bill to this effect in the light of objections by the opposition. Thus it was now easier to cast those who still called for its restoration as a small minority of extremists whose demands did not elicit any tangible response from the great majority. (*The Japan Times* 12.2.1960; *The Mainichi* 12.2.1960)

Although the revival of *Kigensetsu* was widely discussed in the press, this did not affect the image of the Emperor as such, other than turning people's attention indirectly to the features that had been characteristic of this image during the war years. On the contrary, the treatment of the Imperial Birthday became progressively more formulaic towards the late 1950s, repeating the same things from one year to the next. This also meant that the characteristics of the image of the Emperor which has persisted throughout the decade were reinforced still further. Thus the birthday articles in the *Asahi Shimbun*, *Mainichi Shimbun* and *Yomiuri Shimbun* in 1957, for example, all reviewed the Emperor's scientific activities in more or less the same words, and the accompanying picture, which was the same in all the papers, including the English-language ones, showed him bent over his work on his new research vessel, the *Hatagumo*. The papers reported on the work that he was doing on his new ship, the possibilities that it opened up, his modest nature as he worked away, dressed in his old clothes, the process of collecting and examining samples and identifying new species, his future publication plans and the help that he received from his family. Some mention was also made of the Emperor's everyday life at the palace, the signing of documents, the audiences with foreign visitors, research work in his laboratory, walks in the garden, watching the television and more research work in the evenings and the Sundays spent with his family. The papers also carried details of the day's festivities and instructions for members of the public going to the palace. The reports of the events of the day published afterwards similarly conformed to a fixed pattern. Only the *Yomiuri Shimbun* stood out from the other papers published in Japanese by mentioning the celebrations held in various parts of the country on the lines of the former *Tenchō-setsu*, although without commenting on them. The image of the Emperor as an extremely active, diligent person again served as a good example to the people.

The Imperial Birthday of 1959 was exceptional in the sense that it was the first time that the Emperor greeted the crowds together with his family, the Empress, Crown Prince Akihito, Crown Princes Michiko, Prince Yoshi and Princess Suga. The record number of visitors, 132,000, was evidently due to the presence of the Crown Prince and Princess following their marriage on 10 April. *The Japan Times* and *The Mainichi* did not comment on the occasion as such, but simply noted after the usual report that the whole imperial family had been there and that the number of visitors had been exceptionally large. (*The Japan Times* 29.4.1959, 30.4.1959; *The Mainichi*: 29.4.1959, 30.4.1959) The *Asahi Shimbun*, on the other hand, went through the day's events in more detail than the English-language papers, as was the case with the Japanese papers in general, and reported on how busy the Emperor was with the manuscript of his latest book, a further reference to his scientific work. (*Asahi Shimbun* 29.4.1959) The *Mainichi shimbun* emphasized the family aspect of the Emperor's image, describing the meals that they had together on Sundays and the Emperor's love for walks in the garden, and for his garden in general, his desire to pass its secrets on the Princess Michiko and the homely, popular side of his nature in the form of his great interest in sumo wrestling and baseball, the latter of which was also mentioned by the *Yomiuri Shimbun*, alongside his research work. (*Mainichi Shimbun* 29.4.1959, *Yomiuri Shimbun* 29.4.1959)

The image of the Emperor in the period following the restoration of Japanese sovereignty in 1952 may be seen to reflect the problems and aspirations of the times, and also the changes that took place in the country's international position. At first it had retained the feature reminiscent of the war years of the Emperor encouraging his people in their reconstruction efforts, sharing their hardships and serving as an example to them all by his diligence. One prominent element in the image throughout the decade was his rôle as a scientist, which, particularly at the early stages, must have reflected the idea of him setting an example to the nation in peaceful international cooperation. The reporting of his birthday was probably motivated by the desire to find new means of strengthening the bond between the Emperor and the people and to bring out the respect that the nation felt for their Emperor in the context of the new democratic constitution. A further typical feature was the stressing of the human side of his personality, with its fears, uncertainties, paternal feelings, homely moments spent with his family and towards the end of the decade popular interests such as sumo and baseball.

The newspapers published in Japanese usually went through the birthday ceremonies in greater detail than did their English-language counterparts, because these meant more to Japanese readers. There was also a clear difference towards the end of the decade in that the English-language papers, particularly *The Japan Times*, were highly critical of the possible effects of the increased self-confidence of the Japanese as expressed in the demands for the restoration of the *Kigensetsu* festival, banned during the occupation, and of the *Tenchōsetsu* in its traditional form, whereas the Japanese-language papers were very much more cautious in their handling of this subject. This was a delicate matter and one which was apt to provoke outspoken opinions, and it was evidently for this reason that attempts were made to avoid stirring the matter up. This consideration was not so important in the English-language papers, of course, in fact it was important to demonstrate that there was no question of the atmosphere that had prevailed before and during the war being revived. In this sense the image of the Emperor was even exploited in support of democracy, as it had been in some cases in the 1920s and 1930s.

BIBLIOGRAPHY

Nippon Times (from 1957 *The Japan Times*)
The Mainichi
Asahi Shimbun
Mainichi Shimbun

Brown D.R., (1955) *Nationalism in Japan: an introductory analysis*, Berkeley: University of California Press.
Fält O.K., (1993) The Status of the Emperor as a National Symbol in the

Fifteen Year War Period, 1931–1945, in I. Neary (ed.) *War, Revolution and Japan* Folkestone: Japan Library, 93–106.

Kosaka M., (1982) *A History of Post-war Japan* Tokyo: Kodansha.

Woodward W.P., (1972) *The Allied Occupation of Japan and Japan Religions*, Leiden: E.J. Brill.

19

Prime Ministerial Leadership in Japanese Foreign Policy*

BERT EDSTRÖM

INTRODUCTION

The rôle of leadership is one of the perennial questions that political scientists have discussed back and forth in countless treatises. At the one extreme are scholars who argue that leaders do not count for much in foreign policy. A classical case is that of J. David Singer who, in a seminal article, argued that the international system so shapes and constrains policy that individual policy-makers can have little impact (Singer 1961: 77–92) At the other extreme are scholars and analysts who find that the importance of foreign policy decision-makers exceeds that of any other factors in determining foreign policy. (Shapiro and Bonham 1973: 147–174) For those who hold that the policy-maker matters, it is also an open question whether it is the role that is of decisive importance or whether it is the political leader's personality that has the greatest bearing on foreign policy. Those who emphasize the *role* argue that the leader is but a representative who reflects the views and beliefs of the constituency he represents. Famous is the dictum that 'where an individual sits in the process determines. . . the stand that he takes. (Halperin 1974: 17) Those who find it impossible to disregard the impact that *personality* has on the foreign policy enacted by the decision-maker argue that it matters whether it is one politician rather than another who is in charge. In an

* Revised version of a paper presented to the 7th International Conference of the European Association for Japanese Studies, Copenhagen, August 22–26, 1994. I would like to take this opportunity to thank Kazuki Iwanaga as well as Ernst Lokowandt and other seminar participants for their comments on this paper

empirical study of succession in democracies, as well as in socialist countries, Valerie Bunce demonstrated that the election of a new leader means that the policy implemented by the government is affected and she concluded, 'Who rules does indeed make a difference.' (1981: 256)

The problems characterizing analyses of leadership are also to be found in descriptions of Japanese foreign policy. On the one hand are those who claim that Japanese foreign policy has been characterized by a singular lack of leadership. In his memoirs, for instance, Henry Kissinger characterized the style of Japanese leaders representing their country internationally as 'understated' and 'anonymous' (1979: 324) and Gerald Curtis once described Japan's foreign policy as 'essentially defensive and reactive and characterized by pragmatic responses to international developments as they unfold'. (1979: 22)

On the other hand, the view that leaders have had an impact on the formulation and execution of Japanese foreign policy also has vocal proponents. After studying the negotiation process that resulted in Sino-Japanese normalization in 1972, Haruhiro Fukui concluded that the Prime Minister and the Foreign Minister participated actively in this process on the Japanese side, while all other cabinet members were almost completely shut out of the decision process. According to Fukui, it was abundantly clear that it was the Prime Minister who had played 'the first fiddle' in this case. (1977: 100)

The most common view, however, is reflected in the claim that, while some leaders have demonstrated leadership, most have failed to do so. Frank McNeil, a long-time observer of Japanese politics, remarked in a recent analysis: 'The conventional wisdom among Euro-American observers, and among many Japanese as well has been that Prime Ministers lack leader- ship. That judgement reflects insistence on defining leadership in Western terms – as a charismatic or, as in the case of Truman, a take-charge type. In those terms only Yoshida, Kishi, and Yasuhiro Nakasone fit the bill. (1993: 37) McNeil's view is similar to a conclusion that Watanabe Akio drew in 1977 from his comparative study of US and Japanese foreign policy decision-making. According to Watanabe, most Japanese premiers failed to exert leadership in foreign policy. Only Yoshida Shigeru, who governed as Prime Minister during eight years after the Second World War (1946–47, 1948–54), and Hatoyama Ichiro, Prime Minister between 1954 and 1956, could be said to have exerted leadership, according to Watanabe: Yoshida earned his reputation for leadership during the negotiations for the peace treaty that was concluded in 1951, while Hatoyama showed that he was a leader during the negotiations with the Soviet Union that resulted in the normalization of diplomatic relations between the two countries in 1956. (1989: 83)

DEFINING LEADERSHIP

As hinted at by McNeil in the passage quoted above, the answer to the question of whether Japanese Prime Ministers have demonstrated leadership in foreign policy hinges on how leadership is defined. One problem for any study of leadership interpreted is that the concept itself is elusive. (Blondel 1980:9) As pointed out by Lewis J. Edinger, one of the foremost scholars of leadership, a troublesome problem for anyone searching for generally acceptable working definitions of political leadership is that studies associate it variously with such concepts as power, influence, command, authority, and control in confusing, if not contradictory terms. (Edinger 1990: 510) Chong-do Hah and Frederick C. Bartol noted in a review article of studies of political leadership that such studies have almost exclusively been concerned with 'leaders', and thus, with the drive of certain individuals to assume leading political roles. (Hah & Bartol 1983: 100)

Basically, there are two approaches to the definition of leadership to be found in the literature. One is the *positional* approach: leaders are defined by the position they occupy. A leader is a President, Prime Minister, chairman of political party, etc. The other type of definition is *behavioural*: leaders are defined by the actual and effective part they play. It seems reasonable to state that it is not the position as such that constitutes leadership, but the behaviour associated with the position. 'Indeed', Jean Blondel has noted, 'a moment's reflection shows that titles and positions are means of acquiring leadership, or sources of leadership: they are not leadership itself.' (1987: 11) A leader is someone who influences a group whether or not he or she happens to be formally at the head of that group. This is captured in Robert C. Tucker's description of leadership 'as a kind of activity that leaders seek to perform in their capacity as leaders.' (Tucker 1981: 13) One definition of political leadership explicitly linking position and behaviour has been presented by Edinger, according to whom it can be defined as 'a position or – in the language of the cognitive approach to role analysis – the location of an actor or actors in a group, characterized by the ability of the incumbent to guide the collective behavior of this group in the direction of a desired authoritative distribution of values in a political community.' (1972: 217) According to this definition, the core of the concept is not the position but the behaviour associated with it.

THE BASIS OF PRIME MINISTERIAL LEADERSHIP

Taking Edinger's definition as a starting-point, the first matter to decide in any study of leadership is who the leader(s) is/are. After surveying the foreign policy literature, William Wallace concluded that '[t]he conventional wisdom of academic inter-pretation, it would be fair to say, remains that foreign policy is an élite process, dominated by the executive' (1971: 40) This is true of Japan, where formal decision-making power is vested in the Prime Minister, the government, the parliament, and the Ministry of Foreign Affairs, although a number of other actors can influence foreign policy, among them the political parties and their factions, interest groups, public opinion, and the mass media. (Fukui: 1977: 4) According to the constitution, the government is charged with the management of foreign as well as domestic affairs. Article 73 of the constitution reads: 'The Cabinet, in addition to other general administrative functions, shall perform the following functions: (i) Administer the law faithfully; conduct affairs of state; (ii) Manage foreign affairs. Conclude treaties. However, it shall obtain prior or, depending on circumstances, subsequent approval of the Diet [. . .]'. It follows from these constitutional provisions that it is the government which occupies the central position in foreign policy-making, while the parliament controls rather than deter-mines foreign policy. This is reflected in the literature on Japanese foreign policy, in which a fairly general view has been that the parliament has not played a significant role in foreign-policy formulation, at least not in the initial decades of the post-war period. (Sato 1977: 387) For a long time after the war, the parliament was no more than a ratifier of decisions that had been taken by the Prime Minister and his colleagues. (Baerwald 1974:139–141;1977:37) The internal structure and processes of the parliament rendered it relatively impotent in foreign policy-making. The most important factor limiting the role of the parliament was the cleavage of the political parties into two opposing blocs, one consisting of the Liberal Democratic Party

(LDP) and the other of the opposition parties. The divergence in the foreign policy goals of the LDP and those of the dominant opposition party, the Socialist Party, was considerable and left little room for compromise. Up to mid-1993, it was clearly the LDP which had the upper hand in foreign policy. The party commanded a solid position as the largest of the political parties and was, by and large, able to implement its policies without having to be too concerned with its rival parties, which seemed to be doomed to eternal opposition.

The constitution assures the Prime Minister control over government administration. Article 72 of the constitution reads: 'The Prime Minister, representing the Cabinet, submits bills, reports on general national affairs and foreign relations to the Diet and exercises control and supervision over various administrative branches.' The central role given to the Prime Minister by the framers of the constitution is also clearly seen in the provision of Article 74, which stipulates: 'All laws and cabinet orders shall be signed by the competent Minister of State and countersigned by the Prime Minister.'

The pre-eminent position of the Prime Minister within the political system is made abundantly clear by Article 66, which stipulates that the premier is the head of the government, Article 68, which states that it is the prerogative of the premier to appoint as well as dismiss the ministers, and Article 72, which stipulates that the premier represents the government. These provisions can be seen as the basis of the powers vested in the prime minister. The government is a decision-making collectivity, but once in power the Prime Minister as an individual is in a relatively strong position *vis-à-vis* his cabinet colleagues. (Destler 1976: 61; Drifte 1990: 17) The background to these provisions was the conviction of the authors of the post-war Japanese constitution that the pre-war administrative structure's vague definitions of personal authority and responsibility had contributed to Japan's international behaviour during the 1930s and 40s, a recurrence of which they were determined to hinder. (Angel 1988–9: 586)

The stipulation that the government shall 'conduct affairs of state' and 'manage foreign affairs' endows it with the power to make decisions as well as set the agenda. The central role assigned to the Prime Minister in the constitution gives him the potential of exercising these functions together with the government. Furthermore, the stipulation in Article 72 that the Prime Minister represents the government gives him the additional role of national spokesman – when acting in the international arena.

Decision-maker

The Prime Minister's central rôle for decision-making is based on his constitutional position as the chief executive of the government. The provisions of the constitution have given the Prime Minister primacy in decisions concerning major foreign policy issues both in fact and institutionally. (Hellman 1988: 353) As the leader of the executive ministries of government, the Prime Minister has the potential to direct and command the organizations and people who do the bulk of the planning and implementation of public programmes. During the long period in which the LDP was the ruling party, the premier had powers which could not be matched by other actors. His position was based not only on the provisions of the constitution and the fact that he was elected to his office but also due to the fact that he had been elected president of the party that dominated Japanese politics.

The Prime Minister's pre-eminence in foreign policy is highlighted by the fact that certain foreign policy matters are dealt with by the prime minister alone – as witnessed by Hatoyama Iichirō, who was minister of foreign affairs at the end of the 1970s. (Hirano 1980: 11) One who excelled at autocratic decision-making was Yoshida Shigeru, who is often called 'the father of post-war Japanese foreign policy'. His style was in contrast to that of other Japanese Prime Ministers in the post-war period. He was considered by his contemporaries to be so domineering that he was frequently referred to as 'One Man' whose rule was 'almost arbitrary'. (Kawai: 1960: 114)

The pre-eminence of the prime minister in his capacity as decision-maker has been seen as even more striking on some occasions in the past, when the incumbent has demonstrated an ability to act as what the Hermanns have named 'the ultimate decision-maker' in the sense that he has 'the ability to commit the resources of the society and, with respect to a particular problem, the authority to make a decision that cannot be readily reversed.' (Hermann & Hermann 1989: 362) In the context of domestic political affairs, one such agenda-setter was Ikeda Hayato, prime minister between 1960 and 1964, who has been described by a leading political figure as having exercised 'creative political leadership in 1960, when he made his decision to commit Japan to doubling its income within a decade. Not many people believed it was possible. He set the basic course for the next twenty years or more.' (Wataru 1989:42)

A number of other post-war premiers are associated with crucial and sometimes agonizing foreign-policy decisions. Writing in 1972, Donald C. Hellman noted:

Whether by design or not, each Prime Minister has assumed personal responsibility for, and identity with, one principal policy achievement during his administration, and inevitably major foreign-policy decisions have fallen into this category. 'Normalization of Soviet relations' (Hatoyama), 'renewed security alliance with the United States' (Kishi), and 'return of Okinawa' (Sato) have all come to be seen as keystones in the respective administrations. Because these critical decisions acquire a personal definition, the full prerogatives of office are employed to bring about their achievement. . . (1972: 56)

The foremost figure in this respect is no doubt Yoshida Shigeru. Few Japanese would deny Yoshida's importance for post-war Japanese foreign policy. The former top diplomat who became Prime Minister in 1946 remained in office until the end of 1954, a long reign interrupted only by a break from May 1947 to October 1948. In many descriptions of post-war Japan it is claimed that it was Yoshida who created the underpinnings not only of the foreign policy of post-war Japan but of post-war Japan itself. Although public opinion and many of his fellow politicians expressed a desire for Japan to pursue an independent policy line, Yoshida, on behalf of Japan, consented to the sub-ordination of Japanese policy to the Cold War strategy of the United States by signing the mutual security treaty with that country in 1951. He had concluded that, as an occupied country, Japan had no choice but to yield to the wishes of the United States in order to attain the goal that had been given top priority during the occupation years of 1945–52: the end of the occupation. Yoshida's decision was of a momentous importance and shaped Japanese foreign policy. (Edström 1993: 85–140)

In retrospect, Yoshida has been viewed by many as a statesman who personally determined the course Japan would take in the post-war world. That he was personally responsible for this was demonstrated during the peace treaty negotiations in San Francisco in 1951, when Japan signed not only a peace treaty with 48 other countries, but also a bilateral security treaty with the United States: Yoshida was the only Japanese delegate to sign

the security treaty, while all the members of the Japanese delegation signed the peace treaty. Yoshida himself claimed later,
moreover, that his intention had been to personally assume
responsibility for the security treaty. (Yoshida 1963: 159)
However, his fame is maybe misplaced: whether Yoshida had the
choice of refusing to sign the peace treaty is not at all certain.
Even the most vocal of Yoshida hagiographers has claimed that
'[t]here existed no choice for Japan outside of an alliance with
the United States.' (Kosaka 1989: 298) I have argued elsewhere
that, were the result inevitable, its achievement could not in fact
have been the great accomplishment that Yoshida's ardent
believers maintain it to be. (Edström 1992: 19) Nevertheless,
there seems to be general agreement in Japan that Yoshida's feat
was of singular importance in the sense that he not only gained
admission to the Western camp for Japan on the basis of its ties
with the United States, but also laid the foundations for the
economic success and prosperity that Japan enjoys today. (Iokibe
1989: 29) As the Japanese post-war success story continued to
unfold, Yoshida was increasingly given the credit, and developments were seen as the result of his leadership.

A question raised by Margaret G. Hermann in 1978 – 'Must
the times be right for the man or will the man be a great leader
regardless of the times?' (Hermann 1978: 50) – would probably
not make sense to Yoshida's admirers. Nevertheless, Nishimura
Kumao, a high-ranking Japanese official who worked for Yoshida
in the negotiations with the US that brought about the end of
the occupation and, hence, Yoshida's elevated standing among
most Japanese, indicated in an interview that under different
circumstances than those prevailing after the war, Yoshida would
not, perhaps, have been considered the great man that he was
generally seen to be: 'Yoshida was the right man for those hard
times', Nishimura said in the interview. 'He was decisive, strong,
stubborn, and secretive. Of course, these same qualities would
make him less suitable for a normal peacetime democracy
. . . But back then, the times were tough and Yoshida was the
sort of leader that the country needed.' (Yoshitsu 1983: 32)

In the study by Watanabe Akio referred to above, the author
drew the conclusion that Yoshida's successor as Prime Minister,
Hatoyam Ichiro (Prime Minister 1954–56), also passed the test
of having exercised leadership. Watanabe based his verdict on the
determination that Hatoyama displayed in securing the normalization of Japan's relations with the Soviet Union. At the outset,
the Japanese Ministry of Foreign Affairs was not enthusiastic

about the negotiations, partly because the premier dealt directly with the Soviet Union, bypassing the ministry, and partly because ministry officials did not want to initiate negotiations against the wishes of the U.S. government and former Prime Minister Yoshida. (Hosoya 1989: 27) In order to win the domestic political support needed to achieve his overriding diplomatic goal – a normalization of relations with the Soviet Union – Hatoyama resigned his post as Prime Minister. In the eyes of Watanabe, this was a personal sacrifice which testified to Hatoyama's political leadership.

One of the few premiers to explicitly comment on his leadership was Tanaka Kakuei, Prime Minister between 1972 and 1974. Typical of Tanaka as a political leader was a remark he made in his maiden policy speech to the parliament as newly appointed Prime Minister: 'The politics of the 1970s,' he said, 'require strong leadership.' (Naikaku Seido: 1986: 853) Tanaka's use of the outlandish term *ridashippu* was a way to show himself to be a dynamic leader in the context of a new kind of politics, replacing his predecessor, the staid and cautious Sato Eisaku. Tanaka knew that his prime attraction for Japanese voters was the fact that he was seen as a new type of political leader with a bold vision for the future, who offered the Japanese a bright future and new options. He understood well the instrumental function of a leader, which is 'to set the goals of the group and direct its members towards the achievement of such goals.' (Ike 1978: 52) The role of the politicians, Tanaka said, was to make practical goals clear to the people, indicate limitations, and make all-out efforts to realize those goals. (Naikaku Seido 1986: 853)

Another premier who explicitly commented upon leadership was Fukuda Takeo, Prime Minister between 1977 and 1979. In a policy speech to the parliament he stated: 'Our country's responsibilities towards international society are now extremely heavy, and as [we] move towards the 1980s, [Japan] is being urgently called upon to play a leading role.' (Naikaku Seido 1986: 985) It is evident from this that Fukuda did not like Tanaka's talk of *ridashippu*; being a task for the Prime Minister, but instead indicated that it was Japan as a nation which was called upon to be an international leader. The term used by Fukuda to indicate the kind of role that Japan was called upon to play was *sendōteki*, i.e., 'leading' in the sense of 'guiding'. Thus, he saw Japan as a prospective leader, in the sense of guiding. This was in line with his view that Japan was 'a new type of great power', with a position based not on military power as had been the case with the old powers, but on economic power and moral virtues. (Edström 1988: 189–90) In the Japanese parliament, the Prime Minister declared his determination 'to make every possible effort to ensure that our country is cognizant of this responsibility and fulfills its rôle in response to world expectations. (Naikaku Seido 1986: 983)

As noted above, where McNeil is quoted, one Prime Minister who was widely seen as having exerted leadership was Nakasone Yasuhiro. Like Tanaka, he had a clear grasp of the rôle of the politician: 'The politician must always be a reformer refusing to be satisfied with "business as usual", but also both practical and constructive,' was how he put it in one of his policy speeches to the parliament (Naikaku Seido 1986: 1129) Nakasone was widely regarded as a dynamic leader. As the head of one of the middle-sized LDP factions, he had experienced the severe limitations on the room to manoeuvre in factional politics and resistance against political change that was a result of the existence of factions. He was therefore an advocate for the creation of a direct link between the public and premier that would allow the latter to claim a popular mandate in the exercising of his authority. (Angel 1988–9: 594) By securing public endorsement and national consensus, opposition from the government bureaucracy, from factions within the Liberal Democratic Party and from the official parliamentary opposition could be outflanked. (George 1988: 267) His 'top-down' formula for political leadership envisaged a chief executive with the authority and administrative resources available to US presidents, which would make it possible for the Prime Minister to circumvent the constraints that were imposed on him by factional politics. For many years he had called for a presidential style of government, and when he became Prime Minister he stated that the Japanese Prime Minister should be a presidential one. (Nakasone 1992: 330) He used his time in office to convert prime ministerial power into party power in a very concrete way. (Curtis 1988: 105) In retrospect, it has been said that Nakasone's top-down style led to a 'presidentialization' of the prime ministership (Kusano 1989: 84) Looking at Nakasone's successors as Prime Minister, it is hard to find confirmation of such a verdict, as several of the premiers who assumed office after Nakasone turned out to be quite weak; one of them, Kaifu Toshiki, was even nicknamed 'the teflon politician' for his ability to adjust his opinions to the power game being played within the Liberal Democratic Party, and another, Miyazawa Kiichi, fell from grace for his inability to act decisively when needed.

National spokesman

The second important role played by the Prime Minister is that of national spokesman in international arenas. It is well illustrated by the case of Nakasone. It has been claimed that Nakasone's period in the Prime Minister's office was prolonged because of 'a common perception that strong "Western-style" leadership was needed in the face of intense foreign pressure for basic changes in economic policy' (Stockwin 1988: 20) While incumbent, he was hailed as a politician who not only was able to stand shoulder-to-shoulder with the leaders of the major Western industrialized countries, but who had also ensured that Japan's presence on the international political stage was one that loomed larger than ever before in the post-war period. Other post-war premiers have also explicitly alluded to their capacity as national spokesmen. In his policy speech in the parliament on 17 June, 1958, for instance, Prime Minister Kishi Nobusuke stated:

> As required by the entire Japanese populace I have been vigor-
> ously advocating this [disarmament] for a long time to the
> whole world and, based on this kind of perception, have strongly
> promoted its realization on every occasion and by every means.
> The Government is determined to continue, in close cooper-
> ation with all like-minded countries of the world, to work
> unremittingly to bring about a total ban on nuclear weapons by
> appealing to the common sense of mankind. (Naikaku Seido
> 1986: 591)

The premier's function as national spokesman was also eloquently expressed by Prime Minister Suzuki Zenko in a speech to the United Nations in 1982. Ogata Sadako describes how the two chambers of the Japanese parliament adopted identical resolutions on the promotion of disarmament, particularly nuclear disarmament, prior to the departure of Prime Minister Suzuki for the special session in 1982. 'The prime minister was fully aware of the domestic significance when he addressed the special session in the following moving terms: "I stand here today in this Assembly Hall, representing the collective will of the Japanese people, as expressed in those resolutions [. . .]".' (Naikaku Seido 1986: 591)

That the premier functions as a spokesman for Japan is also illustrated by cases in which a Prime Minister has made a statement that has subsequently been corrected. One such case occurred in 1972, at the end of Sato Eisaku's tenure as Prime Minister. According to a report filed by Thomas Ross, the Prime Minister had been 'mehrmals mit außenpolitischen Erklärungen vorgeprescht, hinter denen offenbar weder reifliche Überlegung noch Beratung im Kabinett stand.' (Frankfurter Allgemeine Zeitung 8 March 1972) Some of the statements made by the Prime Minister had to be 'promptly corrected' by his foreign minister. (Nakamura 1972) The important information in these reports is that the Prime Minister functioned as a spokesman, and when he conveyed information and views which did not represent his government, they were corrected.

CONSTRAINTS ON THE PREMIER'S LEADERSHIP

As noted above, the authors of the Japanese constitution wanted to endow the Prime Minister with personal authority, but also personal responsibility, for policy-making. However, Japanese foreign policy decision-makers have been acutely aware that situational factors, both domestic and international, severely limit the number of available options. (Hellman 1988: 368–74) The extensive formal powers that the Prime Minister enjoys and the responsibility for policy leadership that is vested in him have in practice been limited, and the extent of his powers is nothing like that of the American president or even the British Prime Minister. (Kawaii 1960: 114; Destler 1989: 111) Juxtaposed to the wide latitude in terms of authority and responsibility given to the Prime Minister under the constitution are a number of constraints which limit his scope of action. These constraints derive from factors operating on a number of levels.

Constraints on the role of decision-maker

The scope of activities open to the Japanese Prime Minister is restricted by factors originating in the political party system. One such factor is a function of the process in which the premier is elected, which has been said to favour a certain type of personality. 'Rather than breeding individuals with pronounced leadership qualities,' Hosoya Chihiro and Usui Hisakazu have argued, 'Japanese political culture breeds individuals with a sense of balance, attaching importance to harmony [*wa*] within the organization, which makes it difficult to produce a leader who promotes active discussion and positively shows the way.' (Haroya and Usui 1985: 91)

Hosoya and Usui are not the only analysts who have noted the importance of psychological factors to the foreign policy of Japan, but it has usually been claimed that such factors reside on a higher level than that of the individual. In a section of his book on Japanese security policy published in 1981, Taketsugu Tsurutani pointed out that 'the character, motivation, and dynamics of Japan's unique political psychology [is] the most crucial source of its external conduct during the past decades.' (Tsurutani 1981: 5) A similar view was expressed in 1979 by Gerald Curtis in a discussion of Japanese foreign policy. He noted that Prime Minister Fukuda Takeo had struck a responsive chord in Japan by using an image of himself as captain of the ship *Nippon Maru*. According to Curtis:

> Foreign policy is seen as a problem of moving Japan between the Scylla and Charybdis of international political and economic affairs, with success being dependent on a combination of skill, fortitude, and luck. This psychological orientation is not conducive either to bold initiatives or to grand strategy; it contributes to a proclivity toward policies that emphasize the minimizing of risks rather than the maximizing of opportunities, and to behaviour that is reactive and defensive. (1979: 70)

Even if it is true that the election process will, in many instances, yield politicians with the special psychological make-up described by Hosoya and Usui, this is not necessarily always the case. Nakasone's personality clearly contradicts the descriptions of politicians referred to above as he is anything but a soft-spoken politician. What was characteristic of his style as premier was, instead, that with his 'commanding presence wherever he goes' he was in every sense the opposite sort of personality to that argued by the aforementioned scholars as typical of Japanese leaders. (McNeil 1993: 37)

The process of electing the Prime Minister also influences his ability to act in a way that differs from that of harmony-oriented personality types. To become Prime Minister, a politician has to command the support of a majority of the parliament. Up to 1993 when the LDP was the dominant party in the parliament, its party chairman was 'automatically' elected Prime Minister. The LDP consists of a number of factions and the party leader is recruited from among those who can best operate in the world of factions, making it necessary for a politician wanting to become premier to win the support of those factions. When selecting a new chairman of the party, and, thus, the prime minister-to-be, more consideration would be taken of his effectiveness as an intra-LDP political operative than as national leader. (Murakami: 1979: 12–13) Writing in 1967, Robert E. Ward described the situation prevailing in the 1960s as follows:

> In conservative circles, it makes very little difference whether a given person is an accomplished public speaker or possessed of a personality with wide popular appeal. The meaningful criteria are more apt to be length of political service, abilities as a fund raiser, skill as a tactician, administrative ability, possession of useful connections, and a personal reputation for loyalty and sincerity. Such a system tends to bring to the fore men of experience, caution, and a generally conservative approach to political problems rather than more brilliant or venture-some types. (1967: 80)

Even if the LDP had comfortable enough advantage over the opposition parties in the parliament, the 'mainstream' factional coalition backing the Prime Minister was volatile, which made the position of the premier insecure and his tenure as premier dependent more on his intra-party skills than on policy commitment or leadership. (Tsurutani 1981: 3) The government was a chance congeries of contending, mutually mistrustful intra-party factions. In order to survive as Prime Minister, the incumbent had to maintain the support of a majority in the parliament, which meant that he had to continue to command the support of a majority factional coalition, and thus had a strong incentive to avoid divisive policy issues, which meant that the premier had to concentrate primarily on intraparty politics. (Angel 1988–9 987; Destler 1976: 61) The premier had to act as a go-between in order to balance the interests of different factions and other groupings within the party, which made it difficult to take bold decisions. Consequently, factional struggle became important to decision-making. (Hanai 1975: 271f)

Thus, the scope enjoyed by a given Prime Minister to play the rôle of a forceful leader was often minimal, as he was expected to be an articulator of consensus. (Hellman 1979: 96) This conforms to the description of one of the tasks of leadership given by Charles P. Kindleberger in his well-known *Power and Money* – 'to seek a consensus among groups, or if that is impossible, a majority view which is tolerable to the minority . . . to retain the support of the group while compromising its interests for the sake of the reconciliation with competing interests.' (1970: 29) This description can be applied to the view entertained by many of the role of the Japanese Prime Minister, including many who occupied the office. In the words of the eminent Japan specialist, Edwin O. Reischauer, a leader, even a Prime Minister, was, or could not be anything other than 'a cooperative team player rather than a soloist.' (1979: 144) In a 1975 study, John C. Campbell noted that:

> . . . as any study of the LDP will show, maintaining his position [as premier] requires keeping a majority of Dietmen satisfied, and balancing off interests of factions and other groupings within the party. The prime minister has most often found that the benefits of strong leadership in domestic policy matters are outweighed by the costs of such a position. (1975: 100)

In line with such views, the Prime Minister has been described as a judicious consensus-builder at best, rather than a forceful advocate, constrained from undertaking independent action. He was expected to move slowly and carefully, articulating the existing consensus on a given issue or nurturing gradual changes in it rather than issuing clarion calls for fundamentally new policies. (Destler 1976: 186) To the extent that he wished to influence the prevailing norms, preferences, or goals, he had to act as an unobtrusive tactician rather than a grand strategist, striving for subtle advances, not innovative moves. More often than not, therefore, a Japanese leader follows, rather than leads, according to Taketsugu Tsurutani. (1981: 124)

While the intention behind the constitutional provisions was to secure a strong position for the premier within the government, they have not worked entirely in that direction. Kyogoku Jun'ichi argues that the fact that the LDP has enjoyed an enduring monopoly of power has resulted in the prime minister no longer possessing 'the political authority to head the state and govern the people on the basis of securing a mandate of the people following victory in an internal war.' He has the legal power to force the government and its agencies to comply with his orders but does not have the necessary leverage to politically dominate the organs of government. (1987: 104) As noted by Charles Bingman, certain countervailing forces have worked in the same direction. While the Prime Minister as president of the governing party exerted great influence, the LDP expected and demanded that he would see to its interests as premier; while the premier and the government were accountable to the parliament, the premier could also use his parliamentary presence to influence and persuade from the inside; while supposedly directing and supervising the ministries, this supervision was seldom a match for the skilled and experienced permanent career staff of the ministries. (1989: 17) Furthermore, throughout the post-war period, the bureaucracy has been one of the three hubs in the three-headed governing 'iron triangle' composed of the business sector, the ruling Liberal Democratic Party and the bureaucracy. Bureaucrats have commanded a central position in the decision-making system as the politicians have been dependent on them for information and analysis. (Fukui 1977a: 4) The system of *ringisei* has in many cases left the drafting of policies to the Ministry of Foreign Affairs and other concerned agencies. (Hanai 1975: 271f; Abe et al. 1974: 37)

The consensus that the Prime Minister *cum* LDP chairman has had to strive for within the party applies to the national level as well. Consensus has been necessary not only among the factions of the Prime Minister's own party, but also among other parties and actors taking part in the foreign policy decision-making system. John Campbell also noted that in system-wide conflicts between the LDP and government and between sub-governments, only the premier has been able to act as go-between. (1984: 318) Hans Baerwald noted a disparity between the *Weltanschauung* of the different political parties in the parliament which was of more than passing significance, given the high priority accorded to consensual decision-making in Japanese society. (1979: 38) According to another analyst, Taketsugu Tsurutani, the consensual culture made the government hesitant to undertake drastic policy changes. (1981: 76) The uproar of 1960 that occurred after Prime Minister Kishi Nobusuke forced the revised security treaty through parliament showed what could happen when consensus was disregarded.

Contraints on the role of national spokesman

Situational factors beyond his control limit the options open to the Japanese premier as a decision-maker. Among these factors, constraints on Japanese foreign policy imposed by the surrounding world and the international system have primarily been those taken into account. In a way, it can be said that the successive Prime Ministers of the post-war period have, almost without exception, been quite vocal proponents of the Singerian view referred to in the introduction, according to which the international system shapes and constrains policy in such a way that individual decision-makers can have little impact on events. Given Japan's historical heritage, this was not unnatural. The Japanese experience with the world, especially since the arrival of Admiral Perry's ships in 1853, has created a sense of isolation in the Japanese. The natural poverty of the nation, coupled with its geographical and historical isolation, has fostered a sense of national vulnerability and even inferiority. (Kyogoku 1969: 170) According to J.A.A. Stockwin:

> Whatever the successes and failures of Japanese economic man-
> agement over the past century, one thing that is certain is that
> national economic imperatives have crucially shaped the
> character of the polity and the perceptions of political leaders.
> Many of Japan's leaders perforce developed certain habits of
> mind and certain kinds of political arrangement adapted to the
> governing of a resource-poor nation, dependent upon making
> the best of meagre natural advantages, so as to survive in a
> competitive economic and political environment [. . .] (1982: 9)

In the initial decades of the post-war period, the politicians emphasized, time and again, that the complexities of the international system were beyond their control, as well as the uncertainties in that system. A few examples should suffice to demonstrate that this stance was a pervasive trait of the world-view of the Prime Ministers.

Being the Prime Minister in the years immediately following the defeat in the Second World War, Yoshida Shigeru preached the necessity of being a 'realist'. The way he viewed it, the mighty ruled the world and nothing could be done about it, least of all by a weak and defeated Japan. Based on his long experience of diplomacy, Yoshida concluded that Japan had no choice but to adapt as best as it could to the conditions pre-vailing in the external environment or prescribed by the workings of the international system. At most it could try to exploit the situation to its own advantage. (1961: 289)

In the policy speeches of Ikeda Hayato, one of Yoshida's disciples and Prime Minister between 1960 and 1964, one can find traces of the insight that the world is 'a given' and has to be accepted the way it is, whether one likes it or not. In his last policy speech to the parliament, for instance, Ikeda stated that the Japanese 'must exercise cool judgement, manifest wisdom

and encourage and actively play a rôle suited to the environment and position in which our country is placed.' (Naikaku
Seido 1986: 701) When it came to influencing its international
environment, Ikeda's successor as prime minister, Sato Eisaku,
saw Japan as having little room for manoeuvre. In fact, he
attributed the past successes of Japan to the fact that the country
had been able to adapt skillfully to changed circumstances and
pursue realistic policies:

> That, after the war, our country could raise itself up from amidst
> the ruins and build up the prestige and prosperity it has today, is,
> I believe, due to [the fact] that the policies of our party and
> government have been realistic and appropriate to [the task of]
> adapting to changes in the internal and external situation.
> (Naikaku Seido 1986: 754)

In contrast to the focus on external factors constraining the
possibility of Japanese premiers functioning as forceful spokesmen for their country in the international arena, a recent
Japanese Prime Minister, Hosokawa Morihiro, pointed to internal factors as posing the obstacle to Japanese leadership on a
global scale. According to Hosokawa, 'Japan must extract itself as
soon as possible from its present mindset in which culture is
considered an "Achilles' heel", and show the world clearly that
it intends to proceed as a cultural leader.' (1993: 6) When he
envisioned Japan as an international leader, it was not primarily
as a leader in the political field but in the cultural field. (1993:
108) Thus, he continued to be a proponent for the traditional
view, according to which there are severe constraints on any
leadership rôle to be played by Japan.

SUMMARY

The present paper has attempted to shed some light on the
nature and extent of prime ministerial leadership in post-war
Japanese foreign policy. The concept of leadership is vague and
elusive and the analysis is based on an interpretation of leadership in terms of two rôles that are enacted by the Japanese
premier, namely his role as a decision-maker and that of national
spokesman, two rôles that are established in constitutional provisions. A number of constraints on the implementation of these
rôles have been identified. The premier's rôle as decision-maker
is constrained by factors operating at different levels. One is the
process in which the Prime Minister is selected, which tends to

favour politicians who tend to prioritise harmony and balance rather than demonstrate strong leadership. Another constraining factor is related to the necessity of the premier to secure factional support in his capacity as party leader, resulting in him acting consensus-articulator rather than articulator of his own views. A third factor is the necessity of the premier promoting consensus not only among his party's factions but among other parties and actors taking part in national decision-making as well. A factor constraining the Prime Minister's rôle as national spokesman is the traditional world view – which has lingered far into the post-war period – according to which Japan is seen as being a mere pawn in international politics, which has to adapt as best as it can to the wheelings and dealings of mightier international actors.

BIBLIOGRAPHY

Abe, Hitoshi, Muneyuki Shindo, and Sadafumi Kawato. (1994) *The Government and Politics of Japan*. Tokyo: University of Tokyo Press.
Angel, Robert C. (1988–89) 'Prime Ministerial Leadership in Japan: Recent Changes in Personal Style and Administrative Organization.' *Pacific Affairs*, 61: 4, Winter, 583–602.
Baerwald, Hans H. (1974) *Japan's Parliament: An Introduction*. London: Cambridge University Press.
—— (1977) 'The Diet and Foreign Policy.' In Robert A. Scalapino, ed., *The Foreign Policy of Modern Japan*. Berkeley, Los Angeles, London: University of California Press, 37–54.
Bingman, Charles F. (1989) *Japanese Government Leadership and Management*. Basingstoke and London: Macmillan Press.
Blondel, Jean. (1980) *World Leaders: Heads of Government in the Postwar Period*. London and Beverly Hills: Sage Publications.
—— (1987) *Political Leadership: Towards a General Analysis*. London: Sage Publications.
Bunce, Valerie. (1981) *Do New Leaders Make a Difference? Executive Succession and Public Policy under Capitalism and Socialism*. Princeton, N.J.: Princeton University Press.
Campbell, John Creighton. (1975) 'Japanese Budget Baransu.' In Ezra Vogel, ed., *Modern Japanese Organization and Decision-making*. Berkeley, Los Angeles, London: University of California Press, 71–100.
—— (1984) 'Policy Conflict and Its Resolution within the Governmental System.' In Ellis S. Krauss, Thomas P. Rohlen, and Patricia G. Steinhoff, eds., *Conflict in Japan*. Honolulu: University of Hawaii Press, 294–334.
The Constitution of Japan. Reprinted in *Kodansha Encyclopedia of Japan*, Vol. 2. Tokyo: Kodansha, (1983) 9–13.
Curtis, Gerald L. (1979) 'Domestic Politics and Japanese Foreign Policy.' In William J. Barnds, ed., *Japan and the United States: Challenges and Opportunities*. New York: New York University Press, 21–85.

—— (1988) *The Japanese Way of Politics*. New York: Columbia University Press.

Destler, I.M. et al. (1976) *Managing an Alliance: The Politics of U.S.-Japanese Relations*. Washington, D.C.: The Brookings Institution.

Dower, J.W. (1979) *Empire and Aftermath: Yoshida Shigeru and the Japanese Experience 1878–1954*. Cambridge, Mass. and London: Harvard University Press.

Drifte, Reinhard. (1990) *Japan's Foreign Policy*. London: The Royal Institute of International Affairs and Routledge.

Edinger, Lewis J. (1964) 'Political Science and Political Biography.' *The Journal of Politics*, XXVI, August, pp. 648–676. Reprinted in Glenn D. Paige, Ed., *Political Leadership: Readings for an Emerging Field*. New York: The Free Press, and London: Collier Macmillan, 1972, 213–239.

—— (1990) 'Approaches to the Comparative Analysis of Political Leadership.' *The Review of Politics*, 52, 509–523.

Edström, Bert. (1988) *Japan's Quest for a Role in the World: Roles Ascribed to Japan Nationally and Internationally 1969–1982*. Diss. Japanological Studies, 7. Stockholm: Institute of Oriental Languages, Department of Japanese and Korean, 1988.

—— (1992) *Yoshida Shigeru and the Foundation of Japan's Postwar Foreign Policy*. Stockholm University Center for Pacific Asia Studies Working Paper 26.

—— (1993) 'Yoshida Shigeru and "the Yoshida Doctrine".' *The Stockholm Journal of East Asian Studies*, 4, 85–140.

Fukui, Haruhiro. (1977a) 'Policy-Making in the Japanese Foreign Ministry.' In Robert A. Scalapino, ed., *The Foreign Policy of Modern Japan*. Berkeley, Los Angeles, London: University of California Press, 3–35.

—— (1977b) 'Tanaka Goes to Peking: A Case Study in Foreign Policy-making.' In T.J. Pempel, ed., *Policymaking in Contemporary Japan*. Ithaca and London: Cornell University Press, 60–102.

George, Aurelia. (1988) 'Japan and the United States.' In J.A.A. Stockwin et al., *Dynamic and Immobilist Politics in Japan*. Honolulu: University of Hawaii Press, 237–296.

Hah, Chong-do and Frederick C. Bartol. (1983) 'Political Leadership as a Causative Phenomenon: Some Recent Analyses.' *World Politics*, XXXVI: 1, October, 100–120.

Halperin, Morton. (1974) *Bureaucratic Politics and Foreign Policy*. Washington, D.C.: The Brookings Institution.

Hanai, Hitoshi. (1975) *Gendai gaikō seisaku ron*. Tokyo: Minerva shobo.

Hellman, Donald C. (1972) *Japan and East Asia: The New International Order*. New York, Washington, London: Praeger.

—— (1979) 'Foreign Policy à la LDP: The 1956 Soviet-Japanese Peace Agreement.' In Murakami Hyoe and Johannes Hirschmeier, eds., *Politics and Economics in Contemporary Japan*. Tokyo and New York: Kodansha International, 93–108.

—— (1988) 'Japanese Politics and Foreign Policy: Elitist Democracy Within an American Greenhouse.' In Takashi Inoguchi and Daniel I. Okimoto, eds., *The Political Economy of Japan – Volume 2: The Changing International Context*. Stanford, Calif.: Stanford University Press, 345–378.

Hermann, Margaret G. (1978) 'Effects of Personal Characteristics of Political Leaders on Foreign Policy.' In Maurice A. East, Stephen A. Salmore,

Charles F. Hermann, eds., *Why Nations Act: Theoretical Perspectives for Comparative Foreign Policy Studies.* Beverly Hills/London: Sage Publications, 49–68.

—— and Charles F. Hermann. (1989) 'Who Makes Foreign Policy Decisions and How: An Empirical Inquiry.' *International Studies Quarterly,* 33, 361–388.

Hirano, Minoru. (1980) *Gaikō Kisha nikki: Hatoyama gaikō no ichinen.* Tokyo: Gyosei tsushinsha.

Hosokawa, Morihiro. (1993) *The Time to Act is Now: Thoughts for a New Japan.* Tokyo: NTT Mediascope.

Hosoya, Chihiro. (1989) 'From the Yoshida Letter to the Nixon Shock.' In Akira Iriye and Warren I. Cohen, eds., *The United States and Japan in the Postwar World.* Lexington: The University Press of Kentucky, 21–35.

—— and Usui Hisakazu, eds. (1985) *Kokusai seiji no sekai.* Tokyo: Yushindo.

Ike, Nobutaka. (1978) *A Theory of Japanese Democracy.* Boulder, Colo.: Westview Press, and Folkstone: Dawson.

Iokibe, Makoto. (1989) 'Kokusai kankyo to Nihon no sentaku.' In Aruga Tadashi et al., *Kōza Kokusai seiji, 4: Nihon no gaikō.* Tokyo: Tokyo daigaku shuppankai, 19–52.

Kawai, Kazuo (1960) *Japan's American Interlude.* Chicago, London, Toronto: The University of Chicago Press.

Kindleberger, Charles P. (1970). *Power and Money: The Politics of International Economics and the Economics of International Politics.* London and Basingstoke: Macmillan.

Kissinger, Henry. (1979) *The White House Years.* Boston: Little, Brown & Co.

Kosaka, Masataka. (1989) 'Nihon gaikō no benshō.' In Aruga Tadashi et al., *Kōza Kokusai seiji, 4: Nihon no gaikō.* Tokyo: Tokyo daigaku shuppankai, 293–323.

Kusano, Atsushi, (1989) 'Taigai seisaku kettei no kiko to katei.' In Aruga Tadashi et al., *Kōza kokusai seiji, 4: Nihon no gaikō.* Tokyo: Tokyo daigaku shuppankai, 53–92.

Kyogoku, Jun'ichi. (1969) *Gendai minshūsei to seijigaku.* Tokyo: Iwanami shoten.

—— (1987) *The Political Dynamics of Japan.* Tokyo: University of Tokyo Press.

MacDougall, Terry Edward, ed. (1982) *Political Leadership in Contemporary Japan.* Michigan Papers in Japanese Studies, No. 1. Ann Arbor: The University of Michigan, Center for Japanese Studies.

McNeil, Frank. (1993). *Japanese Politics: Decay or Reform? The Consequences of Political Stagnation and the Prospects for Major Change.* Washington: The Carnegie Endowment for International Peace.

Murakami, Hyoe. (1979) 'The Making of a Prime Minister.' In Murakami Hyoe and Johannes Hirschmeier, eds., *Politics and Economics in Contemporary Japan.* Tokyo and New York: Kodansha International, 3–21.

Naikaku seido hyakunenshi hensan iinkai, ed., *Rekidai naikaku soridaijin enzetsushu.* (1986) Tokyo: Okurasho insatsukyoku.

Nakamura, Koji, (1972) 'New Power Balance in East Asia: Japan's Hard Options.' *The Times of India,* March 18.

Nakane Chie. (1970) *Japanese Society.* Berkeley: University of California Press.

Nakasone Yasuhiro. (1992) *Seiji to jinsei. Nakasone Yasuhiro kaisoroku.* Tokyo: Kodansha.

Ogata, Sadako. (1985) 'The Changing Role of Japan in the United Nations.' In Joshua D. Katz and Tilly C. Friedman-Lichtschein, eds., *Japan's New World Role.* Boulder and London: Westview Press, 29–42.

Reischauer, Edwin O. (1979) 'Their Special Strength.' *Foreign Policy, 24,* Spring, pp. 142–153.

Ross, Thomas. (1972) 'Japans Außenpolitik ohne klaren Kurs: Die Autorität der Regierung Sato schwindet dahin.' *Frankfurter Allgemeine Zeitung,* March 8.

Satō, Hideo. (1989) *Taigai seisaku.* Tokyo: Tokyo daigaku shuppankai.

Satō, Seizaburo. (1977) 'The Foundations of Modern Japanese Foreign Policy.' In Robert A. Scalapino, ed., *The Foreign Policy of Modern Japan.* Berkeley, Los Angeles, London: University of California Press, 367–390.

Shapiro, Michael J. and G. Matthew Bonham. (1973) 'Cognitive Process and Foreign Policy Decision-Making.' *International Studies Quarterly,* 17, 147–174.

Singer, J. David. (1961) 'The Level-of-Analysis Problem in International Relations.' *World Politics,* XIV:1, October, 77–92.

Stockwin, J.A.A. (1982) *Japan: Divided Politics in a Growth Economy.* 2nd ed. London: Weidenfeld and Nicolson.

—— (1988) 'Dynamic and Immobilist Aspects of Japanese Politics.' In J.A.A. Stockwin et al., *Dynamic and Immobilist Politics in Japan.* Honolulu: University of Hawaii Press, 1–21.

Tsurutani, Taketsugu. (1981) *Japanese Policy and East Asian Security.* New York: Praeger.

Tucker, Robert C. (1981) *Politics as Leadership.* Columbia and London: University of Missouri Press.

Wallace, William. (1971) *Foreign Policy and the Political Process.* London: Macmillan.

Ward, Robert E. (1967) *Japan's Political System.* Englewood Cliffs, N.J.: Prentice-Hall, Inc.

Weinstein, Martin E. (1989) *The Human Face of Japan's Leadership: Twelve Portraits.* New York, Westport, Conn., London: Praeger.

Yoshida, Shigeru. (1961) *The Yoshida Memoirs: The Story of Japan in Crisis.* London, Melbourne, Toronto: Heinemann.

—— (1963) *Sekai to Nihon.* Tokyo: Bancho shobo.

Yoshitsu, Michael M. (1983) *Japan and the San Francisco Settlement.* New York: Columbia University Press.

20

New Directions in Japanese Politics

J.A.A. STOCKWIN

We have swallowed the Socialists and we have them in our stomach. All that remains is for the gastric juices to digest them. (Tokyo Insideline 30 July 1994: 1)

These remarks attributed to the former Prime Minister. Takeshita Noboru, suggest a cunning plot to restore the essence of LDP hegemony, which had been so rudely snatched away with the formation of the Hosokawa Government in August 1993. According to this hypothesis, the reform ambitions initiated by the Hosokawa coalition government (August 1993–April 1994) are close to foundering with the return of the LDP to power, in a coalition with the Socialists, at the end of June. Another way of putting the same thing is to say that Ozawa has been defeated by Takeshita: that the ambitious reformer who wanted to remake the system of politics has been defeated by the old-style politician who wishes to restore the *status quo*.

The principal purpose of this paper is to examine this view in the light of recent and earlier events. I shall argue that despite current appearances what has happened since August 1993 means that the old system cannot be put together again in anything like the same form as before. The genie has escaped, and cannot easily be returned to the inside of the bottle. Although the process of changing the system has proved (predictably) a rocky one, the system – for good or ill – is experiencing a period of substantial change, though the end result may well not satisfy many of the proponents of reform. In arguing thus, I am conscious of having some heavyweight opinion against me, as the prevailing opinion seems to be that political reform has stalled, or even, failed.

In order to come to grips with what has happened over the past year (1993–4), I want to go back into the 1980s, when Nakasone was in his own way trying to reform the way politics was conducted by setting up a range of commissions and think-tanks in order to shift policy in a range or areas including defence and education. Although he had a certain amount of success in pushing defence policy somewhat in the direction he wanted it to go, and although he was accorded a longer period as Prime Minister than any of his predecessors since 1972 and any of his successors, although he won the 1986 election with a handsome majority, ultimately his policy successes were very limited. (Watanabe 1993; 1994)

None of the four LDP prime ministers between Nakasone and the party's loss of office in 1993 could be regarded either as reformers or even as particularly successful leaders. Indeed Kaifu, who in some ways may be regarded as the least unsuccessful of them, had to concentrate on exercises of damage-limitation following the comprehensive LDP defeat in the 1989 House of Councillors elections, which followed on the heels of the Recruit Scandal. Let us now go on to look briefly at the reasons for the LDP loss of office in 1993, and the subsequent political events.

The collapse of the 38-year-long rule by the LDP in August 1993 was preceded by a split in the pivotal Takeshita faction of the ruling party, and a consequent weakening of central control within that party. This in turn was accompanied by a series of corruption scandals, one of which led to the disgrace and effective withdrawal from politics of Kanemaru Shin, who had been the Takeshita faction's most dominant and effective leader. As a result, the Takeshita faction split, and that section of it led by Hata Tsutomu and Ozawa Ichirō became an increasingly dissident voice within the party. The Takeshita faction (formerly the faction of Tanaka Kakuei), which had essentially controlled the LDP for more than a decade, was fatally weakened. If erosion of the central leadership, and a crescendo of revelations about corruption, were the backdrop, the proximate cause of collapse was the decision by the Miyazawa Cabinet in the early summer of 1993 not to proceed with a plan to reform the electoral system for the Lower House, or House of Representatives.

In protest, two separate groups, the larger of which was the dissident half of the old Takeshita faction, broke away from the LDP and formed new parties. The larger of the two was to be called *Shinseitō* (Renewal Party), and was the party of Hata and

Ozawa. Ozawa, a highly controversial reformist politician, came to be seen as the brains behind new programmes of reform. The other party, more on the left, called itself *Shintō Sakigake* (New Harbinger Party), and was led by Takemura Masayoshi. As a consequence of these defections, the LDP lost a motion of no-confidence in its government, the Miyazawa Cabinet dissolved Parliament and held new elections in July 1993, which it lost.

To general surprise, a new government was formed under the prime ministership of Hosokawa Morihiro, a former prefectural governor who had formed the *Nihon Shintō* (Japan New Party) of political outsiders about a year before. The government consisted of no fewer than eight separate parties. The largest of these parties was the Social Democratic Party of Japan (formerly Japan Socialist Party or JSP, though its title in Japanese had not changed, remaining *Nihon Shakaitō*. For consistency and clarity we shall continue to refer to it as the JSP). Although it was the coalition's largest party, it had lost many seats in the July elections. The other main parties constituting the coalition were the Renewal Party, the Japan New Party, the *Kōmeitō* (a long-established party linked with the Buddhist group *Sōka Gakkai*), the Democratic Socialist Party and the New Harbinger Party. Of the former parties of opposition, only the Communists, with a mere 15 seats in the Lower House, remained aloof.

The Hosokawa Government embarked upon an ambitious programme of reform, including reform of the electoral system, an anti-corruption law, deregulation of industry and commerce, reform of the tax system and decentralization of power to local authorities.

By the end of 1993 the new Government found itself in difficulties, both because of divisions within its own ranks and because of pressure from the LDP, which remained by far the largest party within Parliament, though it was now in opposition.

Part of the problem lay with the reactions of the JSP, which found itself badly divided on the modalities of electoral reform, as well as on other aspects of reform, particularly tax reform and liberalization of rice imports. An even more serious problem was that the new government's Chief Cabinet Secretary, the Chairman of the New Harbinger Party, Takemura, soon found himself at odds with the Prime Minister, Hosokawa, as Hosakawa was drawn more and more into the orbit of the maverick and manipulative Ozawa, whom Takemura plainly disliked.

Early in 1994 the crucial Lower House electoral reform bills were accepted by Parliament, but they had been substantially modified by comparison with the Government's earlier proposals. Since this was such an important part of the Government's reform programme (and because failure to effect electoral reform was the immediate cause of the LDP's fall from power), we need to dwell a little on the technicalities of the bill. The new electoral system for the House of Representatives was to be based on 300 single-member, first-past-the-post constituencies, and 200 seats contested in 11 regional constituencies under a list system of proportional representation. This would replace the existing system, based on a single non-transferable vote (SNTV) in multi-member constituencies, which was widely held to be responsible for competitive factionalism within large parties, and thus for a great deal of corruption. It was also hoped that, by completely redrawing electoral boundaries, the gross imbalance in the value of votes that had been allowed to develop between many rural and many urban constituencies, would be eliminated.

Considerations of party advantage informed much of the quarrelling that took place in late 1993 and early 1994 over the precise modalities of the new electoral law. The initial proposal had been for equal numbers of single member and proportional representation seats (250–250), but pressure from the LDP and from elements in the Government (especially Ozawa) that favoured competition between large and cohesive, rather than small and fragmented parties, led to the former type of seat being increased at the expense of the latter. The division of the proportional representation seats between 11 regional blocs rather than, as in the early proposals, within a single national constituency, was also thought likely to be disadvantageous to the smaller parties, and was therefore opposed by them. The Socialists, however, were particularly enraged at the increase in the number of 'British-type' seats, which required a plurality of votes to win.

Even though the electoral reform bill successfully passed through Parliament, the early months of 1994 saw ever increasing strains within the coalition Government. A tax reform bill, designed to reduce direct taxation but compensate this by an increase in indirect taxation (largely consumption tax) foundered on the opposition of JSP dissidents in the Upper House. An attempt by the Prime Minister to reshuffle his Cabinet in order to remove Takemura from his politically sensitive position likewise had to be abandoned.

In addition, ancient money problems were being dragged up by his opponents to discredit Hosokawa, who unexpectedly tendered his resignation in April. He was replaced as Prime Minister by Hata Tsutomu, the head of the Renewal Party, which also harboured within it Ozawa Ichirō. Although the composition of the Hata Cabinet was initially identical to that of its predecessor, Ozawa had hatched a scheme to amalgamate most of the non-Socialist parties into a single new Reform party (*Kaishin*), upon the announcement of which the JSP immediately pulled out of the coalition. The New Harbinger Party also distanced itself from it.

The Hata–Ozawa Government lacked a majority in Parliament, and lasted a mere nine weeks. Its main task was to pass the national budget, which had been delayed in its passage through Parliament by political instability. The Socialists declared a truce until the budget was passed, but upon the budget being approved in June the Hata Government was faced with an unwinnable no-confidence motion and tendered its resignation.

The subsequent outcome astonished most observers. After more than two weeks of fruitless negotiations between the Socialists and Hata Cabinet (which remained in a caretaker role), a new Government was announced consisting of the LDP, the JSP and the New Harbinger Party. It was not particularly remarkable that the LDP should have returned to office after just under a year in opposition, given the chaotic state of politics under the Hosokawa and Hata prime ministerships. What stunned observers, however, was that it was the JSP, the long-time scourge of LDP policies, that had become its principal partner in government, and most particularly that the new Prime Minister was to be a veteran Socialist, the 69 year-old JSP Chairman, Murayama Tomiichi. Murayama had been little known outside his party until September 1993, when the annual JSP Congress decided to punish its previous leaders for the party's poor showing in the elections, and replace them with a new team, headed by Murayama as Chairman.

On the face of it, the LDP/JSP/NHP combination appears like a strange fantasy out of Lewis Carroll. On closer inspection, however, it is perhaps not so weird after all, though it is certainly unfamiliar. There are a number of reasons for taking this view.

Firstly, by late June 1994, it had become evident that the Hata Government was incapable of restoring its parliamentary majority. Over a period of some months, Ozawa had played a double game with the Socialists, seeking at times to attract sufficient numbers of dissident Liberal Democrats over to the coalition. The LDP faction leader. Watanabe Michio, had been very tempted by Ozawa's overtures, but in the end could not persuade enough of his followers to join him to create a parliamentary majority for the coalition. When all these attempts failed, Ozawa tried once again to pull the JSP back and restore the coalition's majority, but he was unable to dispel the acute Socialist suspicion that his earlier tactics had incurred. A numbers calculation, therefore, left marriage between Liberal Democrats and Socialists the only possible base for a government that could enjoy a parliamentary majority.

Secondly, for many years the parliamentary JSP had been relatively conservative on many areas of policy, though there remained a small rump of labour union left-wingers much influenced by Marxism (as well as some radical activists from citizens' movements). The same could not necessarily be said for the party's rank and file, but as with other Japanese parties, parliamentarians retained the predominant influence. The re-writing of the party's basic document in 1986 had largely removed the Marxist ideological legacy from the party, leaving it able to occupy the political centre-ground on many areas of policy. The JSP ideological legacy was most apparent in matters relating to the Constitution, defence, foreign policy and the rôle (and legitimacy) of the Self Defence Forces, but even this had suffered some erosion with the ending of the Cold War.

Thirdly, and following on from the last point, it seems in retrospect that the Cold War had been in some considerable part responsible for freezing the Japanese ideological map in an icy mould, which the demise of Cold War rivalries has gone a long way to thaw out. Now that the Constitutional axis of Japanese political competition is no longer set in the pattern of bipolar international rivalry, greater flexibility is possible in politics and new thoughts may be thought.

Fourthly, although JSP electoral fortunes have fluctuated wildly since the late 1980s, the party has to some extent reestablished its position as a credible political force, and of course the emergence of a Socialist Prime Minister may well consolidate this. It has shown itself to be an indispensable element in two coalition governments, those of Hosokawa and of Murayama himself. There is a sense that after four decades in the political wilderness, the JSP is on transforming itself into some kind of Establishment party, though whether the electorate will reward or punish it for taking this path remains to be seen.

Fifthly, the Deputy Prime Minister and Foreign Minister in the Murayama Government is Kōno Yōhei, elected President of the LDP after its fall from power in 1993. Kōno himself has moderate reformist credentials, and it was he who led the one and only substantial defection of parliamentarians it experienced in its 38 years tenure of office – that of the New Liberal Club, formed as a reaction against the Lockheed scandal in 1976. The Murayama-Kōno combination places the Government firmly in the centre of the political firmament.

Finally, despite the drubbing that the JSP received from the electorate at the July 1993 elections, and despite the appalling strains to which the party has been subjected by its first experience of participation in government for nearly forty years, it remains the case that the party has largely held together as a single organization. This contrasts with the recent experience of the Liberal Democrats, who suffered numerous defections during 1994 in addition to the major defections of 1993, and it also compares reasonably well with any of the parties now out of power, with the possible exception of the *Kōmeitō*, which has a firm organizational base in the *Sōka Gakkai*. In many ways the JSP has a form of organization which is comparable to that of the LDP, in the sense that it has strength at local level, based on local political machines. The JSP is not, of course, remotely as rich as the LDP. On the other hand, while much of its political weakness has stemmed from the fact that, being for ever out of power, it had little access to patronage, that disadvantage has now – perhaps temporarily – been rectified.

If we have given some reasons for believing that the LDP/JSP/NHP coalition may not be quite the unnatural hybrid that many portray it as, it still remains to consider the implications for the progress of reform to the system of politics.

On the one hand, there are several reasons that may be adduced in support of the proposition that the formation of the Murayama Government spells the end of serious reform.

Firstly, the arguments put forward above could well be interpreted as implying that if the LDP/JSP/NHP alliance is a natural one, then the agenda is bound to be that of the largest party in the coalition, which is the one most nostalgic about the former *status quo*, namely the LDP.

Secondly, the chaotic performance of the Hosokawa and Hata governments did much to discredit reform, and ultimately led to the defeat of Ozawa, who was its most enthusiastic and resourceful proponent. Without the dynamism which Ozawa had injected into the process of reform, what hope had it of ultimate success?

Thirdly, after a few weeks in office the new Socialist Prime Minister, Murayama Tomiichi, announced publicly some fundamental changes to the most deeply entrenched shibboleths of Socialist Party policy. Henceforth the Government, and with it the JSP, would regard the Self Defence Forces as legitimate in terms of the Constitution. The Japan–US Security Treaty would be accepted. The participation of Self Defence Force contingents in UN peacekeeping missions would be proceeded with. Unarmed neutralism would no longer be the basis of JSP foreign policy. The controversial anthem *Kimigayo* and the rising sun flag would become official in state schools throughout the land. This appeared to be an astonishing climb-down from long-established JSP policy, and understandably caused ripples within that party itself. Takeshita's digestive analogy, mentioned above, was given substance by the new Prime Minister's surprising statements.

Fourthly, there was some evidence that the ever-opportunistic *Kōmeitō* was contemplating changing sides, so as to position itself to join the three-party coalition government. (Tokyo Insideline 30 July 1994)

On the other hand, arguments were by no means lacking on behalf of the view that the emergence of the new government did not spell the ending of reform.

Firstly, the various Murayama statements could with some plausibility be regarded as a possibly belated recognition that some parts of the traditional JSP message were out of date in the post-Cold War world. A poll of JSP parliamentarians in the *Asahi* showed a surprisingly high degree of support for the changes, even though some who supported them saw them as a concession to the inevitable rather than as something to be welcomed with open arms. (*Asahi Shimbun* 27 July 1994) It could be argued that by coming into the mainstream on defence matters, the JSP would be better placed to pursue peace-related causes from a standpoint of realism as well as idealism.

Secondly, some of the JSP cabinet ministers (as well as Takemura of the NHP, who was given the Finance portfolio) were proving quite effective as ministers, while the Prime Minister was praised by some observers for his shrewdness and eloquence, and even for his charisma. Not all non-LDP parts of the Government appeared to be undergoing a process of alimentary absorption.

Thirdly, if the Maruyama Government is to continue for a reasonable period of time, the logic of the system suggests that the presence of the JSP will at least dilute LDP hegemony. Indeed, it seems quite possible that certain ministries may ultimately become JSP monopolies, or at least become heavily influenced by JSP-related interests.

Fourthly, given the fact that the Murayama Government enjoys a parliamentary majority, it seems unlikely that other parties (such as the *Kōmeitō*) would be allowed to dilute what in effect is a minimum winning coalition. This would, of course, cease to be the case if there were further serious defections from the LDP, but that must have become less likely now that the LDP is once more in government, and can once again enjoy the spoils of office.

Fifthly, there is manifestly a constituency for political reform among many younger parliamentary members of both the LDP and the JSP, who found themselves seriously excluded from advancement under the old system of LDP one-party dominance. The government, like its immediate predecessor, has also included, it is true, some personages afflicted with unreconstructed views on sensitive issues, as shown in the recent affair of the statement by Sakurai, Minister in charge of the Environment Agency, on the subject of war responsibility. The Prime Minister acted promptly to force the offending Minister to resign. (*Asahi Shimbun* 16.8.1994)

Sixthly, it is important to understand that the orchestra of reform has not always played in harmony. The differences became quickly apparent in the days of the Hosokawa Government, when the tune played by Ozawa failed to harmonize with that being played by other elements in the coalition, notably the Socialists. Essentially, what Ozawa was pursuing was the goal of a party system in which a small number of large parties would be able to alternate in power, and debate on real policy issues would determine electoral outcomes. On defence and foreign policy issues Ozawa pursued the aim of a 'normal' state, without constitutional restrictions on the deployment of a conventional defence policy or on the ability to pursue national interests on the world stage. By contrast, many Socialists and the New Harbinger Party, among others, wished to maintain constitutional safeguards so far as defence was concerned, while on the future shape of the party system they sought to defend the rights of smaller parties by extending the proportional representation element in the new electoral system.

Finally, against the expectations of some, Murayama announced, shortly after his administration was formed, that the electoral reform proposals would be pursued, and no attempt would be made to preserve the existing system. It had been thought among some observers that the LDP and JSP, once they were in government together, might combine to resuscitate the old system, and use it to their joint advantage. Whatever may have been the temptations of such an approach, the new government forbore to pursue it.

CONCLUSION

In concluding this paper, I wish to argue the proposition that the natural condition of Japanese party politics is fragmentation, the disadvantages of which require clever organizational stratagems to avert. While fragmentation creates political instability, it is also conducive to more dynamic politics than that which follows from a successful attempt to overcome fragmentation.

Japan's first post-war decade (1945–55) provides ample evidence of both party fragmentation and of political dynamism. Many of the most important policies of the post-war era were devised (admittedly with a little help from the Americans), in this period, which was characterized by a high degree of intra-party competition. The most dynamic periods of LDP rule between 1955 and 1993 were those where factional competition was at its height. In contrast, the 1980s were a period of dominance by a particular faction and rigidly controlled seniority system for party and government promotions. It was also a period characterized by massive corruption and a great deal of policy immobilism.

Party fragmentation and fluidity suddenly and unexpectedly returned with the fall of the LDP from office in August 1993, and suddenly radical change seemed possible. The startling changes in JSP policy initiated by the Prime Minister are merely the latest evidence of a transition to policy dynamism.

The problem with the long period of LDP dominance, was that inter-party competition became essentially perfunctory and as a substitute intra-party competition between factions in the ruling party became the principal mechanism to keep the system dynamic. Now that the LDP has lost its secure majority in both Houses of Parliament, a new mechanism is required to try to ensure that the natural condition of party fragmentation shall not sow the seeds of political anarchy. The trick, however, is to improve on the stability-creating mechanisms which the LDP so expertly perfected, in such a way as to ensure not only political stability, but also true competition and dynamism in the creation of policy.

To this end, reform of the electoral system is crucial. The essence of a desirable solution is one where a realistic fear of losing office acts as an effective stimulus to the party or parties in power at a particular time to take the policy needs of the electorate into account in the formulation and implementation of policy. It implies that policy rather than simply patronage should be to the fore in the minds of most politicians, and that a balance be struck between national and local concerns. It certainly involves a reduction in bureaucratic power and an increase in political power, but without a concomitant loss in political responsibility. Whether the proposed electoral reforms will bring about such a result is probably the subject of another paper.

BIBLIOGRAPHY

Asahi Shimbun, various editions, 1994.
Tokyo Insideline, no. 30, 30 July 1994.
Watanabe Osamu, (1993) *Nakasone Yasuhiro and Postwar Conservative Politics: an historical interpretation* Oxford: Nissan Occasional Papers, 18.
Watanabe Osamu, (1994) *Seiji Kaikaku to Kenpō Kaisei* (Political Reform and Constitutional Revision), Tokyo: Aoki Shoten.

21

Ozawa Ichirō:
The Making of a Japanese Kingmaker

DAVID WILLIAMS

> *There is nothing so difficult, or so improbable of success, as to inaugurate a new order of things.*
>
> Machiavelli

INTRODUCTION

Comparisons are invidious. Let us make a few. Born on 24 May 1942, Ozawa Ichirō is post-war Japan's answer to Talleyrand. Like the servant of almost every French government from the Revolutionary Directory to the restoration of the monarchy after Napoleon, Ozawa is a great political survivor. Nursed on the no-nonsense 'democracy-is-about-numbers' logic of the era of Tanaka Kakuei, Ozawa would later play a key role in bringing Tanaka's reign to an end, thus securing the premiership for the eternally patient Takeshita Noboru. Ozawa helped to make and then break Kaifu Toshiki, ensuring that the latter's exposure to the politics of prime ministerial impotence was mercifully brief. Ozawa buffeted and then defeated the hapless regime of Miyazawa Kiichi in 1993.

The fall of Miyazawa brought to an end almost 38 years of unbroken one-party domination of the Lower House of the Japanese Diet by the Liberal Democratic Party. Having split the LDP, Ozawa has repeatedly sought to shatter the fragile unity of the Japan Socialist Party (JSP) which together with the LDP had formed the two pillars of the 1955 system. Ozawa was the indispensable kingmaker of the Hosokawa government which came to power in August 1993. When Hosokawa resigned in anxious frustration in April of the following year, it was Ozawa who ensured that Hata Tsutomu, his long-time friend and fellow member of the Diet class of 1969 (when they were both first elected), assumed the premiership in May 1994.

Thrust from power by an unholy alliance between the LDP and the JSP in June of that year, Ozawa is still pursuing his vision of a Japan governed by a two-party system in which both groupings are sufficiently conservative to permit easy transfer of power between them. In power or in opposition, Ozawa continues to give unrivalled direction and drive to the contemporary transformation of Japanese parliamentary democracy.

This extraordinary career has made Ozawa one of the most important politicians of his generation. His impact on the course of party politics has been little short of astonishing. It allows one to argue that Ozawa has already left a more substantial stamp on Japanese government than such influential prime-ministers as Kishi Nobusuke, Ikeda Hayato, Satō Eisaku, Nakasone Yasuhiro or Takeshita Noboru.

Indeed, barring a fateful turn of what an Elizabethan tragedian once called 'the rolling wheele of chaunce', that is political fate, Ozawa may some day be regarded as one of the great shapers of Japanese politics since Meiji, fully comparable in influence to Tanaka Kakuei or even Yoshida Shigeru. History is a fickle muse, but Ozawa is a force of nature. This is, after all, the man who broke the mould of postwar politics. Only his health may stand in his way.[1]

About this man, there had existed almost nothing that a historian would call primary or secondary sources until 1993. There is no equivalent of the records of the Tanaka trial. A multi-volume study of Ozawa to match *Tanaka Kakuei Kenkyū* by Tachibana Takashi has yet to appear. Despite Ozawa's importance, few journalists have reported about him in a sustained manner in the English-language media. Hundreds of articles have been written about the man and his politics in both the quality and tabloid press in Japanese, including the six-part series on Ozawa which appeared in the *Asahi Shinbun* in June 1994, but until recently, to my knowledge, no books had been published in Japanese about him. (*Asahi Shinbun* 14–18 June 1994)

Here I would like to focus on three of the most important of these recent publications: the biography of Ozawa by Ohshita Eiji, the biography of Hata Tsutomu, also by Ohshita, and *Nihon Kaizō Keikaku*, by Ozawa Ichirō, which has appeared in English under the title *Blueprint for a New Japan: The Rethinking of a Nation* (1994). (Ohshita 1993a; 1993b; Osawa 1993, 1994) Despite their status as official biographies, Ohshita's two works are important not least because they will form the natural point of departure for any student of Ozawa for some time to come.

Given that nearly all Japanese reporting and commentary has concentrated on what might be called the mature Ozawa, this article takes the young Ozawa as its focus. Here I have drawn on Ohshita's biographies which have unique value despite their obvious and not-so-obvious flaws. As for *Nihon Kaizō Keikaku*, I have chosen to provide a close reading of Ozawa's text because those reviews of the English translation that I have seen have failed to penetrate the heart of Ozawa's programme of political and policy reform.

THE YOUNG OZAWA

The son of the father

Ozawa worships heroes. His taste for samurai drama and action films is merely the outward sign of a pronounced psychological stance. This is a clear-eyed romantic who has chosen to make his life and career among Japan's conservative political caste, where sentiment, sacrifice and the grand gesture serve to elevate the gaze from the often sordid business of governing a great and wealthy nation. Kanemaru Shin, the power behind the throne of numerous prime ministers, and the politician with whom Ozawa is best compared, cultivated a life-long identification with his distant relation, Takeda Shingen, the famous samurai. Whatever illusions may be at work in such psychology, one must begin with heroes.

Ozawa is a reader with a weakness for historical novels, particularly those which celebrate the triumphs of the Meiji Restoration. Of all the leaders from the past two centuries, Ozawa judges the greatest to have been Okubo Toshimichi, Itō Hirobumi, Hara Kei and Yoshida Shigeru. It is revealing that after a childhood infatuation with the nobility of failure dramatized by the rise and fall of Saigo Takamori, it is Ōkubo, the man who centralized the powers of the Meiji state, with whom Ozawa came most closely to identify. As a child, Ozawa first seized on examples of local ambition and achievement. These included three of the most successful sons of Ozawa's hometown of Mizusawa: Takano Chōei, the scholar of *Rangaku* or Dutch learning, Gotō Shinpei, the mayor of Tokyo, and Saitō Makoto, the pre-war prime minister. Ozawa passed the houses of Takano and Gotō every day on his way to elementary school.

From such exemplars, Ozawa absorbed an unflinching confidence in the ability of people from the margins of national life to shape Japan at its centre. This is a lesson as old as the key rôle played by Satsuma and Chōshū in the downfall of the Tokugawa *Bakufu*. The scions of rural power bases exerted commanding influence over the Meiji state. Like Balzac's Rastignac, Ozawa has mastered the weapons required to challenge the forces of metropolitan domination and entrenched power. But even after he came to manipulate some of the pivotal levels of national politics, he remained loyal to his Iwate roots. In return, Iwate has rewarded Ozawa's undisguised affection with thundering electoral approval.

Ozawa's rise offers a potent reminder that the sacrifices which rural Japan has made to Tokyo's mastering energies include not only manpower and investment but talent. Like most US presidents, Japanese leaders continue to spring from rural backgrounds far removed from the urbanized reality of contemporary life. Despite Japan's post-war demographic revolution, which has concentrated the younger generation, and therefore the future, overwhelmingly in urban and suburban communities, political figures with rural ties, such as Ozawa, Hata and Hosokawa, may be seen to link, in their very different ways, an early post-war experience of provincial life with Japan's present sense of itself.

Ozawa's childhood offers no exception to the rule that a son's first and most important hero is his father. One thinks of Ozawa's uncompromising advocacy of single-seat constituencies as forming the novel spear-point of his reform programme, but Ozawa Saeki, Ichirō's father, was a forceful proponent of the single-seat constituency during Ichirō's youth. Saeki was a lawyer. He was not one of the former bureaucrats who dominated conservative politics during his career but rather a pure party politician (*tōjin seijika*). The second son of a poor Mizusawa horse-coach driver, Saeki left Iwate to study at Nihon University at night while working during the day as a 'red cap' at Ueno Station. Afterwards, he opened a law office in Okachimachi, in what was then Tokyo's Shitaya ward (now Taitō ward). He made it one of his missions to satisfy the legal needs of Tokyo's poorer citizens. He served as both a Tokyo City Councilman (*Tokyo Shikai Giin*) and Tokyo Prefectural Councilman (*Tokyo Fukai Giin*). Benefiting from the Occupation purge of many conservative veterans from the political process, Saeki won a seat in the national Diet in Japan's first post-war election in April 1946.

Almost immediately, an impressive parliamentary career began to unfold. Saeki became transport minister in the second Yoshida cabinet in 1948. Jobs as communications minister and a dual portfolio as minister of posts and communications (*Teishin daijin*) followed. Later, Saeki served as construction minister in the fifth Yoshida cabinet. Such involvement at the very heart of cabinet government had its light side. When one of the young's Ozawa's Keiō University classmates telephoned the Ozawa home, politely announcing that 'This is Ikeda calling', one of Ichiro's sisters answered with the confidence of practised familiarity, 'Oh, is that Prime Minister Ikeda?' (Ohshita 1993a : 64)

The choice of the name 'Ichirō' was a direct result of his father's early electoral experience. Saeki came to regret the three-character elegance of his personal name because some voters found it difficult to remember when they entered their choices on the ballot sheet. Saeki's later campaign posters carried his personal name in the *hiragana* syllabary, rather in Chinese characters. Indeed, so mindful was Saeki of the ballot-box usefulness of simple names, that he insisted that his son, on the slight chance that he, too, might become a politician, not be burdened with a *kanji* flourish such as Saeki. In fact, Saeki at first wanted Ichirō to be called just '*Ichi*' (one), and only compromised with 'Ichirō' at the urging of his wife. In his biography of Ozawa, Ohshita exploits this incident with effect in his title *Ichi o Motte Tsuranuku*.

All this, of course, means that Ozawa Ichirō is, like Hata Tsutomu, a second-generation or *nisei* politician. Being the son of a politician is a mixed blessing. If the second generation later succeeds as a politician, his success is always shadowed by the suggestion that he has not made it on his own ability. The *nisei* always wants to be able to say, like the American intellectual Susan Sontag, 'I did it all by myself'. But even if a political career is not pursued, the child of a politician, especially one representing a close-knit rural community, such as Mizusawa, must always be on his best behaviour, much like a clergyman's daughter. Competitive, physically strong and short-tempered, Ichirō was ever mindful of his exposed position as his father's son at school and in the constituency. Self-control was one of the disciplines of childhood. Such burdens are often forgotten by the critics of second-generation success stories.

In fact, despite Ichirō's name, Saeki consciously sought to insulate his son from the demands of political life. One result is that when Saeki suddenly died in May 1968, Ichirō had to make strenuous efforts, despite the long involvement of his mother in

her husband's election campaigns, to win over the leaders of
Saeki's political base or *jiban*. This was because, on Saeki's death,
Ichirō was an unknown quantity in the circles that counted in
Mizusawa.

Despite his father's ministerial career, Ichirō first visited the
Diet on the occasion of the memorial address for his father. As
a young man, Ichirō had never made the rounds of Japan's
corridors of power despite the fact that he had lived in Tokyo
for many years, having moved to the capital from the third year
of junior high school. Although he had been educated at Keiō
University and Nihon University, Ichirō needed a driver to
navigate him through the Kasumigaseki traffic when he paid his
first official visits to key ministries after being elected to the
Diet in December 1969. It would be unwise, however, to
exaggerate Ichirō's ignorance. He may not have known where
the Construction Ministry was located on that day devoted to
protocol, but he made Saeki's favourite ministry his first port of
call after taking up his father's seat.

There is another price that the son of a national politician
pays for the paternal career: fatherly absence. The phenomenon
of *tanshin-funin* has further exacerbated the domestic consequences of the long work day of Japanese fathers by sending
them into solitary exile, at home or abroad. One result has been
the much discussed psychological condition of a generation of
Japanese urban children who suffer from one form or another
of a disability known in the vernacular as '*papa kon*' or (absent)
father complex. Long before this became a mass phenomenon,
the children of rural Diet politicians had to learn to cope with
the effects of paternal absence.

Japanese fathers know the price that their children may pay
for their residence elsewhere, but most believe that they have no
alternative. In national politics, the centralizing impact of Tokyo's
influence has been so great that it is Nagatachō commonsense
that, if you want to meet anyone politically important from
Shimane or Kagawa or Iwate, then you will find him (influential
women are extremely rare) in the capital. The result is an
imperative to maintain a more or less constant presence in
Tokyo. Gotō Shinpei, Ozawa's childhood hero, set out the
double-bind involved in this modern version of the *bakufu*
system of official hostages (*sankinkōtai*) when he observed: 'I
shall not build a grave in Mizusawa, but, in exchange, I shall leave
my home and family there'. (Ohshita 1993a : 33)

The Road to Mejiro

Having missed his father during early his life and then having played only a small part in Saeki's political campaigns in Iwate, Ozawa lost his father at the comparatively young age of 25. This gap was filled, definitely but not at once, by a kind of father figure, one who would involve Ozawa fully in his political affairs. The surrogate was Tanaka Kakuei.

The rapid rise of Ozawa in Tanaka's affections and trust belies the difficulties the young man had in making his way to Tanaka's door. If Japanese social practice conspired with the taboos of Diet political culture to keep Ichirō in the dark about the deteriorating state of his father's health, Ozawa was subsequently pulled in contrasting directions by the uncertain nature of Saeki's legacy. For one thing, Saeki's death found Ozawa caught up in the demanding business of passing the national equivalent of bar examinations. Ozawa was determined to become a lawyer, partly out of respect for paternal precedent, and partly at the urging of his mother who did not wish him to pursue a political career.

Neither of these concerns took into account Saeki's heavy investment in his precious Iwate *jiban*. Ozawa hoped to finish his examinations before having to think seriously about becoming a politician, but the longer a potential heir leaves the decision to contest the seat once held by his father, the more arduous the task of keeping the seat in the family becomes. At this crucial phase in Ozawa's career, a mentor appeared. His name was Suzuki Seishichi. Suzuki was a formidable election tactician. He curbed the well-intended but, in his view, unhelpful interference of Michi, Saeki's widow, while directing Ichirō away from the Fujiyama faction, to which Saeki had belonged, and towards the faction of Satō Eisaku, upon which the young and dynamic Tanaka Kakuei was working a transforming magic.

The key struggle was to win recognition for Ozawa as an official LDP candidate. Suzuki secured this goal only by pledging personally to see the young Ozawa through to electoral victory. Although he understood that conventional wisdom judged Ozawa to be hampered by his youth, his unmarried status, and his lack of *jiban* exposure, Suzuki was confident that these supposed disadvantages could be made to work in Ozawa's favour if the young man was prepared to focus all his energies on winning the first time that he stood, campaigning on the theme of youth and political renewal. This required Ozawa to renounce his legal ambitions.

Suzuki's assessment carried weight because he had master-minded the brilliant campaign of Yamaguchi Toshio to recapture the old Diet seat of Yamaguchi's father nearly six years after the latter's death.[2] It was through Suzuki that Ozawa began to nurture a bond of special intimacy with Yamaguchi, who many years later emerged as one of the most effective back-room conspirators of recent LDP politics (responsible in part for the boomlet that made Kaifu prime minister). Afterwards, Yamaguchi won unique status as an unofficial television spokes-man for the Hosokawa and Hata administrations, even more useful in this capacity than Lord Archer has been to the wobbly Tory governments of recent years. Plagued during 1995 by a financial scandal much more serious than that which recently troubled Archer, Yamaguchi offers a warning against Ozawa taking the reins of official power into his hands lest the public prosecutors and the mass media turn on him.

Such concerns were long in the future when Ozawa formally announced his intention to stand for election in Iwate at the end of 1968. Smarter clothes replaced the school uniform that he had favoured while at Keiō University. He made his first trip abroad, with stops in the Middle East, Nepal and Hong Kong. Most important, he drew together an electoral team under Suzuki's astute guidance. And he waited, for many months, for the call from Tanaka which alone would confirm his status as an official party candidate.

When that call finally came, Ozawa made his way alone to Tanaka's spacious Tokyo residence in Mejiro in April 1969. It proved to be the defining encounter of Ozawa's political life. Tanaka's relentless pace, intelligence and command of the tough realities of Japanese party politics left an indelible impression on Ozawa, who would later speak of the man having an aura. In the beginning, however, Ozawa was just one face in a crowded picture. On that first April visit, Ozawa waited for hours, amid a throng of perhaps 50 petitioners, for his turn to meet Tanaka who was known to grant audiences to 300 people a day.

Tanaka peppered such encounters with an impressive mixture of vigorous 'boosterism' and pithy pieces of practical election-eering advice. He demanded that Ozawa master his election district down to the last tree. He was to visit 30,000 homes and shops. Only when the candidate fully surrendered to the fact that he was entirely on his own in this battle would victory become a possibility. After two further brief meetings in Mejiro, Tanaka ordered Ozawa to assemble his inner core of *jiban* loyalists. Ozawa returned with over 200 people who travelled up to Tokyo from Iwate on five buses. Tanaka's *aisatsu* or welcoming remarks turned into an hour-long speech. Ozawa won official LDP backing and in due course became a member of the Satō faction. From such beginnings came into being one of the most formidable alliances in post-war Japanese politics.

Ozawa Ichirō was born to win elections. Only his first offered him serious difficulty. Unlike Hata Tsutomu who has a ready appetite for pressing the flesh, for the banter and gossip of campaign encounters with the public, Ozawa is more private, more reserved, and more completely a strategist. In Hata, the urge to serve is so strong that it is never lost on the electorate. Ozawa is made from a different mould, but he does know how to work an Iwate crowd with skill. Indeed, it was the unbeatable combination of tactical boldness and the forceful projection of a fresh image that won him his first contest. Nothing speaks more convincingly of Ozawa's gifts as a campaigner than this immediate and total mastery of the lessons that Suzuki taught him during that first trial of strength in 1969.

To fund his campaign, Ozawa sold a large portion of the Tokyo property that he had inherited from his father (whose clients tended to pay for his legal services with pieces of land rather than with cash), and thus raised the minimum sum required: roughly 20 million yen. (Ohshita 1993a : 86) But the election battle itself proved more difficult. For one thing, Suzuki was simultaneously working for both Ozawa and Yamaguchi, who was standing in Saitama. Suzuki's conflicting commitments prevented him from seeing the unhappy impact that Michi, Ozawa's mother, had on the first phase of the struggle. She had been formed by Saeki's unbroken chain of ten victories, which contrasted with Ichirō's neophyte vulnerabilities. Suzuki managed to persuade Michi to leave tactical matters to him, and then proceeded to devise a high-risk assault on the *jiban* of two of the other six candidates standing for the four seats of Iwate's no. 2 constituency. The targets selected were the precarious *jiban* of Shiga Kenjirō, the conservative veteran also standing with LDP backing, and Kitayama Airō of the Japan Socialist Party.

The ploy worked. As a new, young face with an established name among a field dominated by senior politicians, Ozawa managed to strike a fresh chord across the constituency. He attracted thousands of voters to hear him speak. His final campaign appearance at a gathering of his women's support group in front of Mizusawa station proved to be an emotional triumph.

On a floodlit platform, addressing an audience being lightly dusted with December snow flakes, Ozawa provoked tears and repeated cries of 'Itchan! Itchan!' from the huge crowd which had assembled to hear his last campaign speech. So impressive was this display of energy and organization that the LDP veteran Shiina Etsusaburō abandoned his plans to speak in the same square after Ozawa had finished. (Ohshita 1993a : 118)

A brief but intense struggle of just under three weeks duration had generated a new force in Iwate politics. Ozawa captured an astonishing 71,520 votes, 10,000 more than his nearest rival, while denying Shiga his seat. At the age of 27, Ozawa had become the youngest member to be returned to the Diet, having won a conspicuous place in the celebrated parliamentary cohort first elected in 1969, which included not only Hata Tsutomu and Doi Takako, but also Yokomichi Takahiro, the former governor of Hokkaidō who may yet prove to be the hero of the demoralized forces of the old left of Japanese politics.

Ozawa's victory added lustre to the LDP's 'miraculous triumph' of that year in which it captured 288 seats in the House of Representatives, the more powerful Lower House. More crucial still for the future, more than one-half of the LDP's 44 new Diet members joined the Satō faction. The majority of them, including Ozawa and Hata, belonged to what was known as the Tanaka stream within the Satō faction (*Satō -ha; Tanaka-kei*). The birth of the Tanaka faction was now all but inevitable.

In the summer of 1972, Sato resigned and Tanaka became head of the faction, president of the LDP and prime minister of Japan. The period between the 1969 election and Tanaka's capture of the premiership was perhaps the most important phase in Ozawa's formation as a politician. It is one of the major failings of the Ohshita biography of Ozawa that the author moves so rapidly, and so lightly, through this key chapter in the politician's life. It began when Nakajo Takehiko, then the Sato faction secretary, agreed, at Tanaka's urging, to become Ozawa's personal secretary. It ended with Ozawa's celebrated wedding party in October 1972, when 1,400 guests, a record for the Hotel New Ōtani, gathered to celebrate the marriage between Iwate's most promising son and the daughter of the president of the Fukuda-gumi, one of Niigata's leading construction companies. Perhaps as revealing, many of the leading members of Japan's business élite attended the sumptuous *hirōen*. During the formalities, Tanaka stood at Ozawa's side in place of Ichirō's dead father.

In a manner worthy of the Hapsburgs, the marriage helped to weave a complex and subtle political network for Ozawa. Returning with his bride to Iwate, a further 12 wedding banquets were held, at which none other than Kanemaru Shin, the LDP's supreme master of backstage politics served as the official go-between or *nakōdo*. The younger sister of Ozawa's new wife would later marry the younger brother of Takeshita Noboru. Completing this powerful circle of political marriages, the second son of Kanemaru Shin would marry Takeshita's oldest daughter. In the process, the single-handed domination of Japanese party politics became, as it were, a family affair.

The Nurturing of a Kingmaker

Tanaka's climb to the pinnacle of official political prestige formed part of the a larger shift both within and without Japanese society. The twin 'Nixon shocks' (the devaluation of the dollar and the accommodation with communist China) signalled the new limits to American power. The economics of the 1973-74 oil crisis effectively halved Japan's annual rate of GNP expansion. Pressing ecological problems and the demands of the politics of redistribution began to redefine some of the central concerns of the Japanese policymaker. But, at the level of party politics proper, the passing of the torch from the bureaucrat-politician, who harked back to the polished élitism of the post-war school of Yoshida Shigeru, to the new pure-party politician symbolized by Tanaka was soon reversed by the in-vestigative labours of Japan's print media.

Tanaka's reputation, if not his effective hold on power, was decisively damaged by the publication on 10 October 1974 of the November issue of *Bungei Shunjū*, the influential intellectual monthly. In the first of a brilliant series of investigative articles, Tachibana Takashi, Japan's answer to Woodward and Bernstein of Watergate fame, helped to pierce the thin shield which had guarded against public probing of Tanaka's financial dealings. (Ohshita 1993a : 147)

Revelations about a corrupt web of money politics (*kinsen seiji*) played into the hands of Fukuda Takeo, Tanaka's old rival, who led a successful uprising against Tanaka's domination of the party. One month and 16 days after the appearance of Tachibana's first article, Tanaka resigned the premiership under a wave of relentless press assault. Worse was to follow. On 4 February 1976, the Lockheed scandal broke. At the end of June and the beginning of July 1976, key figures in the affair at All Japan Airways and Marubeni were arrested. Then, on 27 July, Tanaka became the first former prime minister to be arrested since the fall from grace of Ashida Hitoshi in the 1948 Shōden scandal. In response, Kanemaru and Takeshita moved promptly to restore the morale of the stunned Tanaka faction by proposing that Takeshita assume effective leadership of the faction. But by acting with what Tanaka saw as unseemly haste, they incurred his wrath, and their efforts came to nothing.

For Ozawa, then 33 years old, Tanaka's arrest was a blow. In Ozawa's presence, over a game of *shōgi* (a favourite Tanaka pastime), the former premier apparently rejected suggestions that he strip the veil from the complex structure of *kinsen seiji* in a gamble to win public support. (Ohshito 1993a : 148) In this way, he may have prevented the kind of intense media probing that might have destroyed the prospects of those who, like Ozawa, had advanced their careers by Tanaka's empire. Later, when Tanaka refused to abandon his unlikely dream of a political comeback, Ozawa joined hands with Takeshita, Kanemaru and Nikaidō Susumu ('My hobby is Tanaka Kakuei') to ensure that the Tanaka machine continued to dominate the LDP. But the psychological toll on Ozawa of Tanaka's fall from power was inevitably severe.

In an unrivalled demonstration of personal loyalty, Ozawa attended every session of the Tanaka trial, and was apparently the only member of Tanaka's entourage of parliamentarians to do so. (Ohshita 1993a : 156) Ozawa also lashed out in the media at Tanaka's tormentors. (Ohshita 1993a : 177) As Tanaka's problems grew, Ozawa found himself struggling with other problems

As parliamentary vice-minister at the Science and Technology Agency, Ozawa had to help find a home port for the nuclear-powered ship '*Mutsu*'. This job was one of the few government posts (as opposed to party jobs) he has held during his Diet career of a quarter of a century. The lack of cabinet or near-cabinet experience should be seen to reflect not only Ozawa's temperament but his relative youth in a system governed by seniority. Then, in December 1976, Tanaka, Ozawa and the whole of the LDP girded themselves to fight the so-called 'Lockheed election'.

Confronted with a major electoral challenge, Ozawa reacted with characteristic boldness. He announced to his private secretary that he planned to commit himself to helping other LDP candidates win their seats, and therefore he would spend only ten days of the 20-day campaign period defending his own seat in Iwate. Tanaka was as appalled as Nakajō at this proposal, and the former prime minister demanded that Ozawa reconsider this plan. Tanaka knew that Ozawa was putting his seat at risk, but Ozawa's reasoning was powerful. As the youngest member of the huge LDP class of 1969, his lack of seniority would all but guarantee that he would have to wait until all of his 44 *senpai* (the members of his Diet class who were older than Ozawa) had their turn at cabinet posts before his chance would come. Somehow he had to circumvent this barrier to advancement. Ozawa argued also that leaving his campaign to his *jiban* chiefs would force them to achieve new levels of unity and effectiveness. He must have known as well that his strategy would place a heavy burden on his wife, then pregnant with his second child.

Ozawa's gamble paid off. Once again, he was the top winner in the Iwate no. 2 constituency. In the huge Tanaka faction, only one other candidate managed to increase his vote that year. Ozawa's reputation within the ranks of the faction and the LDP soared. He took pride in the fact that only two LDP politicians before him had risked as much by throwing themselves into the re-election battles of other ruling party candidates: Ikeda Hayato and Satō Eisaku. They had come to the aid of their party in this way the third time that they had stood for the Diet, and both had gone on to become prime minister. Ozawa had matched their achievement on his third ballot-box test. The man's career was acquiring a mythical patina.

When Fukuda Takeo established his first administration in December 1976, Ozawa was made parliamentary vice-minister of the Construction Ministry, where his father had served as minister. The senior bureaucrats who had worked for Saeki remembered Ichirō's father with fondness, and warmly embraced his son. They even created an informal association to further his career called '*Ozawa Ichirō o Kakomu-kai*'. This group later included civil servants from the ministries of Agriculture and Fisheries, Labour and Posts, as well as from MITI. Another group of officials formed the '*Kasumigaseki Shiyu-kai*', again centred on Ozawa, which attracted a wide sampling of middle- and high-ranking bureaucrats who had graduated from Ozawa's Koishikawa High School. The impressive membership roster even included Ueda Tetsuo of the Japan Socialist Party. Similar associations were formed among the Japanese business establishment, but Ohshita insists that Ozawa, mindful of the distance that his father was supposed to have kept from individual businessmen, still refused public displays of intimacy with powerful individuals from the private sector.[3]

Ozawa proceeded to make his reputation as an election winner by carrying his Iwate seat by an overwhelming margin every time he stood for parliament. This Ozawa had done in 1969 and 1972, as he did again on 5 December 1976 in the 'Lockheed" election. He confirmed his reputation as a vote winner by capturing more of the electorate than any other candidate in the elections of 7 October 1979 and 22 June 1980. This made him a '*go-kai-sei*' (five-time winner), a factor of some importance because the first member of the Diet class of 1969 entered the first Suzuki Zenkō cabinet in July 1980 as construction minister.

It was Suzuki's sudden resignation in October 1982 which raised the curtain on the first act of the prolonged drama of Tanaka's departure from stage centre of Japanese party politics. After Tanaka's resignation, the prime ministerial chair had been successively occupied by Miki Takeo, Fukuda, Ōhira Masayoshi, and Suzuki. None was from the Tanaka faction, though it remained by far the largest political group within the ruling party. Three of the most important leaders of the Tanaka faction – Kanemaru, Nikaidō and Takeshita – were anxious that the faction reassert its hold on the premiership. But whatever the qualifications of Nikaidō and Takeshita for the job, both were substantially younger than Tanaka. This mattered because Tanaka feared that handing power to the younger generation would, in effect, doom his chances of becoming prime minister again. He warned his faction that any generational change would spell his political death. As a result, no feature of this phase of the Tanaka era came to matter more than the fact that Tanaka and Nakasone Yasuhiro were both born during the Taishō era (1912- 1926), and were therefore of the same generation of politicians. Without Tanaka's personal support, Nakasone's nearly five years as prime minister would have been unthinkable, so loathed was he by the leadership of the Tanaka faction.

Meanwhile, Ozawa continued to mount the heights of the party's organizational pyramid. In December 1982, he became the LDP's youngest ever *Tō-sōmu-kyoku-chō*. In this position within the party secretariat, he served as the front-line organizer of the ruling party's election efforts. At the same time, Tanaka asked Suzuki Seishichi, Ozawa's old mentor, to become the chief election strategist for the Tanaka faction as a whole. In this new

post, Ozawa had to struggle with the sensitive politics of proportional representation in the House of Councillors or Upper
House, while endeavouring to get on with Nakasone, a man he
detested. But Ozawa made a major contribution to a streak of
LDP victories in local and national elections, and his star
continued to rise.

On 20 October 1983, Tanaka was judged guilty for his
involvement in the Lockheed scandal, and was sentenced to four
years in prison and ordered to pay a fine of 500 million yen.
Expecting that Tanaka would be found innocent, Ozawa reacted
sharply, denouncing what he saw as the assertion of judicial
powers over those of the executive. He also blamed what he
called the irresponsible press. Rounding on Tanaka's many critics,
Ozawa reportedly took the uncompromising position that the
infamous 'logic of numbers' was the true 'foundation of democracy'.[4] By the time of Tanaka's fall, Ozawa was well on the way
to becoming a formidable insider within the highest echelons
of the ruling party.

During the decade from Tanaka's conviction until Miyazawa's
resignation brought the LDP's near monopoly on power to an
end, that is from 1983 until 1993, Ozawa emerged the dominant
personality at the heart of Japanese party politics. If Kanemaru
Shin, Ozawa's corrupting mentor, once claimed to have been
the author of the Nakasone, Takeshita and Kaifu cabinets, then
Ozawa may boast his own achievements. He is said to have
personally decided who entered the cabinets of five of the six
governments from Kaifu to Hata, the sole exception being the
Miyazawa cabinet which Ozawa, more than any single
politician, effectively brought down. (*Asahi Shinbun*, 14 June
1994) In creating and then sustaining, almost single-handedly,
the governments of Hosokawa and Hata, Ozawa powerfully
demonstrated that a new Japanese kingmaker had been born.
Out of power since 1994, he remains the most important
Japanese politician since Tanaka Kakuei.

A VISION OF THE FUTURE

In May 1993, Ozawa published his *Nihon Kaizō Keikaku* (a plan
to remodel Japan). Almost certainly ghost-written, this set of
policy proposals had, by the summer of 1994, sold over 700,000
copies. The same year, the book was rendered into English as
Blueprint for a New Japan: The Rethinking of a Nation. A best-seller
which has attracted wide interest outside Japan, *Nihon Kaizō*

Keikaku is one of the most discussed books of its kind since Tanaka Kakuei published his controversial plan to 'remodel the Japanese archipelago' in 1972. Tanaka's vision was also ghost-written and serves, at numerous points, as the model for Ozawa's own effort. As Ozawa's opus has been the object of often bemused commentary, particularly in the United States, I propose to bring three basic questions to bear on *Nihon Kaizō Keikaku*.

First, one must ask what Ozawa tells us about his goals of reforming the parliamentary system and the rules of the electoral contest between the parties. Having already achieved so much, what are Ozawa's remaining ambitions?

Second, one must pursue the stark question: Is Ozawa corrupt? Ohshita's often engaging biography of Ozawa, which appeared in October 1993, carefully skirts this issue. Yet, corrupt practices have the potential to destroy Ozawa's career, just as they proved the undoing of Tanaka, Ozawa's patron. Concerning this issue, rumours still vastly outnumber the facts.

Third, there is the 'A' factor. It is a cliché among Ozawa's left-wing critics to charge the man, often and loudly, with being a fascist. While it is ridiculous to compare Ozawa's career to date with that of Adolf Hitler, Benito Mussolini or even Tōjō Hideki, Ozawa's hunger for power is undisguised. What light does *Nihon Kaizō Keikaku* shed on what Theodor Adorno might have termed Ozawa's 'A' for authoritarianism potential? Do Ozawa's ideas suggest that his ambitions are either illiberal or politically dangerous?

Ozawa's book is divided into three parts: (1) '*Ima, Seiji no Kaikaku o*' (The urgency of political reform), in which he addresses the themes of national ethos and political reform: (2) '*Nihon no Seikinin to Yakuwari*' (Japan's responsibilities and rôle), which contains Ozawa's view of Japanese foreign and defense policy; and (3) '*Itsutsu no Jiyū o*' (Time to realize the five freedoms), in which Ozawa articulates his social vision.

Most foreign reviewers of *Blueprint* have concentrated on the third part of the book in which Ozawa paints his portrait of what he calls 'the Japanese dream'. To realize this Japanese answer to the so-called 'American dream', Japan must, in Ozawa's opinion, embrace five freedoms: freedom from Tokyo, from corporate servitude, from overwork, from ageism and sexism, and from excessive bureaucratic regulation.

Since this agenda touches on some of the most conspicuous challenges facing Japanese society today, readers of *Blueprint* may find it helpful to turn initially to the third section, if only to

discover what Ozawa says about the social status of women.
After all, Ozawa is the man who tactlessly observed, when
discussing coalition partners, that 'It doesn't matter which woman
you sleep with.' (There are at least five versions in Japanese of
what Ozawa reportedly said.) This remark makes an odd bed-
partner, to continue the metaphor, with Ozawa's soothing
advocacy of women's rights in *Nihon Kaizō Keikaku.* So what are
Ozawa's honest views?

To charge that Ozawa's book does not answer the question is
to do more than point out a sharp contradiction. The real goal
of any effort to scrutinize *Nihon Kaizō Keikaku,* or indeed any
other feature of Ozawa's long career as a politician, is to discover
where the balance of truth lies between what Ozawa thinks he
must say to curry public favour and his true feelings on any
sensitive subject, be it constitutional revision, Japanese rearmament or, for that matter, the rights of women. Such uncertainty
colours the book and the life. Having said as much, the views set
out in *Blueprint* on the place of women in Japanese society are
moderately liberal and forward-looking.

As Tanaka sought to do in his book, Ozawa sets out a reform
programme of ambitious scope. He has been advocating some
of these ideas for years. His call for single-seat constituencies, as
was noted above, may reflect the influence of his father.
Certainly from the beginning of the 1990s, Ozawa began to
speak of the need to break the LDP's long hold on power. (*Asahi
Shinbun* 17 June 1994) He wants his country to have a two-
party system in which power changes hands on the American
and British pattern. He also urges enhanced powers for the
prime minister. Ozawa seeks to make the Japanese Diet into a
working parliament, to have the élite core of the party in power
actually govern the country, in cooperation with a refocused
bureaucracy.

None of these ideas would carry even a tinge of reality unless
the Liberal Democratic Party, which has dominated party
politics in Japan since its was founded in 1955, had been driven
from power. But Ozawa achieved this during the summer of
1993. It is his ability to realize his ambitions which had made
him a force in the land. More than any other politician, Ozawa
helped to ensure that the first phase of the political restructuring
process dealt a massive blow to the LDP. After nearly ten months
in opposition, the LDP was able to return to power in June
1994, but only by agreeing to a coalition with its old enemy, the
JSP (initially renamed, but only in English, as the Social Demo-

cratic Party of Japan). The price of this marriage of convenience included making Murayama Tomiichi, a socialist, prime minister.

Is there a key, then, which unlocks the uneasy blend of forceful reform and dark politics that haunt *Nihon Kaizō Keikaku*? The answer, I believe, lies in the two formative moments of Ozawa's career as a politician. The first was the encounter with Tanaka in the late 1960s. The second was the Gulf War. As the details of the precise nature of Ozawa's relationship with Tanaka remain shrouded in mystery, here I shall only touch on his reaction to the Gulf War, which is described in his book.

The day Iraq invaded Kuwait (2 August 1990), Ozawa rushed to the prime minister's office, in his capacity as secretary-general of the ruling party, only to discover that no-one was on duty. (Ohshita 1993a : 332–7) Ozawa's fury at such complacency has never completely left him. This incident may explain why 'crisis management' forms the constant refrain of his book.

It was Ozawa's sense of urgency over the crisis in US-Japan relations provoked by the Gulf War which galvanized him, according to Ohshita, into persuading the Japanese Ministry of Finance to raise 13 billion yen in taxes to help pay for Allied costs (principally American) in the Gulf campaign. But perhaps even more important, the Gulf War confirmed Ozawa's respect for the powers of the American president.

Ozawa is perfectly willing to shift power to the periphery of Japanese life at the expense of central government, if, in return, the prime minister can effectively gather into his hands the kind of leverage which US presidents have always exercised over national security and foreign policy; but which no Japanese prime minister, certainly none since the First World War, ever has.

In short, Ozawa wants to remodel Japanese government to create the kind of top job which might tempt this master of backstage politics to step into the limelight. That a Japanese politician's politician, someone who has been a key player at the very heart of the nation's establishment for 25 years, appears to entertain the daydream of executive power concentrated in the hands of a single institution, let alone the office of a single person, verges on the incredible. It flies in the face of one of the most persistent features of Japan's political culture: the imperative to disperse power. Japanese departures from polycentric government, in ancient, medieval and modern times, have been that rare. (Williams 1994 : 19–26) Even Tojo Hideki would have envied the kind of authority that Ozawa would concentrate in the office of a peacetime prime minister.

Three factors give Ozawa's unlikely proposals a veneer of plausibility. First, Ozawa proposes to redistribute powers between local and central government in such a manner that the periphery will be enormously strengthened in precisely those areas of domestic policymaking which most concern local interests and local administration. Second, historical forces are gradually dissolving the isolationism of post-war Japan. This posture as a diplomatic wallflower has served to insulate the country from the responsibilities and dangers of the politics of the real world. At the same time, the US–Japan alliance may be in terminal decline. Third, Ozawa displays a remarkable confidence in the powers of government to get things done. In this, he harks back to earlier generations of politicians. Modern examples include Theodore Roosevelt, Franklin D. Roosevelt, Harold Macmillan, Lyndon B. Johnson, Harold Wilson, and, of course, Tanaka himself.

Ozawa leaves many Japanese uneasy. Indeed, it is the prospect of a rich Japan, confidently nationalist and proud of its new weight in global affairs, being led by a right-of-centre prime minister with the powers of an American president which has sparked demands in Japan, particularly on the enfeebled left, for what might be called the sixth freedom: the freedom from Ozawa.

This concern brings us to the most discussed aspect of *Nihon Kaizō Keikaku*: Ozawa's plea for Japan to become *'futsu no kuni'* or 'a normal country'. Unlike many of his more right-wing colleagues, Ozawa has made repeated attempts to address the fears among Japan's neighbours about a return of Japanese militarism or overseas expansionism. For someone regarded as a dyed-in-the-wool nationalist (as a young man he considered a career in the Self Defence Forces), Ozawa is refreshingly candid about the facts of Japanese aggression during the 1930s and 1940s. Yet, as in the case of a number of other important issues, the question remains: Is Ozawa sincere?

Typically, when he speaks of Japan's need to become a 'normal country', Ozawa rather self-servingly means several different things. One is a set of policy and institutional adjustments (including the dilution or abandonment of Article 9, the famous peace clause of the MacArthur constitution) that stand in the way of Japan taking up all the burdens of, for example, a permanent seat on the United Nations Security Council. What

Ozawa understands by the term '*futsū no kuni*' should not be translated as a 'normal country', but rather as a 'normal great power' with at least the freedom of Britain and France (as opposed to Germany) to act on the international stage.

The ambiguities and nationalist flavour of this vision of Japan will not reassure those who nurse doubts about Ozawa's ambitions, personality and values. The title of Ozawa's tract, like that of Tanaka's *Nihon Rettō no Kaizō-ron*, echoes uncomfortably the rhetoric of pre-war Japanese nationalism, as does the title given to Ohshita's biography of Ozawa. Nevertheless, the left's reaction has been excessive. Ozawa's *Nihon Kaizō Keikaku* is not post-modern Japan's answer to *Nihon Kaizō Hōan Taikō* written by Kita Ikki in 1919. It is certainly not a Japanese *Mein Kampf*.

All men and women are products of their times. Ozawa came to adulthood during the 1960s. Not much older than Bill Clinton, Ozawa has inevitably been influenced by post-war democratic education. He speaks the language of *post-war* Japanese nationalism, an idiom which departs significantly from the reactionary, even revanchist tone sometimes exhibited by the generation of Nakasone Yasuhiro. Ozawa's psychology is all about forward motion, not a return to the past. True, Ozawa may be one of the most nationalist politicians to dominate the climate of Japanese party politics since Kishi Nobusuke, but there is no convincing evidence, with which I am familiar, to justify the claim that he is fascist.

CONCLUSION

Japan is a graveyard for political prophets. The epigram of former Deputy LDP President Kawashima Shōjirō that '*Seikai wa issunsaki wa yami*' (very roughly, 'The next step in Japanese politics is always shrouded in darkness.') is not cited so frequently for nothing. I shall not attempt to predict here the next turn in what has been called the 'revolving stage' of the new Japanese politics of the 1990s. When I began to write this essay in the spring of 1994, Ozawa had personally selected the cabinets, as I noted earlier, of five of the last six governments and created two successive national administrations. By the autumn of 1994, Japanese pundits were writing his political obituary. In the face of such radical shifts in the assessments of the stature of the man, I would repeat my claim that whatever happens tomorrow, Ozawa Ichirō has already earned the status of one of the most influential leaders of the post-war era. In that sense, his reputation is secure. Fresh triumphs will only strengthen his claim to a place in the history books that remain to be written about the politics of our times.

NOTES

1. The tabloid press in Japan has frequently speculated about Ozawa's health problems. According to one report in the Shūkan Hōseki (23 June 1994), Ozawa is supposed to have travelled to London for heart treatment in September 1993 and, again, in March and May of 1994. Another visit to Britain was reported in October 1994. Ozawa's public outbursts against his critics after Hata became prime minister were blamed by the tabloid press on the side effects of his medication. According to Ohshita, Ozawa's father died of a heart complication (*kyūsei shin fuzen*), albeit at the age of 70. See *Ichi o Motte Tsuranuku, Ningen Ozawa Ichirō*, Tokyo, Kodansha, 1993, p. 76.

2. The defence of a carefully nurtured *jiban* has played a decisive role in encouraging the phenomenon of second-generation politicians who, as of June 1993, may have formed as many as 40 per cent of sitting LDP MPs. According to Ohshita's biography of Hata, it was the *jiban* imperative which finally forced Hata Tsutomu to become a politician, an idea that both he and his politician father had always opposed.

3. For an assessment of Ozawa's links to bureaucratic circles as well as his ostensible coolness towards big business, see '*Ozawa Seiji*', op. cit., Part 5, '*Zai-Kanka, Majiru Kyōkan to Kyorikan*' (Big business and the bureaucracy: mixing sympathy with coolness), *Asahi Shinbun, chōkan*, 13th edition, 18 June 1994, p. 2.

Ozawa's turn to the *Sōka Gakkai* for financial backing underscores the importance of this ambivalence. Japanese criticism of Ozawa for his 'alliance' with Ikeda Daisaku may therefore be seen as a principled attack on Ozawa's willingness to sleep, as it were, with anyone for political gain or an absurdly high-minded refusal to acknowledge that in contemporary Japan a politician confronted with a second make-or-break national election in less than two years time must either go cap in hand to big business or seek alternative ways to finance his election campaign. The sorry fate of the defunct Japan New Party once led by Hosokawa Morihiro highlights the lesson involved.

4. Tachibana Takashi observes, however, that Ozawa's written response to the 1983 *Asahi Shinbun* survey of 84 LDP candidates (with 79 responding) belonging to the Tanaka faction suggests that he was willing to concede Tanaka's guilt. This Tachibana deduces from Ozawa's argument that Tanaka should have quit earlier, thus precluding the necessity for a trial. See Tachibana Takashi, *Rokkiido Saiban to Sono Jidai* (The Lockheed trial and those times), Volume 4: January 1982 to December 1983, Tokyo, Asahi Shinbun-sha, 1994, p. 530.

SOURCES CITED

Asahi Shimbun 14–19 June, 1994. Series of articles entitled Osawa Seiji (Osawa Politics).

Ohshita Eiji, (1993) *Ichi o Motte Tsuranuku*, Tokyo: Kodansha.
Ohshita Eiji, (1993) *Ju ni Shite Go*, Tokyo: Kodansha.
Osawa Ichirō, (1993) *Nihon Kaizō Keikaku*, Tokyo: Kodansha.
Osawa Ichirō, (1994) *Blueprint for a New Japan: the Rethinking of Nations*, trans. Louisa Rubinfien, Tokyo: Kodanasha Int.
Williams D., (1994) *Japan: Beyond the Ends of History*, London: Routledge.

Index